NEO-NATIONALISM IN EUROPE AND BEYOND

NEO-NATIONALISM IN EUROPE AND BEYOND

Perspectives from
Social Anthropology

Edited by
Andre Gingrich and Marcus Banks

Berghahn Books
New York • Oxford

First published in 2006 by
Berghahn Books
www.berghahnbooks.com

Library of Congress Cataloging-in-Publication Data
Neo-nationalism in Europe and beyond perspectives from social anthropology / edited by
Andre Gingrich and Marcus Banks.
    p. cm.
    Papers originally presented at a workshop in Brussels in 2001.
    Includes bibliographical references and index.
    ISBN 1-84545-189-9 (hardback : alk. paper) -- ISBN 1-84545-190-2 (pbk. : alk. paper)
1. Political anthropology--Europe. 2. Political culture--Europe.
3. Nationalism--Europe. 4. Europe--Politics and government. 5. Europe--Social life and
customs. I. Gingrich, André. II. Banks, Marcus.

GN575.N46 2006
306.2094--dc22

2006019278

British Library Cataloguing in Publication Data

A catalogue record for this book is available from the British Library.

Printed in the United States on acid-free paper

ISBN 1-57181-190-2 (hardback)
ISBN 1-57181-189-9 (paperback)

Contents

Acknowledgements

The editors wish to thank a number of individuals and institutions that have made this volume possible. First, in addition to the insight of the volume contributors themselves, we must thank Ulrike Davis-Sulikowski, Mark Potok, Frédéric Saumade and Verena Stolcke for their valuable contributions to the original workshop in February 2002: Ulrike was also instrumental in organising the workshop, while Stefan Rutkowski provided technical and administrative support. Richard Fox, former President of the Wenner-Gren Foundation, who was also present, contributed greatly to the discussion, and we wish to thank him and the Foundation for making the workshop possible. We also wish to thank the Director of the Club de la Fondation Universitaire, Brussels, and his staff for making our stay there so pleasant.

Partial funding for copy-editing and indexing of the book was provided by the Austrian Science Fund's Wittgenstein Award made to AG in 2000, and we are very grateful for this. We are also grateful to Marion Berghahn for her encouragement and support of the project, and to her reviewer who helped us tighten up the volume. Finally, we are indebted more than we can say to Julene Knox who worked valiantly to bring a number of disparate texts into a clear and coherent whole.

Andre Gingrich and Marcus Banks
August 2005

Introduction

Neo-nationalism in Europe and Beyond

Marcus Banks and Andre Gingrich

Introduction

This book has its genesis in a Wenner-Gren sponsored workshop in Brussels – the symbolic and administrative heart of the European Union – in early 2001. Prompted by the near-simultaneous rise to political influence of more than a dozen apparently similar parties across Western Europe, a group of anthropologists from Europe and beyond met to consider the phenomenon and to ask what distinctive contributions anthropology might make to its study. From the outset, Western Europe thus represented a central regional focus of this debate, thereby acknowledging that an assessment of nationalism under the post-socialist conditions prevailing elsewhere in Europe would require a debate of its own. The term 'neo-nationalism' was used from the start and was our central focus although, as we note below, this term requires considerable unpacking. Nonetheless, a variety of other issues were touched on along the way: the legacy of European colonialism, violence and the role of extra-parliamentary right-wing groups, migration and globalisation, and, perhaps less obviously, humour, Armani suits and photo opportunities. By the end of the symposium, and in our subsequent discussions with contributors, we concluded (perhaps unsurprisingly) that anthropologists do have a distinctive contribution to make, both conceptually and methodologically. Conceptually, we elaborated an ability to balance explanations that emphasised historical and structural causes with those that emphasised the agency of persons and events. Methodologically, we combined an ability to see the world as the neo-nationalists see it (while never seeking to endorse those perspectives) with scepticism towards their view of the world.

This is thus a book by social anthropologists, presenting a distinctively anthropological point of view. But we aim to address a broader audience, including other academic specialists such as political scientists or sociologists, as well as non-academic groups and individuals interested in contemporary political phenomena. We regard our approach as complementary to the findings of cognate academic disciplines, a matter we discuss below, but our primary engagement is on two fronts. First, and most importantly, we address the phenomenon of neo-nationalism itself; second, we engage with anthropology's past contribution to the study of nationalism and take these insights forward, a matter to which we turn at the end of this introduction.

What is Neo-nationalism?

The central topic of this book is 'neo-nationalism'. In a nominalist sense, the term clearly implies 'recent and new variants of' nationalism, and by implication this simultaneously refers to a whole range of 'earlier' variants of nationalism, as analysed by social anthropologists and historians. From the outset, such a nominalist understanding of neo-nationalism therefore presumes a historical and logical interrelation between 'earlier' and 'recent' variants of nationalism. However, exploring this interrelation has to be combined with a consideration of some historical continuities and differences between 'earlier' and 'recent' forms of nationalism in Western Europe.

Authors such as Gellner (1983) and Hobsbawm (1990) outline the relatively recent rise of nationalism, but by definition the same could be said, even more so, of neo-nationalism. A conspicuous contrast thereby arises, perhaps more dramatically than already identified by Anderson (1983) for 'earlier nationalists', between the very recent contexts of emergence and the neo-nationalists' own claim to be upholding 'eternal values' and defending 'timeless aspirations'. In turn, this contrast inspires and necessitates, among earlier nationalists as much as among neo-nationalists, explicit efforts towards a continuous 'invention of tradition'. In short, some of the most basic characteristics of earlier variants (Banks 1996: 121–31) also apply to a considerable extent for neo-nationalism.

As a working definition, it thus seems appropriate to specify further the nominalist understanding of neo-nationalism by approaching neo-nationalism as the re-emergence of nationalism under different global and transnational conditions. The end of the Cold War initiated these new global and European contexts, which are often summarised by the ambivalent term 'globalisation'. They entail a wide range of transnational (economic, political and socio-cultural) dimensions (Appadurai 1996; Beck 1997; Hannerz 1996), to which neo-nationalists feel they have to adjust, and to react. Thus the most visible 'new' aspects in current European nationalisms are due to such interactions with, and reactions towards, several of these fairly recent, transnational and global developments in Western Europe. Some of the most conspicuous reactions include the neo-nationalists' stance towards immigration, or on central EU decisions, as well as their populist appeals to the mass cultures of the present. In addition, the neo-nationalists' own social basis differs from that of their predecessors to a certain extent insofar as earlier nationalists in addition to their urban basis could also rely upon a degree of rural support that, due to Western Europe's transformations after the Second World War, has now largely vanished. In turn, many neo-nationalist leaders have been forced, in view of today's urban heterogeneity, to depart from earlier nationalist ideals of cultural homogeneity. In most cases, this reorientation has been achieved through a new emphasis on either 'assimilation' (anathema to most earlier nationalists) or 'separation' of various sorts.

Given such similarities and differences between earlier and current forms of nationalism, neo-nationalism in this volume is first and foremost identified as a social phenomenon. Rather than treating it primarily as an ideology to be traced through the language of political manifestos, it is thus discussed here through an analytical focus on action, interaction and practice, together with accompanying forms of discourse. Such a focus on the practices and interactions of neo-nationalisms in Western Europe raises questions about this phenomenon's wider social and regional contexts: neo-nationalism is neither an isolated phenomenon, nor is it internally coherent.

Some of the wider social and regional contexts of neo-nationalism have been analysed and outlined as 'integralism' by anthropologist Douglas Holmes (2000), under which he subsumes all kinds of chauvinistic, territorially based essentialism in Europe at the end of the twentieth century. At the beginning of the twenty-first century, it seems appropriate to refine this useful but very general concept further, at least for our present purposes. In this sense, neo-nationalists may be loosely and pragmatically distinguished from two other major variants of integralism in Western Europe: regional secessionism and right-wing extremism. Regional secessionism, as a second variant of integralism after neo-nationalism, implies an unavoidable tendency towards violence, insofar as it aims at 'breaking away' from, and thus openly challenging, the existing state domain. Certain factions of the Basque and the Corsican movements in Spain and France represent key examples of this tendency and illustrate that many of these secessionist and radical autonomist cases differ substantially from 'parliamentary' neo-nationalism in their programmes and methods. Examples of intersection between variants, however, include the Lega Nord in Italy or the Vlaams Blok in Belgium, in which radical autonomism may combine forces with, or become identical to, neo-nationalist parliamentary parties.

The third variant is right extremism, which favours illegal and violent means to promote openly racist causes, usually in explicit defiance of parliamentary democracy. In terms of key elements of their ideologies, as well as their hate-speech and views on history, right-extremist groups sometimes show a surprising similarity to specific parliamentary parties from the far right. Yet their actual methods and explicit programmes differ to a significant degree. Right extremists are usually anti-parliamentary pro-fascists or neo-Nazis, while today's neo-nationalist parties from the far right usually are not, even if some (notably in Austria and in Italy) emerged out of predecessor organisations with such backgrounds. In spite of such partial intersections, the distinction is nonetheless valid and necessary. In fact, right extremists seem to have gained ground, together with mob violence, precisely in some of those countries where 'parliamentary' parties from the far right have so far *not* been successful on a country-wide level, such as in Germany, England or Spain.[1] Right extremists and parliamentary parties from the far right thus have more often interacted as rivals, rather than as cooperating 'legal and illegal' branches of a single movement. While it is important to consider all possible forms of interaction between the 'mob violence' and the 'parliamentary' ends of the neo-nationalist and right-extremist spectrum, this volume is focused on the more influential 'parliamentary' side as a mass phenomenon of the late twentieth and early twenty-first centuries.

The neo-nationalist movements discussed and analysed in this volume are therefore associated with far-right but legitimate parliamentary parties. Major differences and parallels among them will be scrutinised along various comparative and 'country by country' case study dimensions. Such a focus on far-right, neo-nationalist parliamentary parties requires one additional qualification: right-wing parliamentary representatives are not necessarily also blinkered nationalists, nor need radical nationalists always come from the political right. Many conservative groups and parties from the moderate right in Western Europe are not nationalist chauvinists, while post-Second World War Western Europe also has its legacy of 'left nationalism'. In the 1960s and 1970s this ranged from the extreme-left nationalism of European Maoism to the main support groups of the Basque ETA and the Irish IRA, but left nationalism also included nationalist elements of the 'parliamentary left' in France, Britain and elsewhere. Today, the continuing strength of the post-communist PDS in eastern Germany, with its ex-GDR 'regional interest' dimension, might in fact signal a new round of further, left (post-communist) regionalist and nationalist integralism among some of the new members from East Central Europe that joined the EU in May 2004. In view of this, it is not self-evident that in Western Europe today the neo-nationalist parliamentary parties mostly belong to the far right of the political spectrum.

Nonetheless, it was the combination of neo-nationalism with far-right populism as a political agenda that gained increasing influence in a number of Western European countries in the 1990s. In turn, this attracted international media attention and public concern for a while. A decade later, however, the topic of neo-nationalism no longer seems so urgent to the wider public in Western Europe and North America.

There are a number of different reasons for the current phase of public disinterest. First, other medium-term concerns have moved to the foreground of global and international awareness. Most notable are the consequences of the U.S.-

led 'war on terror', leading to the 2002 military operation in Afghanistan, the war in Iraq, the increasingly unstable situation in the Middle East and to an extent most recently the bombings in London and Madrid. If a first historical phase after the end of the Cold War was marked by seemingly unbounded, neo-liberal economic priorities, then a second phase since 11 September 2001 has added new, hegemonic political-military accents to that economic thrust. There was strong opposition on various levels to the Iraq war: governments within the EU and civil protest movements in the EU and the U.S. openly opposed it, and the ensuing contradictions between the U.S. administration and several governments within the EU, not to mention between those governments and segments of civil society in those states, have led to widespread reconsideration of the direction in which Western Europe is, or should be, moving. It has thus become obvious that the rise of far-right parliamentary parties was only one among several factors characterising these heated debates about Western Europe's future. Other factors, such as political and economic relations with the U.S., and the seemingly more pro-American stance of some of the new incoming EU member countries, are at least equally important in this process.

Secondly, simultaneous with these contested changes on the global scale, some kind of provisional mutual accommodation has taken place in domestic Western European party politics. A larger European public seems to have accepted the fact that various parties of the far right have successfully established themselves as serious players in several EU countries and likewise in the European Parliament. In turn, these parties have become quite keen to demonstrate to the world that they are not as radical as was anticipated, particularly so after several of them gained positions in national European governments. This accommodation process may or may not turn out to be provisional or superficial, but it has contributed to the declining media profile of this issue in Western Europe in the early years of the twenty-first century.

Finally, the Austrian and the Dutch national elections in 2002 and in early 2003 brought significant defeats for two of these neo-nationalist parties whose earlier successes and rise to government power had shocked world opinion. It is understandable that many interpret these signs of neo-nationalist failure as an additional indication that other priorities may now take over, and indeed this may well prove to be the case for a number of specific political forces and individual actors.

Yet at the same time, the puzzle and the challenge that neo-nationalism poses for the social sciences, including anthropology, remains. This puzzle has several dimensions. The rise of neo-nationalism, for instance, has questioned the premature assumption of many historians and social scientists that by necessity nationalism was intrinsically manifested in young nation states alone. Our working definition of neo-nationalism, as the nationalism of the current phase of transnational and global developments, seeks to move beyond this bias. It allows us to explore the manner in which neo-nationalists present themselves as offering solutions to specific problems of the present both empirically and ethnographically. Another dimension of the 'neo-nationalist puzzle' relates to the fact that much of these parties' public success is owed to rhetorical strategies that manipulated and instrumentalised various notions of culture, and which at the same time dramatised and enacted these strategies in sometimes spectacular media performances. Many other social scientists have often dismissed this side of the neo-nationalist success story as 'superficial' showmanship, or as an ephemeral and sociologically unimportant aspect of the problem. Given their established expertise not only in 'culture' as broadly understood but equally in matters of social charisma, the social power of performance and the aesthetics of social action, it is thus high time that social anthropologists contributed to meeting this specific dimension of the challenge.

These dimensions of the puzzle alone already indicate that the problem of neo-nationalism arises from the interface of structure and agency, a central theoretical concern of contemporary anthropology and the social sciences at large. How far is neo-nationalism to be understood as an outcome of the current phase of accelerated transnational interaction and global developments? And, alternatively, how far is neo-nationalism to be understood as a socio-cultural process introduced and performed, but also opposed and negotiated, by more or less creative agency? These are two of the central questions raised and pursued in different ways by the contributors to this volume. As social anthropologists, the authors put specific emphasis on analysing current and contemporary processes, without ignoring the impact the past has upon the present, by elaborating distinctive anthropological approaches to meet the intellectual challenge of the neo-nationalist puzzle.

Part I elaborates a number of the theoretical and methodological issues touched upon so far in more detail. The empirical case studies which follow in Part II combine these theoretical and topical interests with pragmatic considerations. On the one hand, a regional focus on Western Europe offers the advantage of studying a variety of dense local experiences of neo-nationalism, through the professional expertise of social anthropologists from some of those very countries which are the major context of the emergence of the phenomenon. On the other hand, restricting the empirical analysis to Western Europe alone easily could have resulted in losing sight of a number of important factors, most notably the colonial and post-colonial record and the current phase of globalisation. Out of these comparative, post-colonial and global considerations, therefore, a number of authors have also been invited to contribute on themes and topics with a particular potential to shed additional light on these dimensions. Part III therefore moves on, from the 'country by country' level to dimensions of European-wide and EU-wide relevance, whereas Part IV features comparative case studies from outside Western Europe. In order to provide analyses of the present which duly acknowledge the enduring legacy of a European colonial past, this volume integrates contributions on India and on Australia, where well-known neo-nationalist forces have been active in the very recent past. Part V picks up this comparative, post-colonial and transnational line of argument, by again addressing some of the main insights of this volume through new perspectives on the current phase of globalisation.

The Contribution from Anthropology

Anthropology is often known to other disciplines for its distinctive ethnographic approach, based on long-term fieldwork. Although both the term and the concept of ethnography have spread widely into a range of other social sciences, anthropology is often still understood to derive ethnographic insight from the most long-term, loosely structured, linguistically intense form of fieldwork: the so-called 'total immersion' method. While not wishing to deny the importance of either ethnography or fieldwork, there are two problems with this perception.

First, anthropology is not merely a discipline of method, a toolbox of field techniques to gather data that are then written up into convincing ethnographic narratives of an essentially descriptive nature. The essence of ethnography is a fusion of and a constant dialogue between field data and theory, each informing the other in equal measure. Some of the theory that informs the contributions to this volume is discussed below. Secondly, if anthropology were merely a set of field methodologies then there would clearly be problems for the discipline when facing a phenomenon such as neo-nationalism. Although some of the authors here do indeed base their contributions on traditional fieldwork investigations (Stacul, Seiser, McDonald and to a degree Gullestad), many more do not. Even of those who do, none has conducted fieldwork directly with neo-nationalist politicians and activists themselves, but rather with the ordinary people who may or may not support such politicians. This is not to say that an anthropologist could not do so; although some of the agents and events described in the following chapters might actively hinder such an investigation or pose a real risk of personal violence, there are plenty of anthropologists who have worked in much more dangerous or hostile contexts, whether voluntarily or involuntarily.[2] Equally, although with fewer examples, there are anthropologists who have conducted fieldwork with powerful elites that might normally resent or prevent such intimate access as is required by fieldwork.[3] We would argue that it is more likely that anthropologists have avoided fieldwork with neo-nationalists not because they are unable to gain access but because they do not wish to – for the sake of moral hygiene rather than to avoid bodily endangerment. We return to this point below.

But if we see fieldwork within the context of anthropological analysis more widely then, to a greater or lesser extent, all the contributors have conducted fieldwork in the sense of bringing an anthropological sensitivity to their investigation of primary sources: websites, surveys, autobiographical accounts, interviews, newspaper articles and political manifestos. More particularly, they have brought understanding from other areas of anthropological investigation – often derived precisely from traditional long-term field investigation – and applied it to the neo-nationalist problem. Chief among these areas are those that concern the state and the nation. As anthropologists most of us have conducted field-based research on topics that are normative, naturalised and unquestioned for those we work amongst, and in particular on forms of linguistic, religious and ethnic identification. Especially beyond the European context (but sometimes also within it – for example McDonald's work on Breton ethno-nationalism [1989], or Tone Bringa's [1995] study of Bosnian Muslim identities) and where the state is weak, primary loyalties may be towards kin groups, language communities and confessional or ethnic groups, and indifference to the state is apparent. While in some instances such indifference can be injurious or even fatal (for example, the peasant victims of state violence against counter-state terrorists or revolutionaries in Nepal or Guatemala), in others such indifference forms a bulwark against globalising forces passing through the state's offices (for example, the many indigenous revival movements in the Americas – North and South, and the continued resilience of caste in India). In all cases, fieldwork with such communities grants anthropologists an alternative perspective on the hegemonic claims of many states, which see their nationalist ideologies as often either weak or a rewritten form of ethnic distinctiveness, or both. While nationalism and the state may be the dominant form of political organisation of our age (Banks 1996: 125), they are neither universal nor all-powerful. Anthropologists thus tend to maintain a healthy scepticism towards the state and its power.

Equally, they remain sceptical about the power of political ideologies, at least as those ideologies present themselves, however persuasive or seductive they may be (Gellner 1979). To an extent, this scepticism is rooted in one of the premises of anthropological fieldwork and participant observation, namely, the distinction between a people's claims about their beliefs and their actual practices. Such scepticism does not seek to deny or underplay the very real power such ideologies can have in people's lives but rather to challenge the terms in which such ideologies cast themselves and the actual causes of their success. Plenty of field-based work by anthropologists on state socialism, for example, has shown that socialist states often maintained themselves despite Marxism rather than because of it, as it were.[4] Meanwhile it is equally clear that industrial capitalism does not blindly structure a market – local or global – that in turn structures the state.[5] In their studies anthropologists have identified a number of factors that undermine the self-presentation of nationalism, and now neo-nationalism, as monolithic entities of maximal ideological power.

Foremost among these factors is the persistence of notions of kinship in nationalist and neo-nationalist rhetoric. We are used to the state being represented as 'mother' or 'father' (motherland, fatherland), and key individuals may be represented in this idiom either metaphorically (Saddam Hussein) or mythically ('Mother India'). At other times the state is sometimes conceived of as a huge family, whose members go to war as 'brothers' and 'sisters'. As Eriksen states: 'One may perhaps go so far as to say that urbanisation and individualism [characteristics of the late capitalist state] create a social and cultural vacuum in so far as kinship loses much of its importance. Nationalism promises to satisfy some of the same needs that kinship was formerly responsible for' (1993: 108). Anthropologists are particularly attuned to kinship, not solely as a mode of social organisation, but also as a discursive idiom within which concepts of relatedness are articulated. At one level in particular, an apparent difference between older forms of nationalism and neo-nationalism is rendered comprehensible. Many older European nationalisms sought to present the nation not merely metaphorically but also literally as a family, relying on misguided correlations between language 'families' and ethnicity to argue that members of the nation shared the same blood or ancestry (see Chapman 1992: 16–17). Conversely, much neo-nationalist rhetoric is sufficiently pragmatic to accept that blood-based homogeneity can never define the boundaries of the nation, let alone the state, and seeks instead to generate an argument based upon historical association.[6] Yet at the same time, anthropology has never understood kinship in non-European societies to be solely or even primarily concerned with biological descent and relatedness, and recent research on 'cultures of relatedness' (e.g., Carsten 2000) has shown that other forms of association, for example commensality, can just as easily create kinship.

Equally important to contemporary anthropology is a recognition of the role played by colonialism, not only in the formation of the discipline itself, but also in the attitudes taken today in European nation states towards non-European migrants. Anthropologists have worked on both aspects[7] and all anthropologists today would recognise the obvious points: many migrants, the targets of neo-nationalist opprobrium, come from former European colonies, and many European Union states are still struggling to deal with their reduced global influence in a post-colonial world. In a way, the rise of neo-nationalism in Western Europe thus displays dimensions of 'dethroned' (Gingrich 2002) former colonial powers, i.e., of post-colonial European societies in the process of aggressively readjusting themselves to new immigrant generations from the realms of their former colonial subjects. Not only that, in the present volume most contributors recognise the relationship of neo-nationalism to processes of decolonisation as well as to post-war labour migration; this point is made most clearly in Gullestad's contribution on Norway, an example of a European country without any active colonial past of its own.

The kinship-inflected discourse of relatedness within the nation is mirrored, indeed co-constituted, by a political discourse of power relations between nations. We know who 'we' are and what constitutes our sameness, precisely because we know who 'we' are not and what constitutes our difference from others. Such a sense of similarity and difference or of belonging and alterity (Baumann and Gingrich 2004), fundamental to the anthropological enterprise, is at the root of another core anthropological project: gender. Perhaps surprisingly, gender can act as another analytical vantage point from which to observe the development and process of neo-nationalist ideology. Gendered difference may be embedded within such discourse; a language of 'immigrants' being granted excessive rights within the state often goes hand in hand with claims of (neo-)conservative men that feminism has given women more rights than they deserve or need, while older European fears of miscegenation or 'race mixing' in the colonies are a direct antecedent of contemporary moral panics concerning sexually predatory foreigners. Such discourses of course feed back into ideas of kinship and bio-social purity within the nation.

The remarks above reflect anthropology's often-noted dual perspective: the ability to match micro-perspectives derived from intense field study, with holistic and macro-perspectives derived from inductive reasoning and comparativism (see Gingrich and Fox 2002).[8] The micro-ethnographic perspective complements top-down work by political scientists and sociologists, while holism allows connections to be made between apparently unrelated areas of social experience.

Yet anthropology itself is an ever-changing discipline. While the contributions to this volume set out to address the phenomenon of neo-nationalism by elaborating a distinctive anthropological approach, they simultaneously respond to a number of changes within anthropology. From the outset, previous anthropological assumptions of a naïve kind of holism are being left behind, by carefully considering variations and contradictions that are inherent to the phenomenon. Quite apart from the fact that analytical presumptions of any internal homogeneity would be in danger of uncritically absorbing neo-nationalists' propaganda rhetoric, our contributions also move beyond the first and most obvious task of demonstrating how different neo-nationalist parties relate to different local and historical contexts. Taken together, these analyses outline a number of clustered parallels among the various appearances of neo-nationalism today. Inside Western Europe, these differences include a cluster of such parties (in France, Belgium, Austria and Italy) with a historical context of predecessor groups directly rooted in various post-fascist and post-Nazi elements left over after the Second World War, and another cluster of neo-nationalist parties (in Scandinavia, Switzerland, the Netherlands and Portugal) with very different and more recent historical contexts of emergence. Moving beyond Western Europe brings out another set of parallels, between those neo-nationalist movements with a particularly strong anti-Islamic element (as in India or in the Netherlands), and others with a more diversified political agenda (as in Australia or Scandinavia). In these ways, authors of the present volume also move beyond the particular to discuss wider tendencies and parallels. By responding to anthropology's recent emphasis on transnational perspectives and on methodological sensitivity, the contributions to this volume manage to avoid the collapse of careful analysis into empiricist particularism. Instead, analyses of the particular are pursued with a theoretical perspective on a heterogeneous social-political phenomenon in transnational and global contexts, in which the key actors and main events are only partially connected (Strathern 1991) and interrelated. From this perspective, the contributors therefore address the relationship between structure and agency as a sphere of processual, dialectical and creative tension. All contributors share the structural insight that the wider contexts of accelerated globalisation after the end of the Cold War have favoured and promoted the recent emergence of neo-nationalism, as one specific option of a reclusive and reactive response to these structural conditions. Yet in order to transform this option into reality, specific forms of agency are required. On this topic, a Weberian approach in the social sciences suggests that individuals act and mobilise for the purpose of transforming potential options into social agency. Several case studies in this volume (particularly those on the Netherlands, India and Austria) exemplify the fertility of such an actor-centred approach.

This approach closely corresponds with anthropology's recent emphasis on lived experience, on individuals and on actual everyday lives. For improved understanding of these spheres, anthropology has developed a number of methodological devices that promote a theoretical consideration of personal experience beyond structure, and of agency beyond voluntarism and individualism. This new methodological emphasis on socially and culturally shaped ways of experiencing the world thus extends anthropology's established competencies in elaborating micro-perspectives. The methodological dimensions of several contributions to this volume not only relate to the analysis of neo-nationalist leaders, but also to the rank and file: What is it that makes voters, supporters and members of these parties rally around their leadership? How do they see the world and in what ways do they want their parties to change it? On the basis of which experiences are some people more inclined to follow neo-nationalism for longer or shorter periods, and others less so?

When such a methodological focus on experience and actors' perspectives is thought through for neo-nationalism, however, a number of substantial consequences become apparent for ethnographic fieldwork, that is, for anthropology's central tool kit of methods. Giving careful attention to indigenous voices remains a decisive aspect of fieldwork even when these indigenous voices are those of active neo-nationalists. This specific set of fieldwork contexts, however, belongs to a wider class of cases in which the average anthropological fieldworker may not necessarily sympathise with the 'indigenous' people among and with whom fieldwork is carried out. How, then, is fieldwork best pursued under such conditions, which do not allow for any 'advocacy' by the anthropologist?[9] As a rule of thumb, 'empathy not sympathy' is the appropriate formula for such fieldwork among people one does not like. Sympathy is impossible because the basic orientation of neo-nationalism, despite its claim to be defending (national) culture, is towards cultural exclusion and assimilation, an orientation that contradicts anthropology's basic premise of socio-cultural diversity. Empathy, however, is indispensable for any seriously methodological focus on actors' experiences and perspectives.

While this volume thus represents a concerted effort by anthropologists to engage intellectually with the present, it certainly is not an activists' handbook. It does not propose any models or agendas for how best to oppose neo-nationalism (though note Pinxten's and McDonald's remarks in their chapters that the EU needs to cultivate a stronger sense of common citizenship). Instead, it explores causes, manifestations and tendencies of a mass phenomenon, on the premise that comprehension is necessarily prior to action. On the one hand, therefore, it is suggested that a certain detached scepticism is indispensable for the analysis of any such phenomenon.[10] On the other hand, this does not exclude recognition of passions and emotions. Yet rather than getting the fieldworker emotionally involved prematurely, the contributions underline the need to understand 'indigenous emotions' as part of what the analysis is all about: fears of losing one's job, one's cultural or gender identity, feelings of humiliation and frustration. Hoping and longing for some kind of change are thus part and parcel of exploring and analysing neo-nationalism, among its active supporters as much as among those who resist it.

The Contributions – Themes, Contrasts and Comparisons

History

While for many decades after Malinowski anthropology eschewed the study of history (as a narrativised, chronological sequence of events), the study of historical consciousness has long been a key area of investigation. This is why many contributions in the present volume note the degree to which neo-nationalist ideologies seek to present national history in particular self-serving ways, from the co-option of the Picts and Ancient Britons into neo-nationalist projects in England (Banks) to the universalisation of specific historical moments of national homogeneity in Denmark (Hervik) and France (Gaillard-Starzmann, McDonald). By definition, a strong variant of cultural relativism always informs such tales of national uniqueness. While such retellings can often serve to heighten the importance of specific historical events, they can also serve to downplay them. In most cases, for example, the relationship between colonialism and nationalism (and neo-nationalism) is rarely granted prominence. Gullestad's chapter on Norway is particularly illuminating in this regard for presenting the contrary opinion: lacking an empire, and hence lacking a sense of post-colonial guilt, ordinary Norwegians seem offended by having to shoulder the burden of such guilt, or rather of such European co-responsibility, especially when they understand themselves to have done so much good in the former colonies of others.

While the stories that nations, and neo-nationalists, tell themselves regarding 'history' are fruitful areas of study, the contributors to this volume also recognise that neo-nationalism is itself a historical phenomenon, and one with roots and causes. As we have mentioned above and will return to below, there are both systemic and event-based aspects to this. With regard to the deep roots of neo-nationalist origins we have already mentioned the importance of earlier nationalist thought in Europe and the rarely discussed relationship with European colonialism. Some of the contributions highlight even earlier historical factors, however. For example, in their contribution on the Netherlands Sunier and van Ginkel identify the country's long-standing political culture of negotiating consensual practices, which to an extent is rooted in a long record of denominational coexistence between Protestants and Catholics. In the authors' view, neo-nationalist forces could then exploit the process of erosion of some among these key elements of established political culture in the Netherlands for their own purposes. Stacul, by contrast, indicates the relatively late consolidation of the Italian nation state as a decisive factor in the emergence of an aggressive earlier variant of nationalism in the form of Mussolini's Fascism. In turn, mainstream democratic parties firmly established themselves as caretakers of the centralised nation state after the Second World War, while in several parts of the country regionalist and autonomist forces developed a new local and 'integralist' agenda that continues to build on Italy's record of late national consolidation. Similarly, in India while the arrival of religious nationalism on the democratic political scene is relatively recent, as Banerjee notes, its roots go back to early twentieth-century attempts to redefine 'Hinduism' as a culturally fortifying counterpart to British colonialism. In this sense, a number of case studies presented in this volume illustrate the long-term historical factors that have to be taken into account for a proper analysis and understanding of neo-nationalism today.

Nor should we ignore more recent historical events and circumstances. The majority of the contributions about Europe describe outcomes directly resulting from the rebuilding of Europe after the Second World War and the massive influx of labour migrants from former colonies and elsewhere. As noted above, the decline in European world influence at this time and the transfer of global political as well as economic power to the U.S. combine as factors: a loss on the one hand matched by a gain on the other. More specific and local events must not be underestimated however. As Gaillard-Starzmann notes, the French Republic's attempt to counter the losses of colonial influence through an increasing EU engagement led French mainstream parties to give up a whole range of their established domestic agendas. Consequently, this opened up a space for Le Pen's Front National, in which that party could recruit its new clientele. For Denmark and Austria respectively, Hervik and Fillitz provide similar insights for the specific contexts of Western Europe's small and relatively affluent countries. Meanwhile Pinxten demonstrates how Belgium, first 'forced' by its powerful neighbours, by circumstance as it were, to become a nation in the nineteenth century, encountered considerable difficulties in the post-1945 period as it sought to hold republicans and monarchists, Flemish and Walloons together in the nation, allowing plenty of fault lines for the neo-nationalist Vlaams Blok to exploit.

Nor should these factors be examined solely within the context of party politics. While crystallised in some European states as the agenda of a particular political party, neo-nationalist thinking across Europe is a more diffuse phenomenon, one informed by attitudes towards class and gender, as well as race, ethnicity and nationhood.

The historical records of Western Europe, India and Australia that are examined in this volume demonstrate that older and more recent forms of nationalism were rarely restricted to one or a few parties alone. Rather, nationalism in its various historical manifestations, from its emergence to the present, has always represented one among several basic alternative ways of envisioning collective identities from 'above', i.e., from the perspectives of those in power, as much as from below, i.e., from the perspectives of various classes and segments of society at large, whether or not these are articulated through parties. Likewise, the recent re-emergence of nationalism in Western Europe requires analyses that combine an assessment of those specific parties with an understanding of the wider contexts in which they operate.

These wider contexts were introduced, it has been said, by Western Europe's more subordinate global position after the Second World War, in view of the collapse of colonial empires, of Germany's defeat and division, and with regard to the emergence of two superpowers in the course of the Cold War. The end of the Cold War and the ensuing new phase of globalisation thus indicate the wider European contexts of today's neo-nationalism. Since the late 1980s, these went hand in hand with profound transformations of Western Europe's political and economic landscape, in the form of accelerated EU integration and enlargement. In their contributions, Maryon McDonald and Gertraud Seiser demonstrate the importance of such Europe-wide perspectives 'from above'. In her chapter, Seiser focuses upon agrarian politics as a top priority on the EU's economic agenda, which has resulted in widespread acceptance of the EU by farmers. These efforts to an extent managed to stabilise the living conditions of this decreasing albeit important part of Western Europe's population. By contrast, Maryon McDonald's chapter shows through her analysis of representatives of the European Parliament and bureaucracy that the rise of neo-nationalism indeed has to do with growing insecurities among many other mostly urban segments of the population – insecurities that mainstream parties often fail to address. McDonald in fact demonstrates that all mainstream parties, from left to right, participated in the construction of the EU. Together with the demise of the extreme left, this opened up the space of an anti-EU agenda as a political field for the extreme right. For these reasons, neo-nationalists strive to occupy a space that is more or less involuntarily made available to them by their competitors from other parties. In this volume, these insecurities are analysed along their various dimensions of politics, culture, religion, gender or social status. It is in these contexts that finally, and most acutely felt in recent years, the globalisation of the economies of European states and the increasing globalisation of political power can be said to have led to feelings of insecurity that echo those at the end of the colonial period.

Ideologies of Identity

The insecurities mentioned above are manifested on a number of levels, from that of the individual to that of the nation, but all could be said to revolve around problems of identity or, as recent writing would phrase it, problems of identification (Jenkins 1996). At the level of the individual and his or her relations with others, many of our contributors point to a kind of self-interested conservativism. This point is made explicitly by Gingrich (this volume) with regard to the economy in his notion of 'economic chauvinism' and the finding that it is not so much the unemployed as the precariously employed that vote for neo-nationalist parties, but which also extends to cultural chauvinism ('Why should our children learn about these foreigners' festivals at school?' 'Why should they be allowed to flaunt their religious beliefs by wearing headscarves in the supermarket?'). As Pinxten (this volume) among others notes, 'cultural fundamentalism' (as identified by Stolcke 1996) has often come to replace race in the discourse of neo-nationalists (see also Banks 1996: 171–78).

In many instances, including the Indian and Australian examples (Banerjee, Kapferer and Morris), a series of challenges to individual self-interest are rhetorically linked to a perceived or actual rise in rights and benefits gained by newcomers to the nation, or those previously kept in a position of socio-economic disadvantage, such as Indian Muslims or Aboriginal Australians. As noted above, and in greater detail below, economic insecurities prompted by globalisation are identified at the local level as uncertainties regarding the relationship between persons. While this is clearly manifest with regard to immigration and non-European migrants, uncertainties in other kinds of relationships are also implicated. Most notable among these are gender relations.

Older forms of nationalism shaped and more importantly were shaped by nineteenth-century understandings of gender relations in the respective European states: men, for example, were expected to do their duty at times of war, while a woman's duty was to keep the home fires burning while her husband was away. Naturalised notions of biology as destiny applied as much to citizens' roles within the nation as in any other realm of life, within the family, for example. Within neo-nationalist thought such naturalised gender notions are still to be found, albeit problematically (Banks, this volume), but the entanglement of nation and gender runs much deeper, at a more symbolic level. As Said (1978) and more particularly Inden (1990) have noted, the Orient and especially India were feminised in nineteenth-century European thought, and more generally the idiom of the European colonial project was one of barely disguised active masculine hegemony over passive feminised subjects. In her chapter Banerjee notes that the early twentieth-century reform of Hinduism as 'Hindutva' – the precursor of today's religious nationalism in India – entailed masculinising it, while in recent years a defiantly militarist and masculine representation of the god Ram, the sacred figurehead of Hindutva, has displaced an older, more benign representation.

Anthropologists have noted a general tendency in many societies for 'women' to be considered in the same categorical space as 'other'. While many of the chapters in this volume note the effect of economic globalisation in promoting employment insecurity in European states, this is also accompanied in many cases by insecurities regarding masculinity. If, in late capitalist society, masculinity is at least in part defined by employment, then a threat to one is a threat to the other. It may only be coincidental that post-Second World War labour migration to Europe was coterminous with the growth of employment opportunities for women, but it nevertheless doubles the bruising felt by many men. That women in European states vote for neo-nationalist political parties does not invalidate this line of argument. What the neo-nationalists overwhelmingly offer is reassurance, and masculine reassurance at that: a firm hand that will control things such as rampant immigration, meddling by EU bureaucrats and so forth; in brief, a return to order. The self – usually perceived as adult, healthy, white, male and breeding – was a carefully nurtured project of nineteenth- and twentieth-century Euro-American individualism. Today, it is often perceived to be under threat from a variety of sources that seek to dilute it, remove its autonomy or to promote other forms of sociality – the faith community, for example. Neo-nationalists promise to restore familiar forms of identification for the self, not least the nation itself.

In this sense, the analysis of some of neo-nationalism's limited, previous 'success stories' demonstrate in a particularly revealing manner how neo-nationalist parties managed to use existing political spaces for questioning existing notions of nationhood, while at the same time promising to reassert nationhood in redefined ways. For the Netherlands and for Austria, where these forces were more successful for a while, the chapters by Fillitz and by Sunier and van Ginkel demonstrate how neo-nationalist local leaderships were able to continuously question and challenge established notions of democratic consensus, and prevailing ideas about political correctness. By opening up new discursive fields of conflict, and of radical redefinition, these neo-nationalist leaderships were capable of creating new forms of public awareness about the nation's allegedly insecure presence and future. It was only by creating these new discursive and ideological spaces, and by posing themselves as those who had the courage to do so, that a twofold discursive and ideological goal could be achieved. Enhancing, manipulating and exaggerating existing notions of insecurity about a nation's identity went hand in hand with successfully propagating the remedy for this perceived ill: national reinvigoration and cultural reinforcement against the nation's newly identified enemies. Neo-nationalism therefore urgently needs popular feelings of national insecurity, and fears about loss of cultural identity.

Because of these requirements, neo-nationalism constantly manipulates the diagnosis of national sickness in such a manner that its own therapies and remedies sell best. In turn, the pursuit of these discursive and ideological necessities leads neo-nationalists towards positing concepts like 'the cultural right to self-determination' and related notions, as an absolute. On a discursive and theoretical level at least, anthropologists' encounters with neo-nationalism are far from being concluded.

Globalisation

Historical perspectives on today's neo-nationalism in Western Europe, as discussed so far in this introduction, as well as by the authors in this volume, thus contribute two primary insights. First, they demonstrate that current developments of neo-nationalism in Western Europe have not emerged independently of their local short-term and long-term historical preconditions. This helps to illuminate some of the diversity and heterogeneity in these Europe-wide phenomena. Secondly, however, these historical perspectives also remind us of wider, long-term factors beyond local constellations, and of their impact upon the present. In this sense, nationalism emerged in one form or another as an unavoidable accompanying factor to modern states and market economies, and often continues to be their resource and partner. Against that background, today's neo-nationalism has arisen at a time when Western Europe began to move beyond the collapse of colonialism, and beyond the end of the Cold War.

As much as these historical perspectives therefore enlighten us about preceding and ongoing contexts, they nevertheless lead us back to the present. Today's neo-nationalism in Europe cannot therefore be seriously understood in terms of any 'comeback' by Franco, Mussolini or Hitler, as some historians and political scientists tend to imply. At best, such interpretations represent a well-meaning moralist warning of little practical relevance. Today's neo-nationalist groups use, manipulate and instrumentalise the past of course, but for purposes and goals that are rooted in the present. Most contributors to this volume therefore insist, quite rightly in our opinion, that today's neo-nationalism is best understood in terms of the current phase of globalisation, albeit not wholly caused by it. Indeed, our earlier discussion of 'threatened identities' is complemented by the analysis of 'groups that feel less threatened' by the current effects of globalisation, such as parts of the upper middle classes, of the corporate business elite or many of Europe's subsidised farmers (see McDonald and Seiser, this volume).

To the extent that neo-nationalists build their mass support on rallying 'threatened identities' of all sorts, and on enhancing, manipulating and instrumentalising their concerns and fears, neo-nationalism can indeed be understood as one specific reaction against various effects of the current phase of globalisation. It is by no means the only reaction, though. This is evidenced by the worldwide anti-globalisation or 'alter-globalisation' movements, which represent a structural alternative to the neo-nationalist kind of reaction against globalisation.

If neo-nationalism thus can be identified as an essentialist and seclusive reaction against the current phase of globalisation, then this essentialist and seclusive tendency primarily relates to 'culture'. Attempts to reinvigorate essentialised notions of what is constructed as local culture, in a defensive and often pessimistic manner against alleged centres that pose a threat, are frequently a central element of neo-nationalist ideology and propaganda. Whereas in strictly economic terms, neo-nationalists often pursue business-friendly and sometimes even neo-liberal policies, their cultural priorities cut across this whenever they favour strict state sanctions with regard to new immigrants, illegal alien residents or other local minorities. One may therefore wonder if the pursuit of 'identity politics' and of 'multiculturalism' has not sometimes involuntarily played into the hands of neo-nationalists and their cultural priorities. By identifying and defining minorities, and by isolating special group interests (with the aim of protecting them) from wider social concerns, a tendency towards 'desolidarisation' becomes acceptable from one side, which neo-nationalists are then able to exploit and to enhance from their side. In a similar manner, anthropology itself is well advised to reflect on why neo-nationalists today are able to use such essentialised and static notions of culture that display embarrassing similarities to earlier anthropological concepts. Those coherent, static and self-containing notions of culture as employed by neo-nationalists all over the world today are derived from a legacy to which anthropologists themselves once contributed in the decisive manner of strong cultural relativism, and which they began to criticise and redefine only very recently.[11]

It is important, however, to distinguish the neo-nationalists' rhetoric from the realities of their political practice. 'National cultural values' are instrumental tools for mobilising support, but are not an end in themselves for most European neo-nationalist leaders. In the sense that these leaderships often represent both small and large, local and 'national' business groups, their cultural rhetoric in many cases has the smokescreen effect of diverting public attention away from their actual, socio-economic priorities. That 'smokescreen effect' may sometimes be difficult to identify in individual cases, but it will hardly escape any broader, comparative assessment.[12] This is another reason that makes it especially important to study neo-nationalism in a comparative manner. On the basis of detailed local analysis of the phenomenon, a comparativist approach, as pursued in this volume, contributes additional insights into the specificities, contradictions and commonalities of the phenomenon at large.

This raises the question of whether neo-nationalism is or is not a special development within Western Europe alone. The answers suggested in this volume indicate that it is not. Neo-nationalism may have become particularly loud and conspicuous in Western Europe by the beginning of the twenty-first century, but parallel and comparable movements are simultaneously establishing themselves in Australia, New Zealand and to an extent in Canada. If these countries represent examples of the legacy of Anglo-European cultural and political hegemony, so too does India, albeit in a highly modified form. As Banerjee notes (this volume) the origins of contemporary religious nationalism in India lie in the recent resurgence of a strand of anti-colonial thought that commenced in the early years of the twentieth century. This strand sought the reform and politicisation of religion as a bulwark against the British, but was overtaken by Gandhi's project to reform politics morally through religion, and so faltered in the years leading up to and immediately after Indian independence. The Gandhian weakness, however, was to avoid modernity and to set India on a path (largely successful for many decades it must be said) of economic autonomy; when the country turned to economic liberalisation in the late 1980s the resulting insecurities identified here for European nation states were just as strongly felt. Conversely, in Australia as noted by Kapferer and Morris (this volume), the progress towards neo-nationalism entails a number of ironies, apparent paradoxes and redefinitions of meaning to get to the same point. While Pauline Hanson's One Nation rhetoric reflects the same economic and cultural insecurities found elsewhere, it again builds upon a much older substrate of ideas. In this instance, however, those ideas were anti-state, the result of a people being formed not by the colonial state but through their elimination from it. The resulting ideology of egalitarianism is seen to be under threat, not simply from without but from within, from the 'white cosmopolites' who have sought to introduce difference where none should exist.

These are some of the basic considerations and insights that have persuaded us that in methodological terms, an anthropological assessment of neo-nationalism today is best pursued by combining detailed local investigations with comparative analysis in a transnational perspective. It is this methodological basis that allows an additional, transnational comment on Western Europe, as the regional focus of this volume. In a way, the 'new' forms of nationalism in Western Europe, India, Canada, Australia and New Zealand all share a common historical context after colonialism and after the end of the Cold War, amidst dramatic changes in global economy and politics. What makes Western European development today somewhat different from the other cases discussed here, however, is not only Europe's specific historical positioning with regard to the colonial and Cold War past, but also the role of the state in Europe today.

Whether the current phase of globalisation goes hand in hand with a general weakening of the role of the state (Appadurai 2000) or whether, alternatively, it brings about the increase of at least some states' power (Sassen 2000; 2001) remains an ongoing debate in the social sciences. In whatever way this is going to be assessed on a global level, it is certain that in Western Europe national states have delegated, to a greater or lesser extent, at least some of their former sovereignty to the European Union. When it comes to currency issues, international imports, labour immigration or state subsidies for industry and agriculture, it is no longer the 'national state' alone but to an increasing extent the European Union as well that sets the decisive standards. In this sense, the EU increasingly represents a regionally organised, transnational quasi-state, which is simultaneously a product of globalisation, and in some instances also a bulwark against it.

From this perspective, we may pursue the insights presented by Maryon McDonald and Gertraud Seiser in this volume one step further. The EU as a regional and transnational quasi-state has in fact been accumulating some of those powers that had formerly been held by national states. Neo-nationalists interpret this as a process of disempowerment for nations, i.e., as a process based on the false promise that the future would thus become more secure while it increasingly turns out to be less so. It is the EU's own systemic ambivalence of partially being a protective barrier against, as much as partially being a tool for and product of, globalisation that therefore sets the systemic and structural standards for neo-nationalists' agency. In the long run, the EU's structural tendency to raise expectations and hopes that will ultimately be disappointed is a factor in its own right, which neo-nationalists will continue to exploit in order to reclaim 'their states'.

Performing Nationalism: The Symbolic Dimension

Several of these factors concerning globalisation and the ambivalent role of the EU have already been noted by political scientists, journalists and others. One of those fields to which anthropology makes a unique contribution is its consideration of the symbolic realm, through which both unique events and structural constraints are understood for those involved. For voters, a decision to support one party rather than another is not necessarily a fully willed act, a utilitarian weighing up of means and ends, nor are voters simply passively responding to the mesmerising power of political leaders. Rather, as much anthropological work on political oratory has demonstrated (e.g., Bloch 1975), medium, message and response must find a goodness of fit within a much broader social and cultural environment. Whether by conscious intention or not, neo-nationalist politicians in Europe and beyond have found ways to achieve this goodness of fit. For example, many rely on balancing the shock of transgression with the reassurance of familiarity. There is a constant rhetoric of speaking the plain truth, of saying things that other politicians would not dare to say: for example, that there are simply too many immigrants in the country; that however much one might want it otherwise, 'they' simply cannot assimilate to our ways; that 'they' are in danger of dragging us back to the Middle Ages. Yet at the same time this is balanced with a rhetoric of caring compassion: for example, that more of the state budget will be spent on the elderly and infirm; that there will be a return to living in small local communities free of drugs and sexual deviants; that the faceless, interfering bureaucrats of Brussels will be sent on their way.

In this way, neo-nationalist politicians – as politicians of all hues the world over – aid the voter in identifying and then seeking to protect symbolic capital. As used by economists, this term has come to mean networks and linkages (kinship, friendship) upon which people can draw to support their economic strategies. As used by anthropologists (sometimes in the variant form, cultural capital [Bourdieu 1977]), it covers a broader field, encompassing a variety of intangible and symbolic elements. More importantly for anthropologists, symbols do not exist in isolation ('my home', 'motherhood'), and indeed symbols are not things at all but a set of what are understood to be transcendent truths to which particular signs point.

Symbolisation is the logic by which different fields of cultural activity are brought into relation with one another. This is shown especially clearly in Fillitz' remarks on the cultural policy of the Austrian Freedom Party: in formulating a hierarchy of art forms, one which favours folk and popular art over fine and experimental art, the party sets up a logic by which the far more abstract and ambiguous relationship between the German-speaking majority within Austria and the relationship between the Austrian state and the EU can be understood.

Such symbolic relationships and the identification of symbolic capital cannot, however, merely be confined to party manifestos and politicians' speeches. To have force and power they must be continuously emergent, constantly present threads in the weaving of social life; in short, they must be performed. We mean this in both a literal and a less literal fashion. One thing that marks many of the current generation of neo-nationalists out from many of their political opponents is their showmanship. The Austrian Freedom Party uses a constant series of referendums, despite their political ineffectiveness, to highlight the two-party conservatism that has dominated the Austrian political scene, and to roll out alternative campaigns. The British National Party makes well-publicised visits to towns and cities recently affected by outbreaks of racist violence. Lal Krishna Advani, of the Indian BJP, is photographed posing as Lord Ram, bow and arrow in his hand. Similarly, several prominent neo-nationalist politicians manifest a distinctive style: Jörg Haider poses as a dashing sportsman, perfect white teeth flashing; Pim Fortuyn revelled in his flamboyant lifestyle, which included a chauffeur and butler; even the rumpled veteran Le Pen comes across well on television. With their sharp suits, their media-friendly sound-bite rhetoric, even their occasional brawls (Le Pen, again), the neo-nationalists perform the play of politics with gusto, putting their socialist and conservative opponents in the shade. We are not suggesting that their popularity rests entirely upon these apparently superficial factors – we have outlined a number of additional political, economic and sociological forces above – but neither should these be discounted. Life is lived in the round and needs to be studied as such.

Towards a New Theory of Nationalism?

Although anthropologists, in both a personal and professional capacity, had been concerned with issues of racism and discrimination against migrants in European nation states for many years, it is probably true to say that the rise of neo-nationalist movements, in Europe and elsewhere, caught them unprepared. Some, including some of our contributors, had been working on such issues for many years of course, but within the academy it is apparent to us that existing theories of nationalism are insufficient to grasp the problem and subject it to rigorous analysis; hence the justification for the present volume. But what is the 'problem' that the phenomenon of neo-nationalism poses for established theories of nationalism? In broad terms there are two aspects to existing theory. On the one hand, and by far the more dominant, there are a series of voluntarist explanations, all of which propose that nationalism is a willed construct brought into being for a variety of purposes (to mobilise labour for capital more efficiently, to make a decisive break with the dead weight of the past while seeming to provide continuity with it, and so on). Such ideas are found in the work of Hobsbawm (1990), Eriksen (1993) and others. On the other hand, we have more systemic approaches, which posit that nationalism arises out of a set of structural and historical conditions (a new form of religion after official religion's decline, the transformation of ethnic identities within a capitalist context and so on). Such ideas are found in the work of Durkheim (1960) and Smith (1986). Several authors combine both perspectives, most notably Anderson (1983) and Gellner (1983).

Neo-nationalism poses a problem for both strands. For the voluntarist strand, while neo-nationalism may seem to offer a sense of psycho-social reassurance in a rapidly changing and apparently incomprehensible world, its obvious lack of economic rationality cannot be disguised, no matter how skilful the performances and rhetoric of its proponents. Yet for the systemic approach, while neo-nationalism could be seen as an inevitable outcome of the increasing structural tension between globalisation and older ideologies of nationalism, globalisation seems well on the road to creating an idea of a new 'global nation' with a single ideology of liberal democracy.[13] From this vantage point, neo-nationalism could be seen simply as a phase, a transitional period before the new global order is established. There are two problems with this assessment. The first is a disciplinary caveat: anthropologists are generally extremely reluctant to offer predictions about the development of social trends. The second is that contemporary anthropology is also aware of the need to balance structure with agency, to factor in the singularity of actions and events as transformative of structures. From the current historical vantage point, after the invasions of Afghanistan and Iraq, it seems extremely unlikely that a single global ideology will be established in the very near future, thus giving neo-nationalist ideology plenty of time to take root or mutate.

Yet as anthropologists, we do not feel the need to apologise for what might seem a prevaricating, wait-and-see stance. Over its history the discipline has always maintained a balance between theory or analysis and empirical data derived from field investigation, always seeking to allow one to inform and transform the other. Earlier approaches to nationalism were sufficient for their time, for the known state of play. In the last decade or so things have changed, within Europe and outside, and it is time for theory to change too.

We began this introduction with the statement that neo-nationalism has disappeared from the centre stage of Western European politics, and yet we conclude by indicating that the problem and the phenomenon persist nonetheless. Whether centre stage or waiting in the wings, neo-nationalist forces and parties now seem to be a permanent presence on the political scene in Western Europe and beyond.

From a transnational and global perspective, neo-nationalist forces by the early twenty-first century have managed to establish themselves in a number of the world's large regions and subcontinents. From Australia to South Asia, in both Eastern and Western Europe, comparable parties and movements have positioned themselves in national parliaments and governments, with some considerable impact on state power. These movements mostly operate within legal, parliamentary channels, and they use essentialised notions of local culture to mobilise against real and alleged threats to local identities of status, gender, religion, nationhood and ethnicity. The visions that these movements advocate tend to be seclusive and retrogressive in cultural and political terms, while in economic terms they pursue priorities that call upon heterogeneous interest groups while remaining friendly to domestic business. In contexts of dramatic social mobility, neo-nationalists rely on colourful symbolism and on charismatic performance in order to rally heterogeneous interest groups behind their agendas. These are new variants of nationalism in a new, global era. As more and more parts of the world encounter this new wave of 'constitutional nationalism', then anthropology is well suited to meeting the challenge, empirically and theoretically.

Notes

1. For Germany in particular, this assessment is to a limited extent related to particularly stringent legal regulations on right extremism in Germany, as a consequence of the country's history in the twentieth century. Although two parties, the NDP (National Democratic Party) and the DVU (German People's Union), managed to gain a presence in two state parliaments (Saxony and Brandenburg) of East Germany in 2004, their legal status remains highly contested and they are still best regarded as neo-Nazi organisations.
2. Aside from the 'everyday' risks to health and personal safety posed by harsh environments, disease and so forth encountered by many anthropologists, the work of Philippe Bourgois on New York crack dealers (1995) is a good example of the deliberate undertaking of such challenging subjects; while Nordstrom and Robben's volume on 'fieldwork under fire' (1995) collects accounts of anthropologists often inadvertently caught up in violent and warlike situations. Closer to the subject matter of neo-nationalism, the sociologist Nigel Fielding made 'covert' observations of the British National Front in the 1970s, as well as conducting more 'overt' interviews with members (Fielding and Fielding 1986: 54; see also Fielding 1981 and Banks's chapter in this volume).
3. Examples of such 'studying up', in Laura Nader's terms, range from George Marcus and Peter Dobkin Hall's work with powerful Dallas business families (1992) to Ulf Hannerz' recent work on equally powerful (if perhaps less elite) foreign correspondents (2004), taking in along the way studies of the rich and powerful in Hollywood (Powdermaker 1951) and Bollywood (Thomas 1985), and European Union *fonctionnaires* (McDonald 1996). It has to be admitted, however, that anthropological research on elites is far outweighed by anthropological studies of minorities, the dispossessed and the socially marginalised – see Shore and Nugent (2002).
4. Perhaps the most persuasive example is Katherine Verdery's work on Romania (1991); see also examples in Hann (1993).
5. For this, see the many anthropological micro-studies of actual markets or economic transactions within capitalist and quasi-capitalist contexts, in which the presumed rationalities of neo-classical economic theory (profit maximisation, for example) are entwined with and subverted by other, more socially contingent understandings of value and success. The 'triumph' experienced by

Hungarian Gypsies when they deceive a Gorgio in an apparently negative economic transaction of horse trading is a good example (Stewart 1997: Chapters 9 and 10).

6. Such a position is neither acceptable to nor necessary for extreme right-wing and neo-Nazi groups, which can quite happily entertain their unrealistic notions of ethnic homogeneity phrased in their aggressive hate idiom of 'racial purity'.

7. Approaches towards anthropology's colonial origins are diverse, though all stress that the relationship between the two ventures is by no means as simple as anthropology being a mere 'handmaiden' to colonialism; see Asad (1973), Goody (1995) and Stocking (1991). No less diverse are the discipline's approaches to the study of minority and migrant communities, though many if not all stress the necessity of understanding the 'home' culture prior to migration and the importance of colonialism and its consequences in facilitating migration; see Banks (1996: Chapter 4) for an overview.

8. For a relatively recent survey of such a perspective see the essays in Fardon (1995), James (1995), Miller (1995), Moore (1995) and Strathern (1995), all representing anthropology's understanding of the relationship between the local and the global. More recent work on transnationalism (e.g., Hannerz 1996) has operated within the same set of dual understandings.

9. Given the fieldwork experiences of many anthropologists in the non-Euro-American world, we assume that many are predisposed to take the side of fragile, marginal and politically dispossessed populations. The neo-nationalists themselves could conceivably be described in this way, yet their rhetoric against the more fragile, more marginalised and more dispossessed minority migrant groups in Europe renders them unsympathetic to our contributors. See also Fielding and Fielding's thoughtful discussion of being able – or not – to 'appreciate' the ideas and statements of groups such as the National Front (Fielding and Fielding 1986: 55).

10. Some additional aspects of this methodological discussion are examined in Gingrich (2004).

11. See, for example, Wright (1998). She notes that the term has in part been hijacked by politicians and media types, who, while declaring that they use the term 'in an anthropological sense', effectively claim an authority that has not been bestowed and which forecloses discussion. See also Brumann (1999) who seeks to reclaim the term for anthropology.

12. Harking back to a much older, Marxist sociology, the claim was made by Verena Stolcke at the original workshop that press reports of incidents of 'racist' violence (between natives and migrant workers) in the Spanish intensive agricultural industry served to mask poor pay and exploitative labour relations for all concerned. See also Castles and Kosack's pioneering work on migration and race in Western Europe (1973).

13. Although much challenged, not least by anthropologists, this is the thrust of Fukuyama's 'end of history' thesis (1992).

Bibliography

Anderson, B. 1983. *Imagined Communities: Reflections on the Origins and Spread of Nationalism*. London: Verso.

Appadurai, A. 1996. *Modernity at Large: Cultural Dimensions of Globalization*. Minneapolis: Minnesota University Press.

———— 2000. 'Grassroots Globalization and the Research Imagination', *Public Culture* 12(1): 1–19.

Asad, T. ed. 1973. *Anthropology and the Colonial Encounter*. London: Ithaca Press.

Banks, M. 1996. *Ethnicity: Anthropological Constructions*. London: Routledge.

Baumann, G. and Gingrich, A. 2004. *Grammars of Identity: A Structural Approach*. Oxford: Berghahn.

Beck, U. 1997. *Was ist Globalisierung? Irrtümer des Globalismus – Antworten auf Globalisierung.* Frankfurt/Main: Suhrkamp.

Bloch, M. ed. 1975. *Political Language and Oratory in Traditional Society.* London: Academic Press.

Bourdieu, P. 1977 [1972]. *Outline of a Theory of Practice.* Cambridge: Cambridge University Press.

Bourgois, P. 1995. *In Search of Respect: Selling Crack in El Barrio.* Cambridge: Cambridge University Press.

Bringa, T. 1995. *Being Muslim the Bosnian Way: Identity and Community in a Central Bosnian Village.* Princeton: Princeton University Press.

Brumann, C. 1999. 'Writing for Culture: Why a Successful Concept Should Not be Discarded', *Current Anthropology* 40: 1–27.

Carsten, J. ed. 2000. *Cultures of Relatedness: New Approaches to the Study of Kinship.* Cambridge: Cambridge University Press.

Castles, S. and Kosack, G. 1973. *Immigrant Workers and Class Struggle in Western Europe.* Oxford: Oxford University Press.

Chapman, M. 1992. *The Celts: The Construction of a Myth.* New York: St Martin's Press.

Durkheim, E. 1960 [1933]. *The Division of Labour in Society.* Glencoe: The Free Press.

Eriksen, T.H. 1993. *Ethnicity and Nationalism: Anthropological Perspectives.* London: Pluto Press.

Fardon, R. ed. 1995. *Counterworks: Managing the Diversity of Knowledge.* London: Routledge.

Fielding, N. 1981. *The National Front.* London: Routledge & Kegan Paul.

———— and Fielding, J.L. 1986. *Linking Data: The Articulation of Qualitative and Quantitative Methods in Social Research.* London: Sage.

Fukuyama, F. 1992. *The End of History and the Last Man.* London: Hamish Hamilton.

Gellner, E. 1979. 'Notes Towards a Theory of Ideology', in E. Gellner ed. *Spectacles and Predicaments.* Cambridge: Cambridge University Press.

———— 1983. *Nations and Nationalism.* Oxford: Blackwell.

Gingrich, A. 2002. 'When Ethnic Majorities are Dethroned: Towards a Methodology of Self-reflexive, Controlled Macro-comparison', in A. Gingrich and R.G. Fox eds *Anthropology, by Comparison.* London: Routledge, pp. 225–48.

———— 2004. 'Concepts of Racism Vanishing, Movements of Racism Rising? Global Issues and Austrian Ethnography', *Ethnos* 69(2): 156–76.

Gingrich, A. and Fox, R.G. eds. 2002. *Anthropology, by Comparison.* London: Routledge.

Goody, J. 1995. *The Expansive Moment: The Rise of Social Anthropology in Britain and Africa, 1918–1970.* Cambridge: Cambridge University Press.

Hann, C. ed. 1993. *Socialism: Ideals, Ideologies, and Local Practice.* London: Routledge.

Hannerz, U. 1996. *Transnational Connections: Culture, People, Places.* London: Routledge.

———— 2004. *Foreign News: Exploring the World of Foreign Correspondents.* Chicago: University of Chicago Press.

Hobsbawm, E. 1990. *Nations and Nationalism since 1780.* Cambridge: Cambridge University Press.

Holmes, D. 2000. *Integral Europe: Fast-capitalism, Multiculturalism, Neofascism.* Princeton: Princeton University Press.

Inden, R. 1990. *Imagining India.* Oxford: Blackwell.

James, W. ed. 1995. *The Pursuit of Certainty: Religious and Cultural Formulations.* London: Routledge.

Jenkins, R. 1996. *Social Identity*. London: Routledge.

Marcus, G.E. with Dobkin Hall, P. 1992. *Lives in Trust: The Fortunes of Dynastic Families in Late Twentieth-century America*. Boulder: Westview Press.

McDonald, M. 1989. *'We are not French!' Language, Culture and Identity in Brittany*. London: Routledge.

───── 1996. '"Unity in Diversity": Some Tensions in the Construction of Europe', *Social Anthropology* 4(1): 47–60.

Miller, D. ed. 1995. *Worlds Apart: Modernity Through the Prism of the Local*. London: Routledge.

Moore, H. ed. 1995. *What is Social Knowledge For?* London: Routledge.

Nordstrom, C. and Robben, A.C.G.M. eds. 1995. *Fieldwork Under Fire: Contemporary Studies of Violence and Survival*. Berkeley: University of California Press.

Powdermaker, H. 1951. *Hollywood, The Dream Factory: An Anthropologist Looks at the Movie-makers*. London: Secker and Warburg.

Said, E. 1978. *Orientalism*. New York: Pantheon Books.

Sassen, S. 2000. 'Spatialities and Temporalities of the Global: Elements of a Theorization', *Public Culture* 12(1): 215–32.

───── 2001. *The Global City*. New York: Oxford University Press.

Shore, C. and Nugent, S. eds. 2002. *Elite Cultures: Anthropological Perspectives*. London: Routledge.

Smith, A.D. 1986. *The Ethnic Origins of Nations*. Oxford: Blackwell.

Stewart, M. 1997. *The Time of the Gypsies*. Boulder: Westview Press.

Stocking, G.W. Jr. ed. 1991. *Colonial Situations: Essays on the Contextualization of Ethnographic Knowledge*. Madison: University of Wisconsin Press.

Strathern, M. 1991. *Partial Connections*. Savage: Rowman and Littlefield Publishers.

───── ed. 1995. *Shifting Contexts*. London: Routledge.

Stolcke, V. 1996. 'Claiming Culture Again', *Current Anthropology* 37: 1–36.

Thomas, R. 1985. 'Indian Cinema – Pleasures and Popularity', *Screen* 26(3–4): 116–32.

Verdery, K. 1991. *National Ideology Under Socialism: Identity and Cultural Politics in Ceausescu's Romania*. Berkeley: University of California Press.

Wright, S. 1998. 'The Politicization of "Culture"', *Anthropology Today* 14(1): 7–15.

PART I
Concepts and Methods

Chapter 1

Nation, Status and Gender in Trouble?

Exploring Some Contexts and Characteristics of Neo-nationalism in Western Europe

Andre Gingrich

Introduction

Until recently, the new rise in Western Europe of far-right parties was a major issue of public concern. It made headlines in the international media, mass rallies were held against these parties, prominent politicians from mainstream parties frequently issued public warnings about them, official committees were set up to investigate the phenomenon.

That first period of wider public concern may have passed; it remains, however, for individuals to undertake more profound anthropological analyses of the phenomenon. Anthropologists were among those who initially commented on and criticised the rise to government of these parties. There certainly is nothing wrong with anthropological commentaries on headline topics. On the contrary, the anthropologist's role as a public intellectual may well deserve a higher profile and further substantiation, as Adam Kuper, Ulf Hannerz and others have argued repeatedly (Gingrich 2002b). However, such public comments by anthropologists on current events will frequently and necessarily lack the conceptual wealth and empirical detail indispensable for solid research. When the spotlight moves away from specific events, opportunities for new research increase: with the pressure off, it is possible to take a step back, and assess changes and characteristics from medium- and long-term perspectives.

This is what my contribution will attempt to do: to move beyond public commentaries and study a relatively recent phenomenon with the tools and means of anthropology, which requires empirical and conceptual effort. By definition, empirical efforts by anthropologists imply fieldwork, which is still in its early stages among most authors with an interest in this topic. This volume counts some of the best examples among its contributors. For my part, I have presented results of earlier ethnographic work on the topic elsewhere (Gingrich 2002a; 2004), including methodological reflections on such fieldwork 'among people with whom one does not sympathise'. Out of these first insights and results, some initial conceptual deliberations were offered (Gingrich 2003), which the present contribution will attempt to elaborate further. This chapter is thus based on earlier ethnographic and archival empirical work, and it will elaborate a number of conceptual reflections and suggestions for the purpose of further series of fieldwork.

Here I explore the main contexts and characteristics of Western European far-right parties.[1] These will be pursued through three methodological procedures: first, by comparing certain aspects of the present phenomenon regionally; second, by assessing some historical contrasts and parallels; and third, by examining some aspects of an exemplary case of potentially wider relevance. Regional comparison, historical contrast and exemplary case study are thus chosen as methodological devices to arrive at a more detailed and precise research hypothesis for future ethnographic studies of this phenomenon.

These methodological devices will simultaneously explore three topical dimensions of Western Europe's new far-right parliamentary parties. First, regional comparison will demonstrate that these parties share a new variant of nationalism. It will be shown that certain contexts in Western Europe seem to be more favourable to this variant than others, for which some of the underlying factors will be explored. Secondly, it will be shown through historical contrast how contexts and practices of these new variants of nationalism differ from earlier forms and how, most notably, questions of social status and fears about downward social mobility inform mass support for these parties. Finally, the Austrian case will highlight two additional points of wider relevance: first, conflicting interests among the new nationalists' own clientele have to be overcome and redirected through spectacular campaigns and charismatic performance, in ways that seduce and emotionalise. Second, these efforts towards constant mobilisation not only reconstruct nationhood and reassert social status, but they also reach out towards male voters in particular by enhancing specific aspects of gender roles. These three methodological exercises will lead to the conclusion that in the current phase of globalisation, and in various European countries, these parties manage to address and instrumentalise key questions of national, social and gender identity.

Explorations in Regional Comparison

Douglas R. Holmes (2000) coined the term 'integral Europe' for those heterogeneous socio-political movements in Europe and beyond that combine essentialised visions of selves and some form of local, regional, ethnic, religious or national chauvinism with stereotypes of their 'opponent others'. My own explorations in this section build on those useful insights by Holmes, but they suggest further differentiation using political criteria. The focus in this chapter, and in fact this whole volume, is on those parties from the far right that strive for mass influence primarily through parliamentary, electoral and basically peaceful means. 'Integralist' movements may comprise sub-groups with affiliations across the political spectrum. If we maintain the somewhat worn-out distinction of 'right' and 'left', then it is precisely to point out that the parties discussed here position themselves within a much narrower range of the political spectrum than integralism would allow. These parties therefore try to establish themselves on the far right within the existing political system, while simultaneously manipulating it for their own purposes, in the hope of transforming it according to their own visions and programmes.

For this first step of regional comparison along political lines, I rely on the excellent work of political scientists such as Jean-Yves Camus (2002) and Cas Mudde (1998), although my conclusions differ slightly. In view of Western Europe's diversity, the fact that these parties display parallels other than belonging to the 'far right' actually might be surprising. Indeed, the public self-presentation by these parties continuously emphasises the opposite, by insisting on their respective 'authenticity', 'originality', 'specificity', and on their 'rootedness' in each country's region, history and culture. It is almost by definition that these parties follow ideologies that claim they are 'different'. They also bitterly disagree with one another: Italy's Alleanza Nazionale and Austria's Freedom Party have long avoided contact because of the South Tyrolean/Alto Adige question.[2] Or, to cite another example, most parliamentary far-right parties in Scandinavia do not want to display much open sympathy for the Belgian Vlaams Blok.[3]

Recognising Western Europe's heterogeneity is an intellectual and empirical necessity. Yet to emphasise nothing but difference among the same 'class' of examples would not only amount to empiricism, but would also overlook the necessary task of demonstrating precisely which factors are at work to make these various examples nevertheless belong to the same class. Besides, such particularist empiricism would come very close to reinforcing these parties' self-congratulatory propaganda of 'authenticity' and 'originality'.

At least three major programmatic parallels can be identified among Western Europe's far-right parliamentary parties:

1. A basic populist criticism of any further EU integration, which would take away decision-making power from national governments and imply a heavier financial burden.
2. A general, profound scepticism towards further EU enlargement, particularly in view of the low income and cheap labour markets of potential new EU members.
3. A hard-line orientation against illegal immigrant residents inside the EU and any new immigration from outside, and, at the same time, a particular emphasis on cutting down on social services and cultural expenses by the national state.

Notwithstanding more or less important differences, Western Europe's far-right parliamentary parties share these three orientations. This includes not only those from countries inside the EU (before 2004), but also their Swiss and Norwegian counterparts, with the necessary qualification of them being against their countries' entry into the EU at all. At the very least, these key orientations clarify that some version of *nationalism* is central to these parties' programmatic agendas. They are against 'Brussels', 'immigration' and 'enlargement' if it is seen to affect their countries. On most levels, they seek to reassert nationhood (or ethnic/regional selves in the Swiss German, Flemish Belgian and northern Italian cases) against 'outsiders'.

Identifying a common nationalist dimension among these parties also sheds additional theoretical light upon their respective differences. In fact, one important aspect of these differences relates to the fact that all ideologists of nationality and of nationalism have to present 'their' nation as unique. Benedict Anderson called this one of the basic paradoxes of nationalism, by which 'the formal universality of nationality as a socio-cultural concept' contrasts with 'the irremediable particularity of its concrete manifestations' (1991: 5). This indicates that Western Europe's 'new nationalists' share this paradox with their historical predecessors, as analysed by Anderson. Far from presenting an insurmountable obstacle to the analysis of nationalism, the paradox can be acknowledged as part of any analysis of the topic. For our present purposes, we may state that beyond their unavoidable and necessary differences, these parties share a combination of 'far-right' and 'new nationalist' political orientations.

On this basis we move on to the second step in our comparative regional exploration, in order to find out more about the local conditions in which these parties have thrived. In what kinds of Western European countries, then, have these parties managed to establish themselves? I will confine myself to the fifteen member countries of the EU prior to 2004, and to Norway and Switzerland (members of the European Economic Area, EEA). I chose the two criteria of below or above '10 percent of national voters', and of being or not being a 'national government member' in order to identify the degree to which these parties have managed to establish themselves substantially inside national parliamentary systems.

Until 2003, no far-right parliamentary party had been able to establish itself in the national parliaments of Britain, France, Germany or Spain. Among the 'big five',[4] Italy represents a clear exception in this regard. In Italy, the radically autonomist Lega Nord (2001: 4 percent) and the Alleanza Nazionale (2001: 12 percent) – a successor to the former neo-fascist party – were members of a national coalition government by 2003. In spite of a symbolic 18 percent in the 2002 presidential elections, France, by contrast, features quite a different constellation. There, the Front National and the Mouvement National Republicain (MNR), now divided, hardly manage to come close to 10 percent of votes for the Assemblée Nationale, let alone any government participation. Otherwise among the 'big five', far-right parliamentary parties to date are irrelevant on a national scale. This signals that the rise of far-right parties, despite a relatively successful initial period in Western Europe, has so far not become a mainstream current throughout the EU. In 2005 it is still confined to more specific hot spots in Western Europe, and it is not yet central to developments among the 'big five'.

We are thus led to identify these hot spots in the smaller EU and EEA countries.[5] For that purpose, it is useful to differentiate them from the outset, again, by using economic indicators. Among the 'lower and medium average income countries', Portugal represents the exception. There, a populist far-right party (Partido Popular) is quite well represented (2001: 9 percent) in the national government and parliament. By contrast, the national governments and parliaments of Greece and Ireland do not as yet feature any strong, separate representation by a comparable party. Among the small, affluent 'above average income' countries, however, we find the most important of Western Europe's far-right parliamentary parties: the Danish People's Party (2001: 12 percent, in government); the Dutch List Pim Fortuyn (2002: 17 percent, in government for less than a year before disintegrating and the 2003 elections); the Belgian Vlaams Blok (1999: 15 percent); and the Austrian Freedom Party (1999: 27 percent; 2002: 10 percent, in government). In Finland, Tony Halme's 'True Finns' Party gained a first surprise success (three out of 200 parliamentary seats) in the 2003 elections. To these, one has to add Blocher's wing (UDC) of the People's Party in Switzerland (2003: 26.6 percent, in government), and the Progress Party in Norway (2001: 15 percent, lending substantial support to the government, but not formally a government member). In this group of small, affluent countries, Sweden is the exception to the rule: there, previous attempts by a similar party, Ny Demokrati (New Democracy), met strong opposition and failed. In 1991, very soon after it was founded, the party was voted into the Swedish Parliament. By the next election in 1994 it had gone. After this early failure, there followed a longer period without any serious second attempt (see Hannerz, this volume).

This regional comparison by socio-economic criteria thus leads to an interesting result: it is among the (relatively) 'small and wealthy' countries that these new nationalist far-right parties have found and created more favourable conditions to establishing themselves within the parliamentary system. Given the common elements in these parties' programmes discussed earlier, a few obvious points arise from this 'small and affluent' conclusion. One is that affluent countries pay (or would have to pay) more into the joint EU budget than they receive (or would receive) out of it. Another point is that the same number of immigrants, of course, is not only more visible in a small country but also constitutes a larger minority by proportion. We shall pick this up again at the end of this section.

The 'small and affluent' conclusion has been reached by applying demographic and socio-economic criteria. If we now take a second look at this conclusion, the question arises of whether any other obvious commonalities exist. Do any linguistic or historical parallels among these countries (German-speaking parts of

Switzerland, Austria, Flemish Belgium, the Netherlands, Denmark, Finland and Norway) favour the recent emergence of far-right parliamentary parties there?

Some of these parties' strategists and theorists have already noticed, with pleasure, the strangely 'peripheral Germanic' aspect among most of these more successful movements and their respective countries: with the exception of Finland, one might claim that a 'Germanic' language is spoken by the majorities in each of these countries. In addition, a few among the new nationalist parties from the outset tried to strengthen ties between them and developed a special enthusiasm for such a joint project, precisely for reasons of 'joint Germanic' sympathies and ideologies. Yet the mere fact that a few of these parties' leaders and strategists think about pan-Germanic options, and try to speak about them privately among themselves is not enough to my mind to justify a 'peripheral Germanic' interpretation of the overall phenomenon today. None of these parties has based its success upon explicit pan-Germanic references as central topics in election campaigns. Rather, the opposite is true: any explicit pan-Germanic orientation would be anti-constitutional in each country where these parties strive to gain influence within their legal frameworks and parliamentary systems. Moreover, the majority of their present supporters would simply no longer vote for them were such an issue currently part of their public agenda.

One may wonder, of course, if this could not change all too easily were a similar party ever to gain any substantial influence in Germany. For such a scenario, the present, more or less secret, flirtation with pan-Germanism among a few strategists does remain a somewhat uncertain option for the future; uncertain indeed in view of local voters' sympathies. However, a potential danger for the future remains to perhaps 'try out' pan-Germanism more openly on a national level were things ever to change inside Germany, in such a direction. As an expression of voters' aspirations in the present and in the more recent past, pan-Germanism therefore plays no role in the emergence of far-right parliamentary parties in several small, affluent countries of Western Europe. Nor have the electoral successes, and their social and political roots, anything to do with other pan-Germanic factors that I can identify. I am also sceptical whether any wider parallels to the specific Austrian problem of dealing, or not dealing, with a past under Hitler might be at work elsewhere in these cases – but I leave that question to historians.

If such 'pan-national' orientations are not at work, then we can take this as confirmation of our first comparative excursion into the programmatic parallels among these parties. In addition to socio-economic factors, it is not pan-nationalism but nationalisms (in their state-oriented forms, and in their smaller 'ethno-political' variants in Belgium, northern Italy and Switzerland) that are a second set of interacting factors at work here.

In a final comparative step, I want to consider briefly those cases where far-right parliamentary parties have not yet managed to establish themselves to any significant extent. Apart from the remarkable Swedish experience, a whole range of other factors become visible. In the U.K., a strong parliamentary tradition and an electoral system favouring majorities make it more difficult than elsewhere in Europe for any small party to gain seats in the House of Commons. Simultaneously, parliamentary 'devolution' in the U.K. has begun to provide a certain forum for local nationalists of various sorts, while also containing them, for instance, to the Scottish or Welsh regional levels.

In Germany, mainstream parties have been so markedly engaged and relatively successful in the primary national cause of reunification that few fields of activity remained for any nationwide emergence of a separate far-right party, despite the local success in 2003 of two parties of a right-extremist orientation (i.e., the NDP and the DVU) in the east German states of Saxony and Brandenburg. The 5 percent electoral barrier has also helped, and it prevents easy access to federal parliamentary seats for small parties in Germany. Likewise, the emergence of the post-communist PDS as a party with a strong, far-left, 'regionalist' East German bias might have been a factor here. In addition, public efforts to enhance civil awareness about the dangers of extreme right-wing policies, in view of Germany's past, have undoubtedly left their mark.

In Spain, on the other hand, a wider range of more or less radical 'ethnic nationalists' (autonomists and, in a few cases, secessionists) are basically confined to the regional level; although national governments sometimes have to rely on support from one or another among them. Perhaps, as in the U.K., this imposes a stronger necessity upon political representatives of the Castilian majority population to represent the country's overall unity and to keep far-right nationalism at bay.

In the cases of Greece and Ireland I would suggest that most mainstream parties there have 'national causes' (e.g., historical and present interactions with Turkey and with Britain respectively) so high on their own agendas that this leaves very little room for separate far-right parties to gain any additional profile. As in some cases among the 'big five', this perspective suggests that in fact a 'rightist' political mainstream practice may for some time be able to contain the rise of a separate far-right party.

If, however, we continue this assessment of underlying factors, by reapplying the notion of 'containment through mainstream rightist practice' back to our 'small, affluent' cases, then their own development indicates that such a strategy can in fact be quite short-sighted. In all these cases, mainstream parties tried to control the emergence of new far-right parties by engaging in rightist practices themselves. Ultimately, this upgraded rather than contained or diminished rightist policies and their influence, and thereby prepared the way for the subsequent success of these parties. We may thus conclude, from this third comparative step, that 'mainstream containment through rightist practices' seems to work only if this is supported by other, more systemic factors (reunification, and the 5 percent barrier in Germany, for instance); generally, such a strategy seems to entail at least as many risks as it may promise rewards. It is thus important to differentiate rightist political mainstream practices as an increasingly important factor in Western

Europe from the separate emergence of new far-right parliamentary parties, and to acknowledge the competitive but also mutually reinforcing interaction between both factors.

In several of these small, affluent countries there are right-of-centre plus far-right coalition governments working both formally and informally. In turn, such coalitions have resulted in the implementation of fairly neo-liberal government programmes in many of these countries (Norway, Denmark, the Netherlands, Austria) with a previously strong, Social Democratic welfare state record. In these new 'mainstream far-right' coalition programmes, the far-right nationalists not only impose themselves upon their coalition partners, but it is important to recognise that they themselves are also used for particular causes: as an entertaining diversion from, an excuse for, and sometimes as a more radical tool in support of, the actual agenda. Dismantling the welfare state, or what is left of it, and rigidly implementing the Schengen Treaty, which is anti-immigration, are centrepieces of rightist and neo-liberal policies, with or without the new far-right nationalists. (One may thus also argue that these new far-right nationalists are superfluous, where all this was achieved long ago, as in the U.K. after the 1980s.) This diagnosis does suggest that the new far-right parliamentary nationalists not only pose a specific threat to many but that they also represent a certain 'systemic usefulness' for a few.

When it comes to facing the threat, however, the Swedish experience of 'promoting early failure', the French experience of dividing up the far right, and the Spanish and British experience of containing nationalists to regional levels have all turned out to be more successful than most nationwide mainstream exercises of 'containment through rightist practices'.

In this first section, three comparative steps have thus provided a number of conclusions. The joint programmatic characteristics of the new far-right parliamentary parties were identified as anti-immigration, anti-welfare state and EU-sceptical nationalist. Then, a core group of small, affluent countries was identified where these parties had particular success, in which socio-economic and 'national' (rather than pan-national) factors play a crucial role. Finally, some conditions and strategies were identified that have so far kept the emergence of separate far-right parties at bay in several EU countries, whereas in the small, affluent cases, 'containment through rightist practices' was counterproductive. In the English-speaking world outside Europe, experiences with the One Nation Party in Australia (Kapferer and Morris, in this volume), with the New Zealand First Party and to an extent with the Reform Party in Canada confirm these conclusions.

For Western Europe it was said that specific national and socio-economic factors favoured the early rise of far-right parliamentary parties in many small, affluent countries. In particular, we noticed the relatively large weight of immigration and of (possible or real) payments to the EU in these countries. In addition, I have suggested in more detail elsewhere (Gingrich 2003) that, as a hypothesis for further fieldwork, popular attitudes of 'cultural pessimism' and 'economic chauvinism' may be considered as factors that accompany and support the emergence of these parties in the small, affluent countries of Western Europe. Both notions refer to socially produced sets of attitudes and emotions, which have a somewhat spontaneous basis 'from below' as much as they are instigated 'from above'. Cultural pessimism is centred on feelings and fears about 'what will happen to our small country, in this changing world of Europe-wide and global developments', combined with the pessimistic conviction that this country's 'culture' is doomed to perish if the course of events remains the same. Economic chauvinism, on the other hand, identifies with the achievements of post-Second World War welfare states to the extent that they are regarded as personal property, instead of being seen as shared wealth that has always required negotiated redistribution. Thus economic chauvinism is centred on feelings and attitudes that 'this wealth is ours, and we do not want to share it with anybody'. My hypothesis is that economic chauvinism and cultural pessimism are two critical factors that favour and promote separate far-right parties in Western Europe's small, affluent countries.

Historical Contrasts

In this section, I want to examine nationalism further through historical comparison.

In order to outline some major contrasts and parallels between today's parliamentary nationalists and earlier nationalists in European history, I will focus on three topics: international contexts; nationalists' attitudes towards 'their' states; and mass support for nationalists. These earlier historical contrasts will primarily relate to France, Italy and Austro-Hungary and its successor states before and after the First World War (1900–1930).

The international context of those earlier nationalist movements was clearly the late colonial period. Rivalry between major and minor colonial powers led to the First World War and subsequently, to a profound rearrangement of Central Europe's national boundaries and to a last phase of the late colonial order. Among the dominant powers, earlier nationalists pursued policies of defending and expanding the respective colonial realm, and of being radical supporters of their country's position during the increasing rivalry among European powers. Public support for nationalist rivalry became so enthusiastic that at the outbreak of the First World War even large segments of labour movements gave in, irrespective of their allegedly internationalist programmes. During the First World War, nationalists represented policies of increasing authoritarianism to save 'their nation'. Among the dominated parts of the Austro-Hungarian Empire, by contrast, local nationalists mostly worked for radical autonomy or for independence and secession. Therefore, their support for Austro-Hungary's war was lukewarm and limited at first, but later changed into opposition (Kann 1980: 406–560).

Nationalists' attitudes towards 'their' states differ considerably in the period under consideration. Before and after the First World War, European nationalists' economic programmes were much more coherent than their political agendas (Schorske 1980: 116–80). In economic terms, they supported free enterprise by domestic entrepreneurs in domestic markets that included the state-protected colonial markets (until 1918 for Austro-Hungary). For that purpose, nationalist parties of the early twentieth century were also in favour of a strong economic role for the state, as far as it concerned infrastructure and transportation, customs and trade regulations, and everything else that helped to protect a colonial domestic market from international rivals. (Without the colonial aspect, this also continued to be the case among the nationalists in Austro-Hungary's successor states.) In short, most nationalists of the early twentieth century were economic protectionists.

By contrast, the political agenda of earlier nationalists was much more heterogeneous. It has been said that among the dominant powers during the First World War, nationalists' authoritarian tendencies gradually increased. In Italy this was almost immediately perpetuated after the war through the incipient rise of Mussolini's Fascism. In Austria, for some time pan-Germanists and Austrian loyalists competed in parliamentary form until the late 1920s, when they transformed themselves into pro-Nazis and clerical fascists respectively. In France, the main groups of the nationalist right were obliged to observe a democratic and parliamentary constitution for a longer period until well into the 1930s.

This tendency towards growing authoritarianism had certain parallels in some of the other successor states of the Habsburg Empire, such as Hungary, but not everywhere. In the new Czechoslovak Republic, for instance, mainstream (Czech and Slovak) parties had to pursue 'nationalist practices', in order to strengthen their newly independent country and state. Yet domestically, they were basically political liberals. Freedom of speech, freedom of press, free elections and most other trademarks of classic liberalism were important and serious elements on their agendas. The same element of political liberalism could be found among certain national and nationalist forces in other 'young' independent states after 1918, such as in parts of south-eastern Europe but also in Poland, Finland or the Baltic countries.

This indicates that in 'young' nation states of that era many nationalist forces embraced political liberalism more profoundly, to increase support for their own cause. In addition, the early nationalists of the nineteenth century in Italy, Austria, Germany, France and elsewhere in Western Europe had emerged in coalition with political liberalism (Hobsbawm 1990). Early European nationalists were mostly political liberals, who sometimes developed very strong authoritarian tendencies in later phases of their parties' histories.

If we now compare these historical, international contexts of earlier nationalisms with those of today's parliamentary nationalists, contrasts prevail over continuities. Today's parliamentary far-right nationalists began to gain influence at different times and in different places in Western Europe, but generally it is the decade between the late 1980s (Belgium, France, Italy, Switzerland, Austria) and the late 1990s (Scandinavia and Finland, the Netherlands, Portugal) that was decisive in this respect. Old colonial empires had vanished and the Cold War was over. The despotic rules of an earlier generation of anti-democratic far-right nationalist regimes were a thing of the past in some parts of post-Second World War southern Europe (Portugal, Spain, Greece).

This was the period after the collapse of communist rule in eastern and south-eastern Europe in which the colonial form of global capitalism was substituted by other forms of global economic hegemony (Appadurai 1997). In short, we may speak of the early post-communist and (to a limited extent) post-colonial phase of globalisation. In these wider international contexts, most mainstream parties of Western Europe pursued policies of increased EU integration and EU enlargement (from the early seven to the fifteen members until 2003, up to the present). This process led to the implementation of various treaties (e.g., Maastricht, Schengen and EEA), the introduction of the euro currency and to decisive steps towards integrating east central European countries first into NATO and then into the EU.

In these contexts, today's parliamentary far-right nationalists move into realms that mainstream parties had left unguarded in their attempt to rearrange the domestic European post-Second World War order. The EU project can perhaps best be characterised as both a regional variant of, as much as a regional reaction against, the contemporary phase of globalisation. This requires gradual transfers of power from most national levels to the EU level and a redistribution of wealth, basically from the more to the less affluent countries, and from national towards Europe-wide priorities. While mainstream parties pursue the promotion of these processes, parliamentary nationalists oppose them. They insist on a 'strong' national state in terms of security and, most importantly, in terms of control over immigration, while they simultaneously favour a dismantling of social and cultural services by the welfare state. Their populism clearly instrumentalises classic liberal arguments as well, e.g., when they criticise the 'faraway decision-making processes' of EU and NATO representatives who were rarely elected. At the same time, their 'law and order' agenda on the domestic national level represents a centrepiece of their argument, which has implicit authoritarian tendencies.

A late colonial and First World War context of differentiation among earlier nationalists thus contrasts visibly with a 'post-'colonial and post-Cold War context of emergence among today's new nationalists.

If we re-examine the political and economic agenda of today's far-right nationalists in Western Europe, the overall picture is almost the opposite of that pursued by their predecessors from the early twentieth century. Economically, most of today's parties argue against all kinds of bureaucratic regulations. No matter who imposes these regulations – the World Trade Organisation, the EU or the national state – if they are seen or represented as being an obstacle to private enterprise they are criticised and attacked. Entrepreneurs' social and tax expenses for wage costs, regulations of the domestic labour market, state control over infrastructure, and other segments of the economic sector came under attack, and continue to be attacked by today's parliamentary nationalists. Privatisation of state-controlled economic entities of any kind, including key elements of the welfare state, is pursued and supported, as long as this does not lead too visibly towards any 'sell out' to foreigners, which would be too unpopular among their own clientele. In short, most current parliamentary nationalists in Western Europe are neo-liberals in economic terms, with a protectionist veto card up their sleeves.

In political terms, today's parliamentary nationalists, by definition, are careful to signal their basic agreement with a democratic constitution, parliamentary elections, freedom of speech and of press, and so forth. Some of their leaders in Western Europe are notorious for their apologetic remarks about past nationalist tyrannies and atrocities, and several have a reputation for privately or, less often, publicly considering more authoritarian forms of statehood for the future. Similar to the 'hidden' pan-Germanism among some of them, an illiberal potential cannot be denied and it becomes conspicuous when examining the internal hierarchies of these parties. Yet for the time being a basic recognition of the key principles of parliamentary democracy among these parties has to be acknowledged – even if it may be inspired by the reluctant and opportunistic insight of some of their leaders that anything else would not work among the majority of their voters.

If we thus summarise that a basic, right-wing political liberalism combines with an authoritarian potential, then this potential is acted out not only in matters of internal party organisation but also in the field of law and order. This is the key sphere in which these parties' first strategy of dismantling the welfare state is counterbalanced by the second strategy of a strong 'security and protection' state for the army, police, border control and the like. One may thus argue that today's parliamentary nationalists in Western Europe combine a limited, basic political liberalism with elements of political 'protectionism'.

We have therefore been able to outline a number of important contrasts between European nationalists in the early twentieth and early twenty-first centuries. The fact that both groups pursued similar integralist and mostly secular ideologies of nationhood is important: this alone should justify labelling both groups 'nationalists'. Whereas their ideologies display a number of important parallels and continuities, their practices and contexts reveal more contrasts and differences; therefore I prefer to call today's Western European far-right parliamentary parties 'neo-nationalist'.

I shall end this section by examining, through historical contrast, mass support for nationalist parties. Before the First World War, support for nationalist parties primarily came from two main segments of society. In the cities, these were individual and small enterprise to a large extent, and large enterprise to a somewhat lesser one. In addition, various elements from the rural and agricultural population were more or less sympathetic. These social roots of nationalist support seemed so stable that at times leaders of the labour movement referred to nationalism as a 'bourgeois–farmer coalition' directed against the worker. This changed considerably, however, with the outbreak of the First World War, supported by large segments of the labour movement, and it continued to change even more significantly after the war: large groups of returning war veterans, of impoverished farmers turning towards the cities, and growing masses of the urban unemployed became intrinsically linked to the rise of authoritarian nationalism in Europe between the twentieth century's two World Wars (Gellner 1983; Hobsbawm 1990).

Contemporary Western Europe's neo-nationalists obviously do not gain their initial mass support from hundreds of thousands, or millions of impoverished farmers and unemployed workers. The technological and economic transformations of Western Europe during the second half of the twentieth century have been so profound that 'farmers' and 'workers' in the classic sense have become social minorities. From which groups do today's neo-nationalists draw their support? The fact that large and small enterprise continues to support nationalist parties is highly significant in qualitative terms, but quantitatively this is less important. Support by the employed is what matters most here. From Norway to Switzerland, and from Austria to the Netherlands, the small, affluent countries had very low unemployment rates around the turn of the last century. Most statistical analyses of neo-nationalist voters in these countries thus indicate that mass support comes from the urban, employed voters. The social spectrum ranges from commuters to temporary or part-time employees; from those who work in the growing but highly unstable sector of private services to those active in the 'new economy'; from yuppies struggling with third or fifth attempts at a career to very young proletarians, and so on. The key elements of mass support are thus not derived from 'losers of globalisation' in the sense that these voters have already lost out in the recent past. Rather, key support comes from those who remain precariously employed but who are afraid to lose out in the future.

An Exemplary Case

In this last section, I will explore the topic of voters' support further through the example of Austria, giving specific emphasis to public performance and gender issues. The general characteristics of neo-nationalism, as identified above, all apply for Austria, where they combine with a number of local factors. Some of these are almost unique, while others are merely more relevant locally than elsewhere. (Those interested in more details are referred to Thomas Fillitz' examination of the Austrian case in this volume.)

Five of these factors need particular emphasis. First, all mainstream parties' enduring reluctance, throughout the post-1945 decades, to deal openly and honestly with the Nazi past is almost unique in Europe. (Vague parallels come to mind only with Italy and its record of neo- and post-fascist parties, and for one or two other minor cases.) Second, three decades of socialist-led governments (1970–1999) of diminishing success in Austria represented a more extensive example of similar cases in the EU, i.e., of wider erosion processes in post-1945 domestic political orders. Third, mainstream parties' continuing inability, from the 1970s onwards, to provide sustainable economic alternatives to a formerly very large, but now disintegrating, state-controlled economic sector was perhaps more dramatic in Austria than elsewhere. Fourth, throughout the 1990s Austria had one of the EU's longest border zones with non-, and not yet, EU member countries, which gave more weight to local fears about immigration from outside the EU and, in particular, about the EU's 2004 enlargement. Fifth, a far-right parliamentary political force emerged, the Freedom Party, out of a predecessor group Verband der Unabhängigen (VdU), founded in the 1949 as a pool for former Nazi party members and sympathisers. The Freedom Party's current central personality is one of Western Europe's most intelligent and charismatic neo-nationalist leaders, Jörg Haider.

In view of the exceptional qualities of the Freedom Party's central personality, I will try to show in this section that neo-nationalist voters represent such heterogeneous interest groups that some form of charisma is indispensable, more than for mainstream parties, to forge voters into a stable and growing coalition of support.

In a way, the programmatic neo-nationalist orientation of the Freedom Party made it easier for them, than for mainstream parties (People's Party/Christian Democrats, and Social Democrats), to focus upon and reach out to 'urban crowds'. The Freedom Party does not need to care about farmers, intellectuals and minorities. Major segments of the agricultural population are almost beyond their reach, as Gertraud Seiser shows in this volume. In turn, this gives the Freedom Party the permanent option of attacking the 'enormous waste of funds by Brussels', funds that primarily concern agriculture. In a parallel case, people with access to higher education display, in statistical terms, substantial disinterest and antipathy towards neo-nationalism. This allows the Freedom Party the option of pursuing all kinds of juicy, anti-intellectual populist campaigns. Finally, 'old resident' minorities (Jewish; Croatian-, Slovenian-, Hungarian-, Czech-speaking groups of eastern and south-eastern Austria) and 'new minorities' (first-, second- and third-generation immigrants from outside the EU with or without EU passports) certainly do not represent key groups of potential voters for the Freedom Party. Notwithstanding some recent signs of change, they remain another target group in reserve for populist mobilisation. Taken together, these three groups amount to perhaps less than 10 percent of the overall population of Austria.

It was therefore to groups from the ethnic and social majorities that the Freedom Party turned during its period of rising influence (1986–1999). In their own words, they would primarily address the '*kleinen Mann von der Strasse*', 'the regular guy on the street', who would be an '*Inländer*', i.e., an 'autochthonous' person, which is a legal euphemism for the unspeakable term, 'white' Austrian. This process of establishing themselves with majority voters was pursued with increasing success over one and a half decades. In 1986, when Jörg Haider took over the Freedom Party's leadership, it had merely 5 percent of voters' support at the national level; whereas when the party became coalition partner in the national government of 1999, it had more than 27 percent, thus becoming the country's second strongest party.

Although by their failures and arrogance mainstream parties had prepared the ground well, the Freedom Party's remarkable success throughout the 1990s did not come by itself. The 27 percent included very heterogeneous interest groups indeed. One particularly strong group comprised young male workers, disillusioned by the failure of their socialist parents' promises about permanent progress and growing affluence. Another important group was small family business – which is particularly widespread sociologically in Austria, especially in tourism. A third and probably the most influential group consisted of families and single people from the lower middle classes, with particularly strong ambitions towards upward social mobility. Some of this is also evident in the fact that the Freedom Party gained 35 percent in 1999 among voters under thirty years old. In addition, the Austrian industrialists' association (Industriellenvereinigung) has, for more than 100 years, had a traditional 'nationalist' wing that would deserve a study of its own. Formerly pan-Germanic Habsburg royalist, this wing then became pro-Nazi, and today some members from several of the same key families are declared supporters of the Freedom Party.

Forging young workers, industry, yuppies, small and large tourist enterprises and career-minded middle-class families into a 27 percent voters' coalition is not possible if electoral promises are too specific and pragmatic. It is even less effective in a country like Austria where mainstream party loyalties were quite strong until the 1980s. Instead, building up the voters' coalition required an aggressive, emotional and mobilising intrusion into mainstream parties' eroding and unguarded spheres of influence. This took the form of an endless series of emotional, mocking and angry campaigns against, and for, popular topics. These campaigns made the different sub-groups of potential voters for the Freedom Party believe, and, more importantly, feel that they had common interests. This indeed represents a '*Politik der Gefühle*', politics of emotions, as the Austrian writer Josef Haslinger once put it (1987).

Eventually, some of those conflicting interests among sub-groups of voters became quite obvious, which, in turn, contributed to the party's failure in government. Why, for instance, should a young worker, or an employed couple building a weekend house on loans, vote again for a party that did not fulfil its promise to alleviate the tax burden for lower-income groups? Why vote again for a party that, in spite of its claim to represent the common people, helps to cut down on their future income from retirement pensions by up to 10 percent, allegedly out of budget constraints and necessities? Moreover, why vote for them again if simultaneously the Freedom Party and its partner in government decide to buy out of that same 'tight' budget (of a small neutral country that is not a NATO member) the most expensive fighter jets available on the international arms market, with huge follow-up business deals for local industry? After all, this inability to accommodate such conflicting interests among their own clientele contributed decisively towards the Freedom Party's internal tensions, and to their crushing defeat in the 2002 national elections, which left them with only 10 percent and led to the party's split-up in 2005.

This illustrates how fragile and illusory that voters' coalition of 27 percent was. Likewise in the Netherlands, the fragility of the initial 17 percent won by Pim Fortuyn's party immediately after he was murdered was revealed by the Dutch 2003 elections. In both Austria and the Netherlands, the 'implosion' of neo-nationalist support went hand in hand with new support for the mainstream moderate right. Such fragility of support for neo-nationalist parties and the pressure of mainstream parties to instrumentalise neo-nationalists for their own neo-liberal purposes testify to the point I want to make here: there is an inherent necessity for neo-nationalists to pursue emotional campaigns against stock easy targets.

During the Freedom Party's rise, such campaigns against easy targets were directed against trade unionists with dual incomes from public or union sources; against public funding for fine art with an allegedly immoral or unpatriotic tendency; against allegedly illegal and drug-dealing African immigrants; against the entry of the Czech and Slovak Republics into the EU, without a settlement being reached about the post-1945 enforced emigration of German-speaking refugees from there; against Austria's Supreme Constitutional Judge and his reconsideration of improving existing rules on Slovenian minority rights, and so on.

Thus the first point arising from this exemplary case is that such emotional campaigns, carried out in rapid succession against rotating targets and aimed at mobilising 'white' majority support among the more or less precariously employed, are a necessity for any neo-nationalist party. They are indispensable in luring voters away from their previous electoral preferences or voting abstention, and in cultivating their feelings of anger, fear, insecurity, humiliation, envy and indignation towards 'others'. Simultaneously, these orchestrated feelings downplay conflicting interests among 'themselves'. Given that these feelings are directed towards two clusters of topics, I have suggested classifying and analysing them in terms of economic chauvinism and cultural pessimism.

Out of the need to conduct emotional campaigns that intrude into established spheres of loyalty, superficially uniting conflicting interests, there emerges the need for political charisma and public performance. I have tried to outline how this is met by the public self-presentation of 'a man for all seasons' in Austria (Gingrich 2002a); Thijl Sunier and Rob van Ginkel (this volume) do the same for Pim Fortuyn in the Netherlands. Without an anthropological analysis of campaigning, performance and public charisma little can be understood about neo-nationalism today. Liking, admiring, sympathising and identifying with the charismatic seducer is of course the other side of the same socio-emotional coin. The need for 'politics of emotion' corresponds to another of the basic paradoxes of nationalism, identified by Anderson: 'The political power of nationalisms' contrasts with 'their philosophical poverty and even incoherence' (1991: 5). It is thus because of their shallow visions, related to their claim to represent very different and contradictory interest groups, that charismatic politics of emotion are necessary for neo-nationalisms.

In a sense, we have thus clarified that 'the regular guy on the street' does not exist per se, and that instead he is a construct of socio-emotional campaigning and charismatic performance. This construct operates with a simple, tripartite and hierarchical ideological image of 'us' and 'them'. Its uppermost level, 'them above', comprises 'the powerful and influential' at home and elsewhere (the Supreme Constitutional Judge, the mighty trade union leader, Brussels ...); its lowest levels, 'them below', consists of minority representatives, potential and actual immigrants and their countries of origin (alleged drug-dealing African immigrants, Slovene minority members, newly incoming EU members ...). Sandwiched between these two levels, 'above' and 'below', is 'our nation'; because it is constantly endangered (as, ironically enough, former pan-Germanists continue to warn us), the fuzzy borders towards the upper and the lower levels need permanent reassertion – which, in fact, confirms Gullestad's concept or 'neo-ethnification of national identity' (this volume).

This model is 'encompassing' insofar as 'regular' 'autochthonous' guys and their families represent the nation best, but the model is also open to a few 'segmentary' elements (Baumann 2004) insofar as it allows for a number of 'equals' in similar situations elsewhere. Not surprisingly, these few 'equals' are other small, affluent nations of Western Europe. Basically, neo-nationalism in Austria thus aims to redefine and reassert 'nationhood' by reaching out for 'autochthonous' families in smaller and larger cities, particularly those with fears of downward social mobility. It tends to arouse and reassert secularised family values and popular mass culture, and it contrasts these values to alleged dangers from 'above' and 'below'. Implicitly and incidentally, this constant reassertion also redefines 'nationhood' itself, since 'old' and 'new' minorities with Austrian passports are not usually addressed as 'autochthonous', and since the status of the 'powerful and the influential' with their mysterious international connections is represented as a questionable issue in terms of national loyalties. A redefined nationhood is thus presented as being endangered, and inside this nation it is the precariously employed whose social status is also addressed as being in trouble.

I certainly do not want to imply that nationhood and social status are not going through unpredictable times in Western Europe as a whole. On the contrary, my argument has been that it is precisely the small countries that are confronted sooner than others by problems of national identity in times of European integration and the current phase of globalisation; although acknowledging this fact does not necessarily imply a 'pessimistic' conclusion. Furthermore, I argue that among these Western European countries, it is precisely the precariously employed urban population that is hit by all kinds of very real economic and social insecurities in the present era of globalising 'risk societies' (Beck 1986); but, again, this does not necessarily imply chauvinistic conclusions.

My general point, however, is that these risks are unevenly distributed among different social groups with often conflicting interests. By contrast, neo-nationalism emphasises and initiates feelings of fear against dangers from 'above' and 'below' to the extent that these conflicting interests become invisible, whereas responsibility for those dangers is often misrepresented and projected onto scapegoats. Existing fears of status loss, and of downward social mobility, are thus not only addressed by neo-nationalism in Austria, but, in addition, they are emphasised, exaggerated, distorted and misrepresented by 'economic chauvinism'; existing fears about cultural identity and about socio-political aspirations and formal representation are treated in a similar manner by cultural pessimism.

If it is the precariously employed, 'autochthonous' urban masses that are primarily addressed by neo-nationalist campaigns, then the Austrian case reveals another important point. As the Freedom Party's slogan already indicates rather openly, their 'regular guy' is usually male. For the Freedom Party's more successful years, statistical data are quite unambiguous about this point. Between 1986 and 1999, their influence among voters grew constantly in most national elections and with that rise the numbers of their female voters also grew. If, however, the overall proportion of women among their voters is assessed through time, then the picture is quite different. In this perspective, the proportion of female voters went from an initial high of 52 percent in 1982 (before Haider took over the Freedom Party), through several national elections, down to 42 percent in 1995, then to an all-time low of 38 percent in 1999. By that year, this medium-term development had led to three astounding overall results. First, if only women had participated in those elections, the Freedom Party never would have gained enough support to become part of government. Second, only one out of every three Freedom Party voters was female in the elections that made it Europe's most successful far-right party at the time. Finally, that year the Freedom Party overtook the mainstream parties to become the strongest single party among Austria's male voters (32 percent among Austria's overall male electorate of 1999: Hofinger and Ogris 1995; Plasser, Ulram and Sommer 2000). For the Austrian case, such findings are substantiated by other tendencies, such as increased levels of aggression among young military recruits.[6] Again, particularities of the Austrian case may be at work here. As with most other 'Austrian specificities' discussed earlier, my hypothesis in this case is also that it reflects a wider current among Western European societies, with an impact on the background and support groups of neo-nationalist parties. If this is valid (and I repeat that this is merely a hypothesis for neo-nationalism in other EU countries), then it would complement and support the insights gained so far.

The 'angry white men' of North America have their Western European counterparts within many neo-nationalist parties and among their voters. Neo-nationalist campaigns against rotating targets, propaganda and politics in fact seek to make them even angrier by addressing serious concerns and fears, and enlarging, manipulating and distorting them, with the overall aim of instrumentalising them for neo-nationalist parties' own purposes. Bruised masculinity from various social strata of the 'autochthonous' population is thus addressed, seduced and transformed into 'regular guys' who, it is self-evident, are white and angry: they will never have the role and authority of 'household head' that their fathers and grandfathers claimed to have, and they will never have the more stable and long-term jobs their fathers and grandfathers had in the post-Second World War decades. Instead, the restructuration of Western Europe's economies, with its shifts towards short-term and part-time forms of employment, for instance, on a general level introduces more forms of employment that so far only women and labour immigrants have had to cope with.

The Austrian example therefore highlights three points of potentially wider relevance. First, neo-nationalism, as a newcomer to the political landscape, has to intrude aggressively into established spheres of loyalties and influence to gain mass support. Second, unifying conflicting interests among urban crowds of the precariously employed is achieved through emotionalising campaigns, which require at least a certain level of spectacular performance and charisma. Third, these emotionalising campaigns address and instrumentalise concerns and fears about downward social mobility, loss of status and loss of identity, particularly with regard to a redefined nationhood and bruised masculinity among the majority population.

Conclusion

By 2005, the previous rise of parliamentary neo-nationalism seemed to have reached a certain impasse. This is a phase when no new neo-nationalist party is rising visibly in most of Western Europe. Those that do exist have managed to gain some access to governmental power. It seems likely that this represents the last phase of a 'first period', and perhaps the beginning of an intermediate phase. At the end of this first period, if seen from an EU and EEA perspective, the rise of these parties could be confined to a number of small and affluent member countries of the EU and the EEA, plus Portugal and Italy. Within this effort of provisional containment, dominant political preferences have tended towards accommodating neo-nationalist parties by simultaneously 'taming and dividing' them. This seems to have received some confirmation and encouragement through the experience of the Netherlands and Austria: there, two of the formerly most successful neo-nationalist parties became members of national governments, after which they disintegrated to the extent of severe electoral defeats (in late 2002 and early 2003).

Anthropologists are not sociologists, nor political scientists, and therefore they do not even attempt to predict future developments. It thus remains to be seen whether and how neo-nationalists of Western Europe will try to prepare for a 'second period' of further and perhaps more radical expansion, and whether or not this will be pursued in constitutional, democratic form. Alternatively, it also remains to be seen whether and how they will remain satisfied with stabilising themselves within existing dimensions and political forms. In this context, it will be decisive to see how useful and instrumental they remain for the ongoing 'Thatcherisation of Europe', and with what kind of opposition this will be met. In addition, it is not impossible that some or many of these parties will either gradually disintegrate or suddenly implode. That may happen because of their own failure, or because they become superfluous, or because of resistance against them, or by a combination of several of these factors. The suggestion that arises out of my present analysis is that this will not only depend on the leading neo-nationalist 'actors' themselves, but, more importantly, it will also be strongly influenced by the 'contexts', chances and failures that other actors neglect and thereby offer to them.

We are therefore unable to predict how far neo-nationalism will accompany Europe's future – not least in view of the EU's own orientation, and in view of domestic developments among new incoming EU members from east central Europe during the first decade of the twenty-first century. One theoretically inspired conclusion seems to be particularly pertinent with regard to perspectives on the future, at the end of neo-nationalism's first period; the current phase of globalisation, in its Western European variant, is partially responsible for the emergence and successes of neo-nationalism. Nationhood, social mobilities and gender identities are indeed in question all over Europe. If imaginative and creative visions of second or alternative modernities are not thought through, and do not gain some broader popularity among masses of voters, then it seems likely that neo-nationalism's reactive and retrogressive answers to the current phase of globalisation are bound to persist, in one way or another.

Notes

1. The present contribution greatly benefited from the discussions at the Wenner-Gren-sponsored workshop in Brussels in February 2001, for which I am grateful to all its participants. Revised versions were presented at NYU's anthropology department in April 2002, at the EASA 2004 bi-annual conference, and at Chicago's anthropology department in May 2002, where I received additional feedback, in particular from Arjun Appadurai, Susan Gal, Bambi Schieffelin and Jane Schneider. I am especially indebted to Marcus Banks and to Julene Knox for their detailed suggestions and comments.
2. This predominately German-speaking area was formerly part of the Tyrol in Austria, but became part of northern Italy by the end of the First World War.
3. This has to do with the boycott of Vlaams Blok by all mainstream parties in Belgium, and with its more radical rightist and quasi-secessionist orientation; by contrast, most Scandinavian populists from the far right have established close working relationships with several mainstream parties.
4. According to economic weight and demographic and territorial size, it was common to distinguish, within the EU in its form prior to 2004, the 'big five' (Britain, France, Germany, Italy and Spain) from the 'rest', i.e., from the ten smaller EU countries.
5. Austria, Belgium, Denmark, Finland, Greece, Ireland, Luxembourg, the Netherlands, Portugal and Sweden. EEA member countries Switzerland and Norway would correspond to this group of ten smaller EU countries. I shall ignore Western Europe's mini-entities here, such as Andorra, San Marino or Liechtenstein.
6. A choice between civil or military service is obligatory for all eighteen- or nineteen-year-old Austrian males. Army psychologists' assessments of young male recruits indicate increasing

proportions of aggressive behaviour patterns, on the basis of which the army (in 2003) considered one out of ten among these young recruits as 'unfit' for military service (ZiB 3 2003).

Bibliography

Anderson, B. 1991. *Imagined Communities: Reflections on the Origin and Spread of Nationalism*, revised edn. London: Verso.

Appadurai, A. 1997. *Modernity at Large: Cultural Dimensions of Globalization.* Minneapolis: University of Minnesota Press.

Baumann, G. 2004. 'Grammars of Identity/Alterity: A Structural Approach', in G. Baumann and A. Gingrich eds *Grammars of Identity: A Structural Approach.* Oxford: Berghahn.

Beck, U. 1986. *Risikogesellschaft. Auf dem Weg in eine andere Moderne.* Frankfurt/Main: Suhrkamp.

Camus, J.-Y. 2002. 'Die radikale Rechte in Westeuropa. Vom nostalgischen Aktionismus zum fremdenfeindlichen Populismus', in W. Eismann ed. *Rechtspopulismus-österreichische Krankheit oder europäische Normalität?* Vienna: Czernin, pp. 40–55.

Gellner, E. 1983. *Nations and Nationalism.* Oxford: Blackwell.

Gingrich, A. 2002a. 'A Man for All Seasons: An Anthropological Perspective on Public Representations and Cultural Politics of the Austrian Freedom Party', in R. Wodak and A. Pelinka eds *The Haider Phenomenon in Austria.* New Brunswick: Transaction Publishers, pp. 67–91.

——— 2002b. 'Potential for Transatlantic Communication in Anthropology?' *Anthropology Today* 18(1): 27–28.

——— 2003. 'Urban Crowds Manipulated: Assessing the Austrian Case as an Example in Wider European Tendencies', in R. Pinxten, G. Verstraete and C. Longman eds *Culture and Politics.* Oxford: Berghahn.

——— 2004. 'Concepts of Race Vanishing, Movements of Racism Rising?' *Ethnos* 69(2): 156–76.

Haslinger, J. 1987. *Politik der Gefühle. Ein Essay über Österreich.* Darmstadt und Neuwied: Luchterhand.

Hobsbawm, E. 1990. *Nations and Nationalism since 1780.* Cambridge: Cambridge University Press.

Hofinger, C. and Ogris, G. 1995. 'Achtung, Gender Gap! Geschlecht und Wahlverhalten 1979– 1995 in Österreich', in F. Plasser, P. Ulram and G. Ogris eds *Wahkampf und Wählerentscheidung. Analysen zur Nationalratswahl 1995.* Vienna: ZAP.

Holmes, D.R. 2000. *Integral Europe: Fast-capitalism, Multiculturalism, Neofascism.* Princeton: Princeton University Press.

Kann, R.A. 1980. *A History of the Habsburg Empire 1526–1918.* Berkeley: University of California Press.

Mudde, C. 1998. *The Extreme Right Party Family.* Leiden: University of Leiden.

Plasser, F., Ulram, P. and Sommer, F. 2000. 'Analyse der Nationalratswahl 1999. Muster, Trends und Entscheidungsmotive', in F. Plasser, P. Ulram and F. Sommer eds *Das Österreichische Wahlverhalten.* Vienna: ZAP.

Schorske, C.E. 1980. *Fin-de-Siecle Vienna: Politics and Culture.* New York: Vintage.

ZiB 3. 2003. *Österreichischer Rundfunk-Fernsehen,* 16 July 2003.

Chapter 2

Performing 'Neo-nationalism'

Some Methodological Notes
Marcus Banks

Introduction: Cool and Not-so-cool Britannia

Let us begin with two images. The first dates from mid 1997 and is of Geri
Halliwell wearing a Union Jack minidress on stage with the Spice Girls of which she
was then a member ('Ginger Spice'). The second dates from mid 2001 and is of two
British National Party candidates wearing white gags at Queen Elizabeth Hall in
Oldham, in the north of England, as the general election voting results were
announced.

The first image (Fig. 1) is one of several that epitomised 'Cool Britannia' in the
latter half of the 1990s: an amalgam of journalistic hype, government opportunism
and tourist promotion that lasted through the late 1990s. Originating in a
Newsweek cover story (November 1996) that declared London to be the coolest
capital city on the planet (epitomised by its cuisine, fashion and music scene), the
idea of 'Cool Britannia' quickly caught on and was a potent symbol of an
economically strong and culturally confident nation. For a few brief months the
Union Jack – previously a highly charged yet often ambiguous symbol of
Britishness – was reaffirmed as a symbol of an older, conservative and potentially
benign form of British nationalism that could be embraced by the nation's youth.
'Cool Britannia' did not last, however, and the Union Jack quickly reverted to its
ambiguous status.[1]

The second image (Fig. 2) reflects this ambiguity. Since the Second World War,
the Union Jack – and subsequently the Cross of St George (the red cross on a white
ground that represents England alone) – has been claimed by, and associated with,
extreme right-wing political movements (see Phoenix 1998: 121), most notably
today the National Front (henceforth NF) and the British National Party

Figure 1: Geri Halliwell wearing a Union Jack minidress.
Photo: Richard Young/Rex Features

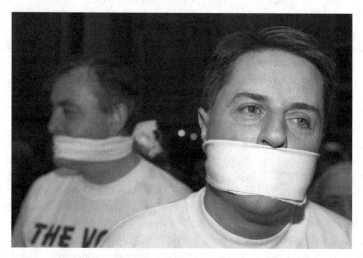

Figure 2: British National Party supporters wearing white gags as the
general election voting results are announced. Photo: ©EMPICS

(henceforth BNP). At the national parliamentary elections in 2001 the BNP fielded candidates in a number of carefully selected seats; particularly targeted were two seats in Oldham in the north of England (Oldham West and Royton, and Oldham East and Saddleworth). These constituencies had seen tension over the previous months between the British Asian population (largely of Pakistani Muslim origin) and the white, largely working-class population; this tension would finally flare into violence later that summer. Neither BNP candidate won the seat contested, but both gained well over 10 percent of the vote (approximately 16 percent and 11 percent in West and East respectively), the biggest share of the vote for such a party since the war. In anticipation of trouble at the election, candidates were not permitted to make their usual speeches at the conclusion of the process, leading to the BNP candidates' self-gagging. Denied the opportunity to wrap themselves in the flag as it were, they symbolically demonstrated its effacement.[2]

Both these images as I describe them here are performances, in a largely literal, everyday sense of the word: both take place on a stage before an audience, for example, but they are also performances – of nationalism – in the more metaphoric sense used by cultural anthropologists and sociologists. In our introduction to this volume Andre Gingrich and I have already discussed the significance of cultural performance in broad terms, noting briefly the performative dimension of neo-nationalist politics in Austria, the Netherlands and the like. In this chapter I wish to expand upon this idea as a methodological strategy, taking one particular case as an example, but intending it to be more widely relevant and applicable for sociological analysis. For the purpose of this contribution, I will use the term performance generally to indicate the fluidity and processual nature of identity expression, to indicate the notion of an underlying norm or script to which performances are thought to relate (but which they also influence), but also more particularly to indicate a degree of self-consciousness in certain types of social behaviour – an element of showmanship, of awareness of an audience, and a manipulation of symbols. In this I follow Schechner and others in seeing the art of performance as transforming experience (real or imagined) into 'palatable' forms, ready for consumption (Schechner 1988: 38). I also hope to demonstrate that performance is not merely a matter of rhetoric turned into action, nor that performances of neo-nationalism are always necessarily successful.

This contribution is not intended as a survey of neo-nationalist politics and activities in the U.K.; rather, it seeks to create a methodological framework for anthropological approaches to neo-nationalism in general that draws upon examples from the U.K. I begin by contrasting conceptions and performances of 'nationalism' as promoted by far-right groups such as the NF and the BNP, and an older stratum of 'nationalism' as a feature of contemporary British society away from the far-right scene.[3] The apparently obvious result of such a comparison – that the far right promotes a form of (neo-) nationalism that is self-conscious and clearly defined in contrast to an older, more liberal-conservative national self-conception (which I shall call 'traditional' nationalism, akin in part to Billig's 'banal nationalism', 1995) – is not, in my opinion, found to be true. Both quasi-fascist neo-nationalism and older 'traditional' nationalism are ambiguous and shifting concepts; both are attractive to certain core constituencies, but both are dependent upon the skilled manipulation of labile and shifting symbols for their power.

Neo-nationalism is Not (Just) Racism

Although the distaste for or rejection of non-white minority populations in the country, manifested in a range of ways from policy statements on voluntary 'repatriation' to violent attacks on the streets, is commonly understood to be the defining characteristic of British and other European neo-nationalist movements, methodologically I advocate the step of setting this aside for the moment in order to see more clearly other aspects of neo-nationalist thought and action. The justification for this is a standard anthropological one: that deeper cultural processes and forms are to be found in the 'backstage' areas behind the arena of public performance; additionally, the anthropological perspective of holism indicates that the specific form of racism or ethnic chauvinism adopted by neo-nationalists will be informed by their perhaps less choate attitudes and opinions in other areas. It is important to remember that in many cases neo-nationalists subscribe to agendas that go well beyond issues of 'race' and immigration; indeed, neo-nationalist political parties that aspire to democratic political representation must of necessity have agendas and policies with regard to the economy, policing, health provision, education and even the arts (see Fillitz, this volume), in addition to statements on gender, sexuality and the correct 'performance' of other, more personal social identities.

Equally, 'traditional' nationalism is by no means entirely formed on the basis of a discourse of 'race' and ethnicity, though these, particularly with respect to the importance of colonialism in the late nineteenth- and twentieth-century manifestations of 'traditional' nationalism, are indeed fundamental. However, to approach both neo-nationalism and 'traditional' nationalism from this perspective alone is to commit a grave methodological error: while categories of 'otherness' may well form the contrastive opposite by which both neo- and 'traditional' nationalisms define themselves, 'alien' others (e.g., immigrant, black, non-European) are by no means the only category of 'others'. Even with regard to 'race' and ethnicity alone, neo-nationalists will have particular ideas about the 'correct' performance of 'whiteness' just as their 'traditional' nationalist predecessors did. In recent years part of the political strategy of neo-nationalist movements in the U.K., for example, has been to identify and stigmatise categories of 'otherness' that have a very broad appeal: the drug dealer, the work shy and the sexual deviant.[4] But while the neo-nationalist position on some non-'race' issues, such as homosexuality, is relatively straightforward, other issues and categories of person cause problems. As I will discuss later on, the definition of 'woman', and hence the correct performance of white femininity is particularly problematic and an ambiguous category item that poses an especial problem for neo-nationalist ideology in the U.K. Elsewhere in Europe the situation is rather different – in Norway, for example, as discussed by Gullestad (this volume) – but the discourse of neo-nationalists is consistently gendered and methodologically deserving of attention.

The Rise of Neo-nationalism and the Definition of Britishness

Although fascist groupings had existed in the U.K. before the Second World War, and while there is a level of anti-Semitism that is centuries old, the rise of modern neo-nationalism in Britain with a particular focus on 'race' and immigration begins with the Union Movement founded in 1948 by the fascist Oswald Mosley. He gained around 8 percent of votes as the candidate for North Kensington in London (which includes the Afro-Caribbean neighbourhood of Notting Hill) in the 1959 general election, following a series of 'race' riots in the area the previous year. The party eventually withered but was replaced in 1967 by the NF,[5] which is still a visible presence today, though a series of splits and infighting in the 1970s and 1980s led to a long period of decline. The more acceptable face, the BNP, was formed in the 1980s as the dominant political wing of the neo-nationalist movement. Initially the party was unremarkable under its 'extraordinarily uncharismatic' founding leader (Griffin 2001), but his successor has recently been highly successful in gaining access to national media and in raising the profile of the BNP in the national consciousness. As with many of the other European neo-nationalist parties, the (male) leadership and elected members wear suits and ties, speak moderately and make every effort to appear reasonable. As indicated, the BNP regularly contests elections – local, national and European – leaving the NF to concentrate on more 'direct action'.[6] At the time of writing (summer 2003) this strategy seems to have led to an ever-greater rift between the two organisations, with the NF criticising the new BNP leader for '[being] on an ego trip',[7] and with the BNP anxious to distance itself from the NF's violent and intolerant image. From the BNP's point of view this can be considered a success: as one woman voter in Heckmondwike, Yorkshire, said in defence of her decision to vote for the BNP in a local council election in August 2003, 'They're not the National bloody Front you know' (*The Guardian* 16 August 2003).

Despite this overt neo-nationalist presence on the political scene, the U.K. is distinctive in Europe, though not unique, in lacking a neo-nationalist presence in central government (see Gingrich, this volume, for the other cases), largely because of the historical embeddedness of the two-party political system and the absence of proportional representation. Yet while instances of racism and ethnic chauvinism in Britain are both a daily occurrence and a central aspect of neo-nationalist political campaigning, a clear neo-nationalist ideology is less apparent than it might be. Certainly, the BNP has achieved some recent successes in the political arena as mentioned above, as well as apparently inserting itself, or at least its ideas, into more mainstream political parties (in the 2001 Conservative Party leadership contest, it emerged that the vice-president of the Welsh campaign team for Iain Duncan Smith, the eventual victor, had links with the BNP, *Observer* 28 April 2002).[8] Despite apocalyptic warnings from the political left, such formal and visible incursions (or performances) of neo-nationalism into the arena of public awareness and discourse tend to be sporadic, highly local and short lived.

At this point it is important to consider quite what constitutes a definition of Britishness for both neo- and 'traditional' nationalisms. For 'traditional' nationalism the problem is initially one of defining the nation itself, and untangling a deep-seated conflation between 'England' and 'the U.K.' or 'Britain'[9] This is of course a problem only to the English and, to some extent, to those outside the U.K. who may not know which term to use: the Scots, Welsh and Irish have always had a clearer sense both of their own distinctive identities and of the distinction between British and English. Following Tom Nairn and others, I have written elsewhere of a particular strategy of certain 'traditional' nationalisms, by which a dominant ethnic group effaces the ethnic distinctiveness of its own identity and promotes these values and features instead as the characteristics of the nation as a whole (Banks 1996: 158–60). This in turn, at least in the British case, serves to reify and sharpen the contours of the sub-national identities – Scottishness, Welshness and so on – making them more rigid, but at the same time more prominent, reducible to an easily identified checklist of culinary items, dress and distinctive speech patterns. In this context, Britishness/Englishness as an identity is vague and inchoate, defined more by what it is not than what it is. On the rare occasions that Britishness is made manifest it is associated with a vague jumble of sentiments and memories invoking past imperial and economic glory, and a strong tinge of nostalgia. The spirit of solidarity and pulling together supposedly characteristic of citizens during the Second World War is sometimes evoked and recreated on a few occasions – happy and sad – such as the monarch's Silver Jubilee in 1977, the death of Diana Princess of Wales in 1997, or the petrol price protests of 2000. Less fixed to time or place are cosy, nostalgic evocations, such as ex-Prime Minister John Major's mid 1990s word picture of Britain as a country of 'long shadows on county [cricket] grounds, warm beer ... and old maids bicycling to Holy Communion through the morning mist'.[10] Behind many or all of these sentiments is an unstated assumption of 'whiteness', although in other contexts – for example, calls from politicians or journalists for Britain to define its place in Europe, or to increase manufacturing output to compete in world markets – 'whiteness' is not especially present. Indeed, the promotion of quasi-American 'hyphenated' identities (Black British, British Muslim and so forth) is a major strand in official policies of multiculturalism, seen, for example, in government-sponsored advertisements for health service recruitment, featuring black, white and Asian nurses.

For the neo-nationalists, however, Britishness is a much more straightforward category, largely through linguistic elision and substitution, in which the word 'British' in (almost) all contexts means 'white'. Although the linguistic shifts and terminological fluidity are, of course, particular to the U.K. case, such problems in including or excluding groups of citizens under the national label are common to many of the other European cases discussed in this volume. In a brief survey of NF literature I have made, the terms 'white' and 'British' both appear frequently, though I have not noticed any instance of a need to qualify 'British' with 'white'. NF literature also makes occasional reference to the somewhat archaic noun 'Briton', thus evoking childhood memories of learning about Boudicca and the Ancient Britons at school (in several contexts this association with ancient ancestry is made explicit[11]). In a similarly brief survey of BNP literature, I have noticed that the adjective 'British' normally stands alone, but every few lines it is rendered as 'white British' to make the exclusivity explicit. Perhaps surprisingly, 'English', 'Englishness', etc. appear rarely in this literature; this may less reflect 'traditional' nationalism's uncertainty about the firmness of the boundaries separating the terms 'British' and 'English', and be more indicative of a political strategy of aiming for the widest possible 'white' audience. Both literatures contain occasional reference to 'Aryans': for example, in the BNP political manifesto context this forms part of its attempts to reconcile the economic necessity of retaining trade relationships with Europe and other 'white' nations,[12] while simultaneously advocating withdrawal from the EU. Here an alliance of 'Aryan' nations is called for to resist the economic might of transnational and global corporations. Methodologically then we can see Gingrich's 'economic chauvinism' played out through rhetoric. But how, if at all, is such rhetoric embodied and made live through performance?

Performing Britishness

The initial conclusion of such a brief and crude survey is that 'traditional' nationalism certainly has shape and form but that these are often fluid, vague, understated and rarely made overt; meanwhile the contours of neo-nationalism are far more clearly defined. If true at all, however, such an assessment would need revising in the light of 'Cool Britannia'. This phenomenon briefly gave solidity and substance to a revived but superficial form of 'traditional' nationalism at a time of national economic prosperity, and during which the neo-nationalist political presence was only just recovering from a period of deep decline, and its members spoke largely to themselves and worked on refining their discourse. However, from the late 1990s onwards, successive waves of Islamophobia, combined with warfare in the Balkans, the military interventions in Afghanistan and the Gulf, and culminating in the current rise in numbers of asylum seekers have given new shape and force to both neo- and 'traditional' nationalisms.

As a result of these post-'Cool Britannia' changes, the then Home Secretary, Jack Straw, commissioned an enquiry from the Runnymede Trust, an independent think tank, 'to analyse the current state of multi-ethnic Britain and propose ways of countering racial discrimination and disadvantage and making Britain a confident and vibrant multicultural society at ease with its rich diversity'. The report, known as the Parekh Report after the commission's chairman, Lord Parekh (one of New Labour's non-white nominees to the unelected upper house of parliament), was published in October 2000 and generated a flurry of controversy (Runnymede Trust 2000).

Many of its recommendations were leaked to the press in advance of publication, where they were taken out of context and frequently misrepresented. On the issue of 'Britishness', for example, the report correctly noted that the term 'British' often contained unspoken assumptions of 'whiteness' (what the report called 'racial connotations') and the authors therefore argued for the *idea* of Britain to be represented as 'a community of communities' (ibid.: 3, 105). They thus indicated a nested conceptual structure in which a series of indeterminately defined (and structured) 'communities', each possessed of their own culture, have equivalence within a wider structure (and possibly within each other);[13] this was misrepresented by the right-wing press as a claim that the term 'British' had 'rac*ist* connotations' and that the report's authors were calling for the very term 'British' to be banned.

One result of the controversy, however, was that the concept of Britishness, and consequently ideas of how to be British (that is, of how to perform Britishness) became prominent in both public and informal discourse; the performances of 'Cool Britannia' were quite clearly no longer adequate and alternatives needed to be sought. Quite aside from the rhetoric of the NF and the BNP, ordinary British citizens – black and white – were forced to confront the idea of adopting the Parekh model of a 'community of communities' or to suggest some viable alternative. At the level of the formal political process a response was shortly apparent. Following the results of a subsequent government report into a series of 'race' riots in the north of England in the summer of 2001 (the Cantle Report, Home Office 2001), Straw's successor as Home Secretary, David Blunkett, advocated the idea of a citizenship test, at least for all new arrivals to the country, thereby setting down a script by which performances of Britishness were to be judged and measured. The BNP immediately, and with some justification, pointed out that questions of language and culture were at the core of long-standing BNP policies that had been 'stolen' by New Labour. As some of the other chapters in this volume demonstrate, especially those concerning Austria, there are certainly occasions when a minority neo-nationalist party proposes what appears to be a vote-winning policy that is then adapted and adopted by the majority party or coalition as a strategy of containment of the minority party or, more cynically, to remain in power.

At a more popular level, judged by letters to the press and informal pub conversation, a rather belligerent resurgence of 'proud to be British' sentiment was apparent; in part this was purely pragmatic, revolving around a long-familiar calculation of taxes paid measured against benefits due (Gingrich's 'economic chauvinism' – this volume). In part, this was also reflected in popular debates and discussions concerning Britain's entry to the ERM and the adoption of the euro. But the Parekh Report, or its echoes, also stimulated a need to justify quite why the mere fact of ancestral or long-term residence in the U.K. entitled one to differential treatment vis-à-vis recently arrived asylum seekers. Language, again, proves to be a key element: command of the English language, one of the key factors in the proposed citizenship tests, is cited as a skill that the native-born not merely have but also need in order to perform their Britishness.

The BNP and NF also have an understanding of 'community'. As with other neo-nationalist parties in Europe they are committed to withdrawal from the EU, and propose a model of government devolved to the lowest possible level: local people holding local jobs in local communities and governing themselves. In part, this is predicated upon notions of descent and biology, but they are aware of the unsteadiness of this as a fundamental principle.[14] The principle of descent can still be claimed as a categorical marker of 'Britishness': the BNP website, for example, states: 'We have lived in these islands near on 40,000 years! ... When we in the BNP talk about being British, we talk about the native peoples who have lived in these islands since before the Stone Age, and the relatively small numbers of peoples of almost identical stock, such as the Saxons, Vikings and Normans, and the Irish, who have come here and assimilated.'[15]

Meanwhile, assorted NF publications variously talk of 'the British', the Aryans or just 'local' people, though again the stress on ancient ancestry is there: for example, on an NF website one image of a very blonde woman in an extremely small bikini and perched on a rock by the sea proclaims, 'All my ancestors were racists ... but they were not cowards or cannibals';[16] although another page of the same site shows a photograph of the Magna Carta (1215) together with a translation, which is certainly a reminder of 'tradition' but hardly a claim about 'ancestors'.[17] Such statements, and many more besides, are rhetorical gestures although their performative power should not be denied – Daniel Miller and Don Slater make a compelling case for websites (in their case, of and by Trinidadians) to be seen as performative extensions of local identities that, seemingly paradoxically in the dispersed and diffuse space of cyberspace, serve to reinforce rather than weaken notions of cultural particularity (2000).

Out in the material world, however, both the BNP and the NF perform their own (quasi-) political identity as organisations easily enough – through marches, demonstrations, media interviews and occasional electoral presence; but, again, these could be argued to be a set of rather formal, ritualistic performances. What both the BNP and the NF excel at is planning the *future* performances of Britishness: in the void of time stretching ahead of them a utopian vision can easily be created.[18] While Britain as a country will be 'white', a sense of which is currently maintained only by contrastive opposition with the non-white population, they recognise that once all the 'non-white' citizens are expelled or purged 'whiteness' will not necessarily be unqualified or unproblematic. Consequently, certain actions currently practised by both white and black British citizens will be outlawed: abortion, homosexuality and anything else that comes under the rubric of sexual deviance. Other things will be practised: the strong nuclear family, for example, and grass-roots governance.

However, in thinking through these issues certain further problems emerge, most notably the 'problem' of women. Within 'traditional' British nationalism there is most certainly an understanding of 'correct' gender relations, with a particular emphasis on the correct performance of womanhood or femininity. These understandings have changed dramatically over the past century, and in particular since the Second World War. Nonetheless, although men and women in British society could scarcely be said to be equal at the end of the twentieth century (in pay, for example), and although there are still bastions of misogyny and occasional 'men's rights' backlash movements, since the 1980s public understandings of a normative set of gender relations have been well articulated and intimately enmeshed with understandings of individual human rights (in part, an enmeshing consolidated during the years of Margaret Thatcher's successive governments, which vaunted individual over collective rights in most arenas).[19]

Up until this point the NF and BNP had largely subscribed to a much older, almost Victorian version of 'traditional' nationalism's understandings which drew heavily on the colonial experience (white women should be protected against predatory black men, for example), and had been more notable in the post-war period for their performances of a particularly aggressive masculinity. Yet, as the U.S. invasion of Afghanistan got underway in late 2001, one of the striking preoccupations of the media in the U.K. (and presumably elsewhere) was the Taliban oppression of Afghan women. All at once, a familiar left-liberal issue of women's rights could be used as a justification for not only military action in Afghanistan, but also as a definition of what constituted 'good' or 'traditional' nationalism. Supporters of the NF and the BNP certainly took advantage of this: there were reports, for example, of attacks on Muslim women that took the form of their headscarves being ripped off. But it also left them on rather shaky ground with regard to their own understandings of, and hence performances of, gender. For some years the NF in particular had been associated with the attitude common among more extreme Aryan Nation-type groups that women are inferior to men in a variety of ways and that they should fulfil their biological destiny of childbearing and rearing. Yet after a half century of dramatic changes in gender relations in British society and the suddenly confusing notion that an attack on a Muslim woman's symbol of her 'alien' religion (ripping off her headscarf) could also be seen as a kind of forced 'liberation', the NF and BNP clearly needed to take stock: how should gender be performed in the new Britain they envision?

Both the BNP and the NF reject prostitution and pornography, and the BNP even advocates wages for motherhood – a very wholesome image.[20] But, as noted above, the NF also uses the mildly titillating image of a scantily clad woman to promote its 'proud to be racist' policy – a rather less wholesome image. It seems that over the last three decades both organisations have wittingly or unwittingly responded to the changing social agenda in Britain, incorporating a variety of issues from the left and Green political agendas (local government for local people, suspicion of global capital, the right of all – men and women – to receive fair wages for fair work); in recent years (post-2000) the shift has become even more marked.[21]

In the popular mind the NF in particular is associated largely with the performance of a certain kind of masculinity: aggressive, shaven-headed and heavy-booted. Through the 1970s and 1980s any women present on NF demonstrations were likely to dress and behave in a similar fashion. On the other hand, however, the largely conservative social agenda of the two organisations today stresses docility, childrearing and home-centred domesticity. A notice in *White Nationalist Report* (August 2000) recently announced a new NF publication, *New Dawn*, for and by women.[22] From the announcement this appears to be a curious mix of traditional women's magazine content and 'traditional' racism, but it also attempts to square previous understandings of biological destiny with contemporary social understandings of gender: for example, it talks of the 'sympathy ploy' to which women are naturally vulnerable, i.e., feeling sympathy for poor, homeless refugees and asylum seekers. While this may be a natural feminine trait, it must be resisted and overcome.[23]

Conclusions

From this brief survey of BNP and NF attitudes and activities in the U.K. over the past few years, some methodological points can be made that have relevance to the study of neo-nationalist movements throughout Europe and indeed beyond. The first is to amplify a point made in our introduction to this volume: ethnographic fieldwork is undoubtedly a defining characteristic of the anthropological approach, and one that yields insights and information simply unavailable by other means. While there are methodological, ethical and – frankly – safety and mental-hygienic issues to consider in contemplating fieldwork with members of or subscribers to neo-nationalist movements themselves, it is or should be possible to devise a fieldwork strategy that involves the study of 'ordinary people' as the audiences of, and perhaps responders to, both neo-nationalist and governmental performative rhetoric on 'national' identity. Nevertheless, beyond fieldwork itself there is also a distinctive anthropological approach to discourse and representation, based in part on the contributions of thinkers such as Foucault, but also deriving from the empirical fieldwork of other anthropologists working in similar or parallel ethnographic contexts. An analysis such as the one above, despite being derived entirely from published sources, can still assess the material in an anthropological fashion.

Finally, my main methodological strategy has been to sidestep the obvious arena of social interaction and discourse: the relationship between white neo-nationalists and their most obvious 'other' and target of their opprobrium, Britain's black population. This is not to deny its importance, but rather to examine the broader context within which neo-nationalist thought operates (following insights from Maryon McDonald 1993, amongst others). Neo-nationalist and racist organisations such as the NF and BNP are as much subject to social forces as any other political or quasi-political body; in forming their distinctive approaches to issues such as 'race' they respond both to history and to current events. However, the Magna Carta and St Alban aside, their attitude towards both history and contemporary society is vague and naturalising: it is a distinctive aspect of their rhetoric that it denies its own construction. The official position (derived, I am sure, from the members' sincerely held beliefs) is to constantly naturalise; they claim not to propose an ideological vision, but merely to tell things as they are, to courageously state the simple facts of nature: for example, that black and white people are simply different and mixing of any kind is socially and biologically harmful (see also Kapferer and Morris on Australian Pauline Hanson's rhetoric in this volume). However, this naturalisation runs into problems when gender is considered. Neo-nationalist movements such as the BNP and the NF must deal with two related contradictions. First, there is a conflict between their earlier understanding of the correct relations between men and women and what the evidence of society tells them today – that the 'biology' of women does not seem to hold them back. Following on from this, even if they choose to endorse a more traditional understanding of correct gender relations, there is a conflict between this and political expediency: some potential BNP and NF supporters who might be recruited clearly have no interest in remaining in the home having white babies. Caught in a bind between 'old' and 'new' ideas of femininity, wishing to blame the 'lesbian Jewish feminist' conspiracy, yet acknowledging its power and achievements, the BNP and NF must simultaneously argue for a woman's right to choose[24] between state-subsidised childcare and wages for mothers at home, while at the same time satisfying some of their male supporters with images of blondes in bikinis. If, as we have seen, the intended racist act of humiliating a British Pakistani woman by ripping off her headscarf can also be interpreted as an act of female 'liberation' then who knows – left or right, fascist or anti-fascist – what is the 'correct' performance of white female Britishness?

As has recently (but only recently) come to be recognised in sociology and anthropology, ethnicity and gender are intimately interconnected and mutually constituting. While earlier studies had demonstrated this linkage between groups normally understood to be 'ethnic' (e.g., non-white groups in the U.K. – see Westwood and Bhachu 1988), the equally recent recognition that 'whiteness' is as much a social construction as 'blackness' (e.g., Lieberson 1985) has meant that the NF and BNP's amoeba-like position on the correct performance of white womanhood also has its counterpart in the academic literature, where the relationship between 'whiteness' and nationalism has begun to be explored (e.g.,

Frankenberg 1993; Phoenix 1998). It is through a process of observing the constant interaction between groups such as the NF and BNP and a wide variety of 'others' (in which I include emblematic moments of history, as well as other individual persons, classes of persons and organisations) that we see the stuff from which they fashion their changing performances, and seek to take control of shifting symbolic territory.

Overall, I would argue that while the dominant and certainly most repugnant aspects of neo-nationalism in Britain are focused on 'race', ethnicity and immigration as they are elsewhere in Europe, it may be in the apparently more obscure corners of neo-nationalist thought, propaganda and performance that anthropologists will find the most illuminating material as to what makes, sustains but may also undermine these movements. Certainly, an examination of these areas through discourse analysis or ethnographic fieldwork reveals both neo- and 'traditional' forms of British nationalism to be at their most labile and symbolically nuanced away from the rigidity of stereotypes that influence academic or journalistic perceptions of neo-nationalism. The neo-nationalists themselves are caught in a cage of naturalised, racist stereotypes, but it is the professional and methodological duty of the academic to look to the wider terrain beyond.

Notes

1. In the summer of 2002, the year of the monarch's Golden Jubilee and England's initial success in the football World Cup, the Union Jack saw a similar – and even more brief – positive revival. At about the same time the Cross of St George also began to be flown as a 'merely' patriotic flag – in England obviously – away from its previous associations with tendencies from the extreme right. It is now relatively commonly seen.
2. 'Wrapping oneself in the flag' is a British English figure of speech denoting the actions of a politician (usually) who cynically appeals to national sentiment in search of popular support.
3. As discussed in chapters by Gingrich and others in this volume, as well as in our introduction, there are some terminological difficulties in using, for example, 'right' and 'left', as well as the very term 'neo-nationalist' (for which the historian of fascism Roger Griffin prefers the term 'ethnocratic liberalism' to distinguish it from other rightist political tendencies, e.g., Griffin 2000: 173). My concern is less with objective precision, however, than with the methodology of mapping out subjective understandings and manipulations of an area of popular discourse and sentiment.
4. Some branches of the NF appear to have a particular interest in allying themselves with anti-paedophile campaigns, for example, seizing upon the *News of the World*'s (a populist Sunday newspaper) 'name and shame' approach to convicted paedophiles released into society at the end of prison sentences. The Yorkshire NF branch has a link to the website of an organisation called 'Noncewatch' (a 'nonce' is a sexual offender in prison slang), which largely consists of lists of names of convicted offenders and rather obsessive investigative journalism, but which has a decided NF tone.
5. Strictly speaking the NF is, perhaps, not a fascist party, and the BNP even less so, having eschewed the fascist ideal of a new social order for an acceptance of the existing liberal-democratic order, only ethnically purified (Griffin 2000). Fielding (1981) provides an extremely lucid account of NF thought in the late 1970s; see also Stan Taylor (1982) for a more journalistic account.
6. The activities of the NF and other even smaller 'direct action' fascist and neo-Nazi groups in the U.K. are regularly documented by the anti-fascist journal *Searchlight* and its associated website (www.searchlightmagazine.com). As with the equivalent if not more extreme extra-parliamentary

groups in the U.S., whose activities are documented by the Southern Poverty Law Center's journal *Intelligence Report* and associated website (www.splcenter.org), the NF and other U.K. groups seem prone to fissiparousness and infighting. It would be unwise, however, as well as methodologically inaccurate, to celebrate this as a sign of weakness and eventual dissolution. Having worked for many years as an anthropologist with an Indian religious tradition that is notorious for its fissiparousness, it is possible to see the regular purges and splinterings as a sign of constant symbolic manipulation and ideological renewal. This is an adaptive process that can simultaneously promote core ideals (racial purity in one case, fidelity to the teachings of the founders in the other) without becoming stagnant, while permitting constant shifts to cope with changed social and political circumstances.

7. www.yorksnf.com/qa10.html (consulted August 2003).

8. The process is, of course, two way, and modern neo-nationalist political parties enjoy a symbiotic relationship with the historically antecedent right-wing political party in most European states, each borrowing policies from the other that appear to have populist appeal. In the U.K. it is commonly understood that the populist right-wing agenda of the Conservative Party under Margaret Thatcher (1979–1990), especially in the later years, led to a marked decline in support for the NF and BNP. In turn, the currently ruling Labour Party has in recent years adopted an increasingly intolerant stance towards issues such as immigration, as discussed below.

9. Stated briefly: 'England' refers to one component of the three-fold 'Great Britain' (England, Scotland and Wales), which together with Northern Ireland makes up 'The United Kingdom' (hence, officially, 'The United Kingdom of Great Britain and Northern Ireland'); the 'British Isles' refers to Great Britain, (the island of) Ireland and a number of smaller islands, some of which (the Channel Islands, the Isle of Man) maintain a degree of political and financial autonomy. 'Britain' is a catch-all term normally equivalent in use to the U.K.' These definitions are important not only to the British Government at Westminster, but also to the NF and BNP, who are committed to defending the retention of Northern Ireland (always referred to as 'Ulster') despite the fact that this rather contradicts both parties' policy that 'immigrants' (including the descendants of first-generation immigrants) should return to live in their own 'home'.

10. Uttered on St George's Day 1993, drawing in part on George Orwell's essay 'The Lion and the Unicorn' (1941).

11. For reasons I will go on to discuss, the whole issue of 'ancestry' and descent is problematic for the BNP and NF. However, there are occasional references in the literature, including websites, to a cultural rather than a biological heritage that white people ought to share. One NF webpage concludes, 'What are ultra-liberal, pro-homosexual teachers telling your children today? Are they being taught about the Bible, St Alban [supposedly the first Christian martyr in Britain], and the early history of Britain?' (www.natfront.com.sleaze.html [consulted August 2003]). See also my discussion of 'culture' as a euphemism for 'race' – Banks 1996: 175ff.

12. The BNP now (August 2003) appears to shun the term 'Aryan', perhaps as part of an attempt to adopt a more 'reasonable' language suited to a party with parliamentary ambitions.

13. In their recent, more moderated public pronouncements, the NF and BNP are anxious to stress that they are not 'racist' in the sense that they do not hate black people (though the websites are full of surveys and summaries of academic studies that 'prove' scientifically that black people are inferior to white people), but merely recognise that different 'races' simply cannot live together and should be separated. Their hatred then is reserved for 'multiculturalism', which they seem to understand as an enforced racial mixing, a kind of melting pot policy (see Banks 1996: 67–71). In this aspect then the Parekh Report's recommendation has some overlap; the crucial difference lying in the fact that Parekh sees the communities as contained within – and politically and legally subordinate to – a transcendent polity.

14. In some respects neo-nationalist thought in Britain cannot fully replace the 'traditional' nationalist understanding of citizenship based upon territory with that defined by blood; although it is by no means clear-cut elsewhere either (for example, see Forsythe 1989 on Germany). The history of the British Isles is simply too messy for this. Although a neat racial binarism can be maintained in some

contexts (e.g., the website lists of academic studies that 'prove' black inferiority), it falls apart when the specificities of the British population are considered: are Irish Catholic migrants in Britain black? No, but they do have a 'home' (Eire) to which they can be repatriated.

15. http://www.bnp.org.uk/faq.html (consulted August 2003).
16. http://www.yorksnf.com/intro.html (consulted August 2003).
17. http://www.natfront.org.uk/magnac1.html (consulted January 2002; the address was not valid by August 2003).
18. Again, Roger Griffin has some very insightful remarks on this phenomenon. Fascists, committed as they are to a vision of a new order, tend to regard themselves as 'living on the threshold of a new age or in a protracted interregnum' (2000: 172); although, as I have said above, the BNP and to a lesser extent the NF are not strictly fascist parties by his definition as their visions are for a new 'ethnocratic' version of the existing liberal-democratic order rather than for a new order per se.
19. A strong commitment to and manifestation of gender equality is a component in the national self-definition of countries such as Norway (Marianne Gullestad, this volume, and personal communication).
20. http://www.bnp.org.uk/faq.html (consulted August 2003).
21. 'We fully support the changes in society over the last thirty years or so which have allowed women a full and equal role in society' (http://www.yorksnf.com/qa10.html [consulted August 2003]); and 'Men or women, we are all British! We recognise that men and women are essentially and inherently different, but this does not make the sexes unequal ... In a BNP Britain, women will have a choice on whether to seek paid employment, and will not be forced to make a decision between children and career' (www.bnp.org.uk/faq.html [consulted August 2003]).
22. http://www.natfront.com/wnr26.html (consulted August 2003); subsequently *New Dawn* seems not to have appeared.
23. The anti-fascist journal *Searchlight* carried a series of stories on women and the NF in 2001; available online at www.searchlightmagazine.com/stories/womenFascism.htm (consulted August 2003).
24. Although I am referring here to the 'right to choose' between going out to work and staying at home with the children (see footnote 21), taking the phrase in the more common feminist sense the BNP has shifted ground from an ambivalence towards abortion (K. Taylor 2001) to an outright rejection.

Bibliography

Banks, M. 1996. *Ethnicity: Anthropological Constructions*. London: Routledge.
Billig, M. 1995. *Banal Nationalism*. London: Sage.
Fielding, N. 1981. *The National Front*. London: Routledge & Kegan Paul.
Forsythe, D. 1989.'German Identity and the Problems of History', in E. Tonkin, M. McDonald and M. Chapman eds *History and Ethnicity*. London: Routledge.
Frankenberg, R. 1993. *White Women, Race Matters: The Social Construction of Whiteness*. New York: Routledge.
Griffin, R. 2000. 'Interregnum or Endgame? The Radical Right in the 'Post-fascist' Era', *Journal of Political Ideologies* 5(2): 163–78.
——— 2001. '"No Racism, Thanks, We're British". How Right-wing Populism Manifests Itself in Contemporary Britain', in W. Eisman ed. *Rechtspopulismus in Europa. Analysen und Handlungsperspektiven*. Graz: Czernin-Verlages.
Home Office. 2001. *Community Cohesion: A Report of the Independent Review Team Chaired by Ted Cantle*. London: Home Office.

Lieberson, S. 1985. 'Unhyphenated Whites in the United States', in R.D. Alba ed. *Ethnicity and Race in the U.S.A.: Toward the Twenty-first Century*. London: Routledge & Kegan Paul.

McDonald, M. 1993. 'The Construction of Difference: An Anthropological Approach to Stereotypes', in S. MacDonald ed. *Inside European Identities: Ethnography in Western Europe*. Oxford: Berg.

Miller, D. and Slater, D. 2000. *The Internet: An Ethnographic Approach*. Oxford: Berg.

Orwell, G. 1941. *The Lion and the Unicorn: Socialism and the English Genius*. London: Secker & Warburg.

Phoenix, A. 1998. 'Representing New Identities: "Whiteness" as Contested Identity in Young People's Accounts', in K. Koser, and H. Lutz eds *The New Migration in Europe: Social Constructions and Social Realities*. Basingstoke: Macmillan.

Runnymede Trust. 2000. *The Future of Multi-Ethnic Britain: Report of the Commission on the Future of Multi-Ethnic Britain*. London: Profile Books.

Schechner, R. 1988. *Performance Theory*. London and New York: Routledge.

Taylor, K. 2001. 'Breeders for the White Race', *Searchlight Magazine* special section on 'Women and Fascism', http://www.searchlightmagazine.com/stories/womenFascismBreed.htm (consulted August 2003).

Taylor, S. 1982. *The National Front in English Politics*. London: Macmillan.

Westwood, S. and Bhachu, P. eds. 1988. *Enterprising Women: Ethnicity, Economy and Gender Relations*. London: Routledge.

PART II
Case Studies from Western Europe

Chapter 3

Imagined Kinship

The Role of Descent in the Rearticulation of Norwegian Ethno-nationalism
Marianne Gullestad

Since the beginning of the era of the nation state in Europe, there has been a tension between a notion of the nation as the bearer of certain civic and political rights on the one hand, and a popular notion of the nation as 'the people' with a particular ancestry, culture, language and history on the other. To build a political nation means constructing a narrative about who belongs and who does not and therefore ultimately depends on a notion of 'the people'. This is so, in different ways, in both the 'German' and the 'French' model of the nation. The national narrative is a moral tale about the people as a moral community and usually involves the suppression of internal difference. Through nation building, minorities in Europe were both created and reified by means of statistics and other modern forms of census taking. At the same time they were rendered invisible and transformed into a residual political category by the new national narrative.

In spite of the suppression of minorities, the tension between the political nation and the ethnically defined people was not publicly prominent in the nineteenth century. With the extra-European immigration after the Second World War, however, this tension has become more pronounced. European societies are de facto plural societies, and a sense of social obligation and moral community is continuously stretched to include new people. At the same time, new attempts at boundary setting are also prominent. Despite different national traditions and political cultures, the current colour-coded externalisation of certain inhabitants as 'them' is surprisingly similar in many European countries. Underpinning this externalisation is a renewed popular emphasis on ideas about culture, descent and 'roots' in the land. Douglas R. Holmes (2000) calls these ideas 'integralism', and has examined their long history in European politics. Integralist ideas can be traced back to the Counter-Enlightenment of the Romantic Movement as resistance to modernity. Durkheim (1933) highlighted similar tendencies when he commented upon the longing for 'mechanical solidarity' based on rootedness in the land, and advanced the notion of 'organic solidarity' based on the division of work in modern society.

Europe is experiencing a revival of integralist ideas, in association with new 'culturalist' justifications of racialisation (the categorisation of people on the basis of characteristics that are assumed to be innate).[1] Right-wing populism is not only gaining parliamentary representation in several small countries, but also considerable ideological influence across the political spectrum. Political entrepreneurs of various kinds (both inside and outside the political parties) mobilise symbolic resources already in circulation when they both play on and contribute to the legitimisation and reinforcement of integralist ideas, images and values.

In this chapter I focus on integralism in Norway at the present historical conjuncture.[2] By looking at politically organised right-wing populism in the light of shifts in the more general cultural climate and social imaginaries, I make a critical analysis of some of the assumptions that are presently underpinning the discussion of issues in the foreground in politics, the mass media and everyday life. By discussing some of the ethnographic specificities of the contemporary Norwegian case in relation to the wider European context, I argue more generally that ideas about family life, kinship, ancestry and descent are central to the political tendencies popularly termed neo-nationalism, and that these ideas are more widespread than their expression in right-wing politics. The value of 'roots' needs to be analytically refocused as being based on ideas about language, 'a common culture' and religion, often ultimately based in assumptions about ancestry and descent. I focus here in particular on assumptions about ancestry and descent, because they seem to be the most taken for granted in current discourses about cultural heritage. Such a contextualisation can help us understand the often self-explanatory nature of many populist ideas at the present moment. My contention is that the assumptions underpinning the debates about 'immigrants' constitute an emerging polarised frame of interpretation, underpinned by rearticulated ideas about descent.

In order to retain and emphasise the notions of the political nation and of citizenship as loyalty to the political constitution, I define neo-nationalism more narrowly and precisely as the neo-ethnification of national identity. The concept of *ethnification* focuses on the use of specific ideas about language, culture, descent and territory in individual and collective processes of identification. Since these ideas are now recombined in new ways in the face of extra-European immigration, I advance the notion of *neo-ethnification* in order to emphasise aspects of both continuity and change when old ideas are rearticulated and gain new importance as social imaginaries in a new situation. In Norway, the Progress Party (Fremskrittspartiet) is the main political vehicle for right-wing populism, and its leaders have no doubt been crucial in articulating and focusing the revitalised ethnification of national belonging, and the accompanying new justifications for racial inequality. I want nevertheless to argue that a focus on this party alone misses the broader and deeper cultural and social basis for ethno-nationalism, as well as the crucial roles played by many other actors in its present rearticulation and reaffirmation.

Norway: A Case in Point

Norway became an independent nation state in 1905 after having been the junior partner in a union with Sweden for almost 100 years and before that a region under the Danish Crown for 400 years. Its new independence was broken in the Nazi occupation from 1940 to 1945 during the Second World War. These historical events are important in order to understand present-day national identification. Nationalism in Norway is popularly considered to be a positive, liberating and democratising force. This is part of the reason why there has been relatively little public self-reflection regarding its actual and potential negative aspects. Instead nationalism is popularly divided into two kinds: a positive one to be found in Norway, and a negative one to be found in some other regions, such as the former Yugoslavia. This national self-image plays down the history of oppressive practices in relation to minorities such as the Sami (formerly called Lapps), the Finns, the Romani (*Tatere*), the Rom (also called Gypsies in English), the Jews and others.

In everyday Norwegian the term 'immigrant' covers both people who have moved permanently to Norway, refugees, asylum seekers, people moving back and forth between the continents – as well as the children and grandchildren of these categories. Extra-European immigrants did not start coming to Norway in any numbers until the late 1960s, later than to many other European countries. Then the proportion of immigrants in the population (both European and extra-European, including more recent refugees and asylum seekers) increased steadily, from 2 percent in 1980, to 7.6 percent in January 2004: 46 percent of these have so far become Norwegian citizens. In 1970, 6 percent of the 'immigrant population' came from Asia, Africa and Latin America; in 2004 the figure was 72 percent.[3] By 1 January 2004 'non-Western immigrants' ('first and second generation') made up approximately 5.5 percent of the total population. More than 100 mother tongues are currently spoken in the schools of Oslo, which is home to more than 40 percent of the 'non-Western immigrants'. Their presence is visible, particularly in some of the inner-city neighbourhoods.[4]

Many 'non-Western immigrants' work in unskilled and semi-skilled service occupations, doing many of the jobs that 'Norwegians no longer want'. They earn considerably less than native Norwegians at the same age and with the same educational level. During the first years after arrival this difference in income is 40 percent, after twenty-five years it is 20 percent (Barth et al. 2004). Educated 'immigrants' often experience difficulties when attempting to obtain appropriate jobs. For white Norwegian employers, a 'strange name' or 'non-Norwegian looks' often signal not sharing basic values and assumptions. Unemployment is three times as high as among majority Norwegians. Both personal narratives (Ali 1997; Johnsen 1996; Wamwere 2000) and research reports (ECRI 1997, 2000; Høgmo 1998; Lunde 2000; SMED 2001: 93; SOPEMI 2000; UDI 2000) document the considerable discrimination that is taking place in the housing market, the labour market and everyday life. These studies suggest that the main problem is not violent extremist and racist groups, but 'more subtle forms of everyday discrimination'. It is argued that this is due to a discrepancy between 'official and unofficial attitudes' (SOPEMI 2000). In other words, that people say one thing officially, and do something else unofficially.

In contrast to this view, I want to argue that the recorded discrimination is rather due to taken-for-granted ideas, images and organising concepts that can be identified in everyday life as well as in official documents. It is thus not primarily a question of presenting different views in different contexts (it may of course be that, too), but that most people in one way or another are influenced by widespread and self-evident cultural assumptions about belonging and non-belonging. These assumptions are simultaneously deeply seated and shifting situationally and over time. Language proficiency (including speaking with a foreign accent), religious adherence, family name and looks are in many situations regarded as more important for national belonging than citizenship and membership of the political nation.

In Norway, groups of violent political extremists (such as self-defined racists and neo-Nazis) are small, comprising only a few hundred individuals (Bjørgo 1997a, 1997b, 1998; Fangen 1998). Even if a number of prominent Norwegians identified with Nazism during the Second World War, as happened throughout most of Europe, present-day Norwegians distance themselves strongly from Nazism and racism. On several occasions, thousands of people have demonstrated publicly against the actions of these marginal groups. Many people in Norway associate the term racism with Nazism, the former segregationist policies in the southern states of the U.S., and the Apartheid regime in South Africa. Nobody, except the very few political extremists, identifies with ideologies that are racist in the traditional sense. As in other European countries, the word is most often mentioned as part of a denial (Van Dijk 1993), such as in the commonplace expression 'I am not a racist, but … '. Fear of being labelled racist is often used as an explanation of some people's blameworthy acts as well as other people's lack of adequate action. Paradoxically, therefore, the word racism is relatively dominant in public debates, at the same time as minority experiences of racial discrimination are usually trivialised by some form of denial ('the problem is not racism, but …'). Because racism is generally defined in individualising terms as hateful intentions, and not as social structures and conventional assumptions influencing more or less everybody, there is a profound majority embarrassment attached to the slightest suspicion of being accused of racism. The embarrassment acts as a barrier against the public acknowledgement of experiences of racial inequality. There seems to be a consensus that the main problem is 'their' religious and cultural difference. I want to argue here that perceptions of cultural difference are often embedded in assumptions about descent, defining who 'we' are.

The Emerging Polarised Frame of Interpretation

In a study of Norwegian public debates on immigration (Gullestad 2001a; 2002a; 2002b; 2003; 2004a; 2004b; 2005), I examined what the debates can tell us about the current reinvention of hegemonic ideas. I scrutinised statements of the Norwegian political and cultural elite (in the widest sense of the term), and I was able to show that even well-intentioned statements often draw on some of the same underlying ideas and stereotypes as the more hateful and discriminating statements of political extremists (Gullestad 2002b). The turn of the decade from the 1980s to the 1990s witnessed the beginning of a remarkable but, nevertheless, largely unacknowledged change in the cultural climate of Norway in the direction of the rearticulation and reaffirmation of integralist ideas. These ideas have different effects in relation to different categories of people. Some new inhabitants are included on the basis of descent. For example, in 1995 new regulations allowed Russian nationals of Norwegian descent to return to the country from where their parents and grandparents had emigrated. After more than 70 years without contact, the Norwegian government decided to offer the descendants of the migrants the possibility to immigrate to Norway, conceived as their 'fatherland'. While this conception of the inherent rights of ethnic nationality is similar to the *Aussiedler* in Germany, its inscription in law is new in Norway. At the same time, other 'immigrants' are being excluded from the Norwegian nation in terms of the very same ideas. In spite of enormous variation in the background and mother tongues of 'immigrants', and many overlapping identities across the categories 'Norwegian' and 'immigrant', the main feature of the new hegemony is a polarisation between 'us' (majority Norwegians) and 'them' ('immigrants'), based on descent. This ideological shift, which is generally not regarded as such, has been reinforced by the reactions to the terrorist attacks of 11 September 2001, and by the media coverage of the murder of a young Kurdish-Swedish woman named Fadime Sahindal by her father in Sweden in January 2002.[5]

According to Hernes and Knudsen (1990), nine out of ten Norwegians associate the word 'immigrant' (*innvandrer*) with what is perceived as 'dark skin colour'. 'Skin colour' (*hudfarge*) is the main term for racial difference in present-day Norway. While everyday life often defies simple dichotomies, the polarity has become discursively more rigidified, especially in the mass media. One example is the image of 'us' as hosts and 'them' as guests (Gullestad 2002b; Hervik 2004). This apparently benevolent and innocent image can function in a discriminating and excluding way when it is used not only in reference to refugees and asylum seekers *as they are arriving*, but also to people born in Norway, or who have lived there for a long time. These metaphors implicitly and self-evidently represent 'immigrants' as outsiders and a burden to Norwegian society. A hierarchical relationship between the social categories, with the majority at the apex, is thus reproduced.

Nevertheless, a few young women with an immigrant background have become publicly celebrated icons in the mass media; they generally focus their attention on the problematic issues within 'immigrant' social circles, such as cases of forced marriage, honour killings and female circumcision.[6] These are very important issues, needing constant and careful public attention in order to protect young people in difficult family situations. At the same time it is also important how these issues are discussed. By only criticising other 'immigrants', the young women do not threaten majority assumptions. In these cases descent is simultaneously very important and not important at all. It is because of their ethnic background that their points of view and experiences are regarded as authentic and so carry weight in the public realm. And because of this authenticity, they are also able to validate the majority self-image of innocence and the one-sidedness in the present targeting in the mass media of whole categories. By identifying strongly and publicly with hegemonic ideas and values, they symbolically transcend their background to become honorary Norwegians. In other words, in exchange for belonging, they are largely expected not to criticise Norway.

The polarisation is well illustrated by two new words in Norway: *fremmedkulturell* (culturally alien) and *fjernkulturell* (culturally distant). These terms are usually considered transparent and neutral, but can, depending on context, function in marginalising and discriminatory ways. The term *fremmedkulturell* first appeared in letters to the editor from racists and right-wing extremists in the late 1980s. Around the mid 1990s it started to be used in editorials and among the general public without any change of meaning (Herbjørnsrud 1998). The municipality of Oslo introduced the twin notion of *fjernkulturell* in 1991 (ibid.: 71). These notions quickly moved into general use and contribute to the discursive hardening of the polarity between 'Norwegians' and 'immigrants'. To be culturally alien or culturally distant is to be associated with a foreign way of life by means of descent. While it is a well-established fact that many 'immigrants' do not want or are not able to become 'integrated' in Norway, this nevertheless becomes a one-sided interpretation when the ability of the majority to accept various forms of difference is not also taken into account. Then it hides the extent to which withdrawal to 'one's own' might be a reaction to discrimination and unacknowledged barriers, to protect both self-respect and important social networks.

Thus, my contention is that Norwegian ethno-nationalism is a close-knit package of specific understandings of geography, history, culture, religion, perceptions of 'skin colour' and descent, and that this close-knit package has recently been reinvented, as it were. 'Foreign' appearance and family name work as markers of cultural difference and social distance. In other words, genealogy in time is interpreted as spatial distance within an imaginary geographical space. Categories, rhetorical strategies and points of view formerly regarded as extremist are now not only in the foreground in the media, but also are to a great extent regarded as a form of self-evident common sense. As in other European countries these assumptions are not confined to the populist right; nor are they solely employed by individuals in particular positions, but consist of signs that circulate, and which are used to express many different points of view. I am thus not focusing on benevolent versus hateful attitudes towards 'immigrants', but on the terms of the debate itself. People who want to express themselves in public about immigration have to engage with the emerging common-sense frame of interpretation.

How did this frame of interpretation develop? This question has many answers, not just one. In the following four subsections, I present four interconnected ideas about why this polarised frame of interpretation has become more or less hegemonic in Norway, as a historical product fashioned by politicians, journalists, researchers and others who participate in the public realm and who play on and rearticulate cultural resources already in circulation (for discussions of the notion of hegemony, see Comaroff and Comaroff 1991: 19–27; Gramsci 1971). I argue that the Norwegian reinforcement of ethno-nationalism has its own specific emphases and timetable, based on national history and unique events. The four ideas are the following: (1) due to historically established values Norwegians are poorly equipped to resist the current rearticulated justifications of neo-ethnification; (2) in the face of wide-ranging social and economic change many people see a need to defend the national moral community; (3) certain unique historical events contribute to the reinforcement of ideas about majority superiority; (4) in addition to the populist right-wing Progress Party, other political actors from other parties and groups have promoted the polarised frame of interpretation. Towards the end of the chapter, I change perspective and analytical level in order to present two empirical examples: one from political life, and one from everyday life. Family, kinship and descent are not only metaphors for national belonging, but also an experiential grounding for the imagining of the national community (Gullestad 1997b) and constitute a key to understanding why and how new forms of ethnic nationalism are becoming naturalised as self-evident.

Living by Values: Stability, Security, Equality, Humanity and the Welfare State

Historically established and deep-seated values influence how people in Norway react to extra-European immigration. The first value that I want to emphasise is stability. Stability provides the basis for *trygghet*, a difficult concept to translate: it is a mixture of safety, security and control over one's life. It can sometimes be closely related to the values of peace and quiet and of homely cosiness (Gullestad 1992). The value placed on stability implies resistance in the face of social changes, and some awkwardness in dealing with them. This also applies to upward social mobility. Contradicting the idea that a person's essence is based in birth, the class traveller seems to have a hard time.

The second value is equality, in association with a stress on boundaries. As already noted, nation building has been interpreted as a liberating force in Norwegian history, at the same time as it has been historically linked to a form of culture building that stressed homogeneity and implied a heavy-handed assimilation of those regarded as different. Everyday life in Norway is often characterised by an egalitarian individualism based on a notion of equality conceived as sameness that I have chosen to call 'imagined sameness'. In social life, it is an unquestioned assumption that people need to be more or less similar in order to get along well. This assumption is expressed in a proverb that is difficult to translate, but is nevertheless self-explanatory to most majority Norwegians. The meaning is something like the following: children who are like each other play together more happily than other children (*like barn leker best*). The focus on sameness as being alike means that difference becomes a problem to be tackled. 'Too much' difference often leads to strategies of avoidance – in social life, in work life and on the housing market. Often it is almost as though an outsider must be found in order for the internal imagined sameness, unity and sense of belonging to be confirmed (Gullestad 2002a; 2002b). Thus the specific form of egalitarian individualism is linked to a passion for boundaries, manifested in tensions between boundary setting and breaking, and in an all-or-nothing quality of many debates and practices that can be characterised as secular pietism, and is historically related to Protestant pietism (Gullestad 1992: 211–30). Boundaries are important in childrearing, home decoration, the mass media, as well as in political discussions about immigration and European integration. Within specific boundaries, the individual is expected to be free to develop his or her potential (Gullestad 1997a). The focus on boundaries thus depends on specific ideas about substance (language, religion, 'culture') and vice versa. Religion, as a repository of traditions of symbols and beliefs, always stands ready to be tapped by those who wish to develop a new framework of ideas about social order (Juergensmeyer 1996). In Norway, Christian religion, in the form of the Lutheran State Church, has gained a renewed importance as an institution uniting even secularised majority Norwegians in opposition to Islam.

The third value is humanity, based on Norway's assumed innocence in relation to colonialism and imperialism. As inhabitants of Denmark–Norway, quite a few Norwegians participated in the Danish colonial venture, including the slave trade. Norwegians also participated in colonialism as explorers, seafarers and, not least, missionaries. The typical Norwegian self-image however is of an innocent and compassionate helper. The public realm thus generally lacks a critical post-colonial perspective on both the past and the present.

Last, but not least, I want to mention the welfare state, containing a structural tendency, as it were, to regard whole categories of people as items of expenditure. Traditionally the redistribution of the welfare state is based on the nation state. The building of the welfare state after the Second World War was legitimated by a national discourse uniting people of different classes and living in both urban and rural areas. The idea is that 'immigrants' disrupt the welfare system because they take away resources that rightfully belong to 'us', and that it is only by closing the borders that Norway can uphold its welfare state, and thus present a political model for the rest of the world to follow. These concerns actualise and reinforce the need to determine who 'we' are, the *folk*. The largely unacknowledged revitalisation of ideas about descent, linked to ideas about language, culture, Protestant religion and territory can be interpreted as a response to this need. The fact that 'immigrant' workers on different levels have become crucial to the functioning of the institutions of the welfare state is not part of popular consciousness.

Defending a Moral Community in the Face of Social and Economic Changes

The second idea concerns the effects of economic neo-liberalism and the current restructurings of transnational capitalism. As in other parts of the world, Norway is undergoing rapid changes related to accelerating transnational flows of capital, information, ideas and lifestyles. Due to global economic restructurings, people in Norway experience changes to working life, and the welfare state is not able to satisfy all their demands. The power of the nation state is under pressure from transnational processes on the one hand, and from regional and local processes on the other. While social democratic welfare ideals are grounded in socialist ideas, the fall of USSR communism and the Berlin Wall in 1989 brought about the end of the power balance of the Cold War, the loss of the Marxian utopia as an ideological counterpoint to unbridled capitalism, and the accompanying fear that hordes of Eastern Europeans would descend upon Western Europe.

Stability is thus a fact of the past, as is the hope of being able to solve all social problems by careful state and municipal planning and social engineering. Norway's economy is among the strongest in Europe because of North Sea oil and its unemployment rate is among the lowest in Europe. While employers' organisations want fewer restrictions on immigration, many people in the unions have feared that 'immigrants' would be willing to work for lower pay and under worse conditions than the so-called ethnic Norwegians, thus lowering the general conditions of work, and making Norway into a more sharply class-divided society than before.

The majority of people have become more affluent, but the gap between rich and poor has also widened over the last ten to fifteen years. In the midst of the affluence, there seems to be a certain dissatisfaction and frustration. Many people are increasingly conscious of living in a global system, while at the same time lacking a clear overview of the forces affecting their life-worlds. There is a fear of downward social mobility, and of not mastering new technologies and the often continuous reorganisation of workplaces. Due to the negative local effects of economic deregulation and the increased power of the investors of capital compared to business managers, politicians and state bureaucrats, Norwegians, like many people all over the world, are now turning to religious, ethnic and national identities as a means of understanding themselves and their situations and defending their interests (Turner 1994: 419). Quite a few people either feel that something valuable is disappearing and should be rescued and defended, or has already gone and should be recreated. For many majority people 'immigrants' and their descendants seem to give these complicated, abstract forces and unwanted social changes a face, and therefore represent a target. 'Immigrants' seem to have become a symbol for the effects of economic globalisation; opposition to immigration can thus function as an organising principle for a much broader protest. This can happen by means of the link that the media continuously make between crime and immigration (Lindstad and Fjeldstad 2005).[7]

In Norway, as elsewhere in Europe, gender and cultural difference have largely replaced social class as the main categories of social conflict in popular consciousness. While class differences have become more important economically and socially, the notion of social class has become almost invalid ideologically. In this soil, ethno-nationalist ideas grow. This is the experiential grounding that political actors (both within and outside the political parties) have given specific interpretations, based on a reworking of ideas and images already in circulation, and capitalising on the fact that people lack alternative concepts and explanations. It is not only what happens that is important, but also how new events are perceived and interpreted.

Using Andre Gingrich's terms in this volume, the present cultural climate is characterised by 'cultural pessimism' and 'economic chauvinism', a fear of losing not only national and individual affluence, but also specific moral values. I would, however, rather use the word *defensiveness* instead of chauvinism, because this word leads us to ask what is being defended. Opposition to 'immigrants' is increasingly argued in terms of a defence of 'our' liberal society against the illiberal fundamentalism of political Islam, with a tendency to see every Muslim as a potential threat. Like in other European countries, what seems to be at stake is a perceived threat to specific national narratives and self-images as a moral community. In the cherished Norwegian national narratives Norway is a *victim* of colonisation (from Denmark), and not a coloniser. Norway has played an important role in various peace negotiations such as in the Middle East, Guatemala, Sri Lanka and Colombia. Norway is among the countries that spend most money per capita on development aid to the Third World, and Norway has gone a long way towards gender equality. The public national self-image is self-congratulatory, seeing Norway as 'the richest country of the world', 'the land of gender equality', and 'a humanitarian superpower'. 'Immigrants' who do not play down their difference threaten such narratives about Norway as a homogeneous, humane, gender equal, tolerant, anti-racist and peace-loving society.

Unique Historical Events Reinforced Ethno-national Ideas

My third idea about the self-evidence of ethno-nationalist ideas involves the effects of two national events. The very successful Winter Olympics at Lillehammer in 1994 strengthened ethno-national self-confidence. Later that same year, a national referendum resulted in Norway remaining outside the EU. Both events fuelled a renewed national pride. The EU referendum again revealed a considerable gap between 'the people' and what was understood as 'the system': the state, the market and the media. However, research has shown no direct statistical correlation between xenophobia on the one hand, and resistance to the European Union on the other, at the time of the referendum (Aardal 1995). In fact, more people who voted for the Socialist Left Party (SV), the Centre Party (Senterpartiet) and the Christian People's Party (Kristelig Folkeparti) voted no to the EU than those who voted for the Progress Party (ibid.). The resistance to the EU spans the political spectrum, and has many different and partly contradictory causes: from pietistic Lutheran resistance to Catholic Southern Europe, to a left-wing focus on the democratic deficit in the EU and the distance to Brussels. Similarly, the opposition to 'immigrants' has many different and partly contradictory justifications: from the focus on family values and traditional gender roles among pietistic Lutherans, through the feminist protest against Muslim gender roles; and from the distance of pietistic Lutherans from Catholics and Muslims, to intellectual post-Christians' lack of understanding for the place of religious belief and practice in human life.

When assessing the importance of the EU referendum for the development of the polarised frame of interpretation, I therefore look more at the terms of the debate than at who voted for whom. National self-determination (*sjølråderetten*) was, rhetorically, a powerful notion in the EU debates (Gullestad 1997b). It is closely related to the container image of the nation state with its focus on boundaries, and, according to Neumann (2001), to powerful and changing ideas about the *folk*. The centre–periphery dimension is also strong in Norwegian politics, based on the perceived social and political distance between the *folk* in the outlying areas and 'the system'. In addition, because of the Union with Sweden from 1814 to 1905, the negative connotations of the notion of the Union in Norway contributed to giving the opposition the rhetorical upper hand (Neumann 2001). The underpinning ideas about the *folk*, I want to argue, are ultimately and unselfconsciously based on rearticulated ethno-national ideas about descent. Different people can defend widely different ideas and values, basing their defence on similar ethno-national ideas.

Not Just the Progress Party

My fourth idea concerns political actors in the widest sense. The organised populist right is a crucial part of a larger ideological movement in which other parties and political actors are also active. Of these, the mass media are especially influential for the rearticulation of social imaginaries that is taking place. The mass media bring events from all over the world into the living room of each household, and have considerable power over the political agenda and the conceptual categories that are used to understand what goes on. The positive aspects of the mass media are breadth, accessibility and immediacy. The negative aspects are lack of depth and complexity. In these respects, the owners' search for profit (in terms of increasing the number of readers and viewers) and the professional criteria of good journalism seem to work in the same direction. Journalists often try to make complex relations immediately recognisable in the light of the experiences of the reader and/or viewer. This almost by necessity implies building on and reaffirming people's prejudices instead of inspiring them to become more reflective. The workings of complicated structural forces are often reduced to simple, concrete and emotionally loaded relations between people. There is an increasing focus on celebrities, sensationalism, polarisation, personalisation and conflict, as well as on entertainment rather than information. Like in other countries, public television and serious newspapers are also influenced by these tendencies. Norway is characterised by a large reading public and many local newspapers, but also by the lack of a high-quality press. There are few journalists with a minority background. With its characteristic blend of entertainment and information, the television medium, in particular, has created a powerful platform for charismatic politicians who simplify and dramatise complex issues. The leaders of right-wing populist parties in Europe, such as Jörg Haider, Jean-Marie le Pen, Pia Kjærsgaard and the Norwegian Carl I. Hagen, master this powerful medium particularly well.

The Progress Party in Norway is a right-wing populist party fighting for lower taxes, fewer regulations, more money to care for the elderly, more police and a more restrictive immigration policy. It was founded under another name in 1973 as a right-wing protest party arguing for reductions in taxes, duties and public bureaucracy and in that same year four representatives were elected to Parliament. The current leader, Carl I. Hagen, has been the unchallenged head of the party since 1978.

The Progress Party is currently the second largest party in Norway, capturing 22.1 percent of the vote at the parliamentary election in September 2005.[8] The leaders of the Progress Party never use explicitly Nazi, neo-Nazi or traditional racist arguments. On the contrary, parts of the populist right, both within and outside the Progress Party, are trying to appropriate the resistance to the Nazi occupation during the Second World War rhetorically, by making an analogy between that occupation and what they consider to be the present-day invasion of Norway by Muslims (Bjørgo 1997a; 1997b).

According to Anniken Hagelund (2003), the abolition of development aid was one of the party's most central demands from the very beginning, and was based on the idea that it is wrong to spend money on total strangers far away when 'our own' old, sick and needy suffer 'here at home'. Together with a strong anti-bureaucratic stance against 'the system' and for 'the people', this idea also underpins their later views on immigration policy. Hagelund further argues that immigration was not made into a fully fledged political issue by the party until the mid 1980s when it was gradually launched as a key issue, focusing mainly on the need to make specific calculations of the costs of immigration to Norwegian taxpayers (*innvandrerregnskap*). At the beginning of the 1990s, the culturalist argument emerged with full force in the party's rhetoric, focusing on the various risks to Norwegian society posed by 'the alien cultures' of 'immigrants'. In 1993 the Progress Party was the first to use the term 'integration politics' in their election materials (Hagelund 2003).

Over time, the term 'integration politics', together with many other ideas first aired by the Progress Party, have become part of the political mainstream. Many people who would never consider voting for the Progress Party have gradually and imperceptibly become receptive to their ideas. The timing of the change in Progress Party rhetoric concurs with the more general changes discussed above. It is difficult to assess how much Progress Party politicians initiated the new political climate, and how much they just played on and reinforced ideas, fears and categories already in circulation. The end of the 1980s and the beginning of the 1990s seem to have been a historical juncture at which specific historical events and more long-term economic and political developments worked together to produce the present hegemony.

Examples of neo-ethnification put into practice can be found in the other parties in the same time period. Some of the ideas of parties such as the Freiheitliche Partei and the Front National have actually become political consensus in Norway. In 1991, the Labour Party politician Rune Gerhardsen launched a campaign against what he saw as the foolish generosity of the state in relation to people on welfare. He did this by applying a neologism first coined by the leader of the Progress Party: *snillisme*, which literally translates as 'kindism', meaning 'kindness to a fault' or 'foolish generosity'. It is perhaps a translation of the English term 'angelism', coined in the Reagan–Thatcher era. The campaign was directed against policies relating to several categories of people on social welfare, but the campaign against practising foolish generosity in relation to 'immigrants' received the most attention. In the same year a social science researcher and politician of the Socialist Left Party (SV) published a book called *I am not a racist, but...* (Brox 1991). In this book his main target was 'the moral elite' who, in his view, refuse to see the problematic aspects of immigration for local workers.

With the import of cheap foreign labour, he argued, there is a serious risk of damaging the pay and work conditions of majority workers and thus of creating a new ethnically based underclass. This is a real problem. However, Brox' solution in this book – as well as in numerous later publications – is a nationalist resistance to further immigration instead of focusing on the need for the unions to strive for equal conditions, regardless of the ethnic background of the workers. Furthermore, when in power in the 1990s, the Labour Minister for Education (and former professor of sociology), Gudmund Hernes, launched a new programme for primary schools in order to refocus and revitalise the canonised Norwegian cultural heritage, as the cement binding the nation together. In addition, he launched a new obligatory hybrid subject in Norwegian schools to replace the former choice between 'Christian religion' and 'worldview'. The pietistic Christians could not accept that the subject was just called religion, so it was named 'Christian religion with an orientation towards worldview' *(Kristendom med livssynsorientering)*, and this has caused much protest by minorities because of its confessional Christian elements. Their case was unsuccessful in all Norwegian courts, but was won when it was taken to the European Court of Human Rights in Strasbourg. In the middle of the 1990s, also, other academics made their influence felt in the public realm (Gullestad 2002b; 2004b; 2005).

Even if the figures are fluctuating, the Labour Party has over the years been losing ground. Norway is currently run by a coalition of three parties from the centre to the right, not including the aforementioned Progress Party, which is so far considered too extreme to be part of the government. There is a constellation of parties in power to which the Progress Party has wanted to present itself as suitable for inclusion in the government. The other parties, however, have so far distanced themselves from the Progress Party. By demonising the Progress Party, they have been able to present themselves as relatively respectable. Hagelund (2003) argues that this constellation of political strategies has implied important checks on right-wing populism in Norway, reducing the party's influence. This is also the point of view of most Norwegian observers. It is a plausible interpretation, in particular in relation to the developments in Denmark where the political climate is more violently anti-immigrant. Nevertheless, in light of the ideological shifts that I have identified in my work, I want to suggest a different interpretation: the political taboo on cooperation with the Progress Party has created the opportunity for many of their ideas to quietly cross the boundary and enter the mainstream. Politicians from the other parties have resisted specific ways of talking that are considered too extremist, more than their underlying frame of interpretation. The words and the tone of voice may be different, but the underlying ideas and concepts are often similar, as well as the associated restrictive politics.

As a result of this quiet process, there are indications that the strategy of the other parties is changing. The Socialist Left Party has been cooperating with the Progress Party regarding 'the integration of immigrants'; because of their position to the left of Labour, their cooperation tends to legitimise that of all the other parties with the Progress Party on this issue. The Socialist Left Party obtained only 8.8 percent of the vote in the election in 2005, while Labour obtained 37.2 percent.[9] As a reaction to media panics in 2002 caused by the aforementioned tragic killing of Fadime Sahindal, politicians of all shades have been competing in proposing new controls on 'immigrants'. In line with the gradually installed hegemonic framework of interpretation, this and other tragic events in Norway are often presented in terms of clashes of culture and religion. Additional and more nuanced interpretations have to a large extent become muted.

Example 1: Home and Family as Political Metaphors

I now change both perspective and analytical level in order to discuss two empirical examples.[10] My aim is to demonstrate that assumptions about descent, kinship and family are underpinning both political and everyday discourse. The first example is from political life, from the period when Labour was still in power. When he took office in the autumn of 1996, the Labour Prime Minister, Thorbjørn Jagland, coined the phrase of building 'the Norwegian house' (*det norske hus*) to give his new government a fresh image. This political slogan was amply criticised and ridiculed, and he was never able to put it into practice; nevertheless it was often referred to at the time. The creation of the political metaphor of 'the Norwegian house' was an attempt at visualising the social-democratic notion of the integrated Norwegian nation state in a new and interesting way. It is not an image of the nation, nor an image of the state, but an integrated image of both, and one that plays on former political discourses and metaphors, as well as on current everyday experiences. As with many political symbols it is vague and polysemous, and can thus embody very diverse experiences and ideas.

My interpretation builds not only on what was explicitly said, but also on what was implicitly evoked in the Norwegian context. The notion of 'the Norwegian house' stresses stability and boundaries. The image of solid house construction promises security and stability in a changing world, the containment of cultural variation within the walls of the national house, and the establishment of national unity and firm boundaries in the face of transnational flows of capital, people, images, ideas, pollution and radiation.

By contrast, the Swedish notion of 'the people's home' (*folkhemmet*), so central to Swedish social-democratic welfare politics in the twentieth century, points to moral qualities based on specific cultural interpretations of family relations. Nevertheless, even if the Norwegian Prime Minister explicitly focused on the materiality of the house, which can, in principle, be any kind of building, including hospitals, schools and factories, he also implicitly assumed the centrality of the home along with all the connotations of close family relations and moral obligation that this notion holds in Northern Europe. He said house, but asked people to think in terms of a home. In a radio interview, for example, he voiced the opinion that only the elite in Oslo were critical of the idea of 'the Norwegian house': 'People around the country understand this very well. We like to think that a society is a kind of home where you can dwell safely and securely.'[11] As a counter-image to 'the Norwegian house', the leader of the Progress Party drew on the same set of symbolic traditions when he evoked the image of 'the Norwegian family' in the spring of 1997. The way he applied this image, it potentially carried a more racialising subtext than 'the Norwegian house': a house, after all, can be filled with all kinds of people, while, according to popular understandings, the concept of the family is based on marriage and filiation.[12]

The rhetorical force of this and similar metaphors relies upon the self-evidence of certain ways of representing family life. The metaphors play down notions of a civil society or a political community outside family and kinship. Feelings of belonging are grounded in kinship relations with an emphasis on those relationships that are apparently not chosen, such as the relations between parents and children. Comparable statements can now be heard all over Europe. Many people return to the ideological cluster of kinship, descent, territory and culture in an attempt to create identity and invoke stability. Using the criteria of family house and national territory, boundaries can be represented as clear and unambiguous. The family home thus seemingly provides a natural, experiential and metaphorical basis for drawing boundaries around 'us' in relation to 'them'.

Example 2: 'Race' Overriding Social and Biological Kinship – the 'Mixed' Person

My second example concerns current interpretations of the 'mixed' child in Norway. In *Ambiguous Ethnicity: Interracial Families in London*, Susan Benson asserts: 'For the mixed-race child, then, even more than for his or her parents, there were problems inevitably rising from an ambiguous ethnicity' (1981: 134). 'The problem of achieving a viable and secure personal identity,' Benson comments, 'is further complicated by the ambiguous nature of their position in the system of ethnic classification that obtains in Britain' (ibid.: 141). For Anglo-Caribbean and Anglo-African couples and their children, problems arising from differences in cultural practice 'were on the whole less significant than the problems that derived from the anomalous status of these families in a racially divided society' (ibid.: 146).

In the following, I present a few quotations to demonstrate the ideas underpinning the present-day Norwegian system of ethnic classification when dealing with the 'mixed' black and white child. For many majority Norwegians, the naturalised meanings of ancestry and descent often lead to interpretations in which people with 'a different skin colour' are regarded as both culturally different and unrelated, sometimes in spite of Norwegian descent. 'Skin colour' is a metonym for many different aspects of a person's looks, the main point being that he or she does not 'look Norwegian', the way this is currently perceived. What is considered a 'different skin colour' symbolises biological unrelatedness, geographic distance and cultural difference within an imagined global geographical space. The world is popularly conceived as a mosaic where people with different looks 'belong' to different places with different 'cultures'. White people are thus regarded as more closely related to each other than to black people. The following excerpt demonstrates how Iselin (a pseudonym), the white mother of a child with a black father originally from Africa, makes use of available cultural resources in order to give the 'mixedness' of her child a positive value:

> They become very strong ... and healthy and able and smart ... And this is because there is a contrast to inbreeding. The further away you go to find a partner, the greater

difference there is in a way in the genes, and the better it is. This is scientifically proved … The point is long distance concerning kinship. (Fredriksen 2001: 91–92, translated from the Norwegian)[13]

As the white mother of a non-white child (and the partner of a non-white man) Iselin is one of the growing number of majority Norwegians who because of love, parenthood and friendship are led to reflect on the social meanings of colour. In the above quote she takes for granted the existence of separate categories that are 'mixed' in the child. Implicitly she reverses a common interpretation: being 'mixed' no longer connotes being unclean, but being strong; however, the categories themselves are not affected by this reversal of value.

In an autobiographical text, Nalubega Asta Busingye Lydersen, a young woman with a black father originally from Uganda and a white Norwegian mother, writes about her own childhood (1999). She was born in Scotland, and then she lived in Uganda for five years and in Kenya for two years as a child. For the rest of her childhood she lived in a small Norwegian town. Nalubega is a clan name given to her by her grandparents in Uganda. This name is not registered in Norway. Busingye is a middle name. Lydersen is a patronymicon that most people in Norway would recognise as 'typically Norwegian', even if it could equally well be Danish. In the text under consideration, she discusses how, in spite of being a Norwegian citizen and speaking Norwegian as her mother tongue, and in spite of having a Norwegian surname (Lydersen) and first name (Asta), she routinely experiences being regarded as an outsider, and this started early:

> My sister and I were the only African children within miles. Among other things Mammy had to explain where she got us. Many people thought that we were adopted. It probably was too absurd for them to think that she had had an African husband, and had given birth to these children herself. (Lydersen 1999: 12, translated from the Norwegian)

A 'different skin colour' is a marker of origin in a distant place ('where she got us'), and of relational distance (a white woman could not be the biological mother of two 'coloured' kids). They 'look different'; therefore they must belong somewhere far away. Lydersen seems to adapt to this when she characterises her sister and herself as 'African children', and not as, for example, 'African-Norwegian' children. This adaptation can be interpreted as a strategy to create *a sustainable self-image* in the face of discrimination (Gullestad 2003; 2004a). Since she is not accepted as someone who belongs in Norway, she roots herself in a different soil, and one considered appropriate to her appearance in present-day Norway. Quite a few young people who 'do not look Norwegian' actually do the same (Gullestad 2004a). They partly inhabit and partly resist the current hegemonic frame of interpretation.

Asta Lydersen also relates how she went to a hospital in Oslo for a medical check-up. When the medical part of the consultation was over, the doctor wanted to fill out some forms for internal use at the hospital. The forms were based on polarised categories that do not fit the current realities. They focused on the patient's ethnic background and language proficiency in Norwegian. One of the categories was 'Norwegian'. The doctor felt that as a woman with an appearance that he perceived in terms of a 'dark skin colour', she also did not fit into this category. Like him, many people today find it difficult to conceive of a black person as 'Norwegian'. At the same time the doctor found that she did not quite fit into the category 'African' (Lydersen, personal communication).

'It belongs to the story', she writes, 'that next time I had an appointment, I met a doctor who called out "Lydersen" in the waiting room, but turned on his heels to re-enter his office when he saw my husband [who is black] and me. Is it not possible to be BLACK and still be called Lydersen?'[14] For the physician, the name 'Lydersen' implied being Norwegian, and being Norwegian equalled being white. Appearance, surname and language proficiency carry normative implications for identity constructions (Lieberson 1985: 163), and in Asta Lydersen's case these are contradictory. In terms of name, citizenship and cultural competence she belongs to one category; in terms of appearance, to another. For the physician, as for many others in Norway at the present historical juncture, 'foreign' appearance trumps a 'typically Norwegian' surname.[15] In spite of her citizenship, and biological and social descent through her mother, Asta Lydersen is often defined as somebody who does not quite belong. This happens in situations in which the parties do not know each other, and therefore categorise each other on the basis of visible and audible signs. Such situations typically occur in the labour market and the housing market. When employers seek new collaborators and house owners seek new tenants, 'dark skin colour', a foreign accent and a 'strange name' signal cultural difference. Because of the deep-seated assumption that 'children who are alike play most happily together', many house-owners and employers seem to avoid people whom they fear are 'too different'.

The examples of 'mixed' children indicate that in spite of their Norwegian ancestors, they are in many situations not considered to belong to the Norwegian people. In these contexts, perceptions of 'skin colour' override biological descent and social kinship. The nature of 'skin colour' and 'race' as a form of *metaphoric kinship* is revealed, and thus the symbolic and socially created character of what is considered naturally given. Social distinctions in the perceptions of looks are translated back into biological kinship, as it were. For this reason I have called this chapter 'Imagined Kinship'.

Closing Note

Within social Darwinism and the eugenics movement the word 'race' was often used interchangeably with 'nation' and 'folk' (Wodak and Reisigl 1999). Today ideologies based on these concepts can both overlap and reinforce one another by being each other's framing conditions (Miles 1993: 53–79). The main point of this chapter is that we cannot understand the appeal of right-wing politics if we do not take into account how this rhetoric is underpinned by and embedded in rearticulated neo-ethnic ideas. Descent is the principle by which one is connected to a national territory and a cultural heritage, and descent is popularly related to 'skin colour'.

In the context of current extra-European immigration, 'descent is thus becoming more relevant for the construction of national identity, involving the belonging of some inhabitants and the non-belonging of others. By constructing people 'who do not look Norwegian' as outsiders in terms of descent, 'skin colour' is, as it were, domesticated and made to serve national ends: Norwegian national identity is often implicitly but effectively configured as white.[16] The colour-coded nature of this discursive boundary justifies the term neo-ethnification to characterise what goes on.

These ideological shifts and continuities are occurring in the context of an increasing 'biologisation' of common-sense thinking about social relationships. While new technologies constantly challenge the conceptual boundary between nature and culture, they also reinforce conceptualisations of biological processes as 'the really real'. One's 'roots' are largely defined in terms of specific combinations of ideas about kinship, culture, religion, language, history and social space. Seemingly a temporal concept, descent is, as we have seen, often defined in both racial and spatial terms.

From the nineteenth century onwards, modern ideas about the nation state have generally emphasised boundaries, in contrast to the ideologies of polities organised around dynastic or religious centres with shifting spheres of influence and diffuse boundaries (Anderson 1983). As we have seen, however, the ideological emphasis on boundaries is complemented by specific ideas about substance. Ideas about religion, language and descent add substance to the imagining of 'the people', and are implicated in specific cultural interpretations of history and geography. At the present moment the balance between political and expressive identities seems to be altered: the idea of the political nation, so central to a modern democracy, is ideologically receding, while transformed ethno-nationalist assumptions are gaining new ground.

Notes

1. According to recent theories, 'culture' now replaces the notion of 'race' in the rhetoric of the political right (see, e.g., Balibar 1991; Barker 1981; Gullestad 2003, 2004b, 2005; Hervik 1999; Stolcke 1995). The new ideologies, theorists maintain, foreground cultural differences without explicitly saying that some 'cultures' are better than others.
2. This chapter was written as part of a larger project on debates about immigration in Norway (Gullestad 1997a; 1997b; 2002a; 2002b; 2003; 2004a; 2004b; 2005). The research was funded by The Research Council of Norway's IMER programme. The interpretations draw on almost thirty years of research in Norwegian society, including two long-term fieldwork experiences in the city of Bergen (Gullestad 1979; 1984; 1992), and detailed analytical work on a collection of

autobiographies written by 'ordinary people' (Gullestad 1996a). Revisions were made during my stay as 'the guest of the rector' at the Netherlands Institute for Advanced Study in the Humanities and the Social Sciences (NIAS) in the spring of 2003. I also thank Otto Dann, Nina Dessau, Fredrik Engelstad, Håkon Lorentzen and Iver Neumann for their comments.

3. After an immigration ban was imposed in 1975, newcomers have only been accepted if they are experts, family members (family reunification), students (with the expectation that they will return home after graduation), and refugees and asylum seekers.

4. Source: Statistics Norway. Since 1994 the official statistical analyses in Norway use the following definition of 'immigrants': 'The population of immigrants comprises persons with two parents born abroad. The population of immigrants includes *first-generation immigrants* who have themselves immigrated, and *second-generation immigrants,* who are born in Norway from two parents born abroad' (Bjertnæs 2000: 10, translated from the Norwegian, italics as in the original). The categories underline the cultural emphasis on descent.

5. The murder received much public attention in Scandinavia. There was, however, a difference in the way the murder was debated in the media in Norway and Sweden. Even if Fadime's family was a secularised Christian family, in Norway the murder was interpreted as a consequence of Muslim religion (Dessau 2003).

6. The most notable example is Shabana Rehman, stand-up comedian and regular columnist for *Dagbladet,* a boulevard newspaper (dependent on sales to non-subscribers) with certain traditions of cultural and political debate. Her writings focus on the oppression of women within Muslim social circles in Norway (Dessau 2003; Eriksen 2003). For example, in *Dagbladet,* 31 March 2003: 47, Rehman strongly supports Oriana Fallaci's views about Muslims, and recommends the Norwegian translation of the book *The Rage and the Pride* (2002) for Norwegian readers.

7. Some issues that are not debated are also significant. One example is 'paperless' or illegal immigrants. While there are a number of illegal immigrants in Norway, first and foremost in Oslo, this is so far not a political issue. In fact, the word 'paperless' is not used in Norwegian in that sense. By calling immigrants 'paperless' one indicates that they are human beings without the right kind of papers. By not having another expression than 'illegal', one focuses only on the illegality. When illegal immigrants are not even recognised, the least favoured group of *legal* immigrants become the 'underclass' in public consciousness, with the accompanying stigmatisation. I thank Nina Dessau for making me aware of this point.

8. In October 2002 the figure was as much as 32.8 percent. Source for all the figures: Bernt Aardal, Institute for Social Research, Oslo, Norway.

9. Before April 2005 the Socialist Left Party had its lowest percentage of the vote in January 2000 (14.2) and its highest in September 2004 (17.5). Labour had 25.9 percent in April 2004 and 30.8 percent in January 2005. Source: Bernt Aardal, Institute for Social Research, Oslo, Norway.

10. I have also used the first example in Gullestad (1997b).

11. NRK P2 *Politisk kvarter.* January 1997.

12. These metaphors can also be used for entirely different political purposes. For example, in English there is 'the family of humankind', in Norwegian 'the Olympic family', each emphasising universal rather than particular values.

13. The example is borrowed from an excellent MA thesis by Magrethe Fredriksen (2001).

14. Lydersen, personal email correspondence in January 2002, translated from the Norwegian. I thank Nabulega Asta Busingye Lydersen for the permission to use her experiences here. I also thank her for her comments on the first draft of my analysis of her experiences.

15. For further evidence of racial ideas in Norway, see Gullestad (2001; 2003; 2004a; 2004b; 2005).

16. See also Gullestad (2005) on the public dispute about the word *neger* in Norway, through which people of colour were politely but effectively regarded as outsiders to the Norwegian nation.

Bibliography

Aardal, B. 1995. 'Ideologi på tvers?', in A. Todal Jenssen and H.Valen eds *Brussel midt imot: Folkeavstemningen om EU*. Oslo: Ad Notam Gyldendal, pp. 165–86.

Ali, M.-R. 1997. *Den sure virkeligheten*. Oslo: Tiden.

Anderson, B. 1983. *Imagined Communities: Reflections on The Origin and Spread of Nationalism*. London: Verso.

Balibar, E. 1991 [1988]. 'Is There a "Neo-racism"?', in I.E. Balibar and I. Wallerstein eds *Race, Nation, Class: Ambiguous Identities*. London: Verso, pp. 17–28.

Barker, M. 1981. *The New Racism*. London: Junction Books.

Barth, E., Bratsberg, B. and Raaum, O. 2004. 'Identifying Earnings Assimilation of Immigrants under Changing Macroeconomic Conditions', *Scandinavian Journal of Economics* 106(1): 1–22.

Benson, S. 1981. *Ambiguous Ethnicity: Interracial Families in London*. Cambridge: Cambridge University Press.

Bjertnæs, M.K. 2000. *Innvandring og innvandrere 2000*, Statistiske analyser 33. Oslo: Statistisk Sentralbyrå.

Bjørgo.T. 1997a. 'Racist and Right-Wing Violence in Scandinavia', unpublished Ph.D. thesis, University of Leiden.

———— 1997b. '"The Invaders", "the Traitors" and "the Resistance Movement"': The Extreme Right's Conceptualisation of Opponents and Self in Scandinavia', in I. Tariq Modood and P. Werbner eds *The Politics of Multiculturalism in the New Europe*. London: Zed Books, pp. 54–72.

———— 1998. 'Entry, Bridge-Burning and Exit Options: What Happens to Young People Who Join Racist Groups – and Want to Leave?', in J. Kaplan and T. Bjørgo eds *Nation and Race: Developing Euro-American Racist Subculture*. Boston: Northeastern University Press, pp. 231–58.

Brox, O. 1991. *Jeg er ikke rasist, men … .* Oslo: Gyldendal.

Comaroff, J. and Comaroff, J. 1991. *Of Revelation and Revolution*. Volume 1. Chicago: University of Chicago Press.

Dessau, N. 2003. 'Nå skal ingen motsi oss', *Samtiden* 2: 28–39.

Durkheim, E. 1933. *The Division of Labor in Society*. Glencoe: Free Press.

ECRI (European Commission Against Racism and Intolerance). 1997. *Report on Norway*, Brussels.

———— 2000. *Second Report on Norway*, Brussels.

Eriksen, T.H. 2003. 'The Young Rebel and the Dusty Professor: A Tale of Anthropology and the Media in Norway', *Anthropology Today* 19(1): 3–5.

Fallaci, O. 2002. *The Rage and the Pride*. New York: Rizzoli.

Fangen, K. 1998. 'Living Out Ethnic Instincts: Ideological Beliefs Among Right-Wing Activists in Norway', in J. Kaplan and T. Bjørgo eds *Nation and Race: Developing Euro-American Racist Subculture*. Boston: Northeastern University Press, pp. 202–30.

Fredriksen, M. 2001. 'Hvithetens semiosis – en antropologisk studie av hvithet som medium', unpublished MA thesis, University of Bergen.

Gerhardsen, R. 1991. *Snillisme på norsk*. Oslo: Schibsted.

Goldberg, D.T. 1993. *Racist Culture: Philosophy and the Politics of Meaning*. Oxford: Blackwell Publishers.

Gramsci, A. 1971. *Selections from the Prison Notebooks*. London: Lawrence and Wishart.

Gullestad, M. 1979. *Livet i en gammel bydel*. Oslo: Aschehoug.

——— 1984 (2nd edn 2002 with a new foreword by Daniel Miller). *Kitchen-Table Society*. Oslo: Scandinavian University Press.

——— 1992. *The Art of Social Relations: Essays on Culture, Social Action and Everyday Life in Modern Norway*. Oslo: Scandinavian University Press.

——— 1996a. *Everyday Life Philosophers: Modernity, Morality and Autobiography in Norway*. Oslo: Scandinavian University Press.

——— 1996b. 'From Obedience to Negotiation: Dilemmas in the Transmission of Values between the Generations in Norway', *The Journal of the Royal Anthropological Institute* 2(1): 25–42.

——— 1997a. 'A Passion for Boundaries: Reflections on Connections between Children's Everyday Lives and Discourses on the Nation in Norway', *Childhood* 4(1): 19–42.

——— 1997b. 'Home, Local Community and Nation: Connections between Everyday Life Practices and Discourses on the Nation in Contemporary Norway', *Focaal* 30–1: 39–60.

——— 2001. 'Each Person his family', in Franois de Singly ed. *Etre soi parmi les autres, Famille et individualization*, vol.1, Collection Logiques Sociales. Paris: L'Harmattan, pp. 23–36.

——— 2002a. *Det norske sett med nye øyne. Kritisk analyse av norsk innvandringsdebatt*. Oslo: Scandinavian University Press.

——— 2002b. 'Invisible Fences: Egalitarianism, Nationalism and Racism', *Journal of the Royal Anthropological Institute* 8(1)(March): 45–63.

——— 2003. '"Mohammed Atta and I": Identification, Discrimination and the Formation of Sleepers', *European Journal of Cultural Studies* 6(4): 529–48.

——— 2004a. 'Tales of Consent and Descent: Life Writing as a Fight Against an Imposed Self-image', in John Eakin ed. *The Ethics of Life Writing*. Ithaca: Cornell University Press, pp. 216–43.

——— 2004b. 'Blind Slaves of Our Prejudices: Debating "Culture" and "Race" in Norway', *Ethnos* 69(2): 177–203.

——— 2005. 'Normalizing Racial Boundaries: the Norwegian Dispute about the Term *Neger*', *Social Anthropology* 1: 1–20.

Hagelund, A. 2003. 'A Matter of Decency? The Progress Party in Norwegian Immigration Policy', *Journal of Ethnic and Migration Studies* 29(1): 47–65.

Herbjørnsrud, D. 1998. 'Dunsten av den norske tidsånde – og 1990-tallets nytale', *Samtiden* 5/6: 67–77.

Hernes, G. and Knudsen, K. 1990. *Svart på hvitt*, Rapport 109. Oslo: FAFO.

Hervik, P. ed. 1999. *Den generende forskellighed: Danske svar på den stigende multikulturalisme*. Copenhagen: Hans Reitzels Forlag.

——— 2004. 'The Danish Idea of Unbridgeable Differences', *Ethnos* 69(2): 247–67.

Høgmo, A. 1998. *Fremmed i det norske hus*. Oslo: Ad Notam Gyldendal.

Holmes, D.R. 2000. *Integral Europe: Fast-Capitalism, Multiculturalism, Neofascism*. Princeton: Princeton University Press.

Johnsen, Ø. 1996. *Gode nordmenn*. Oslo: Cappelen Forlag.

Juergensmeyer, M. 1996. 'The Worldwide Rise of Religious Nationalism', *Journal of International Affairs* 50–1: 1–20.

Lieberson, S. 1985. 'Unhyphenated Whites in the United States', *Ethnic and Racial Studies* 8(1): 159–80.

Lindstad, M. and Fjeldstad Ø. 2005: *Av utenlandsk opprinnelse: Nye nordmenn I avisspaltene.* Kristiansand: IJ-forlaget.

Lunde, H. ed. 2000. *Rikets tilstand 1999.* Oslo: Antirasistisk Senter.

Lydersen, N.A.B. 1999. 'Sjokosjokk', in H.C. Solheim and H. Vaagland eds *Råtekst.* Oslo: Aschehoug.

Miles, R. 1993. *Racism After 'Race Relations'.* London: Routledge.

Neumann, I.B. 2001. *Norge – en kritikk: Begrepsmakt i Europadebatten.* Oslo: Pax Forlag.

SMED. 2001. *Underveis mot et bedre vern 2001: Senter mot etnisk diskriminering sitt bidrag til kunnskap om art og omfang av etnisk diskriminering i Norge.* Oslo: Senter Mot Etnisk Diskriminering.

SOPEMI. 2000. *Norway: Trends of Migration to and from Norway and the Situation of Immigrants in Norway.* Oslo: The Ministry of Local Government and Regional Development.

Stolcke, V. 1995. 'Talking Culture: New Boundaries, New Rhetorics of Exclusion in Europe', *Current Anthropology* 36(1): 1–24.

Taguieff, P.-A. 1987. *La force du prejugé.* Paris: Gallimard.

Turner, T. 1994. 'Anthropology and Multiculturalism: What is Anthropology that Multiculturalists should be Mindful of?', in D.T. Goldberg ed. *Multiculturalism: A Critical Reader.* Oxford: Blackwell.

UDI. 2000. *Art og omfang av rasisme og diskriminering i Norge 1999–2000.* Rapport, Oslo: Utlendingsdirektoratet.

Van Dijk, T.A. 1993. *Elite Discourse and Racism.* Sage Series on Race and Ethnic Relations. London: Sage Publications.

Wamwere, K.W. 2000. *Hjertets tårer: et portrett av rasismen i Norge og i Europa.* Oslo: Aschehoug.

Wodak, R. and Reisigl, M. 1999. 'Discourse and Racism: European Perspectives', *Annual Review of Anthropology* 28: 175–99.

Chapter 4

The Emergence of Neo-nationalism in Denmark, 1992–2001

Peter Hervik

In November 2001 Denmark went through an election campaign for Folketinget (the Danish Parliament) and local government. The key theme of the campaign leading up to the election on 20 November was immigrants and refugees.

Here are some quotes and paraphrasings of opinions presented to the press[1] during the months prior to the election:

'Muslims are just waiting for the right moment to kill us.'
Mogens Camre, MP, Fremskridspartiet (The Progress Party)

'Certain people pose a security risk solely because of their religion, which means that they have to be placed in internment camps.'
Inge Dahl Sørensen, MP, Venstre (Denmark's Liberal Party)

'If you try to legislate your way out of these problems [Muslim organisations], it is a historical rule that rats always find new holes, if you cover up the old ones.'
Poul Nyrup Rasmussen, MP, Socialdemokratiet (The Social Democrats)

'We need to prevent immigrants and their descendants from finding their spouses in Turkey, Pakistan and Somalia.'
Birthe Rønn Hornbech, MP, Venstre

'After nine years with Nyrup [the former Prime Minister] refugee and immigrant problems are bigger than ever. More than every second immigrant is without work. The number of people under the family reunification law is increasing and increasing. Danish values have come under pressure from fundamentalist groups ... Second-generation immigrants are responsible for a disproportionate share of crime and violence in Danish society.'

Anders Fogh Rasmussen, Venstre

As the final example from the election campaign I refer to a political commercial appearing in two Danish popular magazines. Two days before the election the magazines showed a photograph of six children of immigrants charged with gang rape as they came out of the courthouse, while a veiled young woman made an obscene gesture to bystanders. The pictures had been taken a year earlier in connection with the trial. The picture in the magazines, which had been approved by Anders Fogh Rasmussen (the then political leader of Venstre and future prime minister), was given the headline 'Time for change'.

Rather than simply representing 'exotic' illustrations within a debate on the themes of immigration and refugees, these examples, chosen from among many, are better understood as expressions of the neo-nationalism that has emerged in Denmark in the course of the 1990s, and which perhaps peaked during the election campaign. Central to this nationalism is the redefinition of a Danish nation consisting of people who rightfully defend themselves against people from non-Western countries, particularly Muslims. These non-Westerners choose spouses from outside Europe, pose a risk solely by virtue of their religion and may behave like rats and rapists. An enemy image of Muslims is clearly in play and is represented by these politicians and others as threatening Danish values and society.

Neo-nationalism captured much attention, diverting it from other issues of importance during the election, for instance, Denmark's ambivalent relationship to the European Union, which was largely omitted from the campaign.[2] At the end of election day, voters across the political spectrum had suspended their traditional preference and voted for the right-wing parties with their nationalist agendas. The voters' prime focus was the relationship between the positively identified 'we the Danes' and the negatively defined 'others' (primarily Muslim immigrants and their descendants). The nationalist politics and rhetoric were decisive for the outcome of the election and the right won an overwhelming victory. This allowed the Liberals and the Conservatives (Venstre and Det Konservative Folkeparti) to form a coalition government, supported by the ultra-nationalist party Dansk Folkeparti (Danish People's Party), which had split from Fremskridtspartiet (The Progress Party) in 1995 choosing opposition to immigrants, immigration policy and the European Union as the core defining feature of its political identity.

The purpose of my chapter is to show the gradual emergence of neo-nationalism that preceded the election and began ten to fifteen years earlier. While the neo-nationalism outlined in the introduction to this volume is formed through local reactions to larger events and processes predominantly within this post-1989 world (Donnan and Wilson 1999),[3] I am concerned with some of the specific events that formed the trajectory of the Danish version of neo-nationalism. On the basis of the Danish case, and the Scandinavian experience more generally, I argue that the emergence of neo-nationalism as a response to the restructuring of Europe since 1989, as well as global processes, may have started out as a right-wing phenomenon, but has moved on to become one that dominates the entire political spectrum and the large majority of the population today.

The prefix 'neo' in this context is employed to indicate a revitalisation of nationalism in the post-1989 world. This nationalism occurs within an established nation state and thus differs from the nation building in Denmark that took place in the eighteenth century. That process began among Copenhagen's emerging bourgeoisie, which had acquired some wealth and education during the relatively peaceful and economically prosperous eighteenth century, but which was witnessing the king and the aristocracy, with German assistance, firmly in power. *Grundloven* (the constitution) was passed in 1849, thus ending absolute monarchical rule. A few years later in 1864 when Denmark was defeated in another war with Germany, the country lost all its former power, which resulted in the loss of territory including Norway, Sleswig, Holsten and Lauenborg, leaving 170,000 Danish speakers outside its territory. For the first time, (almost) only Danish speakers lived within the borders. In 1920 the lost territory in Southern Jutland was voted back in a referendum reuniting most of the segregated Danish speakers in Germany. Nation building, transformed during the last third of the nineteenth century, spread from the elite to the peasants and later involved workers and smallholders. Nationalism at the time was motivated by the enemy image of Germany but was mainly aimed at gaining social and political power within the country.

A nation can be seen as the imaginary of a community of people, real or construed, who consider themselves culturally homogeneous, depending on the constant ideological innovation and reproduction of its existence. Nationalism consists of those actions and arguments based on the claim that this community of people should be given certain and special rights within the state (see the introduction to this volume for a further discussion of definitions). People who are not part of this community do not have the same rights. Accordingly, the idea of an imagined community of cultural homogeneity implies that some people are included and others excluded and that those who hold this idea in common decide these matters. Those who belong are identified as having particular origins, often with certain racial features as well, and are part of a certain horizontal comradeship. Since the inclusion/exclusion dichotomy tends to fall along 'cultural' and/or 'racial' lines, we can claim that neo-nationalism and neo-racism are two sides of the same phenomenon (Anderson 1983; Hervik 2002; Miles 1993).

While national elections and referendums can be seen as the hallmarks of democracy, according to the Danish experience they are also events at which neo-nationalism and neo-racism are emerging. The public debates that preceded the elections not only polarised the population but also revealed increasingly hostile attitudes and policies towards people of ethnic minority background. The referendum in 1992, when Denmark voted on the Maastricht Treaty, is the first event I deal with in which signs of emerging neo-nationalism can be seen.

Voting on the Maastricht Treaty of the European Union

In the late 1960s a historical new migration took place in which unskilled labourers from outside Europe were invited to work in Western European industry. As elsewhere, this migration provided the impetus for a new understanding of the concept of culture. 'Cultural difference' soon came to refer to the differences displayed by these new workers and their families. Although the migration was formally halted in 1973, the number of migrants kept growing steadily in Denmark throughout the 1980s and 1990s when family members joined each other under the Family Reunification Act. These guest workers and their families were represented positively in the media until the late 1980s.[4]

Following the dramatic events of 1989, Europe in 1990–1991 witnessed a drastic increase in racially motivated violence and polarised attitudes towards immigrants, refugees and asylum seekers: for instance, in the Saxon town of Hoyerswerda, in former East Germany, skinheads and neo-Nazis attacked guest workers and asylum seekers in September 1991 (Peck 1995: 316). Such events were met by demands for tougher policies restricting the number of non-Westerners coming into Western Europe and tougher requirements for those already within the European Union. Leading politicians' warnings about hungry Russians and Africans threatening the 'safety' of the Western European middle class perhaps gave new strength to the idea of the newly expanded 'Fortress Europe' with its vanishing internal and fortified external borders.

The relationship between international turbulence around the disappearance and reappearance of state borders had a profound influence on public debate and the outcome of the referendum on the Maastricht Treaty. In December 1991, in the Dutch city of Maastricht, the leaders of the member states of the European Community had agreed on a treaty that paved the way for a fuller integration of its twelve members' military, economic and foreign policies. The treaty was to be ratified by each of the member countries based on their individual procedure.

The first country that decided to hold a referendum was Denmark and 2 June 1992 was set as the day. The domestic debate ran at fever pitch during the campaign with arguments apparently launched to scare people into voting either 'yes' or 'no' to the treaty. A clear outcome was expected since 130 of the 179 members of parliament recommended 'yes' to further integration. However, the result of the referendum came as a major surprise, and as had been predicted by some, the nation plunged into an economic and political crisis. The 'no' side won a narrow victory: 51 percent opposed and 49 percent in favour. Waves of shock paralysed the otherwise highly vocal EU politicians throughout Europe. The media coverage was extensive and left Danes in a euphoric state of national pride. Some said that the

Danes had defended democracy for all Europeans. National pride received a further boost when, shortly after the referendum, Denmark stunned Europe by winning the European football championship. The Danes had not qualified for the championships, but had replaced banned Yugoslavia a few weeks previously.

The debate leading up to the Maastricht referendum, a second referendum less than a year later that ended in a narrow 'yes', the European football championship and the foreign media blitz on Denmark are all factors that boosted the country's national pride but also polarised attitudes towards the political development of the European Union. These are also some of the signs of emerging neo-nationalism among the Danish population. Theirs being a small country, Danes had asked themselves rhetorically during the referendum about what would become of their language and culture in a new Europe where borders disappeared and integration increased. Would the language and cultural identity disappear? What should Danes do? Who would 'we the Danes' be in such a large entity? Answers were difficult to give. Instead, it was easier to argue what the Danes would or should not be like within their own territory, thus creating a possible framework for agents to utilise for their own political ends.

The two Maastricht referendums had signalled that the distance between representatives in public office and the voters was enormous. Politicians had recommended a pro vote, but voters were not following their political parties. Fremskridtspartiet (The Progress Party) and Socialistisk Folkeparti (The Socialist People's Party) had been the political winners of the first Maastricht referendum, since both parties opposed further European integration. In the preparation for the second round, the Socialists played a key role in teasing out four exemptions, or opt-outs, from the treaty that could be used for a new referendum that the party would support. Those exemptions were: common defence, the common currency, EU citizenship and certain aspects of legal cooperation, including law enforcement. It was Fremskridtspartiet however, more than any other party, who argued that a 'no' to the foreign in Europe was a 'no' to foreigners in Denmark. The party had always attacked the presence of Muslims in Denmark and campaigned to play the nationalist card, but they were not able to capitalise on their win until the party's leader, Pia Kjærsgaard, broke ranks with Fremskridtspartiet to form the Dansk Folkeparti in 1995.

Debating Bosnian Refugees

From 1992 to 1995 Denmark received 17,000 refugees from Bosnia-Herzegovina. These refugees are, generally speaking, no longer considered problematic, but in 1992 the anticipation of refugees arriving from the Balkans to Western Europe and Denmark was discussed in the media. The debate went through different phases. At first it revolved around the preparation of the legislation that granted refugees from the Balkans a collective, temporary asylum for two years. Several politicians stressed the importance of helping refugees in situ, i.e., in the Balkans, and they made only one exception: flying the seriously injured to Denmark for treatment. Others stressed that people who fled 'for their own convenience' should not be helped. During the debate the plan of distributing refugee camps around the country rested on the idea that Denmark could accept the refugees, but did not wish to be influenced by their cultural and religious difference (Larsen 1997: 28).

The legislation, passed in 1992, was based on the conviction that the war would end soon and the refugees could go home. According to the law, Bosnian refugees were granted two years of temporary asylum, implying that after two years they would either have returned home or could officially seek political asylum in Denmark. In the second phase of the debate media coverage focused on clashes between Bosnian refugees distributed around the country and local communities. A nationalist argument took this further explaining that to the extent that problems occurred in Danish communities with refugee camps, they were caused by refugees 'who were not really refugees', since people in real need would not cause problems (Larsen 1997: 33–34). The third phase occurred before the passing of another law in 1995 that would finally give the Bosnians normal rights for refugees, implying that they would go through a three-year programme of integration. At this time it was obvious that the war had not stopped within the two-year limit set by the law on temporary asylum.

During the three years of media coverage of the Balkan war and the Bosnian refugees in Denmark, the dichotomisation of Danes and refugees evolved further. On the political scene the aforementioned law allowing the Bosnians to seek asylum in Denmark was passed on 12 January 1995. A debate on the issue took place on 15 December 1994 (as part of the third phase mentioned above) and has been called 'the day of hatred' referring to the sharp division between the right, who did not want to turn Bosnian refugees into immigrants since the Danish population did not want that, and the left, including the governing Socialdemokratiet and Det Radikale Venstre (The Radical Liberals), using humanistic language (Larsen 1997: 85). Pia Kjærsgaard (Fremskridstpartiet) tried (unsuccessfully) during the debate to convince other right-wing parties to call for a referendum on the future of the Bosnian refugees, arguing that more money for refugees would mean less money for the elderly, homeless and other poor people in Denmark (Larsen 1997: 85–95). After the law was passed, Bosnians were integrated into Danish society and their situation became more normal. They had received much sympathy because of the war and the poor living conditions in camps that allowed only an average of 3 m^2 for each person.

Later the Somalis would take the place of the Bosnians as the group dominating political discourse and media coverage. This was the result of the second of two campaigns against immigration and immigration policy by the tabloid paper, *Ekstra Bladet,* and of the establishment of a new political party, Dansk Folkeparti (Danish People's Party). For the newspaper and the party the political situation and the emergence of neo-nationalism were an opportunity to gain more readers and voters. In addition, their campaigns illustrate the point that nationalism does not arise in a mechanical way but rather at the hands of elitist entrepreneurs.

A Campaign Against 'Foreigners'

In the spring of 1997 *Ekstra Bladet* launched its campaign about the presence of immigrants and refugees in the country. According to the chief editor, Svend-Ove Gade, the objective was to create a debate about what the paper saw as the most salient topic for the Danes: the presence of immigrants and refugees (*Ekstra Bladet* 1997a). The campaign was crafted as a call for a debate, or a referendum, on whether Denmark should become a multi-ethnic society. The chief editor argued that the Danes were never asked if they would accept the immigration of foreigners, it simply happened and continued to happen because of the reunification of families. In response to the demand for a free political debate *Ekstra Bladet* started the campaign, which could serve this democratic function (ibid.).

The transformation of Denmark from a peaceful society to a multi-ethnic one is referred to again and again in the paper as a crime committed by politicians against the Danish people. When the eighty-eight pages of the campaign were published as a special issue, few people in Denmark had doubts about what the paper's vote would be in this hypothetical referendum, thus indicating that the campaign was directed against the presence of ethnic minorities. References to the unwanted presence of culturally diverse others were present everywhere in the campaign. One example was the consistent use of the category *fremmede* (literally foreigner or alien) in writing about people of ethnic minority background, thus suggesting they do not belong in Denmark. Contrasting those who belong with those who do not serves the purpose of constructing the world in an uncomplicated fashion. However, second-generation immigrants with Danish citizenship are also called 'foreigners' and contested. The choice of category is attuned to the rationale of the tabloid paper: to create a public stir and to sell papers.

The paper was successful in maintaining and even expanding the gap between a public discourse of tolerance and the private world of frustrations and common-sense understandings that cultural differences are disturbing. The discrepancy between public and private exists regardless of *Ekstra Bladet*'s campaign, but the campaign rested upon the discrepancy and exposed it. Once the gap was exposed and marketed, organised collective political action could capitalise on it and use it as a unique opportunity for political recruitment.

A Political Party Against 'Foreigners'

In 1995 the leader of Fremskridtspartiet, Pia Kjærsgaard, and other central members broke away from the party to form Dansk Folkeparti. The new party's two major political issues were opposition to the European Union and opposition to ethnic minorities and refugees in Denmark. When *Ekstra Bladet* launched its campaign, Dansk Folkeparti was right there. A Protestant, fundamentalist minister, Søren Krarup, who later became a member of parliament, was writing regularly for *Ekstra Bladet* and Pia Kjærsgaard also appeared during the campaign as a guest writer. The party's and the paper's contestations of the presence of people with an ethnic minority background were hard to distinguish. For instance, Kjærsgaard too called for a referendum about whether Denmark should or should not continue to evolve into a multi-ethnic country. Moreover, both the party and the paper positioned themselves as a 'protector' of the voice of the ordinary people.

Letters to the editor of *Ekstra Bladet*, predominately from people overtly hostile towards ethnic minorities, played an important role in the campaign. *Ekstra Bladet*, wishing to let 'ordinary' people speak, tracked down the letter writers for interviews. Then full-blown articles voiced their indiscreet gut-level opinion on politicians and ethnic minorities while the reporter refrained from asking critical questions. Several of these articles turned out to be with Dansk Folkeparti members or sympathisers. For their part, party secretaries also wrote to the letter writers inviting them to join the party. The relationship between paper and party was, in all respects, symbiotic.

Jørgensen and Bülow found two dominant discourses in the campaign articles and advertisements. One discourse is 'critical of the system', and not my object of analysis here, whilst the other is the discourse of culturalism (or culturalist discourse, Jørgensen and Bülow 1999). 'Culture', in the sense used by *Ekstra Bladet* journalists, is essentialised, homogeneous and seen as rightfully and naturally belonging to certain (non-Western) spaces rather than others. Accordingly, when refugees and immigrants arrived in Denmark, they were seen to bring with them a 'culture' that usually did not fit very well there. The 'natural' hostility between 'cultures' that do not belong in the same place would cause confrontations and had to be resolved. Two examples from letters to the editor illustrate this belief:

> Muslims are reasonable people – so are the Germans south of the border. Only when different religions or nationalities have to live together will problems arise. (1997d)

> We [the Danes] will become a minority. The culture will disappear and we will have a civil war … I am not a racist, but my culture is coming to an end. (1997c)

In the first half of the 1990s Denmark had witnessed a growing anti-immigrant sentiment as well as a collective anxiety stemming from events beyond Danish borders. Debates on the Bosnian refugees further directed anxieties caused by events outside Denmark towards groups of non-Danish people in Denmark. In 1997 *Ekstra Bladet* and Dansk Folkeparti decided to capitalise on the emerging dissatisfaction with ethnic minorities and refugees, and the gap between politicians and voters, by attempting to translate the dichotomy between 'us' and 'them' into an increase in the number of readers and voters. During the campaign the membership of Dansk Folkeparti sky-rocketed. The two-year-old party was expected to attract up to 15 percent of the vote in the following national election.

One group of refugees received more negative attention than any other: the Somalis.

Targeting Somali Refugees

Ekstra Bladet is not the sole agent behind the discourse of culturalism and the emerging neo-nationalist division between 'Danes' and 'foreigners'. In November 1996 a provincial paper, *Aarhus Stiftstidende*, published five articles on Somali refugees within one week (Fadel, Hervik and Vestergaard 1999). The purpose of the series was not made explicit, but the common denominator of each article was the question why Aarhus, the second largest city in Denmark, should be burdened with Somali refugees. The idea of a series of articles on the topic of Somali refugees, the number of refugees and the degree of cultural difference was taken up by several other newspapers as well. These papers were also not explicit about the idea behind their series, but common to the various newspaper series was that the Somalis were presented as problematic and very different from the Danes.

In March of 1997, a few weeks before *Ekstra Bladet* launched its campaign, the same story was repeated in different but collaborating papers in four larger cities: Odense, Esbjerg, Aalborg and Aarhus. The story dealt with the approximately 1,000 Somali refugees in each place. The message was that there were too many Somalis and they were so different that the local authorities could no longer fulfil their responsibilities towards them (Fadel, Hervik and Vestergaard 1999). Towards the end of its campaign, *Ekstra Bladet* also featured a Somali story. A Somali man, Ali, had been found to be responsible for nine children, his wife and ex-wife with whom, according to the paper, he was still having children. Only later was he proven to have received 6 percent more money than he was entitled to, but because of the moral panic in the public sphere at the time Ali's case was taken to parliament, where legislators discussed the idea of an 'Ali-loft', i.e., a limit to how much money can be received in welfare benefits (Hervik 1999a).

The coverage of the presence of Somali refugees and the media's coverage of the *Ekstra Bladet* campaign showed clearly that most newspapers and most politicians from the right and many from the left, including the Socialdemokratiet, took part in the contestation of the Somali refugees.

Another sign of the split between 'Danes', who saw themselves as rightfully belonging to Denmark, and 'others', who were regarded like the Somalis as invaders and irreconcilably different, came from the government. The government coalition of Socialdemokratiet and Det Radikale Venstre chose to introduce a new Minister for the Interior to meet and curb the growing anti-immigrant feeling and the rapidly rising voter support for the new Dansk Folkeparti. The new minister was a retiring mayor and hardliner on questions of immigration, Thorkild Simonsen, and his key responsibility would be to pass a new act on integration.

New Integration Act

The purpose of the Integration Act, which took effect on 1 January 1999, was to enable immigrants to become productive citizens on equal terms with the Danes. A number of initiatives were taken: new, improved courses in Danish language and the workings of Danish society, special programmes to introduce immigrants to the job market, forced county acceptance of a certain centrally determined number of refugees with asylum and a binding geographical distribution of immigrants.[5] Despite the fact that the Integration Act was, controversially, directed at people of ethnic minority background, simultaneously increasing their obligations whilst reducing their rights and having no implications for Danes, it has generally been seen as an improvement. Among the controversial aspects of the legislation was the ruling that refugees and others accepted into the country and entering the official programme of integration or naturalisation would receive far less welfare money than Danes on welfare. The implication was that they were second-class citizens. This contentious piece of economic discrimination was quietly taken out of the Integration Act thirteen months later.

Morten Ejrnæs has shown that the lower welfare payment was a direct response to *Ekstra Bladet*'s editorial call for a reduced rate for newly arrived foreigners (2001). He identified further support for the legislation in reference to the much-discussed case of the Somali refugee, Ali (see previous section and Ejrnæs 2001). As has already been discussed, the story created much moral panic and the case was used in parliament in the reasoning for the lowered payment to newly accepted refugees (Ejrnæs 2001; Hervik 1999b; Jørgensen and Bülow 1999). Ejrnæs' argument shows that the government, at the time Socialdemokratiet and Det Radikale Venstre, was ready to respond to and control parts of the explosive growth of support for Dansk Folkeparti as shown in the opinion polls, by including some strict anti-immigrant policies that would not stand closer scrutiny in terms of national or international legal conventions. Former Minister for Foreign Affairs, Uffe Ellemann-Jensen (Venstre), who was close to becoming the new Prime Minister, had previously warned against letting identity politics and the ensuing nationalism become the major theme of national elections, since this would inevitably lead to racist arguments and eventually overt conflict (*Politiken* 1997). He refused to take political advantage of the growing neo-racism. Nevertheless, the government's adoption of a tougher politics towards immigrants was an important factor in the parliamentary election on 11 March 1998.

After acknowledging his narrow defeat in the election, Uffe Ellemann-Jensen stepped down and Anders Fogh Rasmussen took over the leadership of the party, thereby becoming the new candidate for heading a right-wing government. Unlike

Ellemann-Jensen, Rasmussen would welcome the question of immigrants and refugees as the prime theme of the election campaign leading up to the parliamentary election on 20 November 2001. Before the government decided to call the election in November 2001 other events had occurred that further strengthened the country's neo-nationalism.[6]

Enemy Image of Muslims

Four months prior to 11 September 2001 a group of young Danish Muslim citizens was represented in the media as supporting the Taliban in Afghanistan and the late Ayatollah Khomeini in Iran. Muslims and Islam were already the prime enemy of Danish neo-nationalism, best seen in the representation and presentation of Muslim identity as irreconcilable with Danish cultural identity and democracy by a large majority of the Danes (Hervik 2003). These assertions came primarily (but not exclusively) from a story intensely covered by the Danish media in the last half of May 2001. Two tabloid papers covered the story in April 2001, but it did not break more widely until the national television news of *Denmark's Radio* launched its prime-time evening news on 17 May 2001.[7] The story dealt with Muslim politicians of Pakistani background who were seeking political influence within Det Radikale Venstre (one of the two parties in the government coalition at the time) while maintaining their membership of the international Pakistan-based Muslim movement, Minhaj-ul-Quran, or sub-units of it. The story was based on one-sided, uncritical use of sources, partially incorporating the findings of a biased group of self-appointed investigators within the political party Det Radikale Venstre.[8]

In the news broadcast there was no mention of internal competition within Det Radikale Venstre to be the party's top-ranked candidate for the national election. It was instead dominated by a focus on what was presented as the fundamentalist, extremist and subversive nature of the Minhaj-ul-Quran movement, which was accused of supporting the Taliban and the regime of the late Ayatollah Khomeini. The television news coverage (and a spin-off story on the Muslims' stance on the death penalty issue) showed poor quality documentation and interviewing, but it nevertheless had a huge impact, which could be seen particularly in the alleged but untrue relationship to the extremist Taliban. For three weeks following 17 May hundreds of articles, representing most political parties, demonised the young Muslims, endlessly repeating that being a Muslim believer is to be fundamentalist and not congruent with Western democracy and Danish values.

At stake was the denial of access for Muslims to office at the top levels of the political hierarchy, parliament and Københavns Borgerrepræsentation (the City Council of Copenhagen), by means of references to the alleged implications of their membership of a Muslim movement. Also at stake was the public recognition of their social and cultural identity as simultaneously Danish, Muslim and people of ethnic minority background. With this story the media did the dirty work for a political party, denying the young Muslim rivals political influence. The journalists conveyed a one-sided view of the political aspirations of the Muslim politicians that reproduced the enemy image of Islam already held by the majority of Danes. In this way the television reproduced and further strengthened the antagonistic relationship between those who were presented as 'us' and 'them', where 'us' (or 'we') were identified positively and Muslims negatively (Hervik 2002).

In light of the media coverage in May 2001 it becomes more obvious that the tragic events of 11 September 2001 did not mark a new beginning but rather became a pretext for neo-nationalists to reiterate their arguments against the Muslims in Denmark and Islam more generally. The first three quotes at the beginning of this chapter come from the media coverage in the wake of 11 September; the other comments were made during the parliamentary election campaign that began in late October that year. The election campaign had immigrants and refugees, especially non-Westerners and Muslims, as its main theme. Political candidates for parliament competed in challenging the limits of how far they could go in placing tough demands on people of ethnic minority background in Denmark. Venstre (Denmark's Liberal Party) adopted the same arguments as the ultra-nationalist party Dansk Folkeparti and won the election with a landslide. The new government was formed by Venstre and Konservative (The Conservatives), and was supported by Dansk Folkeparti.

Conclusion

I have historicised the emergence of neo-nationalism in Denmark since the early 1990s by emphasising the major events shaping the particular Danish development of the phenomenon. The fall of the Berlin Wall and the dissolution of the former Soviet Union also changed the rhetoric in the media about immigrants and refugees. The newcomers from mainly non-Western countries, and children born in their new homelands, were more and more frequently presented as people who did not really belong in Denmark with their distinct ways of dressing, practising religion and physical appearance.

Two rounds of Maastricht Treaty votes meant that Danes discussed Danish cultural identity within the context of a larger European Union for more than a year. The votes showed that the European project, supported by the majority of politicians, had moved towards further European integration without the support of half of the Danish voting population, thereby building a formidable foundation of dissatisfaction to be tapped into by any entrepreneur, whether politically, culturally, commercially or nationally motivated. Questions about the future of the Danes in Europe and in relation to increased globalism and decreased Danish control of economy and migration were raised in discussions about the legal and social position of 17,000 Bosnian refugees. Left and right ended up agreeing on a 'waiting room' solution that temporarily placed the Bosnian camps outside normal activities of integration.

The seven years from 1989 to 1995 can be regarded as a period in which a foundation necessary for the development of neo-nationalism and neo-racism evolved. Then from 1995 on these two 'isms' came out of the closet. The first indication of a stricter treatment of refugees and immigrants came during the final discussions about the future of the Bosnian refugees as the two-year period, in what had seemed a permanent time-out situation, came to an end. Parliament was not only divided between right and left but the Social Democrats were internally divided as well. The issue debated was whether Bosnian refugees should be granted asylum, or if some condition should be attached to the legal statutes that would compel the Bosnians to return to their home country when the war ended.

A second indication, and a forerunner of the breakthrough of neo-nationalism, is the establishment of the Dansk Folkeparti in October 1995. Once established, the party could jump upon the opportunity provided by the media's huge coverage of *Ekstra Bladet*'s campaign, 'The foreigners', which voiced anti-immigrant opinions to an unprecedented degree. The campaign was a gift to the party, and the party was ready to collect the reward in the parliamentary election on 11 March 1998: Dansk Folkeparti won thirteen seats (7 percent of the vote) in what was their first election. During the election campaign the party had mainly focused on nationalist issues, calling for a tougher policy towards immigrants and refugees and for Denmark to leave the European Union. The ultra-nationalist success, however, was not sufficient for winning the close election. The leader of Venstre, Uffe Ellemann-Jensen, who had refused to allow his party to focus exclusively on nationalist issues, stepped down. The new chairman, Anders Fogh Rasmussen, had already proven willing to go far in his dealings with refugees when he supported the controversial (if not unlawful) call for a lower level of welfare support for newly arrived foreigners (*Ekstra Bladet* 1997b).

The governing Socialdemokratiet and Det Radikale Venstre hoped that the new Integration Act would contain the popular neo-nationalist, anti-immigrant stance. Even though the new Minister for the Interior, Karen Jespersen (Socialdemokratiet) suggested ever tougher measures towards immigrants and refugees, the neo-nationalist, neo-racist tendency kept attracting more and more voters. On this issue Jespersen's view could not be separated from that of Dansk Folkeparti to the extent that Kjærsgaard openly declared that Jespersen would be welcome to join her party. Rather than seeing this as part of a larger tendency to become more right-wing, I argue that the neo-nationalist stance is spreading and grabbing hold of the entire political spectrum, as well as the voters. In the lead up to the election on 20 November 2001 neo-nationalism had become the decisive factor and successfully mobilised voters across traditional party loyalties. Surveys further revealed that more than 80 percent of Danes welcomed neo-nationalist calls for a tougher policy towards 'foreigners' in Denmark (Hervik 2004; Hervik and Jørgensen 2002; *Morgenavisen Jyllands-Posten* 2001). Support for the neo-nationalist measures comes just three years after the Integration Act took effect (1 January 1999), which at the time was considered one of the strictest in Europe.

Notes

1. These opinions were repeated many times in many different newspapers.
2. The EU question posed a threat to the right's ambition of forming a government together. Dansk Folkeparti (The Danish People's Party) opposes the European Union, whereas Venstre (Denmark's Liberal Party) and Det Konservative Folkeparti (The Conservatives) are pro-EU.
3. In John Comaroff's words this is 'an age of revolution' (1996).
4. Danish political scientist Hanne Fugl has shown a clear shift in Swedish newspapers' presentation of migration and migration policy in the late 1980s, from a largely positive view of migrants to a view of them as a cultural, political, social and economic threat to the Swedish host society (1997). Her data suggest that even though the assassination of Prime Minister Oluf Palme in 1986 may have contributed to this shift, international events and processes are the most feasible explanation for it, suggesting that similar patterns can be found in countries such as Germany, France and United Kingdom (Fugl 1997).
5. The refugee is assigned to a specific county and not allowed to move elsewhere.
6. A government in Denmark is elected for four years, but can be called to election strategically prior to that.
7. The full analysis of the story can be found in Hervik (2002), based on research for the Danish Board for Ethnic Equality. The report is written in Danish but includes a summary in English. The story about the young Muslims in the media is being prepared for publication by the EUMC in Vienna as a case study of bad practice.
8. Six months later the Danish Press Council declared that the television news did not provide adequate documentation for the assertion that the Minhaj-ul-Quran movement supported the Taliban or the regime of Ayatollah Khomeini. Many other sources had been available to the television news and the party, but they had chosen a single secondary source as the basis for this assertion.

Bibliography

Anderson, B. 1983. *Imagined Communities: Reflections on The Origins and Spread of Nationalism.* London: Verso.

Comaroff, J.L. 1996. 'Ethnicity, Nationalism, and the Politics of Difference in an Age of Revolution', in E.N. Wilmsen and P. McAllister eds *The Politics of Difference: Ethnic Premises in a World of Power.* Chicago: University of Chicago Press, pp. 162–84.

Donnan, H. and Wilson, T.M. 1999. *Borders: Frontiers of Identity, Nation and State.* Oxford: Berg.

Ejrnæs, M. 2001. 'Integrationsloven – en case, der illustrerer etniske minoriteters usikre medborgerstatus', AMID Paper Series, 1. University om Aalborg.

Ekstra Bladet. 1997a. 'Danskerne og de fremmede.' Editorial by Sven Ove Gade. 31 March. In reprint June.

——— 1997b. 'Debatten er indeklemt og lummer.' Interview with Anders Fogh Rasmussen. 8 May. In reprint June.

——— 1997c. 'Der bliver borgerkrig.' Interview with author of letter-to-the-editor. 31 March. In reprint June.

——— 1997d. 'Letter-to-the-editor'. 17 May.

Fadel, U., Hervik, P. and Vestergaard, G. 1999. 'De "besværlige" somaliere', in P. Hervik ed. *Den generende forskellighed.* Copenhagen: Hans Reitzels Forlag, pp. 171–213.

Fugl, H. 1997. 'The Securitization of Migration: A Case Study of the Swedish Presentation of Migrants 1970–1995', unpublished thesis, University of Copenhagen.

Hervik, P., ed. 1999a. *Den generende forskellighed. Danske svar på den stigende multikulturalisme.* Copenhagen: Hans Reitzels Forlag.

—— 1999b. 'Nyracisme – politisk og folkelig', in P. Hervik ed. *Den generende forskellighed.* Copenhagen: Hans Reitzels Forlag, pp. 108–32.

—— 2002. *Mediernes muslimer. En antropologisk undersøgelse af mediernes dækning af religioner i Danmark.* Copenhagen: The Board for Ethnic Equality. Available at www.nel.dk.

—— 2003. 'Det Danske Fjendebillede', in M. Sheikh, F. Alev, M. Noman and B. Baig eds *Islam i bevægelse.* Copenhagen: Akademisk Forlag, pp. 181–98.

—— 2004. 'The Danish Cultural World of Unbridgeable Differences', *Ethnos* 69(2): 247–67.

Hervik, P. and Jørgensen, R.E. 2002. 'Danske benægtelser af racisme', *Sosiologi i dag* 32(4): 83–102.

Jørgensen, R.E. and Bülow, V.S. 1999. 'Ali og de fyrretyve k(r)oner. En analyse af Ekstra Bladets kampagne "De fremmede"', in P. Hervik ed. *Den generende forskellighed.* Copenhagen: Hans Reitzels Forlag, pp. 81–107.

Larsen, J.A. 1997. 'Bosniske krigsflygtninge i dansk offentlighed', report, University of Copenhagen.

Miles, R. 1993. *Racism after 'Race Relations'.* London: Routledge.

Morgenavisen Jyllands-Posten. 2001. 'Svært at stramme.' Background by Hans Davidsen-Nielsen. 17 November.

Peck, J.M. 1995. 'Refugees as Foreigners: The Problem of Becoming German and Finding Home', in D.E. Valentine and J.C. Knudsen eds *Mistrusting Refugees.* Berkeley: University of California Press, pp. 102–25.

Politiken. 1997. 'Uffe: Undgå fremmedhad.' Indland, Christine Cordsen. 28 September.

Chapter 5

'At Your Service!'

Reflections on the Rise of Neo-nationalism in the Netherlands

Thijl Sunier and Rob van Ginkel

Introduction

The Netherlands, 6 May 2002. Late afternoon news bulletins report that Pim Fortuyn, leader of the newly established political party List Pim Fortuyn (LPF), has been shot. Soon after, they announce that the 54-year-old former sociology professor has died at the scene of the crime. The alleged murderer, a white animal-rights campaigner, is arrested. People respond with disbelief, abhorrence and shock, and wonder how this is possible in a country that has not witnessed political violence for many years. Fortuyn's death came just nine days before the Dutch parliamentary elections. Opinion polls had predicted that he would win enough seats to lead one of the country's largest political parties. Earlier that year, after standing as a candidate in municipal elections, Fortuyn had been very successful in his hometown, Rotterdam, the country's second largest city, and one that Labour had ruled for more than fifty years. He won more than one-third of the votes, capturing seventeen of the city council's forty-five seats. It gave a boost to his self-confidence. He made no secret of his ambition: he repeatedly stated that he wanted to become prime minister, nothing less, and that he would indeed be the next prime minister. Several bullets silenced his dissident voice.

His death could not prevent the Dutch political landscape from changing drastically on 15 May 2002. The 'Purple Coalition' of the Dutch Labour Party (PvdA), Liberals (VVD) and Liberal Democrats (D66), which had constituted government for eight years, suffered a serious blow. Newcomer LPF gained an unprecedented 18 percent of the vote (26 out of 150 seats in parliament), thus becoming the second largest party, and it formed a new conservative coalition government with election winner, the Christian Democrats (CDA, which went from 29 to 43 seats) and election loser VVD (which retained only 24 of its 38 seats). The Labour Party lost dramatically, tumbling from 45 to only 23 seats in parliament, while the Liberal Democrats went from 14 to 7 seats. Only a year earlier no one would have imagined that this level of support were possible for a newcomer to party politics, and a populist one at that.

In a country whose intellectuals had been boasting for many decades that the Dutch are not nationalist, how can this landslide victory for a neo-nationalist party be explained? Political analysts and politicians alike were stunned by Fortuyn's success. In 2001 they expected a battle over political leadership between Liberals and Social Democrats. The economy was still booming, unemployment was at an all-time low and the large majority of voters claimed they were satisfied with 'purple' policies. The Christian Democrats were confronted with an internal conflict over party leadership and were losing ground in voter polls, while the List Pim Fortuyn did not exist as yet. Politics was still firmly rooted in the practice of consociational and deliberative democracy (Daalder 1971) in which political decisions were negotiated by all sorts of stakeholders. Every government for decades had been a coalition. Every view was taken into account, so long as it was broadly democratic. If anything, politics was stable, predictable and hence fairly dull. Many felt that elections had become somewhat meaningless since forming coalition governments necessarily implied making compromises, and party discipline numbed most parliamentary debate.

Into this scene of utter political tranquility, Pim Fortuyn emerged as the Young Turk who did not abide by unwritten political conventions and so-called political correctness. His slogan was 'I say what I think and I do what I say'. His provocative contribution made the electoral campaign livelier than it had been for decades. He received massive media exposure, especially on television. Fortuyn loved the camera, and the camera loved him. The established politicians did not have a proper answer to his unconventional performance and provocative statements. His behaviour and his message made him the talk of the town throughout the Netherlands. Journalists vied to interview him. Part of their curiosity had to do with the ungraspable character of Fortuyn, a man replete with paradoxes. Upon his death and after the elections, many scholars and journalists made attempts to analyse what had happened in the Netherlands, yet many questions remain unanswered. For example, how could one man single-handedly turn the seemingly stable Dutch political scene upside down? Why did his views appeal to a nation whose boast was that it despised nationalism and embraced multiculturalism? How does Fortuyn's party compare with right-wing or neo-nationalist political parties elsewhere in Europe? In this contribution, we attempt to present some tentative answers, but, doubtless, many puzzles and paradoxes will remain unsolved for some time to come. Before going into recent events, we will briefly deal with the development of Dutch political culture and how it related to issues of nationhood and political, cultural and ethnic diversity.

Political Culture: Discourses on Nationhood and Multiculturalism

The unified Dutch state started to appear on the political agenda in the late eighteenth century. Previously, ideas about the Dutch as a distinct people existed in elite circles only and were mostly supported by myths of origin and images of enemies. By 1780, a national awareness began to manifest itself in various publications concerning the characteristic nature, morals and customs of the Dutch. This self-image included such traits as tolerance, independence and open-mindedness. Yet it was only in the second half of the nineteenth century that state formation and intensifying contacts, increasing interdependencies and civilising missions at national level led to growing national integration.

At the same time, however, the politico-religious compartments or pillars, of Liberals, Catholics and Protestants, emerged. They extended to all organisational spheres, not just to churches and parties per se. The leaders organised their followers tightly, and pillars demanded the right to run their own affairs through the principle of sovereignty in one's own domain. This brought about a compartmentalised civil society based on an institutionalised form of power sharing. Compartmentalisation also had consequences for interpretations of history and views of nationhood and national identity. Each compartment had its own version of 'Dutchness'. Nonetheless, Liberals, Catholics and Protestants, and later Social Democrats, wanted to maintain an impression of a national community. They gave an appearance of a conciliatory attitude and had quite a sound awareness of the national bond that existed alongside the bond to their particular pillar. In fact, their supra-local organisations contributed to national integration.

In the second half of the twentieth century the image of Dutch individuality became invariably more diffuse and, as a result of secularisation, decompartmentalisation and political pragmatism, became less allied to politics and philosophical convictions. Yet today the political culture of accommodation and pacification is still common practice and the history of peaceful coexistence legitimises present integration politics. History textbooks, for example, show how the Netherlands managed to organise a peaceful cohabitation of religious and other minorities by not making an issue of the differences, but rather by 'playing them low-key'. Religion is in a way conceived of as a matter of opinion, culture as a matter of subculture and lifestyle, ethnicity as a matter of background. Toleration, participation and inclusion are the keywords. Dutch history is portrayed as a continuous growth and refinement of an inclusive consultative democracy. The message would seem to be that differences should not be highlighted, but that they are there to be handled and overcome (for a more thorough analysis see Schiffauer et al. 2004).

With this last point we return to actual politics, particularly those issues that dominated the election campaigns of both 2002 and 22 January 2003. In both cases the integration of immigrants was one of the prime themes during the campaigns, particularly on the right wing of the political spectrum. To understand the tone of the debates one must know the background.

Until the end of the 1970s the cultural and religious background of migrants did not play any significant role in debates about their position in society. Migrants were temporary residents. The Netherlands did not yet officially conceive of itself as a country of immigration. Towards the beginning of the 1980s a turning point was reached: for the first time the government acknowledged that the idea of a temporary stay was unrealistic. In 1983 it issued a report outlining a new policy. It was at this point that the concept of 'integration with the preservation of identity' was introduced (Minderhedennota 1983: 38–42). Migrants were granted basic rights to live according to their own cultural background, while at the same time they were expected to take part in society. This became the typical Dutch trajectory towards full citizenship. An important aspect of this discourse was that a relationship was constructed between participation on the one hand and cultural background on the other. 'Guest workers' were relabelled 'ethnic minorities', 'cultural minorities' or 'ethnic groups' and later on 'allochthons' (as opposed to 'autochthons'). In other words, a shift in the definition of the situation took place. From an economic category, 'migrant' turned into a cultural one, and cultural background thus became a relevant factor in integration policies.

During the 1980s the government adopted a lenient attitude towards cultural specificities. Instead of assuming that this was rooted in compartmentalisation and multiculturalism as was assumed in debates in the course of the 1980s and 1990s, it must be traced back directly to the American assimilationist perspective as developed in sociology in the 1950s and 1960s. Preservation of cultural identity was only a temporary situation, a transitional phase to complete assimilation. One of the measures taken was the incorporation of migrants' organisations (including Islamic ones) into integration policies. These organisations were considered an important bridge between migrants and the host society. This contributed to a steady growth in the number of ethnic and religious associations (Sunier 1996: 8). Early critics stated that this could have a negative effect on integration (Vuijsje 1986), but the idea underlying these policies was that when integration was complete, these organisations would become obsolete.

The new integration policies took shape at a time when, in the Islamic world itself, dramatic events were taking place, such as the Revolution in Iran and the assassination of the Egyptian president Sadat. Suddenly migrants from countries such as Turkey and Morocco were 'discovered' as Muslims. 'Muslim migrants' emerged as a new cultural category. Islam increasingly became the explanatory factor not only for the specific (collective) behaviour of, but also for all kinds of societal problems faced by Muslims. This has been phrased as the 'Islamicisation of the discourse' (Rath and Sunier 1994: 57). As a result, a specific image of Islam, based on the idea that Muslims were the least integrated migrants, made its way into public discourse. Islam was not just a new and strange religion, but also one known for its allegedly anti-modern character. Muslims were seen as passive, fatalistic people, turned inward and facing difficulties keeping up with the pace of modern society. For that reason it was believed that they tended to fall back easily on their faith. After the Rushdie affair and subsequent events, another image of Islam appeared. According to this image Muslims were not only conservative but also radical and a potential threat to society. This image became dominant, of course, after the events of 11 September 2001. It was in this political climate that Pim Fortuyn launched his criticisms of Islam.

Since the early 1980s the discourse on Islam, ethnic minorities and immigration has led to a revival of the discussion on national identity. In general, the political and intellectual elites embraced postmodern ideas like relativism and multiculturalism, but recently a growing number of intellectuals have argued for a deepening and dissemination of national awareness and protection of Dutch cultural identity, both in relation to the presence of ethnic minorities and European unification (see, e.g., Scheffer 2000; Schnabel 1999; van Praag 2000). Among the dissenters was Pim Fortuyn, who in 1997 (at which time he was not yet active in party politics) published a book entitled *Tegen de islamisering van onze cultuur. Nederlandse identiteit als fundament* ('Against The Islamicisation Of Our Culture. Dutch Identity as Foundation') that was generally reviewed quite unfavourably. Although Fortuyn focused on Islam, his main point of concern was Dutch national identity, hence the subtitle of the book.

In that sense Fortuyn's critique fitted within a general change in the political climate that took place in the 1990s. The main idea is that the Dutch seem to be at a loss when they have to define the Dutch nation precisely. What is Dutch about Dutch national culture? What does it comprise? Why is the nation (still) an important frame of reference? The answers are equivocal (van Ginkel 1999). The cultural feeling of national belonging has become so 'natural' in the Netherlands that for a long time many thought it hardly needed contemplating. Some have mistaken this self-evidence for a lack of national consciousness, and even a denial of 'Dutchness'. This poses a dilemma for ethnic minorities: if they are willing to integrate into the nation, what is required of them? Exclusion may be a consequence of not knowing how to be included in a concept that is deeply hidden. How can they become fully fledged citizens when it is hard to know how to play by cultural rules that are unclear and constantly changing? How can you become a member of Dutch society when it is unclear what this membership implies? In general, the discourse on minorities was characterised by the rhetoric of multiculturalism, with an implicit expectation that ethnic minorities would assimilate, while separateness generally was the reality.

Yet, until recently at least, the multiculturalism discourse itself reflected a mode of debate that is very much in line with Dutch political culture. Sociologist Frank

Lechner raises the question of how Dutch policy on minorities reflects and transforms a sense of national identity. He writes:

> Dutch minorities policy ... has 'managed others' in keeping with the code of national identity. It operates by consensual methods, strives for egalitarian inclusion, advocates a form of pluralistic tolerance, constitutes a major state project, and contributes to a Dutch conversation about what the Dutch nation is. It also, though, reflects changes in the meaning of membership and identity ... Minorities policy has helped to create a new form of citizenship; it has articulated a new sense of nationhood. (1999: 20)

The debate on the multicultural character of Dutch society and the need for and prospects of integration of ethnic minorities was well underway when Pim Fortuyn burst onto the political scene.

A Maverick Political Leader: 'Professor Pim' and His Followers

Born in 1948 to a conservative, Catholic family in Velsen, a small town in the northwest of the country, Fortuyn went to the (Protestant) Free University in Amsterdam in the 1970s to study sociology. After graduation he became a lecturer at the University of Groningen where he taught Marxist sociology and defended his Ph.D. dissertation on social and economic developments in the Netherlands from 1945 to 1949 (Fortuyn 1981). He joined the Dutch Labour Party (PvdA), but his wanderings in a leftist milieu did not deter him from wearing fancy suits and developing a taste for expensive cars. Contracts with the government followed after he left the University of Groningen in 1988 and he established himself as a management consultant. At that time he left the Labour Party. In 1990 Fortuyn obtained a one-day-a-week professorial post teaching social sciences at the Erasmus University in Rotterdam. There, it was said, he lived up to what had become known as 'Fortuyn's Law': wherever he worked, he brought about controversy and acrimony, on this particular occasion in 1995 (Chorus and de Galan 2002).

By the 1990s he was writing a socio-economic column for the weekly *Elsevier*. His political conviction had moved to the right and his social network was beginning to take in the business community. He disliked the dominant Dutch practice of conflict avoidance through consensus seeking, which, in his view, numbed debate. His outspoken ideas were well received among the nouveaux riches, entrepreneurs and dissatisfied citizens, and he turned into an oft-invited speaker and television chat show guest who did not refrain from making blunt and controversial statements. These activities made Fortuyn well known in the Netherlands long before he became active in politics. They also earned him sufficient money to lead a flamboyant lifestyle, including a chauffeur-driven car and a butler. Fortuyn was gay and proudly so: he boasted of his promiscuity, of nights spent in the back rooms of gay bars, and the delight he took in the male prostitutes he kept around the house, including boys whose ethnic background was not Dutch.

Fortuyn was convinced of his leadership qualities. In several publications that appeared in the 1990s he portrayed himself as a 'shepherd' who would be able to lead the 'orphaned' and 'defenceless' Dutch people if only they would let him. He would show the way in a time during which the Dutch supposedly did not know how to relate to their 'Dutchness' and Dutch national identity (e.g., Fortuyn 1995: 238). His ideal was to dispense with redundant bureaucracy, social benefits and the culture of consultation in the economy (or the so-called *poldermodel*) and clear the way for entrepreneurs and the free market much in line with Thatcherism and Reaganism. He despised the bargaining power of organised groups and stakeholders and instead felt that society had to be made up of individuals entering into voluntary contracts; at the same time he advocated a conscription for young men and women, not into the military but into public service, so that people with different sexual preferences, genders, social and ethnic backgrounds would learn how to deal with one another in a civil manner and give meaning to their Dutchness, thus reinforcing the process of nation formation (Fortuyn 2002: 176). Fortuyn also called for stricter law enforcement. He was a Euro-sceptic who frequently called for the abolition of the European Parliament, more control at the European Union's internal borders, quitting the Schengen Agreement, and the renationalisation of the Common Agricultural Policy. Through his publications Fortuyn attempted to change the Dutch political climate. Though he was ambitious enough to enter the political stage, no party invited him to take on a ministerial post or other important political position.

It was not until November 2001 that Fortuyn became leader of the newly established and supposedly radical Leefbaar Nederland (Liveable Netherlands Party). Leefbaar Nederland was an amalgam of two successful local parties (Leefbaar Utrecht and Leefbaar Hilversum) that had been hammering away at local issues mostly to do with security in the public domain, breaking up the closed politics of the established parties, and policies and decisions that went against the wishes of citizens but which were nonetheless pushed through. Fortuyn accepted his election as party leader with the pathetic words 'At your service!' He guided the party towards the right, slamming bureaucracy in public services and challenging long-established Dutch political norms. The party rose sharply and quickly in voter polls under his leadership. His relationship with Leefbaar Nederland was, however, to be short-lived: in February 2002 he was expelled by the party's board for coming down harshly on Muslim immigrants in an interview (Poorthuis and Wansink 2002: 13) and suggesting that the Dutch Constitution's article one, banning discrimination, should be changed if he could not say what he wanted.[1]

Two days later he set up his own party, List Pim Fortuyn. A huge part of the electorate that had supported Leefbaar Nederland followed Fortuyn, and in opinion polls his party, or rather the leader himself, swiftly gained potential votes.[2] What about Fortuyn's political stance? He blamed the established politicians for neglecting the country's real problems and for losing contact with 'ordinary people'. He despised bureaucracy and railed against the ever-increasing restrictions on Dutch life and commerce imposed by the imperious and undemocratically appointed European Union bureaucrats in Brussels. He campaigned for harsher penal laws, less tax, a leaner bureaucratic apparatus, more government accountability to voters and fewer decisions made behind closed doors by an isolated, self-appointed political elite dishing out jobs. Fortuyn promised to solve problems in healthcare, education and public security without increasing budgets or creating additional jobs in the public sector, while at the same time promising to take a firm line with large-scale bureaucracy. What aroused most attention, support from many dissatisfied voters and resentment from proponents of multiculturalism, however, was the fact that he emphasised time and again that Dutch politicians had been too soft on immigration.

Most controversial was Fortuyn's position on Islam, a culture he dubbed 'backward' in an interview with the national newspaper (Poorthuis and Wansink 2002),[3] as well as his hard-hitting anti-immigrant views. Fortuyn wanted to reduce significantly the number of immigrants and asylum seekers arriving in the Netherlands each year, from 40,000 people in the mid 1990s to just 10,000 'in no time at all'. According to him 'enough was enough', and with 16 million inhabitants the Netherlands was already a very densely populated country. 'This is a full country', he said, 'We are already overcrowded, there's no more room and we must shut the borders' (Poorthuis and Wansink 2002: 13). Those immigrants already in the Netherlands could stay but had to integrate as quickly as possible. 'Professor Pim', as he liked to be called, shocked the Dutch political establishment in February 2002 with a call for the repeal of the first article of the constitution, which forbids discrimination. His argument was that the Netherlands used to be and still was a liberal, tolerant and freedom-loving country where people could freely express their opinion. He feared that with an expanding Muslim minority these permissive values would be at stake. He himself supported gay rights, the legalisation of soft drugs and prostitution, the very hallmarks of permissive Dutch society. In an interview with BBC reporter Kirsty Lang, Fortuyn contended: 'Muslims have a very bad attitude to homosexuality, they're very intolerant ... And women. For them women are second-class citizens' (Lang 2002a). Explicitly referring to Samuel Huntington (1996), he continued: 'What we are witnessing now is a clash of civilisations, not just between states but within them ... I have gay friends who have been beaten up by young Moroccans in Rotterdam. We need to integrate these people; they need to accept that, in Holland, gender equality and tolerance of different lifestyle is very, very important to us' (Lang 2002b). In the same interview (Lang 2002a), he went on to say, 'In Holland, homosexuality is treated the same way as heterosexuality. In what Islamic country does this happen?' Fortuyn's fundamental point was: 'Why embrace them if they won't embrace you?' The Netherlands, he claimed, is a modern, tolerant European culture admirably free of the sectarian and religious violence of countries like Ireland, Spain, most of Eastern Europe and the Middle East. In another interview, he said: 'For Muslims, as a homosexual, I am less than a pig. I am proud that in the Netherlands I can come out for my homosexuality and I'd like to keep it that way' (Graff 2002). A key feature of the new Islamic spirit, he said, is religious evangelism that seeks to convert infidels, meaning anyone who is not a Muslim.

With this kind of statement Fortuyn breached the generally restrictive 'speech code' regarding ethnic minorities and consequently aroused strong opposition from all established parties, particularly from the left. His opponents were quick to point out that his ideas were akin to those of extreme right-wing politicians elsewhere in Europe, among them Filip de Winter in Belgium, Jean-Marie Le Pen in France, Jörg Haider in Austria and Umberto Bossi in Italy. Fortuyn strongly resented being mentioned in the same breath as them or being dubbed a 'neo-fascist' or 'racist'. Fortuyn felt he was being 'demonised' by left-wing politicians, unjustly so. He denied that he was a racist and religious bigot; he said he was a pragmatist concerned about the rapidly expanding numbers of immigrants demanding full social benefits at the expense of taxpaying citizens. Immigrants were to him consumers who gave nothing back to the country that sheltered and fed them, and they sent the money they received directly overseas to their families. He stressed time and again that he defended the permissive, open, libertine culture that the Netherlands is known for. That is why Fortuyn deemed it of the utmost importance that immigrants had to integrate into (read: assimilate to) the prevailing Dutch society and culture as quickly as possible and embrace its democratic values. 'My policies are multi-ethnic and certainly not racist', he said, 'I want to stop the influx of new immigrants. This way, we can give those who are already here the opportunity to fully integrate into our society' (CNN.Com World 2002).

So Fortuyn employed the culturist argument, claiming that he wanted to protect and preserve Holland's supposedly distinctive culture of tolerance and liberty. Fortuyn was certainly not the only one to do so. There were other pleas for a kind of 'enlightened' nationalism, even from left-wing intellectuals, as we have seen (Scheffer 2000). However, what made Fortuyn's viewpoints different was the fierceness with which he opposed Islam and Muslim immigrants. He claimed that the Dutch had to close ranks to withstand 'the dangerous other' (Fortuyn 1997: 16). National unity was required to survive the 'clash of civilizations', i.e., Islam versus Judaeo-Christian Humanist culture. In his view, cultural relativism and multiculturalism eroded the existing shape of national culture and identity. He attempted to turn the attitude of 'let's celebrate our differences' into a 'let's stick with what we know' spirit of nationalism: 'The problems [in Dutch society] concentrate on those fellow citizens who hail from culture areas that are distant to very distant from ours' (Fortuyn 1997: 183). In addition to this culturist argument, Fortuyn and his followers saw immigrants as a financial burden: they constituted a threat to the country's economic prosperity, and the healthcare and prison systems would be less overburdened without the presence of ethnic newcomers.

Fortuyn's anti-Muslim views, calls for limiting immigration, and pledges to come down hard on crime struck a chord with voters despite the country's celebrated reputation for liberalism and religious tolerance. Sentiments like 'they take our jobs', 'they eat our welfare', 'they want my wallet, my wife, our daughter' gained ground. Fortuyn's agitation against Muslim immigrants exploited an anti-Muslim atmosphere that had been encouraged by Western governments and media in the aftermath of 11 September 2001, and by extensive media coverage of the opinions of some radical imams and incidents with the problematic or delinquent behaviour of small groups of youths of Turkish and Moroccan descent in several of the major cities. Those who felt threatened by immigrants applauded Fortuyn's generalising and stigmatising view of Islam as a backward culture. He had broken the taboo on talking about ethnic difference and found ways to air his ideas, and those who bore a grudge against immigrants felt henceforth free to express their opinions too.

What is the background of LPF voters? The LPF found support among voters who would traditionally veer to the (far) right, but also among those weary of the existing political landscape and centre-left government and its 'back-room decisions'. The LPF also had a particularly strong appeal among the young and the poorly educated: nearly half of eighteen- to thirty-year-olds recently polled wanted to see no Muslim immigration at all and 56 percent of LPF voters enjoyed only advanced elementary or lower vocational education. The party also gained a considerable number of votes in urban settings with a high percentage of ethnic minorities, but also in 'white-flight' suburbs. Interestingly however, a considerable percentage of LPF voters are immigrants and once in, they seem to develop an interest in keeping other newcomers out for fear of having to share jobs and welfare benefits. Among the mourners queuing at Fortuyn's house in Rotterdam after 6 May 2002 were many people whose ethnicity was obviously not Dutch. Many traditional non-voters also decided to vote LPF. They felt that for the first time in years someone had voiced their discontent unequivocally. Upon Fortuyn's death many commented that he spoke the unspeakable, broke taboos and voiced the concerns of ordinary people that were swept under the carpet by mainstream politicians. Then there were the sympathy votes.

Without a doubt, Fortuyn was a charismatic leader. Unprecedented scenes accompanied his burial, with thousands and thousands of supporters along the route to his grave weeping, throwing flowers at the hearse, flying banners or national flags. The ceremony was broadcast live by several national television and radio networks. Fortuyn's critics were blamed for demonising him, and by association being guilty of his assassination. 'The bullet came from the left', as an LPF board member insisted. Some left-wing politicians received hate mail and death threats in the wake of the murder. Surely the political climate had turned sour. Established politicians refrained from tackling LPF points of view for fear of being accused of besmirching 'Pim's political legacy'. Rhetorically, LPF politicians began talking frequently about 'the national interest' (*het landsbelang*) and claimed that the party represented 'the people's voice' and 'the people's will'. Who 'the people' are is left obscure; they certainly do not include all 16 million or so inhabitants of the Netherlands.

Fortuyn *was* his political movement. Without its leader the List Pim Fortuyn was rapidly confronted with internal conflicts and mayhem. None of the elected MPs was of his stature; a real programme, a sound party organisation and discipline, and hence coherence, were lacking, and there was no 'natural' and uncontroversial successor accepted by the vast majority of LPF politicians and party members. Although it continued to hammer away at the issues of immigration, security and healthcare, it soon became apparent that the LPF was inclined to give in to the practice of consensus politics that so many of its voters despised.

The Christian Democrats and Liberals skilfully encapsulated their coalition partner and neutralised much of its political appeal by emphasising equally some of the themes that had led the LPF to electoral success. To the dismay of its voters most of the energy of LPF MPs was consumed by intra-party quarrels. It began to disintegrate as soon as it entered political centre stage. Only hours after the presentation of the new coalition government, a junior minister, Surinam-born Philomena Bijlhout, had to vacate her post because she had concealed having worked in a paramilitary militia in Surinam, at the time when the junta liquidated eight of its opponents.[4] There were also well-publicised conflicts over faction leadership in parliament and within the party board. When the conflicts spread to the ranks of the appointed members of government it was clear that the party had lost its position as an acceptable coalition partner. When two LPF ministers were forced to resign by the other LPF members of government, coalition partners CDA and VVD lost confidence and decided that the government would resign. It fell only eighty-seven days after it had been installed. Some commentators had predicted that this was likely to happen. For example, BBC Europe correspondent Angus Roxburgh stated that, 'It could be the worst of all worlds – a hard-right party holding the balance of power, but led by political pygmies and novices' (2002). Dutch social scientists point out that post-war, extreme right-wing parties are usually rapidly confronted with schisms and as a rule of thumb have been rather unsuccessful (e.g., van Donselaar 1993).

As a consequence of the turmoil in government, the dubious statements of some LPF ministers about a variety of issues, and the internal party squabbles, the electorate's support for the party quickly diminished to less than a possible six seats in parliament. During the campaign for the January 2003 elections the party made an effort to invoke, once again, the heritage of Pim Fortuyn, referred to as *de geest van Pim* (Pim's spirit) or *het gedachtegoed van Pim* (Pim's ideas), but with just eight seats they finished far below their previous twenty-six.[5] The LPF will reappear in parliament for years to come as a small party on the right side of the political spectrum. In the January 2003 elections, the Labour Party was victorious and regained many seats lost less than a year earlier (forty-two seats, an increase of nineteen). The Christian Democrats and the Liberals, the coalition partners of the LPF, also won some seats and ended up with forty-four (an increase of two) and twenty-eight (an increase of four) respectively. Apparently, after a turbulent year in Dutch politics the electorate yearned for stability again.

Conclusion: A Nationalism of Sorts

In recent studies on nationalism it has been argued that the spread of neo-nationalist ideology in Europe must be understood in relation to important post-Second World War developments such as mass immigration and unification of Europe (see Eriksen 1993; Schierup 1997). Wicker (1997) argues that the type of nationalism witnessed in Western Europe today is internally rather than externally oriented. Modern nation states do not have to struggle for recognition vis-à-vis other states such as in the case of independence movements in the colonial era, or post-communist Eastern European states (see also Billig 1995). The question is to what extent these factors can account for the initial electoral success (and subsequent demise) of the LPF.

As we have argued, the relative success of the LPF and the popularity of Pim Fortuyn must indeed be understood partly against the backdrop of these developments. It is the Dutch version of processes encountered throughout Europe. Fortuyn's neo-nationalism was based to a large extent on anti-immigrant populism; its central tenets were keeping 'the external Other' out and culturally colonising 'the Other within'. Despite differences of style and emphasis there is a common set of ideas underlying the resurgent populist or right-wing movements in the Netherlands, France, Belgium, Italy, Austria, Denmark and elsewhere. This consists of ending or even reversing immigration and restoring at least part of the powers that are being, or may be, taken from nation states by the European Union; in the Netherlands and Denmark, for example, this has already resulted in much tougher immigration and asylum policies. From being ardent supporters of European integration, the Dutch population and conservative politicians are recently more reluctant to support the European idea, for example, in connection with the expansion of the European Union and the accession of new member states.

Yet, Fortuyn drew on some of the central tenets of the discourse on Dutch political culture and national identity, tolerance, liberty and democracy to expound his views regarding immigrants. He propagated these mythical core values of Dutch society and wanted to instil them into immigrants so that they would become assimilated (not just integrated) into Dutch society. Unlike politicians like Le Pen however, Fortuyn did not propose forced remigration and preferential treatment for the native Dutch population. Whereas other political parties would point to 'integration problems' as justification for anti-immigration policies, he went further and was explicit in his cultural nationalism: for example, as we have seen, the title of one of his books is 'Against The Islamicisation Of Our Culture', i.e., Dutch culture (Fortuyn 1997). In the three decades before Fortuyn's political star rose there had been other political parties that adopted anti-immigrant and nationalist or even racist views; among them were the Nederlandse Volksunie (Netherlands People's Union) established in 1971, the Centrumpartij (Centre Party) established in 1980, and the Centrum Democraten (Centre Democrats) established in 1984. Though they sometimes succeeded in getting seats on municipal councils, their role in national politics was limited (van Donselaar 1991). None of these parties has ever gained more than three seats in parliament. They were characterised by internal strife and their leaders did not appeal to a broad public. They were even considered to be the best remedy in minimising their own impact. The media were generally reluctant to provide a platform for their viewpoints and the taboo on open discussion of ethnic difference was still firmly in place. Racism and discrimination were strongly condemned. In this sense intolerance was not tolerated, at least not in public.[6]

A reason for the initial success of the LPF is the particular circumstances under which the party, or rather its leader, gained support. The backlash of the 11 September attacks, in combination with the very explicit opinions of Fortuyn about Islam, played a decisive role. In that respect the landslide victory of the LPF was contingent upon a combination of specific circumstances. It is precisely the political climate produced by the 11 September backlash that made it relatively easy to challenge the dominant discourse in which open reference to integration issues was a political taboo. The year 2002 will be recalled as the year in which almost every politician put Islam and the integration of Muslims high on their priority list. On the other hand however, the success of Fortuyn cannot be assessed only in relation to international developments, and unlike many other extreme right-wing parties the LPF was not a single-issue party. There is a typical Dutch edge to the movement. By 2002 transformations in Dutch society had brought about an atmosphere in which a man like Fortuyn and his ideas could move to the political centre stage.

First, depillarisation, along with the abandonment of socialist ideology by Labour leaders (as exemplified by Wim Kok's statement in 1995 that the Labour Party 'had shed its ideological feathers'), meant that the pluriform but stable segments in Dutch society lost much of their meaning and became increasingly porous. Concomitantly, political and religious leaders lost their grip on their traditional rank and file, resulting in a large proportion of 'floating voters'. Party loyalty has increasingly crumbled away, a symptom of which is that party membership has generally been in decline for decades. Whereas the media had long served the interests of particular segments in the pillarised Netherlands, this has changed considerably over the past thirty years or so. Commercial television and radio stations were established without any ties binding them to particular pillars, and broadcasting companies and newspapers linked with specific ideological or religious segments cut themselves loose under the influence or as part of the depillarisation process.

Second, with the diminished role of ideology many votes went to politicians not so much for their politics but for their appearance, presentation and media appeal. Once in the political limelight, Fortuyn stood out as a remarkable television personality, whereas most other leading politicians performed rather poorly. Without the old ideological bounds, Fortuyn became heavily mediatised and favoured appearing in live broadcasts on commercial television so that his words 'could not be twisted'. Fortuyn fitted well within what Elchardus (2002) has called 'drama democracy', in which the media play a crucial role. The 2002 campaign was probably the most media-dominated up until then. It was clear that some political leaders had serious problems with this type of campaigning, most notably Labour leader Ad Melkert and Liberal leader Hans Dijkstal. Their successors as party leaders, Wouter Bos (Labour) and Gerrit Zalm (Liberal), did much better in this 'mediacracy', Bos in particular.

Third, since the 1970s the ethnic composition of Dutch society has changed considerably with the influx of migrants from the (former) colonies and immigrant labourers hailing from Morocco and Turkey. Though in the 1980s and 1990s some intellectuals and politicians raised the question of what the implications might be for 'dominant' Dutch culture and identity, the issue was hedged about by taboos. Nevertheless, there were growing anxieties in urban and 'white-flight' suburban settings as regards multi-ethnic society. These 'gut feelings' had much to do with a sense of alienation, with being increasingly unfamiliar with the languages spoken in one's environment, with the smells, sounds, dress modes and codes and so on. Having the political climate on his side, Fortuyn fuelled these fears, which had been simmering for some time. Given his outward appearance he did not seem like other Dutch nationalist or racist politicians that had been rather unsuccessful in the 1970s and 1980s. His twin 'solution' for what he deemed the undermining of national identity – halting immigration and stimulating integration of ethnic minorities – met with growing consent among an increasing proportion of the electorate.

Fourth, with the economy booming there was a general feeling of economic security. However, this favourable situation went hand in hand with growing anxieties and dissatisfaction regarding one's own personal position. One reason for dissatisfaction was that with economic growth in the Netherlands and increasing income differences came social inequality. The layer of wealthy people at the top was growing richer and richer due to disproportionate advances in wages and profitable option schemes; yet, many entrepreneurs felt restrained and pressured by the consensual politics regulated and controlled by the state bureaucracy. Fortuyn appealed to them because of his critical stance towards the politics of deliberation and compromise seeking, and his call to cut bureaucracy. For the poorly educated working population and those depending on welfare benefits, incomes hardly increased, if at all, and upward mobility seemed impossible. Losers, or potential losers, in the economic upsurge blamed the politics and politicians of the Purple Coalition and the corporatism of trade unions that agreed to self-restraint in wage demands, and believed that Fortuyn voiced their discontents. It turned them into vindictive voters. They paid the establishment back by voting for the LPF.

Fifth, although the integration issue dominated the political scene, what made Fortuyn particularly popular was his crusade against the established political parties. Bashing 'old politics' and blaming it for real or imagined problems was his favourite pastime, and many could find some elements to agree with in what he proposed as 'new politics'. Fortuyn's focus on the supposed wrongdoings of the political establishment appealed to a large proportion of the electorate. It is this kind of 'anti-political politics', i.e., 'turning against the powers-that-be but doing it by manifesting popular *ressentiments* in and through electoral behaviour directly related to the mechanisms of representative democracy' that 'is a significant motivational factor from which much populist nationalism in contemporary Europe draws its sap' (Hedetoft 2002: 7). Fortuyn emphasised over and over again that he would bring politics back to the *burgers* (citizens) and the *burgers* back to politics. The campaign of 2003 brought this contradiction between 'old' and 'new' politics to the centre of public attention.

The last and certainly not least crucial Dutch aspect of the Fortuyn movement is the redefinition of some of the central concepts of Dutch political culture. As we have shown above, toleration, permissiveness, inclusion and participation have been key concepts for quite some time now. At first sight it seemed as if Fortuyn rejected these central tenets altogether. His famous slogan 'I say what I think and I do what I say' in practice meant that he did not avoid confrontations and controversial statements at all. He loved to kick ass and break taboos. In the eyes of many right-wing conservatives, his behaviour, especially his libertarian ideas about sexuality, was unconventional if not shocking, but this went to the heart of Fortuyn's ideas about tolerance. His critique of Islam and Muslims was motivated by their alleged anti-homosexual ideas. He often stated that a growing presence of Islam in Dutch society would jeopardise 'our' tradition of tolerance, permissiveness and inclusion. What is at stake here is not whether Fortuyn was right or wrong, rather the crucial point is that both Fortuyn and his adversaries referred to the same set of principles, defining them differently. The present leaders of the LPF hardly refer to these ideas when invoking 'Pim's spirit'. By the elections of January 2003, the party had developed into a small, ordinary, right-wing conservative law-and-order party.

Should the sudden rise of Fortuyn's neo-nationalist party be regarded as an isolated incident, a whim of political history that will soon disappear into oblivion? It is clear that the List Pim Fortuyn was inextricably tied to its eponymous founder and that upon his death its driving force and cohesion were undermined. Though the country is not short of aspiring populist politicians, no leader of Fortuyn's stature and charisma has taken his position. The LPF and the other right-wing parties established in the meantime have not been successful in the January 2003 elections and it is highly doubtful that they will be able to recruit a mass following again in the near future. However, the discontent that surfaced in May 2002 has not disappeared and is not likely to disappear for some time to come. It gave rise to a form of conservative and populist neo-nationalism that combines elements of an open, liberal, market-oriented welfare society with a strong emphasis on national, and particularly ethno-national, interests. The discontents have found another locus.

Following the 2002 political landslide in the Netherlands, popular disgruntlement was channelled into mainstream politics. The Christian Democrats and the Liberal Party would currently seem to be the champions of tougher immigration policies. Using the 'voice from below' as justification, they arrived at new terms of inclusion and especially exclusion vis-à-vis prospective immigrants. They proposed a restrictive aliens policy and stated that illegal immigration should be fought with vigour. Insofar as immigrants are still admitted, they have to complete an integration course (*inburgeringscursus*) successfully and on time, and they must pay for it themselves. The course aims at achieving fluency in the Dutch language, acquiring insight into Dutch society and its 'core values', and knowledge and skills necessary to be self-supporting through employment. Christian Democrat Prime Minister Jan Peter Balkenende openly doubted the desirability of a multicultural Dutch society. He felt that his and Fortuyn's political views had much in common, and he had a tacit agreement with Fortuyn not to attack one another in the 2002 election campaign (Chorus and de Galan 2002). In the campaign for the January 2003 election, Liberal leader Gerrit Zalm, like Fortuyn, stated that the Netherlands is 'full'. Labour and the small left-wing parties also toughened their stance on public security, immigration and integration. As a consequence, neo-nationalism has spread to some of the mainstream political parties, which have thus been able to absorb a considerable fraction of the dissatisfied electorate that supported Fortuyn. Again, this response is much in line with Dutch political culture: at least since the 1960s the political and administrative establishment's response to contestation has been to incorporate and tone down rebellious ideas, thus neutralising opponents (Kennedy 1995). Although the role of List Pim Fortuyn in Dutch politics is now marginalised, its name-giver has controlled the political agenda of the January 2003 elections from beyond the grave.

Notes

We thank Gerd Baumann for his thoughtful comments on an earlier version of this chapter. Thanks also to Julene Knox who did a wonderful editing job. Since we submitted our contribution in June 2003, several books and scores of articles have been published about Fortuyn and the aftermath of his violent death. We would like to mention Pels (2003), Wansink (2004) and de Vries and van der Lubben (2005). Although we did not have the opportunity to use these recent publications for our chapter, we think that they would not have changed our analysis in any fundamental way.
 1. Thus reiterating a view he had already voiced in 1995 (Lucardie and Voerman 2002: 40).
 2. In the May 2002 elections, Leefbaar Nederland got just two seats in parliament. In the January 2003 elections the party lost these seats.
 3. Earlier he had expounded this view at length (Fortuyn 1997). In a column he stated that, 'The greatest threat for world peace is Islam, whereby the distinction between liberal and fundamentalist Islam is only relative' (Fortuyn 2001).
 4. There were several other ethnic minority members on the party list who were elected to parliament, possibly to counter allegations of racism.

5. Of those who voted LPF in 2002, almost a quarter (24 percent) did not cast a vote in 2003; while 18 percent switched to voting Liberal, 14 percent Christian Democrat and 10 percent Labour.
6. Backstage things were different. For example, unemployment figures of ethnic minorities were, and still are, disproportionately high.

Bibliography

Billig, M. 1995. *Banal Nationalism*. London: Sage.

Chorus, J. and de Galan, M. 2002. *In de ban van Fortuyn. Reconstructie van een politieke aardschok*. Amsterdam: Mets & Schilts.

CNN.Com World. 2002. 'Pim Fortuyn: Man of paradox', *CNN.Com World* 9 May, http://europe.cnn.com/2002/WORLD/europe/05/06/fortuyn.profile/.

Daalder, H. 1971. 'On Building Consociational Nations', *International Social Science Journal* 23: 354–70.

de Vries, J. and van der Lubben, S. 2005. *Een onderbroken evenwicht in de Nederlandse politiek. Paars II en de revolte van Fortuyn*. Amsterdam: Van Gennep.

Elchardus, M. 2002. *De dramademocratie*. Tielt: Lannoo.

Eriksen, T.H. 1993. *Ethnicity and Nationalism: Anthropological Perspectives*. London: Pluto Press.

Fortuyn, P. 1981. *Sociaal-economische politiek in Nederland 1945–1949*. Alphen aan den Rijn: Samsom.

———— 1995. *De verweesde samenleving. Een religieus-sociologisch traktaat*. Utrecht: Bruna.

———— 1997. *Tegen de islamisering van onze cultuur. Nederlandse identiteit als fundament*. Utrecht: Bruna.

———— 2001. 'Koude oorlog met islam', *Elsevier* 25 August 2001, http://www.pim-fortuyn.nl/columns/column.asp?ID=69.

———— 2002. *De puinhopen van paars. Een genadeloze analyse van de collectieve sector en aanbevelingen voor een krachtig herstelprogramma*. Rotterdam: Speakers Academy.

Graff, J. 2002. 'Hostage to Fortuyn', *Time Europe Magazine*, 18 March, http://www.time.com/time/europe/magazine/article/0,13005,901020318–216388,00.html.

Hedetoft, U. 2002. 'The Politics of Belonging and Migration in Europe: Raisons d'Etat and the Borders of the National', http://www.socsci.auc.dk/institut2/nopsa/arbejdsgruppe19/ulf.pdf.

Huntington, S.P. 1996. *The Clash of Civilizations and the Remaking of World Order*. New York: Simon & Schuster.

Kennedy, J.C. 1995. *Nieuw Babylon in aanbouw*. Amsterdam: Boom.

Lang, K. 2002a. 'At Home with "Professor Pim"', *BBC News* 4 May, http://news.bbc.co.uk/1/hi/world/from_our_own_correspondent/1966979.stm.

———— 2002b. 'Obituary. Pim Fortuyn: Maverick Dutch Rightwinger Poised for Electoral Success', *The Guardian* 7 May, http://www.guardian.co.uk/obituaries/story/0,3604,711097,00.html.

Lechner, F.J. 1999. *Managing Others: Minorities Policy and National Identity in the Netherlands*, Halle Institute Occasional Paper. Atlanta: Claus M. Halle Institute for Global Learning, Emory University.

Lucardie, P. and Voerman, G. 2002. 'Liberaal Patriot of Nationaal Populist? Het gedachtegoed van Pim Fortuyn', *Socialisme en Democratie* 59(4): 32–42.

Minderhedennota. 1983. *Minderhedennota*. Den Haag: Ministry of Internal Affairs BiZa.

Pels, D.L. 2003. *De geest van Pim. Het gedachtegoed van een politieke dandy*. Amsterdam: Anthos.

Poorthuis, F. and Wansink, H. 2002. '"De islam is een achterlijke cultuur"', *de Volkskrant* 9 February, p. 13.

Rath, J. and Sunier, T. 1994. 'Angst voor de islam in Nederland?', in W. Bot, M. van der Linden and R. Went eds *Kritiek. Jaarboek voor socialistische discussie en analyse 1993–1994*. Utrecht: Stichting Toestanden.

Roxburgh, A. 2002. 'The Paradox of Pim Fortuyn', *BBC News* 16 May, http://news.bbc.co.uk/1/hi/world/from_our_own_correspondent/1977511.stm.

Scheffer, P. 'Het multiculturele drama', *NRC Handelsblad* 29 January, p. 6.

Schierup, C. 1997. 'Multiculturalism and Universalism in the United States and EU-Europe', in H. Wicker ed. *Rethinking Nationalism and Ethnicity: The Struggle for Meaning and Order in Europe*. Oxford: Berg, pp. 111–27.

Schiffauer, W., Baumann, G., Kastorjano, R. and Vertovec, S. eds. 2004. *Civil Enculturation: Nation-State, School and Ethnic Difference in Four European Countries*. Oxford: Berghahn.

Schnabel, P. 1999. *De multiculturele illusie- Een pleidooi voor aanpassing en assimilatie*. Utrecht: Forum.

Sunier, T. 1996. *Islam in beweging*. Amsterdam: Het Spinhuis.

van Donselaar, J. 1991. *Fout na de oorlog. Fascistische en racistische organisaties in Nederland 1950–1990*. Amsterdam: Bert Bakker.

―――― 1993. 'Post-war Fascism in the Netherlands', *Crime, Law and Social Change* 19: 87–100.

van Ginkel, R. 1999. *Op zoek naar eigenheid. Denkbeelden en discussies over cultuur en identiteit in Nederland*. Den Haag: Sdu.

van Praag, C. 2000. 'Op zoek naar de grenzen van multicultureel Nederland', *Socialisme en Democratie* 57(3): 115–17.

Vuijsje, H. 1986. *Vermoorde onschuld. Etnisch verschil als Hollands taboe*. Amsterdam: Bert Bakker.

Wansink, H.A. 2004. *De erfenis van Fortuyn. De Nederlandse democratie na de opstand van de kiezers*. Amsterdam: Meulenhoff.

Wicker, H. ed. 1997. *Rethinking Nationalism and Ethnicity: The Struggle for Meaning and Order in Europe*. Oxford: Berg.

Chapter 6

Neo-nationalism and Democracy in Belgium

On Understanding the Contexts of Neo-communitarianism

Rik Pinxten

Introduction

This contribution sketches two contexts that function as background for understanding the substantial rise in popularity of extreme-right political parties and movements in Belgium: the historical context of Belgium as a nation state, and the socio-political context of Belgium as a European country in the present era of globalisation.

During the past two centuries the nation state has been a primary identity vehicle in Western Europe. Belgium was created in 1830 and the international context at that time was that of European inter-state wars between England, France and Germany. The young Belgian state invested heavily in patriotism in order to develop a stable national political structure that would be able to defend the obvious economic interests of the emerging bourgeoisie. This development yielded particular internal oppositions, which were expressed in nationalist and regionalist political movements over the period of the two World Wars. The success of extreme-right parties can be understood in part against this historical background and I will develop this in the first section.

Since the Second World War, international globalising economic and political movements have deeply altered internal nation state power relations; new economic opportunities and problems emerged and impacted on the local and national situation. On the one hand, new wealth was created, but established national interests and political privileges came under attack, on the other. The particular way 'old' nationalism is ideologically reformatted against this global background gives us an insight into the reasons for the success of extreme-right, anti-democratic and often anti-universalistic movements in a country like Belgium; this is the focus of the second section. Finally, I will draw some conclusions on the relevance of a cultural anthropological perspective in the study of extreme-right movements and parties.

Former work (Pinxten 2002; Pinxten and Cornelis 2002; Pinxten, Cornelis and Rubinstein 2003) on these topics has led me to believe that a series of issues are lumped together in much of the current discussion of neo-nationalism.[1] Economic globalisation is an important factor in evaluating contemporary socio-political restructurings, but cultural and ideological traditions have equal impact. The grand theory of Castells (1996) offers a framework that integrates the globalising tendencies of the Information Age with the surge of identity movements and neo-nationalism in many regions of the world in a most interesting way. It allows us to describe how present economic globalisation and political regionalisation go hand in hand in spite of appearing to be opposites.

Adopting a single cause model (e.g., as in traditional Marxist as well as in neo-liberal theories) denies this contradictory complexity and only adds to misunderstanding through reductionism. To understand what is happening in terms of identity processes (parallel to Castells 1996, especially Part II), I propose to distinguish between the two aforementioned contexts here. Only by becoming conscious of at least both of these will we, as researchers, understand the nature of present-day neo-nationalism in Belgium. This will also help us explain why its success will not easily fade.

Belgium's National Political History

Belgium was founded as a constitutional monarchy in 1830 when the French-speaking bourgeoisie revolted against a generation of occupation by the Dutch state. As emerging capitalists in Europe they rejected Dutch authority with the support of English allies. Brussels and the Walloon part of the new country were booming industrial and financial areas, and the industries of coal and steel in the Walloon area were its main source of economic power. Meanwhile the Flemish/Dutch-speaking part was poor, rural and culturally backward. For almost a century most of the public domain (government, courts, educational institutions) was uniformly French-speaking, and Flemish labourers were exploited by the French-speaking upper class. Further examples of this discrimination are that during the First World War 80 percent of Belgian casualties were ordinary soldiers of Flemish origin and no Flemish was spoken in higher military ranks. These facts gained historical significance in the decades that followed; Flemish intellectuals started focusing on the linguistic divide as a political issue that caused social discrimination (De Wever 1998). The growing resistance to capitalism was canalised by emerging Flemish political groups (including some workers' unions) during the inter-war era in opposition to the French-speaking upper class.

Throughout the nineteenth century, financial power was located exclusively in Brussels and some Walloon cities. The new Belgian capitalist groups rapidly gained a place on the international scene of bankers and industrialists, thus making the young country the second state to be industrialised in Europe, after England. All economic power was in the hands of French-speakers, and the dominant Catholic Church as well as the Royal Court repeatedly expressed the opinion that the Flemish population was not capable of being properly educated, partly because of its language. At the same time the discrimination against soldiers during the First World War, which had been bitterly fought in the 'fair fields of Flanders', continued to inspire Flemish nationalism against the Belgian state. In response the French-speaking minority in power granted some of the Flemish majority's demands such as higher-grade schooling in Dutch and the right to be tried in one's own language.

When the Second World War broke out various groups collaborated with the German occupation. Some Flemish leaders saw the German occupants in the late 1930s as 'liberators' and perceived the Nazi regime as primarily anti-Belgian (i.e., French-speaking Belgian). Flemish nationalists persuaded thousands of young men to go and fight the communists at the eastern frontier of the Third Reich under German officers (De Wever 1998). Hence patriotic resistance during and after the war turned not only against German occupation but also against Flemish collaboration.

The Flemish collaborators justified their alliance with the Nazi regime by stressing that Flemish culture and language were more akin to their German than their French and Romanic counterparts. In some cases fascist ideology was the basis of political collaboration (for example, the Rex movement under Leon Degrelle in the Walloon provinces, or the Socialist Hendrik De Man's loyalty to the Belgian king, Leopold III), but, especially in Flanders, the so-called 'Germanic roots' of Flemish culture and language were frequently invoked as sufficient basis for collaboration with Hitler's regime at the beginning of the war. After the war hundreds were convicted as traitors; however, their trials did not mark the end of the process.

Several historical factors help to explain the present-day success of neo-nationalism. After the war, the Benelux and the nucleus of what was to become the EU were initiated, and in both cases Belgium was co-founder. Moreover, in less than fifteen years the Flemish part of the country became the new centre of financial and industrial power, thus usurping the old industries of the Walloon area. According to economistic ideological theories this growth should have brought about a shift in ideology – economic interests are expected to sweep away the 'false consciousness' of nationalism – however, the case of Belgium, and especially that of the Flemish subordinated majority, shows otherwise, and therefore it is especially interesting in the context of my attempt to understand how and why neo-nationalism proves successful in contemporary Europe.

In the 1950s a Flemish nationalist party, the People's Union (Volksunie), emerged with democratically elected parliamentarians, and in the 1970s they took part in governments and gradually moved towards social, liberal and moderately federalist positions. Belgium was gradually restructured into a federal state with considerable autonomy for the Flemish, Walloon and Brussels regions, and by 2000 Belgium had no fewer than six governments ruling the country.[2] In the 1980s all national parties split into regional ones: Flemish and French-speaking political parties with the same ideology went their separate ways, sometimes collaborating in the federal government, sometimes fighting their sister parties across the so-called linguistic divide in one of the regional governments. This meant that Flemish- and French-speaking identities were gradually adopted by each and every democratic party in the country. With the federalisation of Belgium the cultural and linguistic autonomy of the Flemish- and the French-speaking communities has been realised, and the format of Belgium as a unified state has weakened considerably. However, in line with my critique of economism, this is still not sufficient cause for the rise of neo-nationalism.

Notwithstanding the growing wealth of Flanders, and its increasing autonomy, a group of hardliners split from the People's Union in the 1970s. They established themselves as a separatist Flemish party: the Flemish Block (Vlaams Blok). After some moderate success, the Flemish Block aligned with the exclusivist, extreme-rightist ideology of the Front National under Le Pen in France and started focusing on the 'plague' of immigrants and refugees. This line won them massive support – winning an average of 14 percent in the election of 1999, and 33 percent of the vote in Antwerp in the elections of 2003. This populist party owes much of its success to the aftermath of globalisation, which leaves national governments ever more powerless in making economic and financial decisions. However, the extreme right does not focus on this economic logic but instead blames everything that goes wrong in the wealthy Belgian state on a cultural and religious 'Other', who is polluting the cultural heritage and hence threatening to destroy Belgium's self-made wealth. Populist references to cultural essence and the attack against immigrant and refugee groups have proved to be a successful strategy for winning support. My point is that the focus is on cultural identity and this proves to have great appeal. Whether or not these arguments hold water is not the issue here; rather, that this agenda can gain such massive support is what concerns me.

Another aspect of Belgian political history is equally important when considering extreme-right success. Since 1945 and right up to 1999 the Christian Democratic Party (CVP, now CD&V) has been in power at all levels of government almost without interruption. In terms of the present discussion, it is important to mention that it has systematically avoided dealing with questions of amnesty and coming to terms with Flemish collaboration with the German invader, especially during the Second World War. This is partly because the party backed King Leopold III after the war in a major national crisis over the monarchy. Even when it became clear that the king had actively worked towards a pact with Hitler and had refused to side with the Allies, the Christian Democratic Party, with greatest support in Flanders, backed the king and moved against the Walloon-dominated Socialist Party on the issue. The country slid into a pre-revolutionary state in 1950, with massive violence and uproar in the streets. Only the abdication of the king (in favour of his young son) finally eased the conflict. However, in the referendum that led to the abdication, the 'socialist' Walloon population had voted decisively for a republican system, while the 'Catholic' Flemish population had chosen to preserve the monarchy.

Yet another historical point should be introduced here: over the five decades since the end of the Second World War, during which Christian Democrats have been in power (most of the time in coalitions), governments in Belgium (and in many other parts of Europe) systematically ruled in favour of village life and against metropolitan life. The city was represented as a place of chaos (or even of evil) and of uncontrolled cultural life, and consequently it was not developed or supported in the long period of Christian Democrat government. In practice this meant that suburban and village life were heavily supported through development of transport infrastructure and cultural centres and leisure facilities, with at best a meagre subsidy for the larger cities in Belgium. Furthermore, a European perspective on the densely populated and urbanised region of Flanders as being caught between Amsterdam, Paris and Frankfurt was completely lacking.

Today we are witnessing an influx of (legal and illegal) refugees to the EU, who settle first and foremost in cities. The National Institute of Statistics gives us regular information on the number of people asking for political asylum: 2002 and 2003 saw some 20,000 asylum dossiers per year (Lesthaeghe 2003). However, given that asylum procedures were changed and made more cumbersome in the legislation of 1999–2003, the actual number of illegal immigrants and refugees would be more informative. Research at my centre[3] indicates that this number could easily be three or four times that of legal applications. This estimate is based, however tentatively, on a series of indicators. First, court officials responsible for abandoned refugee children report that nationwide 'a few thousand' such children are found each year (personal communication). Senior officials of the Justice Department tell of gangs who systematically recruit would-be refugees in the Balkans and former Soviet countries, making this illegal human traffic into a very lucrative business. Secondly, directors of city services in Ghent and Antwerp, which help official or so-called 'regularised' refugees, frequently have to turn away people in need who have no papers (personal communication). Meanwhile, NGOs can hardly cope with the demand for food, lodging and medical care. Regional governments (such as the Brussels and the Flemish governments) organise help via these NGOs in spite of the fact that the illegal refugees they help do not show up in official statistics and hence do not exist according to the federal government.

Another problem presents itself in the urban context: 'regularised' refugees helped by city services speak a great variety of languages. In a small city like Ghent (300,000 inhabitants) the refugee population speaks no fewer than 80 non-

European languages. In Antwerp (600,000 inhabitants) over 100, and in Brussels (1,600,000 inhabitants) over 175 non-European languages are spoken in the refugee population. New approaches and ingenious methods are needed to deal with this (e.g., Pinxten, Pyliser et al. 2001). Typically, of course, refugees are attracted to cities as work is more easily found there and they have a greater chance of meeting relatives or compatriots. Because cities had been negatively valued and insufficiently subsidised by governments for a long time, and given that since the 1970s the influx of newcomers has not been adequately managed (first Muslim immigrants, and, since the 1990s, refugees), the most severe problems with integration, exploitation and inter-cultural clash occur in these same cities. Hence populist extreme parties find their greatest appeal there as well.

A final historical factor is that the Flemish region has gained relative autonomy since the 1980s with the development of a Flemish parliament and government, media, cultural and scientific policies, and an independent Flemish education network, etc. As part of that process Christian Democrat politicians have very heavily emphasised Flemish culture and Flemish tradition. The net result has been the development of a pettiness and short-sightedness in culture and politics that feeds subliminally on anxiety about foreigners and anything from outside. For example, the media and politicians systematically focused on Flemish rather than Belgian or foreign stories and heroes. A series of 'famous' people from Flemish music and television became household names, and a small group of politicians quickly gained power by appearing on the same chat and quiz shows as them. In the two decades since the 1980s, Flemish identity was thus systematically promoted, and as a result the younger generation today takes the primacy of this identity for granted.

Recent studies (Elchardus et al. 2002) have shown convincingly that this narrow focus in media and cultural policy has a direct impact on the success of the Flemish Block. Individuals and groups cut off from former social networks and structures (which collapsed or dissipated) increasingly relate to Belgium and the wider world through the media, which presents them with a narrow 'typically Flemish' source of political, moral and aesthetic values. Elchardus and his group of sociologists found that in the poorer and less educated sections of the population, this leads to heightened feelings of insecurity, isolation and even anxiety, which encourages people to vote for anti-foreigner, anti-democratic Flemish Block candidates (Elchardus et al. 2002).

With the growth of globalisation and its threat to job security, each and every political party promotes the newly created Flemish identity as a safe haven. In past decades the American federalist model was often used as a reference point, but the preference shown in the current discourse of democratic parties (at the time of writing in 2003) for the devolution of foreign policy and responsibility for health and social security to the regional rather than federal level goes beyond that: it comes close to separatism and implies the implosion of the Belgian state in a series of constitutional reforms. Flemish independence, however, was a defining feature of the Flemish Block programme from the outset. So, exactly as some Flemish

Block representatives emphasise time and again, the democratic parties have, over the years, taken up at least several Flemish Block causes. At the same time the democratic parties have not adequately coped with the effects of globalisation or with the shift towards multiculturalism.

Brussels itself is an important aspect of the Belgian historical context under discussion here. The power of 'old capital' was in the hands of the French-speaking bourgeoisie throughout the nineteenth and twentieth centuries, and their political dominance in that city posed a problem. After the Second World War the harbours and new industrial areas of Flanders (Antwerp, Courtrai) flourished and rapidly outgrew the industrial power of the Walloon area and Brussels. Nevertheless, financiers, captains of industry and local Brussels politicians continued to play the card of 'French-speaking descent', to the humiliation of the new industrial management.[4] A political deal was forged that reserved a threshold power in Brussels for Flemish political representatives, thus making the consent of this powerful minority necessary in several areas of federal decision making. In this context the People's Union had an important role for a long time, as it represented a crucial percentage of Flemish votes for Brussels, and hence the Belgian political equilibrium.

In 2002, however, the People's Union split. One group emerged to form a right-wing democratic party called the New Flemish Alliance (Nieuwe Vlaamse Alliantie, NFA), and a socialist-liberal group went separately under the name of Spirit. Typically, NFA finds support in Flemish villages – where Flemish Block now sees it as a real threat to its local power – because it usually focuses on Flemish identity and neo-conservatism (against drug use, against permissiveness, and for strengthening family ties). However, at the national level the party had only one person elected in the 2003 elections (instead of the expected four or five). Spirit has an urban focus and its support is concentrated in the few larger cities of Flanders and in Brussels. It presents a young and progressive Flemish image, which should be appealing to young voters who have grown up with a Flemish identity and belong to the middle class. In the 2003 federal elections it formed a loose coalition with the Social Democrats and won a landslide victory. The Green Party was decimated in the same elections.

Now, for the first time, there is a new and curious political landscape in Belgium, which plays out the cultural identity issue in a fresh way. The two dominant government parties are centrist and do not have a clear profile in terms of cultural identity: the Flemish Liberal Democrats (Vlaamse Liberalen en Demokraten, a conservative, non-confessional party led by the Prime Minister) and the Walloon Socialist Party (Parti Socialiste, a workers' party with a leftist past). In addition there is the Flemish centre-left coalition 'Socialist Party–Spirit' (made up of the Flemish Socialists and the progressive Flemish identity proponents) and the Brussels–Walloon centre-right Reformative Movement (Mouvement Réformateur, with an anti-Flemish, and definitely pro-French-speaking tendency). The last two are clearly regional parties with local power primarily in the cities, while the first two are instead supporters of the state and are established in rural areas. The extreme right-wing and anti-democratic Flemish Block did not win any government positions.

Local Belgian, Flemish and Walloon identities alone do not explain the rise of neo-nationalism at the end of the twentieth century in Belgium, but local history informs our discussion since it offers recognisable labels and categories for the electorate. The long-term humiliation of the Flemish is not per se responsible for the growth of particularism and the support for extreme-right politics, but it seems to be used and manipulated with great success by populist leaders in this particular region of Europe.

Wider Forces of Economic and Political Globalisation

It is widely accepted that Europe (in the form of the European Union) is one of the largest democratic 'states' in the world, however, evidence from some socio-cultural areas could be seen to show otherwise (e.g., De Gaay-Fortman 2002; Maier 2002). First, the anti-democratic, neo-communitarian political parties, which reject the European Declaration of Human Rights (Austria, Flanders, Denmark, Norway, northern Italy and Germany[5] all have strong extreme-right movements now), are having increasing success with voters. Secondly, there are no policies to deal with immigrants and their rights (or with the waves of refugees coming into the EU), which are agreed upon by all states of the EU and guarantee a systemic respect for human rights. The various ways of dealing with newcomers in different countries allow substantial leeway for malignant groups who smuggle refugees. Not all members of the EU respect the Schengen Agreement, and the agreement itself may not be optimal in terms of human rights. Finally, there are growing numbers of neo-racist movements in the EU and no adequate way to combat them at the level of democratic political parties, states or European institutions. Some analysts conclude that the policies of EU states are such that they institutionalise forms of discrimination and racism rather than combat them (Verlot 2002).

The lack of a European identity is problematic and the lack of clarity in any European concept of citizenship, even on a minimal European societal and political basis, causes much confusion in the minds of citizens. What does European identity amount to, beyond a unified market? What is the link with Enlightenment values? What are the benefits of the respect for and the institutionalisation of diversity (most visible in the safeguarding of all official languages in the EU enterprise)? Does the citizen know and appreciate the particular form of institutionalised solidarity (through a neutral, community-controlled system of health and social security, in contrast with, for example, the U.S. system) as a typical European asset?

It is not that a European 'nationalism' of some sort should substitute waning nation-state ideologies; it is not clear how such an ideology should be developed, let alone implemented. Moreover, any such nationalism could become a new, exclusive or 'fortress' ideology causing violent conflicts with other states, much like its predecessors did throughout the past two centuries. What I mean by 'European identity' is a minimal political project, recognisable for and endorsed in daily practice by every citizen.

Such a minimal political project could be based on Europe's current attempt to define citizenship within the context of its diverse reality, which combines the three principles of freedom, equality and solidarity with a vow to respect diversity. Obviously, this potentially tension-ridden combination in one integrated political structure is far from self-evident. Furthermore, it is currently a matter of principles and values rather than being part of community practice and it should be taught and practised in schools throughout the European Union in order for it to become viable and successfully adopted by citizens. A lack of clarity or even knowledge of this EU project endangers the EU itself. Furthermore, it produces insecurity among the increasing number of newcomers in EU countries about their rights and obligations, and about realistic expectations vis-à-vis European institutions. Finally, this lack of clarity allows the extremist, anti-European, racist and anti-democratic political parties to proliferate and (to some extent) dictate the public discussion about European identity and otherness.

Nation states in Europe emerge from two or three hundred years of nationalism and patriotism. Institutions such as the educational system, law enforcement and the army but also public discourse and the cultural atmosphere have built up a strong tradition of national identity. This has led to the strengthening of economic life within national boundaries, as I illustrated in the previous section for the case of Belgium. However, it has also brought about wars with surrounding nations, several of which have been particularly bloody. Lives have been given for the nation. The Second World War may have ended the line of great wars between European nation states, but local wars at the borders of the European construct keep the nationalistic fires burning (former Yugoslavia, Greece and Turkey).

In the EU space a new identity and new vehicles of belonging have to be developed; meanwhile national frames of reference do not easily disappear from the educational system or the minds of citizens. The narratives in ritual and cultural events might be good test cases in this context (for example, in sport events or scandals such as that surrounding BSE). The globalising economic world leaves governments powerless and a large proportion of citizenry with a feeling of unease; the diminishing scale of national economic power and independence corresponds less and less to the scope and promises of nationalistic ideology. Belgium has seen some 'symbolic' cases over recent decades: under European market pressure the Walloon coal and steel industries have been closed down by the national government; only three years ago the national airline, Sabena, was taken over and bled to death by an international financial group, in the process of which ministers of the federal Belgian government were deceived under the very noses of the national press.

At the same time, the substitution of nation-state ideology by a significant European identity is not happening: the EU is more a bore (more rules, more bureaucracy) than a blessing. At the highest level a bureaucratic super-state rules, often against national interests (or so it is felt), and at the lowest level the citizen and his or her local politician are becoming less powerful. There is a European Parliament now, but the Commission and the Council of Ministers are not really democratically accountable. The numerous cases of elected members of the European Parliament who resign in order to take up a national governmental mandate indicate that European parliamentary work is not serious, or at least does not confer real power. There is a deficit in democracy from the point of view of the citizen, who gradually comes to see the EU as the 'Other'.

Furthermore, refugees and new immigrants are flocking to the EU because of its manifest economic prosperity. Add to this the wars and other conflicts in the countries of origin of refugees and it is to be expected that newcomers will continue to find their way into EU space. However, the political and cultural frameworks to deal with diversity in cultures, religions and lifestyles from outside the European sphere are lacking; this has resulted in national programmes for dealing with refugees and immigrants (somewhat uniform within Schengen countries) with quite different requirements and sanctions in different member states of the EU. In addition, countries confront each other over these issues (e.g., the U.K. fining Belgium or France when illegal immigrants are found, for example, amongst cargo) and produce policies that are only in the national interest (e.g., Germany reducing the right to political asylum and at the same time searching for skilled immigrants from Asia specialised in high tech). The more or less concerted 'hunt' for illegal immigrants and refugees is a high priority for national governments throughout Europe today, while a genuine and uniform EU policy does not exist. Extreme-right parties have focused almost exclusively on this situation and hence directed public discourse to accept versions of the 'fortress Europe' ideology. Refugees are treated at worst as potential criminals or enemies, at best as victims. In Germany a recent national election focused heavily on the immigration issue, and in Belgium the growing success of Flemish Block (climbing from 3 percent to 15 percent in just twenty years) coincides with its almost exclusive focus on campaigning against foreigners. Over the same period the campaign for integration instead of assimilation has dwindled and the black market in cheap labour by, often illegal, refugees has spread in all cities.

Finally, extreme-right parties have been developing a Europe-wide policy during the 1990s, emanating from the French study centre GRECE (see Gerald Gaillard-Starzmann's contribution in this volume for the origins of GRECE) in order to redefine the old communitarian ideology of 'our people first' (picking up basic elements of Italian Fascism of the 1930s such as solidarism and a culture-as-race discourse, etc.; Pinxten, Verstraete and Longman 2004; Verstraete and Pinxten 2001). Different trends can be seen within this development (from anti-universalism to neo-paganism, for example), but the one that feeds on anxiety about globalisation and blames all evil effects on 'foreigners to our culture' has resulted in the greatest success in terms of power and election results. Strikingly, in some smaller regional (not national) areas of Europe this seems to develop in a particular way: Carinthia (in Austria), the north of Italy, Flanders and the prosperous regions of Denmark, Norway, Sweden and so on show a massive vote for extremist parties.

Conclusion

A sensible interpretation of the Belgian case should take into account a number of economic, political and cultural parameters. Against the European economic and political background sketched above I pitch the particular Belgian features discussed in the first section. The result is a complex picture with the following basic elements. Flanders is (within Belgium, and even more so within the EU) a small region with a history of relative poverty and political insignificance during the nation-state era. It has grown to local and international economic prominence over the past few decades, more or less despite the Belgian state (or so it is felt and expressed in political discourse). Flanders is not the heart of, and does not even belong to, a strong and centralised nation state; rather, it is part of an artificial construct that is in conflict with the linguistic, cultural and religious identity markers of the Flemish citizen. The younger Flemish generation overwhelmingly opts for American or Flemish cultural heroes and ignores the icons of the French-speaking half of the country. Over recent decades the newly found affluence in the Flemish part of the country has contrasted sharply with the poverty and deterioration in the Walloon cities (Liege is called 'Palermo at the Meuse', and Charleroi is considered the centre of car theft and child abuse). The media and political parties in Flanders have been spreading the news for years now that all that is good is the product of Flemish industriousness and the Flemish mental make-up. Consequently captains of industry and cultural heroes have been promoted as examples of genuine Flemish stock, thus disregarding the role of international economic powers in the development of harbours or industries. This all leads to a petty mentality in the context of new-found prosperity.

Against the globalising backdrop and the historical perspective sketched above I now want to evaluate the rise of neo-nationalism in Flanders. Looked at in this multi-perspectival way it is indeed a new phenomenon and one that fits well with an ideology of refusal. It refuses the increasingly urbanised world of Flanders, while continuing to preach and actually deploy modernity at a village level; the slogan of one of the winning groups in the election of 2003 in Belgium was, 'we want to keep it cosy in the main street of the village' (the chair of the Socialist Party–Spirit coalition announced this slogan in the May 2003 election). A more pronounced denial of modernity and European internationalism is hard to imagine: the reference to a larger context is excluded and the reduction of human interests to short-term private privileges is striking. Knowing that this was the slogan of a 'democratic' party that won by a landslide and knowing that in the same elections the anti-democratic Flemish Block had greater success than ever before stresses the relevance of cultural or so-called 'soft' parameters in the struggle for power. The very terminology employed by democratic politicians in this campaign indicates that politics is presented to the citizen as a matter of selfishness, pettiness and private interests rather than a vision of openness to the world and diversity. My conclusion is that the general political climate of Belgium is one of turning inward, of minding one's own business. It remains to be seen whether democracy will survive as a form of political practice in the next generation.

Suggestions for the Future

It is important to understand how culture is playing a role in the rise of the extreme right in Belgium. Anthropologists have been speaking about 'cultural fundamentalism' (Stolcke created this concept in 1996, see also Hannerz 1996) in describing the far right in Europe. The point is well taken: the notion of race is substituted by that of culture, yielding an exclusivist ideological stance on both national and European political formations (Pinxten, Verstraete and Longman 2004).

My suggestion is that anthropologists should address the cultural topics in this political configuration. They should analyse the essentialist notion of culture that is so characteristically advocated by the neo-communitarian extreme right and the equally nonsensical use of the cultural difference of people from a non-European background. This kind of discourse suggests that these people can best be treated as if they were a different (biological) species. Furthermore, anthropologists can inform policy makers and the lay public about the intricacies of inter-cultural communication and interaction, and the learning processes required to become knowledgeable and well versed in inter-cultural negotiation strategies. We have some competence in these matters at the level of individuals and groups (unions, schools and so on, Pinxten and Cornelis 2002), but we need more research to determine what the successful mechanisms are at community levels.

Notes

1. The distinction between neo-nationalism and neo-communitarianism is not very clear in the Belgian context. In general, the democratic parties advocate a moderate communitarian position without a manifest nationalism. They did not strive to split Belgium up into two nations, for example, but they did want each community to be fully autonomous and therefore free to develop its own policy for culture and education. The extreme rightists did and do link neo-communitarianism and neo-nationalism and work from a very explicit nationalistic perspective to flesh out their communitarian ideology.
2. The loss of the colonies did not have a documented effect on Belgian politics. The study by Johannes Fabian (1987) of the perception of Flemish-Walloon oppositions in the colonies gives us a hint of the relevance of colonialism, but till this day no English source on the impact of decolonisation on Belgian politics is available.

3. The Center for Intercultural Communication and Interaction, University of Ghent, Belgium: reports for the Flemish Government on refugees, trajectory building for coping with refugees, and publications on racism in Europe (Evens Foundation 2002).
4. Brussels' political identity is changing in its current wider context; both as the centre of the EU and as the European headquarters of NATO it has an important role that goes way beyond local politics.
5. Germany has no extreme-right political party of any importance today, but it does have a strong neo-Nazi scene operating outside of the parliamentary system.

Bibliography

Castells, M. 1996. *The Information Age: Economy, Society and Culture*, 3 vols. Oxford: Blackwell.

De Gaay-Fortman, B. 2002. 'Racism and Poverty in a Human Rights Perspective', in Evens Foundation eds *Europe's New Racism? Causes, Manifestations and Solutions*. Oxford: Berghahn, pp. 71–84.

De Wever, B. 1998. *Greep naar de Macht*. Tielt: Lannoo.

Elchardus M., Huyse, L. and Hooghe, M. 2002. *Het maatschappelijk Middenveld*. Brussels: VUB Press.

Evens Foundation. eds. 2002. *Europe's New Racism? Causes, Manifestations and Solutions*. Oxford: Berghahn.

Fabian, J. 1987. *Language and Colonial Power*. Berkeley: University of California Press.

Hannerz, U. 1996. *Transnational Connections*. London: Routledge.

Lesthaeghe, R. 2003. *Vluchtelingen in België. Een demografische studie*. Brussels: Department of Demography VUB Reports.

Maier, R. 2002. 'Does a Supranational Europe Stimulate and/or Combat Racism?', in Evens Foundation eds *Europe's New Racism? Causes, Manifestations and Solutions*. Oxford: Berghahn, pp. 85–104.

Pinxten, R. 2002. 'Identité, diversité et nécessité d'un projet social commun', in *Une Europe de la Création*. Hannut: Edition Luce Wilquin, pp. 207–26.

Pinxten, R. and Cornelis, M. 2002. 'What Interculturalism Could be a Solution to Racism?' in Evens Foundation eds *Europe's New Racism? Causes, Manifestations and Solutions*. Oxford: Berghahn, pp. 211–32.

Pinxten, R., Cornelis, M. and Rubinstein, R.A. 2003. 'European Identity: Diversity in Union', in K. Bybee et al. eds *Constructing Civic Virtues*. Syracuse University: Campbell Public Affairs Institute, pp. 115–33.

Pinxten, R., Pyliser, C. et al. 2001. *Vluchtelingen in Vlaanderen, een overzicht*. Ghent: CiCi report.

Pinxten, R., Verstraete, G. and Longman, C. eds. 2003. *Culture and Politics*. Oxford: Berghahn.

Stolcke, V. 1996. 'Claiming Culture Again', *Current Anthropology* 37: 1–36.

Verlot, M. 2002. 'Understanding Institutional Racism', in Evens Foundation eds *Europe's New Racism? Causes, Manifestations and Solutions*. Oxford: Berghahn, pp. 27–42.

Verstraete, G. and Pinxten, R. 2001. 'Culturele eigenheid als proces', in L. Walckiers ed. *Noord-Zuid Cahier*. Brussels: NCOS Publisher, pp. 9–16.

Chapter 7

'Being the Native's Friend Does Not Make You the Foreigner's Enemy!'

Neo-nationalism, the Freedom Party and Jörg Haider in Austria

Thomas Fillitz

The 1990s were successful years for the Freedom Party and Jörg Haider, and the decade reached its momentous climax when the party won around 27 percent of the vote at the federal elections of 1999.[1] As a result it became Europe's largest right-wing populist party, as well as the first to be part of a federal government. Haider was not only the party's chairman, but also its political motor and the nexus of all its political claims and activities. Youth-oriented and dynamic, anti-establishment, a defender of tradition, with allusions to the Nazi times, he also claims to represent the 'ordinary man' with his aggressive, anti-immigrant rhetoric, and a preference for economic deregulation (see Gingrich 2002).

Introduction

When discussing the success of the Freedom Party, several factors have to be taken into account. The first concerns the concept of an Austrian patriotism and an enduring two-party system characterised by a politics of consent that goes back to Austria's state-centred nation building after the Second World War. This Austrian patriotism was consciously opposed to a pan-Germanism, and was shared by the three major parties of the time: the Christian Democrat Party (ÖVP), the Socialist Party (SPÖ) and the Communist Party (KPÖ). Though minorities had to be recognised in the State Treaty of 1955, monoculturalism was nevertheless at the core of that patriotism (Bauböck 2002: 236). The peculiarities of the party system and electoral behaviour are also relevant within this context. Until 1983 political power was concentrated between two major parties: the Christian Democrat Party and the Social Democrat Party. The Freedom Party (FPÖ), founded in 1956, would not gain political power for the first time until between 1983 and 1986 when it was a junior partner in a coalition government with the Social Democrat Party. This mainly two-party system began to change after the elections of 1986 when the Freedom Party succeeded in doubling its share of the vote to 10 percent, and the Green Party (then Grüne Alternative Liste) entered the Federal Parliament with a little less than 5 percent (Pelinka 1994: 15). The most important characteristics of that pre-1983 political system were consent and cooperation rather than conflict, dissent and competition. As Pelinka mentions, this political landscape was traditionally characterised by long periods of coalition government (ibid.). This was combined with an institution known as 'social partnership', which was made up of the Austrian Trade Union (Österreichischer Gewerkschaftsbund), the Chamber of Commerce, the Chamber of Workers, as well as the Association of Industrialists.[2] In addition, Austrian society was divided into respective Christian Democrat and Social Democrat fields of influence.

A second factor is Austria's immigration and foreign policy. Beginning in 1956 with an influx of Hungarian refugees and characterised by openness, in the 1990s the Freedom Party increasingly dictated the country's immigration policies, which shifted towards reluctance to help. Regarding the European Union, between 1989 and 1990 the Freedom Party switched from having a determined pro-EU position to being an anti-EU party – a change reflected in the transfer from pan-Germanism to Austrian-ness. At the same time the Christian Democrat and Social Democrat Parties started contesting the leading role as 'the European party' in Austria. Key EU events were the official application for membership in 1989, the so-called 'Letter to Brussels' by the SPÖ-ÖVP government, the 1994 federal plebiscite about Austria's integration into the European Union (65 percent yes; 34 percent no), and the 1996 elections to the European Parliament, in which the Freedom Party won 28 percent of the vote.

Finally, in reflecting on the success of the Freedom Party, the role of Haider himself is crucial. His rise to the position of chairman of the party in 1986 was made possible by the massive support of pan-German delegates as against the more liberal faction that had supported the previous chairman Norbert Steger. As a result of this change, the then chancellor, Franz Vranitzky (SPÖ), dissolved the coalition with the Freedom Party in the same year. In the early 1990s Haider was elected Governor of Carinthia, one of the nine regions of Austria, for the first time; however, in 1992 he had to resign because of one of his innumerable, positive references to the Nazi era – however, he remained chairman of the party. Haider was elected Governor of Carinthia for a second time in April 1999.

From 1996 onwards, having significantly improved its share of the vote, the Freedom Party became one of the three major political parties in Austria. After secret negotiations between Haider and leading Christian Democrat politicians, the Freedom Party joined with the Christian Democrat Party to form the Federal Government on 4 February 2000. By the end of that same month, Haider surrendered the position of Party Chairman to the then vice-chancellor Susanne Riess-Passer. Nevertheless, in September 2002 Haider attacked the government and specifically Freedom Party government members in such a way that the coalition government collapsed, and federal elections were called. Together with close supporters he had attempted to force them to change political decisions, for example to make tax reductions in place of funding a large-scale national assistance programme for those afflicted by a dramatic flood in the north-east of the country, or to use their veto against the integration of the Czech Republic into the European Union.

The main thesis of this contribution is that in spite of its xenophobic rhetoric, the Freedom Party actually draws heavily on liberal-democratic ideas. Constructions of the self and others by means of shifting contexts appear to be a major strategy of the party. At first we will focus on ideas about foreigners and immigrants, which experienced a radicalisation between 1989 and 1993. I suggest that these ideas contributed to stricter immigration regulations, which were actually implemented by Social Democrat Ministers for Interior Affairs up to 2000, and thereafter by a Christian Democrat minister. Although such radical, xenophobic constructions of foreigners and immigrants constitute a defining feature of the Freedom Party, other liberal-democratic claims form another, which actually seems highly valued by voters: an opposition to the politics of consent, which for decades was exemplified by the other two major parties, and the enhancement of basic democratic decision making.

The construction of the self will be analysed in the context of how Haider and the Freedom Party perceive the relationship between the various social groups considered to constitute the Austrian population. The shift from pan-German identity towards Austrian-ness continues to play a role in self-ascriptive connections to German-speaking minority groups outside the state's territory. This leads us to an examination of the Freedom Party's narrative on culture as fundamental to the relationship between social groups. The importance that the party attaches to culture is evident from the fact that Haider, as Governor of Carinthia, took on the agendas of culture and art. Culture, furthermore, is central to the Freedom Party's ideas about minority groups. One could be forgiven for expecting them to have a homogeneous, bounded concept of culture with a strong emphasis on tradition, but their concept actually operates on various levels, whether that of a minority group, a region, the Austrian state or larger units, such as the European Union, or the pan-German vision under consideration. These continuous shifts of contextualisation constitute one of the fundamental features of the party's discourse on culture, and of the relationships between the various minority groups.

The Politics of Immigration: Redefining Others

In order to contextualise the actions and words of political actors after 1990, it seems appropriate to mention the large migration movements to and through Austria during the Second Republic (1945 to the present). In 1956, Hungarians fled the Soviet invasion and by 1957, 180,288 had reached Austria. Though all were granted asylum, only about 10 percent stayed in the country (Höllinger 1999: 75). Next were the Czechs in 1968, who came when Soviet tanks brought the Dubcek government to an abrupt end. By 1970, there were 12,000 Czechs in Austria and 162,000 had fled via Austria to other destinations. The third major refugee movement was that of the Poles in 1980 and 1981. Approximately 130,000 came to Austria; of those, 33,000 applied for asylum and it was granted in the vast majority of cases (ibid.: 77). In contrast to this apparent openness or humanitarianism Höllinger points out that the readiness of the local population to accept refugees was dependent on how long the migrants appeared to be planning to stay: if too long, rumours began to emerge about the costs of such humanitarian gestures.

The readiness to give humanitarian assistance began to change in 1990 when a wave of Romanian immigrants was greeted with openly expressed aversion. This change in public opinion was, arguably, connected to government strategies. Out of 12,199 applications for asylum, only 303 were successful. The situation further deteriorated when in 1991 and 1992 a group of 80,000 Croats and Bosnians fled the war in Yugoslavia to Austria. At the outset there was widespread public approval for granting asylum, but the longer the refugees stayed the more outspokenly negative public opinion became. In this specific case Höllinger's aforementioned criterion of time was aggravated by another factor: politicians of all parties, as well as civil servants, contributed to the growing negativity by speaking publicly of the exhaustion of resources (ibid.: 79).

Bauböck (2002: 248) attributes this change in the politics of immigration to two further factors. First, whereas the Federal Ministry of Social Affairs and the social partnership, i.e., social institutions, managed immigration in the 1970s and 1980s, responsibility for these matters was later transferred to the Federal Ministry of Interior Affairs and thus came under the control of the state's executive power, the police. Secondly, an internal as well as an external security discourse emerged at the time of the breakdown of the Eastern European socialist regimes. Intensifying border controls was believed to impede illegal immigration from the east. This question was also relevant to Austria's debate about its membership of the European Union at that time. The newly created accord of Schengen (1990), regulating free mobility within the European Union, required intensified control at the external borders, i.e., including Austria's borders with Eastern European countries.

The idea of immigrants as being like humanitarian refugees, and welcomed only temporarily, or as asylum seekers, and therefore as potential abusers of the system, was adopted by the Christian Democrat, the Social Democrat and the Freedom

Parties alike. All three exaggerated the numbers of immigrants in order to promote the idea that Austria's capacity to receive new immigrants had been exhausted. Sometimes administrative mistakes, such as placing large immigrant groups in small villages, would further feed the aversion of the local population (Höllinger 1999: 80). The ruling Social Democrats and Christian Democrats condemned only the xenophobic tones of the Freedom Party, meanwhile enacting anti-immigration laws and going along with anti-immigrant rhetoric (Bauböck 2002: 248).

In 1991 and 1992 the ruling coalition of Social Democrats and Christian Democrats passed new laws relating to immigrants and the reuniting of immigrant families. These were more restrictive and aimed to minimise abuses common under the existing system (Höllinger 1999: 123). Both the Social Democrat Minister for Interior Affairs, Franz Löschnak, as well as leading Christian Democrat politicians, praised the positive effects of the law as the number of asylum applications, as well as the number of asylum approvals, went down. If in 1991, under the old law, there were 27,306 applications, there were only 4,744 in 1993 under the new law. Whilst 2,469 applications were approved in 1991, only 1,193 were successful in 1993 and the number continued to decrease over the next four years (Höllinger 1999: 83, data published by the Federal Ministry of Interior Affairs). However, Höllinger suggests that it was not primarily the new law that was responsible for such drastic reductions, but rather the accompanying measures, such as deportation and direct rejection at the border (ibid.).

In parliament the Freedom Party had voted with the government for the new law. However, shortly afterwards Haider called for reforms. On 21 October 1992, Haider gave the government an ultimatum, and issued twelve demands. In the event that these demands were not met, Haider threatened to call a referendum on closing Austria to immigration. This referendum, 'Austria First' (1993), was the momentous climax of a continuous radicalisation of the Freedom Party's position on foreigners, and particularly immigrants, during Haider's chairmanship. Two declarations, the 'Lorenzener Declaration' and the 'Resolution on Foreigners', made in October 1989 by the regional Freedom Party of Burgenland, may be taken as the starting point. The first identified Austrians with a 'pan-German culture area' (*Deutsches Volkstum und Kulturraum*), which was based on a strictly essentialist concept defining the group (*Volk*) by descent and territory. The second declaration differentiated between three types of foreigners: German minorities outside the German nationalist and culture area, European foreigners, and non-European foreigners (Gärtner 2002: 21).

On 18 December 1989 the Freedom Party had issued another declaration on what they perceived to be the foreigner problem. It listed eight demands including compulsory visas for all foreigners on Austrian soil, 'no sell out of the rights of citizens', no fast track to naturalisation, the adoption of a seasonal worker system,[3] reform of compulsory school education,[4] and the creation of an Eastern Europe Academy in order to increase opportunities and improve quality of life within Eastern European countries themselves (Höllinger 1999: 122). The aim was a double strategy of demarcation. First, potential immigrants should be kept out of Austria, either by directly contributing to social transformation within their countries of origin, or by discouraging them from thinking of Austria as a possible destination. The second strategy reinforced the first and concerned people classified by the party as foreigners already living within the boundaries of Austria. Control of this group would be enhanced by means of visas and restrictions on their citizenship; consequently, monoculturalism (along with monolingualism) would be secured.

This double strategy differentiated all people (inside and outside Austria) into three groups. Two 'pure' groups are made up respectively of Austrians and people living in their countries of origin. These two groups are not only spatially but also hierarchically distinct. The latter group is made up of potential migrants, whereas the former is not and this group is therefore structurally and morally positioned to give humanitarian assistance. The third group is made up of foreigners already living in Austria and is differentiated by being placed in an area of moral danger. Within the logic of this demarcation strategy the group's first transgression was to migrate to Austria; once in the country, it is on the threshold of a second transgression, i.e., undermining the so-called 'culture area' of the local, essentialised population. Access to the rights conferred on citizens is therefore made more complicated. For example, the recommended reforms of the education system would result in structurally regulated and restricted access to this social sphere. Multicultural experience and competence are thus given a negative cultural value.

The radicalisation is obvious if one compares the eight points published in 1989 with the newly formulated twelve points of 1992.[5] First, Haider suggested that the slogan 'Austria is not a country of immigration' be included as an article within the constitution; secondly, that all citizens from Eastern European countries should be viewed as potential transgressors. Consequently, it was proposed that the Eastern Europe Academy should no longer work to improve quality of life in the respective countries (as in 1989), but it should instead aim to hinder migration movements. Moreover, he called for improved permanent border protection to be enforced by customs and police rather than the army. Thirdly, Haider suggested that all foreigners living in Austria should be treated as potential criminals, e.g., identity cards should be compulsory, dedicated police forces should be properly staffed and equipped, and deportation should be made easier.

This new twelve-point strategy put all foreigners into one category and emphasised the distance that must be safeguarded for the sake of those living in their country of origin. Foreigners are potential migrants and as such are intrinsically dangerous to the Austrian community. If in 1989 the aim was to restrict access to citizenship for foreigners living in Austria, now the intention was to get them out of federal territory. Potential criminalisation, and exclusion from local social networks and education would serve as means to this end. In line with this strategy, in 1995 Haider created a new slogan: 'the right of natives to *Heimat* is more important than the right of immigrants to family life' (Bailer-Galanda and

Neugebauer 1997: 180).[6] With this slogan Haider addressed the issue of the reunification of immigrants with their spouses and children still living in their country of origin, and it suggested that this kind of immigration should be stopped. In the same year, to underline this, he demanded that Austria leave the European Convention on Human Rights on the grounds that it was too liberal in its regulations concerning the reunification of families (Höllinger 1999: 126).

From 1997 onwards immigration was to be further impeded by the major parties in government (SPÖ and ÖVP). Leading politicians spoke of the new law as an 'integration package' and as such the question was no longer whether or not foreigners could migrate to Austria, but rather how to handle those who had already settled in the country (Höllinger 1999: 83; Huber 1997). Again, Haider fuelled the debate, this time by responding to these new regulations with a promise to reduce the number of foreigners employed in Austria. He proposed that within two years a reduction of one third would be achieved: first, by expelling unemployed immigrants or those having entered Austria in the last three years; second by reducing the number of work permits issued; and third by no longer renewing expired work permits (Höllinger 1999: 127).

The current situation in Austria is that there is a new law, and a so-called 'integration package' drawn up by the coalition between the Freedom Party and the Christian Democrat Party in 2002. The aim is for immigration of any kind to be brought to a halt, and for regulations enforcing assimilation of residents from foreign countries to be supported by various sanctions, including deportation. During the election campaign of 2002 the Christian Democrat Minister for Interior Affairs, Ernst Strasser, created new restrictive regulations concerning asylum applicants and their return to their countries of origin. Haider's response, as Governor of Carinthia, was to call for a shorter asylum procedure, a drastic reduction in the number of residents' permits issued on humanitarian grounds, and no possibility of appeal at the administrative tribunal for applicants (*Der Standard* 2002: 10).

The Politics of Referendums: Who Votes for the Freedom Party and Why?

The skirmishes about immigration policies outlined above may give the impression that the immigration question has, since the late 1980s, been the defining issue of the Freedom Party. Furthermore, election campaigns in the 1990s underlined the importance of the issue for the Freedom Party: whether federal or regional, they were highly focused on representations of foreigners as abusers of the humanitarian immigration system, or as potential criminals, and aggressive, xenophobic and even racist overtones in advertisements and the public speeches of party officials were common.

However, restricting an analysis of the success of the Freedom Party to the topic of xenophobia/racism would be a mistake. In the 1990s there was a huge and rising dissatisfaction within the Austrian population with the old two-party system, and, moreover, a politics of nepotism in which important jobs were attributed less according to suitability and more according to party affiliation. Haider's Freedom Party presented itself instead as dynamic, youth-oriented and competitive.

After he became chairman, Haider encouraged more direct democratic participation by the population, and from among the three constitutional possibilities he chose the institution of the referendum (*Volksbegehren*) as his primary means. Anybody can initiate a referendum either with around 8,000 supporting signatures from citizens, or with the support of at least eight parliamentary deputies, or four deputies from three regional parliaments. A referendum lasts for a week and if more than 100,000 signatures are obtained

Table 1: *The nine most popular referendums 1964–2002 (total of 29 referendums)*

Issue	Supported by	Year	No. of Signatures	Ranking
Against the construction of a conference centre in Vienna	All ÖVP deputies of all regional parliaments	1982	1,361,562	1
Against genetic engineering in agriculture	8 Green Party deputies	1997	1,225,790	2
Anti-Temelín, EU veto	FPÖ 16,562 supporting signatures	2002	914,973	3
Anti-abortion	Action for Human Life 762,664 supporting signatures	1975	895,665	4
Regulation of working hours (40-hour week)	74 SPÖ deputies	1969	889,659	5
Independent broadcasting law	34,841 supporting signatures	1964	832,353	6
Social welfare state in the constitution	38,212 supporting signatures	2002	717,102	7
Acknowledging women's rights	23 deputies of SPÖ and Green Party	1997	664,665	8
Against buying new tactical aircraft	18,325 supporting signatures	2002	624,807	9

Sources: Bundesministerium für Inneres, *Volksbegehren,* Homepage of the Federal Ministry of Interior Affairs, April 2003.

parliament has to address the topic, though it is not compulsory for it to act. Twenty-nine of these were called in the period up to October 2002.[7]

The referendums called by the Freedom Party relate to key issues for them (see Table 2). 'Austria First' and the anti-privileges vote deal respectively with the anti-foreigner issue and abuses of power by the two mainstream parties; the vote about keeping the national currency (schilling) as against the euro relates to Austrian patriotism; and the referendum on the abolition of the broadcasting monopoly relates to neo-liberal deregulation. The only high-ranking Freedom Party referendum was held in January 2002. The question put to the vote was whether Austria's right to veto within the European Union should be used to oppose the membership of the Czech Republic, if necessary, in an attempt to enforce the closure of the Czech nuclear power station at Temelín. However, Temelín/anti-nuclear power cannot be considered as a primarily Freedom Party issue. Many of the voters in the 2002 referendum were mainly and resolutely opposed to nuclear power, and particularly to that power station, rather than having any special affiliation to or sympathy with the Freedom Party.[8]

Given that the Freedom Party had consistently achieved more than a 22-percent share of the vote at federal elections since 1994, and in particular that its referendums had always been held after periods of intense and aggressive demagogy, the results of these referendums appear to be serious failures. It is

Table 2: *The Freedom Party referendums 1987–2002 (total of 29 referendums)*

Issue	Supported by	Year	No. of Signatures	Ranking
Anti-Temelín, EU veto	FPÖ 16,562 supporting signatures	2002	914,973	3
Federal law for protection of animals 1	35 FPÖ and Green Party deputies	1996	459,096	11
Austria First	More than 8 FPÖ deputies	1993	416,531	12
Schilling vs euro	9 FPÖ deputies	1997	253,949	16
Anti-privileges	All 18 FPÖ deputies	1987	250,697	18
Nuclear-free Austria	9 FPÖ deputies	1997	248,787	19
Abolition of broadcasting monopoly	All FPÖ deputies	1989	109,197	28

Sources: Bundesministerium für Inneres, *Volksbegehren*, Homepage of the Federal Ministry of Interior Affairs, April 2003.

reasonable to conclude that the Freedom Party referendums did not prove popular with the electorate.[9]

However, public participation represents only one aspect of the political value of referendums. Freedom Party officials obviously used referendums, in spite of their apparent lack of appeal to the electorate, as part of a political strategy aimed at putting pressure on the other parties, specifically the two mainstream ones. In that respect, not only results are important, but also the announcement of a referendum and the campaign leading up to it. The more a theme is amplified in political discourse, the higher the public profile of Freedom Party politicians and the more the other parties feel forced to react.[10]

Although the Freedom Party is not successful in mobilising opinion on certain topics by means of referendums, it is interesting to consider voting attitudes in relation to the main issues at federal elections. Plasser, Seeber and Ulram (2000) have analysed these in the case of the federal elections of 1999. Social Democrat as well as Christian Democrat voters cited economic, political and social stability as major reasons for voting the way they did. They also stated that their chosen party would either best represent their interests, or that their choice was made simply out of habit. Green Party voters mentioned first the environment, second human rights, concern for women and the socially disadvantaged, and third the party's active opposition to hostility towards foreigners and right-wing radicalism (Plasser, Seeber and Ulram 2000: 107). Freedom Party voters mentioned as decisive first that the party would relentlessly uncover scandals and privileges, and secondly that it would be a breath of fresh air and bring about change (ibid.: 230).

As stated earlier, however, their immigration policy is not the main reason for voting for the Freedom Party. The issue ranked only fifth in importance amongst their voters in 1990, third in 1994 and second in 1999 (Plasser and Ulram 2000: 229). Since 1990, the exposure of scandals, grievances and privileges, as well as the drive for political, economic and social transformation, continually holds first place as a reason for voting for the Freedom Party. Bailer-Galanda and Neugebauer characterise Freedom Party voters as being weary of the existing political system dominated by the two mainstream parties (1997: 120). According to the authors, a vote for the Freedom Party is a vote against these parties and their politics of consensus, against the grand coalition as governmental form, juridical regulations conveying economic privileges to politicians, distribution of jobs according to affiliation to one of the two major parties (SPÖ and ÖVP) and, of course, against foreigners and immigrants (1997: 120). They also assert that Freedom Party voters often exhibit authoritarian tendencies.

Altogether, Freedom Party voters may be attracted by the party's strategically extensive thematic connections as well as the fact that their style of politics promotes a culture of conflict and competition, which apparently opposes the major parties in a number of respects. The party also plays on voters' emotions in claiming to protect the 'ordinary man', to be hostile to immigrants and to support an Austrian patriotism that is supplanting rather than erasing a right-wing pan-Germanism.

Data relating to socio-demographic factors are also interesting. In the elections of 1999, the Freedom Party's 27 percent was made up of the following shares in different groups: 32 percent of all men, but only 21 percent of all women; 35 percent of all people under thirty, but only 23 percent of those over sixty (Plasser and Ulram 2000: 232). According to profession, 47 percent of low-income workers voted for the FPÖ, 33 percent of the self-employed and freelancers but only 20 percent of civil servants and 10 percent of agricultural workers and farmers. In terms of education, the majority of Freedom Party voters attended technical colleges and vocational training schools (31 percent of these groups), followed by graduates of compulsory school education (25 percent); 22 percent of university and high-school graduates voted for them (Plasser and Ulram 2000: 232).

These figures show two things: first, that Freedom Party voters may not be confined to xenophobic or racist sections of the population – the high percentages of youth and the self-employed do not allow such a conclusion; second, that the assumption among opponents of the Freedom Party that housewives, old people, agricultural workers and farmers, low-income workers as well as people with a lower level of education constitute the major social groups connected to the party is quite wrong. The analyses of Plasser and Ulram suggest otherwise. Women are more critical of the Freedom Party than men, and the self-employed and youth are most strongly attracted by Haider. The support of agricultural workers and farmers, a group that is assumed to stand for traditional values such as preservation of the countryside, continuity and Christianity, is extremely low (see Gertraud Seiser's chapter in this volume). Furthermore, education is not a decisive factor. Only the high percentage of low-income workers corresponds to widespread expectation. All in all, these data support the wide spectrum of identities that Haider himself negotiates.

Austrian Patriotism, Regionalism and the European Union

As has already been mentioned, and as many authors state (e.g., Wodak and Pelinka 2002), Haider and the Freedom Party shifted their identity from right-wing pan-German nationalism towards Austrian patriotism during the 1990s. In order to frame this process, it is important to remember that Haider became chairman of the party in 1986 with the massive support of pan-German nationalists. With the launch of the referendum 'Austria First' in 1993, Haider emphasised for the first time that 'Austria First' would be a matter close to his heart, and the expression of a deep relationship between his party and the country. Throughout 1993 he continued to stress that the Freedom Party was 'the Austrian party' par excellence, and a peak in this repositioning was reached in August 1995 when Haider proclaimed the end of pan-Germanism within the party (Geyer 1995).

At that time, Chairman Haider entrusted one of his closest followers, Ewald Stadler, with the conceptualisation of a new party manifesto. It was finalised at the party conference in Linz in October 1997.[11] The manifesto outlined how the former pan-German notion of the 'German people's and cultural community' (*Volksgemeinschaft*) was to be replaced by the 'Austrian people's community', which was defined as an indigenous, organic community that included all the minority communities (*Volksgruppen*) of Austria (Bailer-Galanda and Neugebauer 1997: 56). Furthermore, Haider proclaimed this people's community to be a 'performance oriented community', and defined its driving force as the will to instigate change based on the determined support of the diligent and hard-working people (Westphal 1994: 56). As the substitution of the notion of the German people's and cultural community was not uncontroversial within the party, Haider, in that same month, went on to explain that the new concept of the Austrian people's community first and foremost implied an awareness of Austria; secondly that it represented an Austria-centred cultural freedom; and finally that it implied a devotion to national characteristics, on the one hand to the local German people's and cultural community, and on the other to the membership of a minority such as Slovenian or Croatian (Czernin and Hoffmann-Ostenhof 1995).

The notion of the Austrian people's community was further elaborated in the new FPÖ-Party Manifesto (chapter 4: 7). The Democratic Republic of Austria, including all its federal states and historically settled, autochthonous minority communities with their respective cultures, constituted the 'native land' or *Heimat.*[12] The following groups were included: German, Croat, Roma, Slovene, Slovak, Czech and Hungarian (chapter 4: 7; Höllinger 1999: 60; Mauhart 1999: 255). Although it is tempting, following Stolcke (1995), to consider this conception as essentialist, and one that distributes these cultures spatially within the state's territory, it is instead both regionally distributed and hierarchically ordered. The FPÖ-Party Manifesto (chapter 15: 37) is explicit that those Austrians who speak German as their first language (the large majority) are consequently part of a broader German cultural community (see also Höllinger 1999: 61). Given that they form the largest of the minority communities (it is actually the majority group), it is considered logical by Freedom Party policy makers that German should therefore be the official state language. With such definitions the Freedom Party bypasses the notion of an Austrian nation, a construct that Haider had previously negated, characterising it as an 'ideological miscreation' on the programme 'Inlandsreport' broadcast by the state TV channel, Österreichischer Rundfunk Fernsehen, in 1988.

Gärtner unravels another apparently contradictory aspect of these formulations in connection with the use of the term 'minority communities'. He argues that when the Freedom Party suggests that the official state language should be German, this implies the existence of a German cultural community within Austria, which rules out the possibility of any self-defining Austrian ethnicity (Gärtner 2002: 26). It is important to stress however that language alone is neither constitutive of culture nor of ethnic identity.

One also has to problematise the concept of 'historically settled, autochthonous communities'. 'Autochthonous' implies a relation to soil based on descent, and definitely not one that normally allows for previous immigration. The associated use of 'historically settled', however, acknowledges preceding migration processes as constitutive of autochthony. As the historical part of the formulation is necessarily connected to a generation system, 'autochthonous' is no longer seen as an essential quality per se, but rather is given a temporal dimension. A generational depth determines the autochthonous quality of the communities in question. However, the formulation does not make reference to who decides from which generation onwards a group may be considered as autochthonous rather than as migrant. The intention is obvious: the conjunction of 'autochthonous' and 'historically settled' creates the impression that this generational depth is naturally determined, and not a social or ideological construct. Only on such a premise could Freedom Party leaders claim during their 'Austria First' referendum campaign and later that Austria is not a country of immigrants.

The formulation also seems to suggest an equal status for the majority German-speaking community alongside the other historically settled, autochthonous communities, but in 1991 the Austrian government had defined the notion of *Volksgruppe* differently: as a group that historically has lived in the country, is in numerical minority, has common ethnic or linguistic characteristics that distinguish it from the majority population, and its own cultural identity (Gärtner 2002: 26). In the terms of the Freedom Party however, this so-called 'German minority community' has the same rights as all the other groups within the Austrian people's community, whilst at the same time being dominant, and therefore politically determining. However, this hierarchical relation is argued on the basis of the group's size – reducing political and social power relations to rights based on the criterion of majority.

The consequences of such formulations are numerous. Rights of citizenship and to protection by state institutions, for example, should only be accorded to those historically settled communities that have autochthonous status. Moreover, the notion of the German cultural community could be extended to include those German communities that were, or still are, minority groups in the former Habsburg territories (FPÖ-Party Manifesto chapter 7: 15); as it is defined by both generation and common descent, the quality of autochthony also applies to them. According to Haider the right of return to the territorial confines of the Austrian people's community should therefore be granted (Höllinger 1999: 128). Furthermore, Austria's right to protect these minority groups in neighbouring states such as Italy, Hungary, Czech Republic, Slovakia, Slovenia, etc. is asserted (Gärtner 2002: 26). In the logic of Haider and the Freedom Party it is a patriotic duty to defend these German minorities.

The intention to reposition the Freedom Party as *the* Austrian patriotic party must be seen within the context of gains in votes at elections during the mid 1990s. While the Freedom Party had 17 percent of the vote in 1990, it achieved 23 percent in 1994, and again in 1995 (Bailer-Galanda and Neugebauer 1997: 243). In an interview with the weekly magazine *Wirtschaftswoche*, Haider referred to changes in the electorate, which was no longer sympathetic to the former pan-German tradition (Geyer 1995). According to him, it seemed pointless to keep this tradition alive; furthermore he mentioned the need for a stronger Austrian patriotic profile for the party in the future. In his opinion, the transformed European landscape and particularly the European Union itself were further evidence of the need for this shift and made the creation of a powerful Austrian identity a top priority (Czernin and Hoffmann-Ostenhof 1995; Geyer 1995).

The Freedom Party's discourse on the issue of EU membership also has to be considered in relation to the discourses of the Social Democrat and Christian Democrat Parties. Long before any other party in Austria, the Freedom Party had demanded Austria's membership of the European Economic Community (EEC) in its 'Salzburg Declaration' of 1964 (Schaller 1994: 237). The call was repeated on several occasions, and had been included in the FPÖ-Party Manifesto of 1985. In May 1987, while the other two parties were discussing membership in connection with Austria's neutrality, the Freedom Party demanded full membership within the European Union (Schaller 1994: 241). The Freedom Party also supported Austria's official application for membership in June 1989.

The Christian Democrat Party was moving towards a pro-EU position in the period between 1983 and 1986 when it was in parliamentary opposition. It opted for full membership and in January 1988 it took a dominant role in federal politics on this issue (Schaller 1994: 243). In 1985, there were only a few supporters of EU membership for Austria among Social Democrat Party members, as until 1983 their foreign policy emphasised Austria's neutrality as a means of mediating in conflicts in the Middle East, and only later had been reoriented towards neighbouring countries and Western Europe. For quite some time party officials were instead promoting an 'Austrian way' that consisted of maintaining full neutrality, while cooperating with the EU on specific projects. It was not until April 1989 however that the Social Democrat Party would fully support Austria's membership of the European Union (Schaller 1994: 246).

Shortly after the official application for membership in June 1989, polls revealed a change in public opinion and the Freedom Party began to adopt an increasingly critical stance towards the European Union (Schaller 1994: 169). Another aspect of the Freedom Party's standpoint on the issue was revealed during the decisive parliamentary debate in 1994 that culminated in voting for EU membership: Freedom Party deputies as well as those of the Green Party complained that parliament had not been sufficiently involved in the decision-making processes.[13] Haider conflated this critique of the two major governing parties' understanding of democracy with his party's opposition to the European Union, which he declared to be both a bureaucratic and centralised as well as a culturally homogeneous federal state.

Following these accusations of undemocratic behaviour, the Freedom Party called for greater democratisation and federalism within the European Union, and for a decentralisation of power in Austria away from the Federal Government towards the regions (Schaller 1994: 193). This political argument is based upon the concept of a Europe made up of people's and minority communities, and makes it possible to differentiate at will the connection between larger unit, state and region. In 1996 Haider further developed these ideas in calling for a 'Europe of fatherlands' (Bailer-Galanda and Neugebauer 1997: 193). He argued against what he saw as an increasing homogenisation of Europe in cultural terms. As expressed in the FPÖ-Party Manifesto of 1997, the Freedom Party identified large-scale unification activities as a means of levelling culture – which they saw as essentially damaging (FPÖ-Party Manifesto chapter 3: 5f ; Höllinger 1999: 61). In polls during the plebiscite of 1994, 34 percent of the population voted against membership, and the Freedom Party seems to have sought its electorate within this group. It gained 28 percent of the vote in the elections for the European Parliament in 1996, being nearly as strong as the two mainstream parties (Bailer-Galanda and Neugebauer 1997: 243).

The Cultural Rhetoric of the Freedom Party

Haider repeatedly opposes debates about ideology. For him, these are 'overemphasised ideational representations' (*Aula* 1994: 20; Kräh 1996: 190). Nevertheless it is noticeable that Haider employs a mixture of ideologies and that the actions and statements of other Freedom Party officials can likewise be related to various ideological discourses. Analysts tend to identify three main FPÖ narratives: liberal, pan-German and (right-wing) populist (e.g., Kräh 1996; Reinfeldt 2000: 215). Kräh also argues that one cannot deduce the party's politics from these narratives. Furthermore, he considers the party in the mid 1990s to be a de-ideologised movement (1996: 177–213); according to him, the overriding motivation was to win votes, ideological or value considerations being irrelevant (1996: 217). Instead of classifying the Freedom Party's position according to these narratives, I shall proceed by examining the seemingly central notion of culture more closely.

References to culture played an important role in the construction of the party's Austrian patriotism, in the conceptualisation of the Austrian people's community and in the party's endeavours to create boundaries between immigrants and citizens, as well as between the historically settled, autochthonous minority groups. A first elaboration of the concept of culture is given in the FPÖ-Party Manifesto of 1997, which asserted that Christianity and (Greek) Antiquity created an influential value system that became a cornerstone of European culture. This value system was said to encompass members of non-Christian religions, as well as people without a faith. According to the manifesto, European civilisation has been, and continues to be, constituted by a dual process: on the one hand, the connection to (Greek) Antiquity and Christianity forms its cultural nucleus; on the other hand, there are relational hierarchies in this constitutive process, such as the influence of Judaism and other non-Christian religious communities (FPÖ-Party Manifesto chapter 5: 9; Mauhart 1999: 256).

In another publication, this time by the Political Academy of the Freedom Party (*Freiheitliches Bildungswerk* 1994), the concept of culture is derived from and further clarified in relation to art. Art is not considered to be a monolithic concept, but instead is broken down into distinct forms such as dance, music, fine arts (ibid.: 110). This publication differentiated between 'fine art' (*ernste Kunst*, the old masters and established Modernism), 'folk art' (*Volkskunst*), 'experimental art' (*experimentelle Kunst)* and 'popular art' (*Unterhaltungskunst*, 1994: 110),[14] and postulated that each has a different value system and that there are no common criteria on which to base comparison of them.

All four categories are connected to distinct groups in society (*Freiheitliches Bildungswerk* 1994: 112). Fine and experimental art are connected to the artworld and to the domain of critical intellectuals and cosmopolitans: a 'self-appointed elite of art consumers' (ibid.). Folk art corresponds to provincial social groups, and popular art to all the people and corporations that produce it. The first two categories are considered to be removed from ordinary citizens and are mostly influenced by state intervention (ibid.). Preference is clearly given to the last two categories, which cover the domain of the popular.

The Freedom Party emphasises a fundamental principle of difference between the art forms that applies equally to each and implies a pluralism of truths within the arts (ibid.: 109). With this in mind, the Freedom Party interprets paragraph 17 of Austria's State Fundamental Law (*Staatsgrundgesetz*), which deals with the freedom of art, as implying that art should be differentiated from 'pseudo-artistic activity' or from 'state art' (also 'system's art' *Staatskunst, Systemkunst*), and consequently that any control of artistic expression should be based upon the notion of responsibility (ibid.: 110–16). It also asserts a plebeian 'citizen's culture' (*Bürgerkultur*), and a decentralisation of art away from the existing 'state culture' (*Staatskultur*, ibid.: 116).

For the Freedom Party 'art is always an expression of and means for shaping a specific culture' (ibid.: 108). In order to grasp the meaning of this fully, it seems opportune to follow the argument outlined in the party publication step-by-step. The thesis of the difference and incommensurability of art forms is extrapolated to the cultural sphere: thus the authors conclude that different cultures are fundamentally incompatible. According to them, cultures represent different perceptions of the world, and therefore are constitutive of different worlds. This notion of the impossibility of any common standard must be, according to the Freedom Party, the basis of any respectful relationship between the most different cultures. The sovereignty of other individuals as well as other cultures must be acknowledged (ibid.: 112). To this end, the principle of equality between cultures goes hand in hand with that of their (fundamental) difference. The concept of the decentralisation of art corresponds to that of a federalism of cultures; and the protection of the difference and uniqueness of cultures, as well as of their forms of expression, corresponds to the prevention of monopolies by particular forms of artistic expression. It is not surprising that given such an understanding of culture, 'multiculturalism' can only be understood as a cultural configuration without any characteristics: 'a humanistic totalitarian non-culture' (ibid.: 114).

Just as art is not considered to be monolithic, nor is culture. Culture and the people's community are each internally constituted by fields of tension. Both have to be understood as alternatives corresponding to the principles of difference and equality. It is apparent by now that the most important principle is that of the tracing of boundaries, even if the *Freiheitliches Bildungswerk* stresses that the Freedom Party must combine this 'necessary' boundary tracing with the principle of tolerance (ibid.: 115).

The Freedom Party's concept of culture operates on various levels. It allows for an overarching value system, for example, the party concedes that larger territorial units (e.g., Europe) have a common culture. However, it also encompasses the level of more specific cultural expression, at which each culture has to be acknowledged as unique and sovereign. According to Freedom Party leaders this is only possible by means of the assertion of a fundamental, insuperable difference that necessitates boundary tracing. Furthermore, the recognition of the uniqueness and sovereignty of each culture obliges any communication (as part of the boundary tracing) to recognise the principles of equality and tolerance, be it between various minority groups within state borders, or between different national people's communities across state borders.

This concept of culture is easily related to what Stolcke calls 'contemporary cultural fundamentalism' (1995: 4). What the author calls 'reification of culture' may correspond to the Freedom Party's concept of a value system inherited from Antiquity and Christianity. Stolcke's 'culture as a compact, bounded and historically rooted set of traditions and values' may be related to the Freedom Party's idea of the uniqueness and sovereignty of each culture. The notion of the incommensurability of cultures proposed by Stolcke is a central one in the Freedom Party's call for boundary construction while asserting equality and tolerance, thus also creating the impression of a spatial distribution of cultures and people's communities. These concepts clearly appear in the eight-point statement of the party's immigration politics formulated in 1989. One can also recognise them in Haider's definition of the various minority groups as being constituents of the Austrian people's community, and particularly in his linking of the supposedly German minority within Austria to larger pan-Germanism.

Haider, however, transgresses the cultural fundamentalist approach described by Stolcke (1995: 4). First of all, his conceptualisation of Austrian patriotism does not allow for territorial uniformity: the definition of the historically settled, autochthonous minority groups implies a constructionist conceptualisation of these minority groups as constituting the Austrian people's community. Moreover, while the Freedom Party allows for the uniqueness and sovereignty of each culture, it does not always consider each culture as a homogeneous and shared category. None of the four categories of art nor the Freedom Party's discrimination between a state culture and a citizen's culture allows any reference to compact and rooted cultural values. These rhetorical distinctions are constructed for the purposes of a politics of conflict; their intention is to create an opposition between the Austrian patriotic Freedom Party, and the denationalising, state-abusing mainstream parties, critical intellectuals and cosmopolitans.

Further aspects of this cultural rhetoric are worth noting. On the one hand, culture appears to be unevenly distributed within society instead of being shared by all members in the same way (see Barth 1989); on the other, Freedom Party leaders, and mainly Haider, are using culture as a processual concept. Baumann has proposed a theory of the 'double or dual discursive competence' of people (1999: 93). Instead of seeing both the essentialist view of culture and the processual one as theories that are opposed to each other in social reality, he suggests instead that it is a matter of two coexisting discourses on culture; what matters is the context in which either of the two is activated (ibid.: 94).

A remarkable aspect of the processual use of culture by Haider can be seen in the shift in the party's orientation from a pan-German nationalist position to an Austrian patriotic one, and within the latter towards regionalism. With regard to the first process, Haider had to react to changes in an electorate no longer sympathetic to the Nazi past, but at the same time he had to appease those people who had been his staunch supporters since 1986. For the former group he presented a sense of Austrian-ness as a cultural freedom, whilst for the latter he positioned the notion within the context of the German people's and cultural community. This strategy allowed Haider to appeal to both groups in proposing that Austria would decide its own way within this community, and to extend it to larger communities such as the European Union. In Haider's own words, this cultural freedom would convey to Austria an unmistakable, incomparable and inviolable identity (Bailer-Galanda and Neugebauer 1997: 193; Haider 1993: 300).

In one sense, this notion of Austrian-ness could, for some, be seen as continuous with enduring values of the past. For others, this emphasis on Austria's cultural freedom could be articulated in relation to processes of European integration, or of globalisation. Above all it is a claim for Austria's right to decide its own cultural and social development. Against the backdrop of the global system, Haider's cultural freedom and regionalism emphasise cultural pluralism and the perspective of smaller units. In contrast to processes of cultural homogenisation and the formation of political power centres, Haider's political vision offers something like a concept of a world system of cultures (see Sahlins 1994).

In the context of such a world system, the articulation of Austria's cultural freedom, i.e., the self-determination of its history, gets its relevance. The Freedom Party's vision of Austria not only represents a return to some supposedly perennial values. The continual reference to such past values by party officials is problematic insofar as Haider and the Freedom Party emphasise the uneven distribution of culture. In the Freedom Party's conceptualisation this is much more important than the maintenance and reification of a homogeneous, bounded cultural core. As much as an order of values is conceded for Europe, the actual articulation of culture is seen as happening at the level of a citizen's culture as opposed to that of the state culture, or at the level of the popular, for example, folk or popular art forms, as against fine art and experimental art. In this sense this discourse is less a retraditionalisation in response to denationalisation, but rather it should be considered as a vague formulation of an alternative modernity. The parallel between the Austrian people's community and the so-called German minority group within it and the context of the European Union and the Austrian state is obvious.

This articulation of culture as process within present social networks highlights contextualisation as the central political strategy of the Freedom Party. Contextualisation is a strategy that is opposed to the reification of traditional values, and the Freedom Party above all else praises itself for questioning so-called untouchable social arrangements and informal social contracts. Precisely this aspect has been revealed as the major reason for voting for the Freedom Party between 1986 and 1999 (Plasser and Ulram 2000). Haider and the Freedom Party do not only use a processual theory of culture or a 'double discursive competence' (Baumann 1999). Furthermore, these narratives take place within a non-essentialist reconceptualisation of democratic spaces characterised by the construction of a political context of conflict and competition, and by negotiations within present social networks disregarding persistent past values. Such a proposition may seem astonishing given the party's apparent cultural fundamentalism, and the challenge therefore becomes to explain how a party whose boundary tracing, for example, in the case of the 'Austria First' referendum of 1993, comes close to racism can also utilise such liberal-democratic rhetoric as outlined above.

I would argue that the answer lies in their conceptualisation of social reality. Kräh draws our attention to the use of the notion of 'freedom' instead of 'liberal' by the party: he emphasises that freedom in this sense is connected to the idea of a common national descent of citizens, and always has a collective connotation (1996: 178). This idea of freedom appears in Haider's call in 1990 for the removal from article 4 of the State Treaty of 1955 of the prohibition on Austria uniting with Germany, or when in 1991 he called upon the government to unilaterally revoke the entire State Treaty (Bailer-Galanda and Neugebauer 1997: 64). In that context another dimension is added to the asserted sense of Austrian-ness: Austria is presented as a minority community being suppressed as much by the Second

World War Allies as within the European Union, by means of decisions made outside state territory.

Conclusion

In this contribution, I have followed different paths in reflecting on the success of Jörg Haider's Freedom Party between 1986 and 2000. The first proposition was that their xenophobic immigration policy is not the prime reason for voting for the FPÖ. In terms of concrete policies, instead one has to consider the new political tradition Haider propagates: instead of consent and nepotism, he advocates conflict and competition; instead of considering social, cultural and political values as untouchable givens, he suggests that everything is negotiable.

If his main aim was to increase votes for the Freedom Party by rapidly reacting to public opinion, one can nevertheless discern a theme behind all these activities: the permanent production of difference and sameness, and, within difference, of closeness and distance. This is apparent in the Freedom Party's radical immigration policies, but also in the concept of the so-called egalitarian relationship between the various minority groups and the German-speakers in Austria.

This brought me to scrutinise the Freedom Party's concept of culture, and the various ways it is employed in its political rhetoric. At stake is the concept of the Austrian people's community. This is a community, on the one hand, whose unity is characterised by a seemingly egalitarian spatial distribution of minority groups each having a specific culture; on the other hand, it is qualitatively determined by the dominance of the so-called German (minority) community, which actually constitutes the majority group. This notion of horizontally distributed, egalitarian 'spaces' of culture, which at the same time are hierarchically ordered, is continually reproduced either in smaller units, e.g., within a minority group, or in larger groups such as the Austrian minority community within the European Union, or Austria in relation to the Eastern countries. In such contexts, and according to Freedom Party logic, Haider's pan-German cultural community and Austria's people's community are permanently in danger of losing their freedom and right to independent cultural action.

This is fundamentally different from a processual theory of culture and a non-essentialist conceptualisation of spaces of democracy designed to negotiate the dynamics of basically pluralist social and cultural landscapes. Haider and the Freedom Party reorder socially given, heterogeneous spaces into a plurality of interacting, homogeneous spaces. Within this strategy the intention is not the construction of a common space in which a dynamic between consent and dissent or between difference and similarity becomes possible, rather the aim seems to be to appropriate a dynamic, democratic tool for excluding or including people. The reification of culture happens less in the creation of continuity with some past value system, something that the party actively avoids, but rather in the creation of the idea of an Austrian consciousness, thus positioning the right to self-determination as an absolute category, incommensurable to any other.

Epilogue: The Collapse of the Freedom Party

At the time of writing, the Freedom Party was going through a turbulent phase, and the outcome was uncertain.

Early in September 2002 the tension between a politics of opposition and those conducive to coalition government lead to serious instabilities within the Freedom Party, and to the calling of much anticipated elections by Chancellor Wolfgang Schüssel of the Christian Democrat Party. However, both Haider's and Schüssel's matrices of action were not new. As in 1986 when the party experienced internal power struggles, Haider relied on hardliners strongly influenced by pan-Germanism for support. Schüssel initiated federal elections in 1995 and had provoked the end of the last grand coalition (1999). In 1986, Haider had won his battle, but Schüssel lost his in 1995. However, the federal elections of November 2002 had a different outcome and brought a tremendous victory for the Christian Democrat Party, which increased its share of the vote from 27 percent in 1999 to 42 percent in 2002, becoming for the first time in over thirty years Austria's top party. At the same time, the Freedom Party fell from 27 percent in 1999 to 10 percent. The Social Democrats went up from 33 percent to 37 percent, while the Green Party increased its share from 7 to 9 percent. In 2005, Haider's group broke away from the Freedom Party, while remaining in government.

These results could be celebrated as a serious defeat for Haider's party. However, Christian Democrat Chancellor Schüssel had formed another coalition government with the FPÖ in February 2003. One could of course argue that this defeat marks the end of the Freedom Party's neo-nationalist politics, but not if one considers that Schüssel's team appropriated the rhetoric, strategies and arguments of their partner. Actually, according to Reinfeldt this process began as early as 1996, when the Christian Democrat Party appropriated the Freedom Party's ideological cornerstones: the FPÖ's self-ascription as 'the hard workers' became the ÖVP's 'respectables'; the FPÖ's opposition to foreigners became the ÖVP's opposition to the 'abusers of the social welfare system'; and the FPÖ's attack on the 'privilege-abusing government' (the SPÖ/ÖVP government) was transformed by the ÖVP into the opposition between themselves as the 'efficient' and the SPÖ as the 'wasteful distributors of social care' (Reinfeldt 2000: 198f, 204ff.).

Notes

1. Austria is a federation with nine provinces. There are thus a national parliament (*Nationalrat*), regional parliaments for each province (*Landtag*) and beneath those the communities, with their

local assemblies, (the *Gemeinderat*). All these parliaments have their own elections. Parties are organised in a similar way at the national, provincial and local levels.

2. Social partnership is peculiar to Austria. The members meet when political questions touch on social issues such as unemployment, medical care, social welfare. They are very powerful and no government could do without them.

3. Maximum stay eight months.

4. Including a reduction in the number of foreigners to a maximum of 30 percent per class, and classifying second-generation immigrant children as foreigners.

5. For a detailed discussion see Höllinger (1999: 164–76).

6. 'Das Recht der Inländer auf Heimat ist stärker als das Recht der Ausländer auf Familienleben.'

7. This kind of referendum can also be just regional, in which case the respective regional parliament has to discuss the issue.

8. Nevertheless, the threat of veto is a favourite topic of the Freedom Party.

9. One must acknowledge that an FPÖ-initiated referendum in Linz about the construction of a multi-purpose music venue was highly effective: 60 percent of the local population opted for the Freedom Party's referendum, i.e., against the construction.

10. Zöchling mentions a statement by a former party official, Gernot Rumpoldt, in which he explained the strategy of political exaggeration for achieving one's ends (2000: 207).

11. The authors were prominent right wingers: Ewald Stadler, Karl Brauneder, Jörg Freundschlag, Herbert Scheibner, Lothar Höbelt as well as one representative of each federal state.

12. The Freedom Party's definition of the relationship between historical settlement and autochthony will be discussed later in this section.

13. At that time the Green Party was known as Grüne Alternative Liste and its members actually voted against the application for membership.

14. The authors were fourteen members of the Freedom Party, including politicians, professors of Austrian universities and a diplomat.

Bibliography

Aula. 1994. "'… wir genieren uns nicht, das rechte Lager zu repräsentieren." Aula-Gespräch mit FPÖ-Bundesobmann Dr. Jörg Haider', *Aula* 44(9)(September): 20–21.

Bailer-Galanda, B. and Neugebauer, F. 1997. *Haider und die Freiheitlichen in Österreich.* Berlin: Elefanten Press.

Barth, F. 1989. 'The Analysis of Culture in Complex Societies', *Ethnos* 3(4): 120–42.

Bauböck, R. 2002. 'Constructing the Boundaries of the Volk: Nation-building and National Populism in Austrian Politics', in R. Wodak and A. Pelinka eds *The Haider Phenomenon in Austria.* New Brunswick: Transaction Publishers, pp. 231–54.

Baumann, G. 1999. *The Multicultural Riddle: Rethinking National, Ethnic, and Religious Identities.* New York: Routledge.

Bundesministerium für Inneres. No year. Volksbegehren. Homepage of the Federal Ministry of Interior Affairs, www.bmi.gv.at/wahlen/volksbegehren_historisches.asp (consulted April 2003).

Czernin, H. and Hoffmann-Ostenhof, G. 1995. '25 Jahre Gehirnwäsche. Interview mit Jörg Haider', *Profil* 21/08: 27–31.

Der Standard. 2002. "'40 Euro und kein Ticket: Kosovaren fliegen heim"', 4 October: 10.

FPÖ-Party Manifesto. No year. www.fpoe-klub-ooe.at/download/parteiprogramm.doc (consulted April 2003).

Freiheitliches Bildungswerk. ed. 1991. 'Heimat-Suche. Österreich im Blickpunkt der Völkerwanderung', *Schriftenreihe des Freiheitlichen Forums KONTRO VERS* No. 1, Vienna.

———. ed. 1994. 'Weil das Land sich ändern muss! Auf dem Weg in die Dritte Republik', *Schriftenreihe des Freiheitlichen Forums KONTRO VERS* No. 4, Vienna.

Gärtner, R. 2002. 'The FPÖ, Foreigners, and Racism in the Haider era', in R. Wodak and A. Pelinka eds *The Haider Phenomenon in Austria*. New Brunswick: Transaction Publishers, pp. 17–32.

Geyer, H. 1995. 'Mit der Deutschtümelei muß Schluß sein. Interview mit Jörg Haider', *Wirtschaftswoche* 17/08: 20–22.

Gingrich, A. 2002. 'A Man for All Seasons: An Anthropological Perspective on Public Representation and Cultural Politics of the Austrian Freedom Party', in R. Wodak and A. Pelinka eds *The Haider Phenomenon in Austria*. New Brunswick: Transaction Publishers, pp. 67–94.

Haider, J. 1993. *Die Freiheit, die ich meine: Das Ende des Proporzstaates. Ein Plädoyer für die Dritte Republik*. Frankfurt/Main: Ulstein.

Höllinger, N. 1999. 'Die Ausländerpolitik der Freiheitlichen seit 1986', unpublished MA thesis, University of Vienna.

Huber, M. 1997. 'Ausländer rein und raus, (in cooperation with T. Hofer)', *Profil* 17/03: 32–36.

Inlandsreport. 1988. *Österreichischer Rundfunk-Fernsehen* 18/08.

Kräh, G. 1996. *Die Freiheitlichen unter Jörg Haider. Rechtsextreme Gefahr oder Hoffnungsträger für Österreich*, Mit einem Vorwort von Kurt Sontheimer. Frankfurt/Main: Peter Lang.

Mauhart, A. 1999. 'Die Entwicklung der Freiheitlichen Partei Österreichs aus realpolitischer und programmatischer Sicht', unpublished Ph.D. thesis, University of Linz.

Pelinka, A. 1994. 'Europäische Integration und politische Kultur', in A. Pelinka, C. Schaller and P. Luif *Ausweg EG? – Innenpolitische Motive einer außenpolitischen Umorientierung*, Studien zu Politik und Verwaltung vol. 47. Vienna: Böhlau, pp. 11–26.

Plasser, F and Ulram, P.A. 2000. 'Rechtspopulistische Resonanzen', in F. Plasser, P.A. Ulram and F. Sommer eds *Das österreichische Wahlverhalten*, Schriftenreihe des Zentrums für Angewandte Politikforschung vol. 21. Vienna: Signum, pp. 225–41.

Plasser, F., Seeber, G. and Ulram, P.A. 2000. 'Breaking the Mold: Politische Wettbewerbsräume und Wahlverhalten Ende der 90er Jahre', in F. Plasser, P.A. Ulram and F. Sommer eds *Das österreichische Wahlverhalten*, Schriftenreihe des Zentrums für Angewandte Politikforschung vol. 21. Vienna: Signum, pp. 55–115.

Reinfeldt, S. 2000. *Nicht-wir und Die-da. Studien zum rechten Populismus*. Studien zur politischen Wirklichkeit, Schriftenreihe des Instituts für Politikwissenschaft der Universität Innsbruck vol. 8, series ed. Anton Pelinka. Vienna: Braumüller.

Sahlins, M. 1994. 'Goodbye to Tristes Tropes: Ethnography in the Context of Modern World History', in R. Borofsky ed. *Assessing Cultural Anthropology*. New York: McGraw-Hill, pp. 377–94.

Schaller, C. 1994. 'Die innenpolitische EG-Diskussion seit den 80er Jahren', in A. Pelinka, C. Schaller, P. Luif *Ausweg EG? – Innenpolitische Motive einer außenpolitischen Umorientierung*, Studien zu Politik und Verwaltung vol. 47. Vienna: Böhlau, pp. 27–267.

Stolcke, V. 1995. 'Talking Culture: New Boundaries, New Rhetorics of Exclusion in Europe', *Current Anthropology* 36(1): 1–24.

Westphal, S. 1994. 'Der Populismus der FPÖ unter Jörg Haider. Zwischen politischer Ideologie und Strategie zur Wählermaximierung', unpublished MA thesis, University of Vienna.

Wodak, R. and Pelinka, A. eds. 2002. *The Haider Phenomenon in Austria*. New Brunswick: Transaction Publishers.

Zöchling, C. 2000. *Haider. Eine Karriere*, 2nd edn. Munich: Econ.

Chapter 8

Neo-nationalism or Neo-localism?

Integralist Political Engagements in Italy at the Turn of the Millennium
Jaro Stacul

Introduction

This chapter analyses the appearance of the right in Italian politics in the last few years, and sets out to put forward some hypotheses about the connection between the appeal achieved by the right itself and the associations its supporters make between themselves and right-wing ideologies. This transformation, in Italian as well as in European politics, has given way to particularistic forms of identification that are effacing old forms of identity and altering the ways in which people constitute themselves as collective and political subjects. Such forms of identification have the effect of legitimating a political discourse centred on the notion of culture expressed by a rhetoric predicated on cultural diversity and incommensurability (see, e.g., Stolcke 1995: 4), which essentialises differences of cultural heritage. This discourse, it has been observed (Wright 1998: 14), reflects a 'redefinition of the notion of culture as a political process of contestation on the power to define key concepts' and has been appealed to and mobilised to stress (and create) difference.

In social anthropology and cognate disciplines there have been various attempts at describing and making sense of these particularistic forms of identification. In labelling this phenomenon a 're-parochialization of politics', for example, Bauman (1995: 251) has interpreted it as the expression of an increasingly individualised society on the one hand, and as the result of a 'deconstruction of politics' (1999: 72–78) stemming from the separation of power from the state on the other. Perhaps the most intriguing reading of the advent of the right has been Holmes' (2000: 3); he has described this phenomenon as 'integralism'. He states that at the level of practice integralism is expressed by an exclusionary political economy, which recasts society as a domain of political engagement , as well as by a renewed commitment to a distinct regional culture and to the routines and intimacies of family life (ibid.: 5). At the level of ideology though, Holmes (ibid.: 13) suggests that it cannot be labelled as either 'left' or 'right', but as a form of entangled politics that is *both* 'left' and 'right', because it synthesises apparently incompatible elements of political thought.

One problem that we encounter in Holmes' and other anthropological analyses of the emergence of the right is that while most of them have sought to provide interpretive keys to the phenomenon from the top down, to date very few of them have attempted to give a deep insight into the association people make between themselves and the ideologies of the parties of the right. Especially in the anthropology of Europe, there has instead been a tendency to understand political expression mainly (but by no means exclusively) in terms of the institutions and the currents of political thought that make that expression possible (Smith 1999: 44–45). Thus, if the right legitimated a political discourse centred on the notion of culture, on what is this notion predicated? What meanings does it convey to those who have chosen to identify with the parties of the right? Do social actors look upon integralist politics as both 'left' and 'right'?

A Changing Political Landscape

Italy at the turn of the millennium lends itself very well to the exploration of these issues. Even though it is experiencing the same problem of the emergence of the right as other Western European countries, its current association with the right itself may seem rather striking. This is due to the fact that what attracted many social anthropologists working on Italy until the 1980s was not issues of racism and nationalism but the tension between 'Comrades' and 'Christians', or Communists and Catholics.[1] Italy used to represent the ideal site for the study of the coexistence of strong sub-national political cultures, and it was the Western country with the strongest Communist Party. Anthropologists doing research in Italy from the early 1990s onwards, by contrast, were faced with a very different (and more complex) political landscape, because of the political instability that the country had experienced. The economic crisis, the corruption scandals that led to the demise of the governing Christian Democratic Party (DC), the fall of Communism that brought about the division of the Italian Communist Party into two parties[2] and the subsequent transformation of the Italian party system resulted in a political situation characterised by confusion. These transformations also had the effect of redefining the function of the Italian state, for they went hand in hand with its decline as the dominant framework for the national economy. They were accompanied by several privatisation initiatives across the country and occurred at a time of immigration from countries outside the European Union.

I will not go into all the details of the changes that occurred in Italy in the last few years. Suffice it to say, for the purposes of this chapter, that these transformations occurred when the Italian state's role as the main social, political and ideological container of the people living in its territory was being questioned (for details see Diamanti 1999). Although the waning of the ideological and cultural role of the state reflects a trend of most Western states in late modernity (Trouillot 2001: 130–31), it must be noted that, unlike in other countries, this change has greatly affected the ways in which Italians relate to the political sphere. While the Communist/Catholic polarity informed the organisation of Italian politics until the late 1980s, the early 1990s saw its gradual blurring, a growing disaffection with politics and a retreat to private concerns. More importantly, the last decade of the twentieth century was characterised by the disappearance of the parties that had dominated the political arena until then. It also saw a redefinition of the political doctrine of other parties and the creation and growth of new political formations that inherited the electorate of those that were disappearing, and which quickly adjusted to the demands of a society disillusioned with politics.

Regionalist and autonomist political movements benefited from these changes as they were able to present themselves as being above and beyond the traditional criteria of left and right. Among these movements Lega Nord (Northern League) was the most successful. When it came to the fore in the early 1990s, the party represented a reaction against the malfunctioning of the state; it contested the idea of national identity and the legitimacy of a nation state seen as corrupted (see, e.g., Diamanti 1996 and Giordano 2000). The party had in its agenda the transformation of Italy into a federal state and, for some time, even the territorial division of the north from the south of the country. Its leader, Umberto Bossi, championed the idea of northern Italy as partaking of a 'European culture' because of northerners' supposed attitude to hard work, as opposed to a 'Mediterranean' one of a putative lazy and state-subsidised south (Cento Bull 1996: 177; Giordano 2000: 458–64), which was seen as the main cause of Italy's economic crisis. His party presented itself as 'populist' in that it purported to recreate a lost 'authenticity' in opposition to the centralised nation state and to maintain a traditional *Gemeinschaft*. According to the party, the 'northern Italian culture' was not just threatened by immigration from southern Italy, but also by the influx of migrants from newly developing countries (Giordano 2000: 460). Although political regionalism was not a novel phenomenon in Italy (see, e.g., Romanelli 1991), the appearance of Lega Nord brought to the fore the issue of northern Italian identity (even though it had never been a problem before), and gave it a political dimension by essentialising the idea of a 'northern Italian culture'.[3]

The advent of the Northern League was accompanied by the redefinition of the political discourse of the post-Fascist party, Alleanza Nazionale (National Alliance), and its transformation into a new political subject after a political isolation of about forty years (Roversi 1999: 605–6).[4] Although the party retained in its agenda proposals for the exclusion of migrants, and stressed the need to preserve national identity (Ter Wal 2000: 41–42), it condemned racism and made an attempt to get rid of both its image as an extreme-right party and the legacy of Fascism.[5]

Perhaps the most intriguing transformation in the Italian political arena was the appearance, in the mid 1990s, of the media tycoon Silvio Berlusconi, who created Forza Italia (Let's Go Italy),[6] a centre-right party that protects the interests of entrepreneurs and promotes an Italian version of Thatcherism.[7] Shortly after its creation it captured most of Lega Nord's vote, particularly in the north of the country. It established an alliance with Lega Nord and Alleanza Nazionale despite differences in political programmes; it also led a centre-right coalition that won the national elections in 1994 and governed the country for a few months. The rest is history: the national elections of May 2001 saw the victory, by a comfortable majority, of the same centre-right coalition, which includes Forza Italia itself, Lega Nord, former Christian Democrats, and Alleanza Nazionale, lead by Berlusconi as Italy's Prime Minister.

Integralism From the 'Bottom Up': The Italian Eastern Alps

As can be seen from this descriptive summary of the changing political landscape, the rise of the centre right in Italy is a complex phenomenon, and interpreting it as an expression of 'nationalism' would not do justice to it given the different agendas of the formations that make up the governing coalition. In exploring this new form of political engagement, one problem that we encounter is the definition of its nature. If we were to look at increasing support for the centre right in Italy simply by reference to the concept of ideology, we would be led to assume that it primarily represents a renewed assertion of national identity as a response to a situation of economic crisis and political disorder on the one hand, and to uncontrolled immigration on the other. Yet despite the Alleanza Nazionale's insistence on the necessity of preserving national culture and identity, the meanings of the notion of 'culture' that the centre right employs can hardly be defined as an expression of 'classical' nationalism. Holmes, as we have seen, has labelled this 'integralism', which he defines as 'a protean phenomenon that draws directly on the sensibilities of the Counter-Enlightenment for its intellectual and moral substance' (2000: 8). As he has observed (ibid.: 13), viewing 'integralist' groups as either 'right' or 'left' is misleading because their agendas do not simply involve fidelity to the idea of the nation, rather, they draw authority from a broad range of collective practices that implicate family, language groups, religious communities, occupational statuses, social classes, etc. They create political orientations that defy easy categorisation, because they recombine ideologies such as nationalism, conservatism, liberalism, as well as populism with their identity politics, and are *both* 'left' and 'right'.

The considerations of the complex nature of integralism, as defined by Holmes, apply to Italy, where the electorate no longer identifies with a political party and its doctrine (Cento Bull 2000: 1–2), and where the left no longer appeals to the notion of class. Likewise, if we were to understand support for Berlusconi's coalition by reference to the concept of ideology we would have to assume that such a coalition has a political doctrine that determines the ways its supporters constitute themselves as political subjects. An interpretation of the success of the right in Italy is far from being so simple. As Bourdieu (1977) and de Certeau (1984) have shown, people do not simply enact culture, but reinterpret it in their own ways. The same applies to political ideologies and messages: these are not necessarily superimposed, but are often accommodated to local-level discourses (see, e.g., Sutton 1997: 415) and achieve their appeal when they mobilise themes already existent in 'local culture'.[8] If political messages have a compelling power, what themes do they mobilise?

In an attempt to answer this question and those asked at the beginning of this contribution, I will analyse integralist political engagements not as existing over and above social relations, but rather as being expressed by a set of discourses and practices that form part of everyday life. The context in which I have conducted research on these issues is the Vanoi Valley, an Alpine community in the Trentino region of northern Italy in which the parties of the centre-right coalition gained the majority of the vote in the national elections of 1994, 1996 and 2001. To a certain extent the valley represents a sort of 'homogeneous community' where people were born and have spent most of their lives. The inhabitants of the area may be described as post-peasants as until the 1960s they had been living by a combination of agriculture, forestry and animal husbandry. They negotiate the intrigues of industrial wage work, peasant farming, the bureaucratic apparatus of the Italian state as well as the material (and symbolic) allure of consumerism and globalisation. Most of them engage in migration across central and northern Europe in search of employment, and eventually come back to the valley. They are full participants in the Italian body politic: they vote in national elections, they read the national and regional press, they watch television and in 2001 various people in the valley had access to the Internet at home. Despite their long-standing commitment to wage earning outside agro-pastoral activities, they never developed a working-class consciousness, and they still refer to themselves as 'peasants' (*contadini*).

With the demise of the agro-pastoral economy in the 1960s, the population of the valley steadily declined. The present-day population (scarcely 1,700 inhabitants) includes, for the most part, retired agriculturalists (mainly women) and lumberjacks (men) who earn a pension from the state, and people who work in various kinds of manual trades. They have direct control over some land, even though a substantial part of it has been alienated to the urban dwellers that come to the valley for summer vacations. In the last few years the valley and the surrounding communities witnessed the arrival of immigrants from non-European countries (most notably northern Africa), particularly ambulant traders who visit the villages from time to time and stop in front of the local bars to display their merchandise.

The valley, like most of Trentino, used to be a stronghold of the Christian Democratic Party (DC), the party that could exercise its power through its clientelistic networks and the capillary infrastructure of the Catholic Church. 'Localism' is the term that best describes the political orientation of the people of the valley: this is characterised by allegiance primarily to the community rather than to the Italian state, and it was one of the main tenets of the DC until recently. Thus, a sense of 'our place' is very strong (for details see Stacul 2003). The Italian Communist Party was the DC's major antagonist, but apart from a couple of occasions in the 1970s, it never posed a serious threat to the DC's supremacy in the valley. The post-Fascist party Alleanza Nazionale (formerly Movimento Sociale Italiano or MSI) has never been successful in the area, and it could count on just a handful of supporters. So, until the early 1990s politics was seen as the arena of confrontation mainly between Catholics and Communists. By contrast, when I arrived in the valley in 1994 labels such as 'Communist' and 'Christian Democrat' had virtually disappeared. The DC had just collapsed and there was a general awareness that dramatic changes in the Italian party system were on the way. Yet there was also anxiety at the possibility that the party of the former Communists (Partito Democratico della Sinistra, or PDS) could take over power as a result of the DC's demise. Lega Nord and a regional autonomist party, the Trentine-Tyrolean Autonomist Party, were benefiting from this political disorder: they were making significant inroads, and most of my informants in the valley proudly declared themselves to be supporters or affiliates of one or the other.[9]

The demise of the DC following the scandal of political corruption at the national level had the effect of discrediting the national government. Thus, the people of the valley were increasingly distrustful of the intentions of the politicians in Rome, and welcomed the possibility that the north of the country could have more autonomy from Rome itself. This lack of trust was epitomised by the phrase 'politicians are dirty'. These events engendered the conviction that what Italy actually needed in order to solve its economic problems was not politicians, but experienced entrepreneurs. This idea was also central to Berlusconi's propaganda when his party, Forza Italia, entered the political arena. When this party and its centre-right coalition won the national elections in March 1994, in the valley the news was hailed as the beginning of a new era in Italian politics: as a woman of Caoria told me, as soon as the election results became known, 'At last now things are going to change'. When I heard that, I replied that things were going to change for the worse, given that the victory of Berlusconi's coalition was going to legitimate a right-wing ideology; she responded that this was not true, for the winning coalition was neither 'left' nor 'right'.

Yet national politics was not the main and only concern for the people of the valley, who were witnessing a period of profound change. The main economic activity, forestry, was declining, and the provincial government was proposing to shut down the local sawmill on the grounds that it was unprofitable.[10] There were very few job opportunities in the valley, and as a result most of the able-bodied living there sought paid work elsewhere and spent the working week outside the area. Moreover, the aging population was growing, and after the 1960s the number of deaths exceeded that of births. Thus, there was a widely shared feeling that the community was changing or even on the wane. The other problem was control over land, for a substantial amount of landed property was being sold to strangers who were neither ordinarily resident nor related to the people living there. Although the transfer of land to outsiders (mainly from the nearby Veneto region) was not a novel phenomenon, in the 1990s it took on unprecedented dimensions. Thus, the presence of outsiders was viewed as a breach of a symbolic boundary of the community, as it challenged the idea that the village belonged only to those with kinship ties in the area, and it questioned the widely shared view that a landholding should be owned by the same family group and handed down from one generation to another (Stacul 2003).

The gradual erosion of village autonomy had repercussions for the local political sphere too. At a time of local elections, for example, the preservation of local identity and the necessity of preventing the land from being alienated to non-residents were high on the agenda of those running for election to the municipal council. They were making promises that, if elected, they would strive to prevent the land from being sold to outsiders and call back to the valley the natives who lived and worked elsewhere. In making such promises candidates were also championing a political programme focused on the protection of locality. They were celebrating the community of the 'old days', a mosaic of private properties, ideally inaccessible and controlled by people who were born and bred in the community itself. Their messages drew on the same set of ideas as much of the right-wing, xenophobic political propaganda, particularly on the idea that people should stay in their own places of origin (Roversi 1999: 616). However, while Alleanza Nazionale and Lega Nord deployed this idiom when promising stern measures to curb illegal immigration from non-European countries, local politicians were drawing on the same rhetoric to propose a traditional *Gemeinschaft* in the face of the erosion of 'local culture' and the transfer of landed property to outsiders from nearby regions. In their propaganda candidates were endeavouring to distance themselves from the politicians involved in the corruption scandals, and although their political messages were drawing on the discourses of the right, they were presenting themselves as neither leftists nor rightists, but as apolitical.

To a certain extent the stress upon the 'apolitical' orientation of candidates for election and the emphasis placed upon territorial identity mirrored some of the themes central to the propaganda of Lega Nord, most notably the denigration of the 'corrupted' politicians of Rome. These messages, like most of those Lega Nord propagated, generated various debates among the inhabitants of the valley. For instance, a woman, now in her early seventies, once told me that one of the advantages of living in a mountain village is that there are no foreign (i.e., non-European) immigrants around. Yet apart from the few who expressed a similar opinion, and despite Lega Nord's crusade against immigration from non-European countries, locals do not seem to worry too much about the few northern African ambulant traders who occasionally come to the area. Rather, as I noted, they often express anxiety at the possibility that people from nearby villages or from other Italian regions could settle in the valley and acquire landed property there. In all likelihood this anxiety stemmed from the fact that while no African ambulant trader owns landed property in the area, several Italians from outside Trentino do.[11] Thus, Lega Nord used its rhetoric to champion the integrity of northern Italy vis-à-vis the south, or to oppose immigration from non-European countries, but at the local level this rhetoric was effective for a different reason: it addressed some of the main concerns of the local people, the integrity and ideal independence of the community, and the issue of the protection of local boundaries from outsiders, no matter where they come from (for details see Stacul 2003).

Lega Nord's construction of northern Italian identity and culture cannot be made sense of unless we allow for its interpretations at the local level. Although this construction represented one of the main tenets of Lega Nord's propaganda, in the valley it had the effect of generating a debate on the nature of local identity rather than on the north/south dichotomy. Local identity became an issue soon after Lega Nord came to the fore, and the question of what distinguishes the people of one village from another suddenly became a topic of discussion. Interestingly, distinctiveness was not predicated on differences in language or dialect, but on attitudes towards work. In the villages of Caoria and Ronco, for example, the idea that locals have always been working hard, and that they never asked for other people's help to solve a problem, looms large in local discourse. This view is no idealisation: in the area studied the capacity to sustain hard work is impressive, and is highly praised. It is rare to see people sitting on a bench and doing nothing. The people of these villages often contrast their self-reliance with the presumed inability of the people of neighbouring communities, particularly the municipal seat of Canal San Bovo, to work hard and solve their problems. One shared view is that because many of the people living there work in offices (and do not pursue any manual trades), they are not workers at all. As a Caorian said, they are 'shit put on a stool'. Arguably, in local discourse clerical workers typify state employees (referred to as *statali*), who are usually pointed to as people that 'do not do anything at all' on the grounds that they rely on a wage earned from the state and not on their own means and hard (i.e., manual) work.

In all likelihood this renewed stress upon the capacity to sustain hard work was also a reflection of the recent economic changes. In particular, the economic crisis in Trentino furthered the belief that the economic system inherited from the Italian state, along with the subsidies granted from the Italian state itself, hindered the economic potential of the province instead of giving it a boost (Turato 1998: 105). This made many people believe that Trentino could be better off economically by relying on its own means, and by developing economic relationships with the regions north of the national border instead of with the rest of Italy.

The discrediting of the Italian state and its agencies and the renewed interest in regional and local 'culture' also fuelled a rediscussion of local history, and of widely shared views about the area's past. One theme that was debated was the hardship that locals had to endure in the past as a result of their living in a mountainous area, which engendered an ethic of hard work and self-sacrifice.[12] Interestingly, in their accounts of the local past, social actors did not draw upon the image of a united and harmonious community in which people help each other, an image that often emerges in anthropological accounts of rural communities. What was emphasised instead was a vision of a community inhabited by self-reliant people. This idea is epitomised by the dictum 'Rely on your own means, and God will help you', which would express the values of a 'Protestant' ethic were it not for the fact that the area is Catholic, at least nominally.

Given the valley's proximity to the Veneto region, the differences in cultural heritage between Trentino and the nearby region became another topic of discussion; yet they revolved around very similar ideas. Although similar dialects are spoken in both regions, villagers stated that people across the regional border are different because they have a different 'culture'. The origin of this disparity, an informant said, is the different landholding system: Trentine people have had control over landed property since time immemorial, whereas in the other region farmers used to work on landholdings owned by someone else. In stating this, locals were giving historical foundation to this sense of autonomy: they have always had direct control over land and they did not have to work for absentee landlords. Although this view is partly idealised, it points to the association social actors establish between property and work, and it suggests that autonomous work and property have the same meanings, for they are invoked to stress, once again, the self-reliant character of locals. Yet it also serves to define the nature of local 'culture' as a set of shared ideas centring on the notions of autonomous work and private property.

Although control over landed property is unlikely to ensure economic independence given the small size of landholdings in Alpine ecosystems, it enables social actors to cast work as something that cannot be alienated. This conceptualisation of work is epitomised by the statement 'We are always working, but we do it for ourselves, not for the others.' Work is perceived to be autonomous, i.e., a set of activities carried out to achieve and preserve autonomy on the one hand, and to protect one's private domain on the other. Especially at a time when the supposed inefficiency of the state bureaucratic machinery and its employees was pointed to as one of the main causes of the national (and regional) economic crisis, appealing to the idea of hard work served to reconcile the past and the present. In other words, it served to reconcile the hard work performed in the past in the pursuit of agro-pastoral activities and the capacity (and willingness) to sustain hard work as a requirement for success in late modernity.

So far I have been discussing attitudes towards politicians and immigrants separately, but what is the relationship between such attitudes, and how do they relate to support for the right? Perhaps a discussion of the meanings that the phrase 'eating' conveys can provide a partial answer. There is an interesting parallel in local discourse between attitudes towards politicians and attitudes towards immigrants that revolves to a significant degree around the notion of 'eating'. In the valley, as in most of Italy, this notion is associated with the exploitation of resources or the illicit appropriation of money. That politicians (especially those formerly affiliated to the Christian Democratic Party) are believed to 'eat', stems from the fact that they can avail themselves of substantial amounts of public money, which they have the power to use to pursue private goals. Rather than being looked upon as 'workers' they are believed to be 'fed' by taxpayers. It is not pure coincidence that in the Vanoi Valley the municipal government is referred to as the *laip*, a trough that in the past served to feed pigs. In making this association, social actors project onto the municipal government the characteristics that are deemed typical of the public (i.e., state) administration, those of a domain controlled by people who 'eat' common resources.[13]

To a certain extent the association of the *laip* with the public administration is reminiscent of the stigma attached to immigrants and to those who do not belong to the 'community'. In settling in a place that is not theirs, immigrants are believed to exploit the host country (or community), which in turn has to 'feed' people who wait for subsidies and neither work nor pay taxes. The same applies, to a certain extent, to the outsiders who have bought houses in the valley, on the grounds that they bring everything they need from their place of origin and that they are entitled to receive timber and subsidies from the municipality, but they never go to the local supermarket to purchase foodstuffs. Paradoxically, both politicians and immigrants belong to the same category of people, as they 'eat' resources that are not theirs. Underlying this view, as may be noticed, is the idea of work itself, particularly that of autonomous work carried on outside the public administration, which is aimed at satisfying one's own needs and not at 'feeding' others. Yet while this conceptualisation of work implies a stigmatisation of those who 'eat' without working, it also draws a boundary between a 'community' of workers and another of outsiders along ethnic and cultural lines. In this case it also defines a *territorial* community just as it is informed by the doctrine of neo-liberalism that marginalises those who are not competitive in the labour market.

In the late 1990s the popularity of Lega Nord and of the Trentine-Tyrolean Autonomist Party gradually declined and both their unsuccessful management of the regional government and the advancement at the national and local levels of Berlusconi's Forza Italia dealt them a severe blow. When I revisited the valley in 2000 no one still supported the autonomist parties, and the term 'Lega Nord' had virtually disappeared from the political vocabulary. Yet although the symbols of such parties ceased to be displayed in public places, people's concerns remained the same. The economic condition of the valley was worsening, young people were compelled to look for jobs elsewhere and more and more houses were being sold to strangers. Locals still expressed disillusionment at the agendas of politicians; they were growing suspicious of the centre-left coalition governing the country, which was imposing new taxes, and they deemed the national government responsible for the waves of uncontrolled immigration into Italy. A woman of Caoria expressed her discontent at this situation by displaying, in her bar, a calendar commemorating the dictator Mussolini.

The eve of the national elections in May 2001 found the people of the area caught between a longing for 'order', which only autonomist and regionalist parties were believed to provide, and the awareness that their choice was in fact limited to either the centre-left or the centre-right coalition led respectively by the former mayor of Rome, Francesco Rutelli, and by the Milanese media tycoon Berlusconi. A few days before the elections I heard various discussions about whether it was sensible to vote for Berlusconi, given his failure to clearly separate his business and political interests. There was a widely shared feeling that this was not a real issue, and if anything it was believed that Italy needed an entrepreneur to solve its economic problems, particularly someone who was not a politician. The Roman candidate of the centre-left coalition, by contrast, was not considered suitable, on the grounds that, as a politician, he had never 'worked' in his life. Moreover, it was assumed that a candidate from Rome (as opposed to a Milanese) could not be interested in what happens in the north of the country. Eventually Berlusconi's control of the media, his self-ascribed reputation as a 'worker' and his promise to reduce taxes and raise the minimum state pension proved decisive, and even in the valley his coalition won the majority of votes.

Thus, the north/south dichotomy and the emphasis on work still figured prominently in local discourses despite the declining popularity of autonomist parties. Yet what was particularly intriguing was the changing meaning of politics. Voting for one candidate or another did not entail commitment to any political doctrine. It did not mean involvement in formal politics and public life, but rather involved a withdrawal from these. Supporting a candidate identified as a 'worker' (such as Berlusconi) did not imply belief in class struggle or class-based politics but, on the contrary, entailed support for a coalition that seemed to promise an Italian version of Thatcherism, and achieved its appeal among people who drew on the concept of autonomous work as an important source of identity.[14] A notion of local and regional identity also prevailed that supplants class and a conceptualisation of work as something owned by the worker, from which a politics that is party driven should be kept separate (for a comparison, see Ulin 2002: 704–6). The meanings attached to the idea of autonomous work, as we have seen, fit well into Lega Nord's advocacy of the hard-work ethic as distinguishing the north from the south of the country, and into Forza Italia's advocacy of the idea of a country governed by entrepreneurs instead of politicians.

Conclusion

Although my analysis of the situation in Trentino does not do justice to the Italian situation as a whole, nonetheless it provides at least some answers to the questions posed at the beginning of the chapter. It seems clear from the ethnographic information discussed that the notion of culture on which integralist discourse centred was largely predicated upon the idea of work, both at the level of political rhetoric and at the level of people's understandings. Thus, discourses and practices that are part of everyday life helped people make sense of the political arena. Both Lega Nord and Forza Italia achieved their appeal (albeit at different times) because their messages were accommodated to local-level discourses. However, they also mobilised themes already existent in 'local culture', among which the protection of boundaries and the idea of autonomous work are the most significant. Whilst an ideology of hard work imbued with Thatcherism was heralded by party leaders based in urban centres, it was actually in a post-peasant society that such ideas became appealing because they were congruent with values and beliefs pervading local discourses. Thus, the values of late capitalism legitimated the boundary between those who 'work' and those who are believed to 'eat' by reifying a different cultural heritage, but they also asserted the primacy of the ethic of the market over solidarity.

The other issue raised at the outset was how far we can make sense of the appeal of the right in Italy (and not just in Italy) by reference to the concept of ideology. As we have seen, a construction of the 'Other' figured prominently in the rhetoric of integralist groups, but did not necessarily entail an assertion of Italian identity. 'Nationalism' as defined by Gellner (1983) and other social scientists can hardly provide a description of the Italian political situation and its complexities at the turn of the millennium. Holmes, as we have noted, has described the phenomenon as *both* 'left' and 'right'. While Alleanza Nazionale's doctrine seems to be informed by a nationalist idiom, Lega Nord's rhetoric combines regionalism and populism, and Forza Italia and its policies express the values of neo-liberalism. Yet if we shift our focus from the level of political thought and official discourses to that of people's understandings of such discourses, and to the ways in which they relate to the political arena, we will find discrepancies: while at one level supporting the right may entail identification with a nationalist-like doctrine, at another this is not necessarily tantamount to xenophobia but to a political engagement perceived as *neither* 'left' nor 'right'. What holds this political expression together is a renewed commitment to a distinctive 'local culture', even though this commitment may be useful to an exclusionary political economy. In this sense integralism cannot be merely understood in terms of the currents of political thought that make its expression possible, but we need to consider social actors' relationships with their total social environment, not just the political sphere: integralism as it is lived and understood by social actors represents a dimension of sociality. The individualistic values that both Lega Nord and Forza Italia champion can coexist with a notion of community as long as we acknowledge the fact that this represents a *community of autonomous workers* inhabiting a mosaic of privately owned lots to which strangers should not have access. This constitutes a territorial community, but it can hardly be understood by reference to the concepts of 'left' and 'right', rather, it is a community from which party-driven politics is removed.

While the rhetoric of the parties governing Italy now may be imbued with some nationalist overtones, what these parties legitimate in the area studied is instead increasing commitment to locality. Although Holmes has labelled this phenomenon 'integralism', there are also grounds for calling it 'neo-localism'. This commitment to locality stems from growing anxiety at a globalised world in which peoples and things move, and are no longer in their proper place. More and more outsiders are taking over landed property in the valley, just as more and more immigrants settle in big cities. In both cases a boundary has been crossed, a situation perceived as disorder has been created and the protection of locality and private possessions now holds together political (or apolitical) expression and permeates the messages of vote-seeking politicians (Bauman 1999: 195). Thus, while the principal ideologies of modern times imply the idea of society having a centre (i.e., the state), when such ideologies decline in significance, locality emerges as a focus of attachment because of its concreteness, as opposed to the abstractness of some political doctrines. This is the imagery of a 'privatised' locality, of a site of resistance to the state and state institutions that emerges as a result of the decline of the state as a frame of identification, and which does not express a renewed commitment to national identity. Thus Italian integralism, as well as embodying the values of right-wing politics, may also be a dimension of sociality that expresses the complexities of a new entangled politics of which (neo-)nationalism is just one aspect.

Notes

I owe an intellectual debt to Jane Cowan, Susan Drucker-Brown, John Friedman, Andre Gingrich and Todd Sanders for their feedback and constructive criticism on earlier versions of this contribution.

1. See, for example, Kertzer (1980), Pratt (1986) and White (1980). For a summary of anthropological studies of politics in Italy, see Filippucci (1996).
2. For an anthropological analysis of this transformation, see Kertzer (1996).
3. The other intriguing aspect was that despite the radical-right overtones of its political propaganda, Lega Nord also succeeded in capturing the vote of former supporters of left-wing parties (for details see Cento Bull 2000: 18).
4. This transformation went hand in hand with the rediscovery of the value of patriotism, and this concern emerged after a period when the language of national identity and nationalism was almost the exclusive domain of the extreme right. Despite the emphasis on national unity, this rediscovery turned out to be an attempt, on the part of some centre-right intellectuals, at a reconciliation of Italians with their past, particularly with the Fascist past (Patriarca 2001: 30). Eventually this took on the form of historical revisionism aimed at questioning the parties of the left, and at legitimating the inclusion of right-wing political formations in government coalitions (ibid.: 26).
5. Paradoxically, while Alleanza Nazionale was endeavouring to redefine its image by rejecting racism, the immigration policies pursued by the centre-left coalition that governed the country between

1996 and 2001 did not bring about greater social justice as far as immigrants and refugees were concerned. In the left-wing city of Bologna, for example, the institutional discourses and practices of the left surrounding the process of integration of a group of Rom refugees from former Yugoslavia seemed to reflect a politics of division, and reproduced a macro-process of oppression (Però 1999: 221).

6. It must be noted that 'forza Italia' is the traditional chant of supporters of the national football team.

7. In its propaganda the party asserted the primacy of the family as the centre of solidarity and entrepreneurship, and promised greater choices for citizens as well as competition and efficiency in public life (Ginsborg 2001: 291).

8. Cohen (1996: 803–4) aptly made this point when he suggested, in relation to Scottish nationalism, that the issue is the identification of the difference between official representations of the nation and the individual's interpretations of these representations. While the politician 'collectivises' nationalism, the individual 'personalises' it (ibid.: 805); so the politician must formulate political messages in ways that enable individuals to appropriate such messages for their own requirements.

9. When it emerged, the Trentine-Tyrolean Autonomist Party (PATT) had in its agenda the creation of a European transnational region, between Italy and Austria, encompassing Trentino itself and the neighbouring German-speaking Italian and Austrian regions. Despite the different political programmes, what united PATT and Lega Nord was an emphasis on a local, regional culture and on distinctiveness vis-à-vis the Italian state.

10. The sawmill was shut down in late 2002.

11. A survey conducted by the local credit institution in the early 1990s revealed that over 50 percent of the houses in the Vanoi Valley are owned by people who do not ordinarily reside there.

12. Heady (1999) has provided an exhaustive analysis of the meanings of the ethic of self-sacrifice in the Carnic Alps.

13. Ironically, despite the villagers' emphasis upon self-reliance and their denigration of slack workers, in the nearby communities the Vanoi Valley is referred to as a municipality 'eating' regional subsidies, on the grounds that despite being heavily subsidised by the public administration it does not produce wealth.

14. This situation contrasts somewhat with the rural areas of southern France where, in the face of the changes that have altered societies and cultures in late capitalism, 'class' remains both a subjective and an analytical category (Lem 2002).

Bibliography

Bauman, Z. 1995. *Life in Fragments: Essays in Postmodern Morality.* Oxford: Blackwell.

———— 1999. *In Search of Politics.* Cambridge: Polity.

Bourdieu, P. 1977. *Outline of a Theory of Practice.* Cambridge: Cambridge University Press.

Cento Bull, A. 1996. 'Ethnicity, Racism and the Northern League', in C. Levy ed. *Italian Regionalism: History, Identity and Politics.* Oxford: Berg.

———— 2000. *Social Identities and Political Cultures in Italy: Catholic, Communist and 'Leghist' Communities Between Civicness and Localism.* Oxford: Berghahn.

Cohen, A.P. 1996. 'Personal Nationalism: A Scottish View of Some Rites, Rights, and Wrongs', *American Ethnologist* 23(4): 802–15.

de Certeau, M. 1984. *The Practice of Everyday Life.* Berkeley: University of California Press.

Diamanti, I. 1996. *Il male del Nord. Lega, localismo, secessione.* Rome: Donzelli.

———— 1999. 'Ha ancora senso discutere di nazione?' *Rassegna Italiana di Sociologia* 40(2): 293–321.

Filippucci, P. 1996. 'Anthropological Perspectives on Culture in Italy', in D. Forgacs and R. Lumley eds *Italian Cultural Studies: An Introduction*. Oxford: Oxford University Press.

Gellner, E. 1983. *Nations and Nationalism*. Oxford: Blackwell.

Ginsborg, P. 2001. *Italy and its Discontents: Family, Civil Society, State 1980–2001*. London: Allen Lane.

Giordano, B. 2000. 'Italian Regionalism or "Padanian" Nationalism – The Political Project of the Lega Nord in Italian Politics', *Political Geography* 19(4): 445–71.

Heady, P. 1999. *The Hard People: Rivalry, Sympathy and Social Structure in an Alpine Valley*. Amsterdam: Harwood Academic Publishers.

Holmes, D.R. 2000. *Integral Europe: Fast-capitalism, Multiculturalism, Neo-fascism*. Princeton: Princeton University Press.

Kertzer, D. 1980. *Comrades and Christians*. Cambridge: Cambridge University Press.

——— 1996. *Politics and Symbols: The Italian Communist Party and the Fall of Communism*. New Haven: Yale University Press.

Lem, W. 2002. 'Articulating Class in Post-Fordist France', *American Ethnologist* 29(2): 287–306.

Patriarca, S. 2001. 'Italian Neopatriotism: Debating National Identity in the 1990s', *Modern Italy* 6(1): 21–34.

Però, D. 1999. 'Next to the Dog Pound: Institutional Discourses and Practices about Rom Refugees in Left-wing Bologna', *Modern Italy* 4(2): 207–24.

Pratt, J. 1986. *The Walled City*. Göttingen: Herodot.

Romanelli, R. 1991. 'Le radici storiche del localismo italiano', *Il Mulino* 40(4): 711–20.

Roversi, A. 1999. 'Giovani di destra e giovani di estrema destra', *Rassegna Italiana di Sociologia* 40(4): 605–25.

Smith, G. 1999. *Confronting the Present: Towards a Politically Engaged Anthropology*. Oxford: Berg.

Stacul, J. 2003. *The Bounded Field: Localism and Local Identity in an Italian Alpine Valley*. Oxford: Berghahn.

Stolcke, V. 1995. 'Talking Culture: New Boundaries, New Rhetorics of Exclusion in Europe', *Current Anthropology* 36(1): 1–24.

Sutton, D. 1997. 'Local Names, Foreign Claims: Family Inheritance and National Heritage on a Greek Island', *American Ethnologist* 24(2): 415–37.

Ter Wal, J. 2000. 'The Discourse of the Extreme Right and its Ideological Implications: The Case of the Alleanza Nazionale on Immigration', *Patterns of Prejudice* 34(4): 37–51.

Trouillot, M. 2001. 'The Anthropology of the State in the Age of Globalization: Close Encounters of the Deceptive Kind', *Current Anthropology* 42(1): 125–38.

Turato, F. 1998. 'Il Trentino Alto Adige', in I. Diamanti ed. *Idee del Nordest. Mappe, rappresentazioni, progetti*. Turin: Edizioni Fondazione Giovanni Agnelli.

Ulin, R.C. 2002. 'Work as Cultural Production: Labour and Self-identity Among Southwest French Wine-growers', *Journal of the Royal Anthropological Institute* 8(4): 691–712.

White, C. 1980. *Patrons and Partisans: A Study of Politics in Two Southern Italian Comuni*. Cambridge: Cambridge University Press.

Wright, S. 1998. 'The Politicization of "Culture"', *Anthropology Today* 14(1): 7–15.

Chapter 9

Regarding the Front National

Gerald Gaillard-Starzmann

In tribute to Rachid Taha and the interpretation of 'Douce France' by his group Carte de séjour.

This chapter begins with the history of the extreme right in France from 1945. It then goes on to examine the evolution of the Front National's vote and the reasons for the electoral failure of the left. I show how the Socialist Party has, over the years, helped to build a strong Front National (FN) in order to divide its adversaries. I raise the question of the possibility of an alliance between the FN and the right and put forward the thesis that one of the fundamental reasons for the FN's success is the specific configuration of republican ideals organising social relations in France, and that broad aspects of its programme are in fact traditionally included in the socio-politics of the right, as well as the left, in other countries. The chapter closes with a comment on the possible end of the French Exception and the pessimistic questions: What will France's future hold? Will it desperately try to close itself off with a national welfare state reserved for 'real' French citizens, as suggested by the FN, or open itself up to a modern, savage, uncivilised capitalism compatible with multicultural society?

Chronology

Thirty Years of the Extreme Right (1945–1977)

The nationalistic extreme right in France ceases to exist with the reconstruction of the country following the Liberation in 1944 and 1945. Tied to Vichy's regime, the Catholic traditionalist clan and the political personnel of that older variant of an extreme right in France vanish into thin air. A new phase begins and the country divides itself between the Communist Party and those from the right, purified by the Resistance, who dare not allow themselves to be associated with the extreme right. The renewed right is progressive, secular, environmentalist, culturalist, against any idea of 'human nature', anti-racist and humanist. With the exception of a few names (most notably Marx), the cultural and ideological references of the right are basically identical to those of the left, and nationalist ideologies are unpopular. The extreme right has few intellectuals of any calibre and only survives amongst various monarchist groups and those nostalgic for Pétain. In the early 1950s the state is modernised, while former collaborators progressively resurface.

The war in Indochina (1947–1954) is followed by the North African war (1954–1962), and political instability is chronic. In late 1955 the Legislative Assembly is dissolved and early elections are called. With 11.6 percent of votes in January 1956, the Poujadists, including a 27-year-old Jean-Marie Le Pen, get fifty-two seats at the National Assembly. The Fourth Republic collapses and in May 1958 the National Assembly invests De Gaulle with full powers. The constitution of the Fifth Republic is adopted by referendum with 79 percent of votes. The legislative elections take place in November 1958. De Gaulle is elected President of the Republic a month later. With less than 1 percent the extreme right is thus excluded from parliament.

From the early 1960s, the extreme right begins to reconstruct itself with the founding of the group Occident and the weekly publications *Europe-Action: Le magazine de L'Homme Blanc* and *Les Cahiers universitaires*. The youth is restless, and the declining old populist right supports the candidature of Jean-Louis Tixier-Vignancour during the 1965 presidential elections. Le Pen, meanwhile, is put in charge of the management of supporting committees. In December 1965 Tixier-Vignancour, who hoped to get 20 percent, withdraws having gained only 5.27 percent of the vote. De Gaulle is elected. *Nouvelle Ecole* takes over from *Europe-Action* in 1968, a periodical with a global distribution. In 1969 it is followed by the Research and Study Group of European Civilisation (GRECE), created by Alain de Benoist. GRECE aims to preserve cultural difference and focuses on pushing for all things Indoeuropean in the face of 'the egalitarian, individualistic and universalistic ideology transmitted by Judaeo-Christianity'.

In 1969 Pierre Sergent, a former militant leader of the Pro-French–Algerian Secret Army Organisation (AOS), founds the Action-Youth group in which future cadres of the FN are to form. Meanwhile the majority of associations emerging from the turmoil of May 1968 are banned, including Occident. The legislative elections of June 1969 bring an overwhelming victory for the Gaullists. De Gaulle wants to initiate reforms to complete the country's transformation from a semi-agricultural/semi-industrial society to one of industries and services, but at seventy-nine he is too old to carry this through. He retires and dies in 1970, and Pompidou is elected as the new president. Meanwhile the extreme right does not even put forward a candidate. The following ten years see both great social unrest and the accelerated modernisation of the country.

Two organisations arise from the ashes of Occident: L'Oeuvre Française and Ordre Nouveau. They are inspired by the Movimento Sociale Italiano (MSI), which broke new ground by permitting its members to keep their traditional political membership of other parties. Ordre Nouveau's leader, François Brigneau, defends the strategy of a 'united front' for the French extreme right. Rejected by GRECE and the monarchists (see Lecoeur 2002: 41), the project is picked up by Le Parti de L'Unité Française, Le Mouvement pour la Justice et la Liberté and by Le Rassemblement Européen de la Liberté. Brigneau suggests that Le Pen should be the President of a Front National pour L'Unité Française (FN), which officially appears on the 5 October 1972 with a logo identical to that of the MSI – a three-coloured flame.

Appointed 'Le Pen's Militant Advisor' the cement heir Lambert joins the FN and finances the first campaign, for the legislative elections of 1973. They experience a total defeat and, disappointed, Alain Robert and Brigneau blame Le Pen. They organise a large meeting on the subject of 'savage immigration'. Police guarding the meeting are attacked by militants of La Ligue Communiste Révolutionnaire. The congressmen join in the violence. Both organisations are banned. Alain Robert then creates the Comités Faire Front (see Milza 1987: 45ff.), but some choose to stay in the FN, or to return to it very quickly; among them is François Duprat, the first champion of revisionism in France.

President Pompidou dies in April 1974. The people of 'Faire Front' ensure *service d'ordre*, stick up campaign posters for the candidature of ex-Minister of Economy Giscard d'Estaing and then create le Parti des Forces Nouvelles (Chatain 1987: 14). More successful than the FN, it becomes the FN's main rival until its collapse in 1979 after failure in European elections; its members are divided between the classical right and the FN. Giscard d'Estaing wins the second round against Mitterrand and begins to modernise the law: reducing the call-up period, establishing divorce by mutual consent, legalising sex shops and pornographic cinemas, free contraception, etc.

Encouraged by their new minister, several young *énargues* working at the Ministry of the Interior leave GRECE to create le Club de L'Horloge.[1] Drawing together senior civil servants, academics and corporate managers, the club proposes to defend both liberalism and the French identity, thus creating a platform for the FN's own programme, which also inspires the legitimate right. By means of dinner meetings, conferences and publications 'the horlogers' popularise notions of corporate culture breaking down horizontal solidarities. Readers of Gramsci (see Bourseiller 2002; Dély 1999; Duranton-Crabol 1996c), they set about the semantic work of replacing certain words: 'classes' becomes 'socio-professional categories'; 'capitalism' is translated into 'free spirit of creativity'; 'egalitarianism' is turned into 'levelling'; 'masses' becomes 'people', etc. In September 1976 Lambert dies, making Le Pen his sole heir and consequently the richest person in French politics.

Chirac wins back Paris during the council elections of March 1977, but it is a landslide for the left in the rest of the country, and the legitimate right combines lists with the Frontists in the south and south-west. A small group of Action-Youth members joins the FN. In March 1978 François Duprat, second most active in the party after Le Pen, is assassinated.[2] The legislative elections held that month bring

1.6 percent of votes to the FN whose posters proclaim: 'A million unemployed is a million immigrants too many' (cited by Bresson and Lionet 1994: 381). The slogan's creator, Stirbois, replaces Duprat at the Political Bureau. He plans to develop the FN on the basis of the concept of a national identity defined around the defence of small enterprise and the battle against the 'immigrant invasion'. The FN rediscovers Jeanne d'Arc whose memory it sets out to honour each year.[3]

The Front National Takes Off (1978–2002)

Le Pen wants to run in the presidential elections but he does not get the necessary minimum support.[4] In 1980 his party has only 270 members and goes on to get only 0.35 percent of the vote during legislative elections in June 1981. In April 1981 Mitterrand beats Giscard d'Estaing with the support of 52 percent of voters. After twenty-three years of opposition the left is finally in power. In May Le Pen writes to the President to complain that the media ignored his party conference. In their battle against the governing right 'the FN and the PS are objective allies' (see Faux et al. 1994: 61). After one of Mitterrand's chief advisors and Le Pen have lunch together, the Minister for Communication receives the order that 'for the sake of fairness the FN should not be forgotten' (the letter is reproduced in Faux et al. 1994: 21; Le Pen himself made it public, see Plenel and Rollat 1992: 365). In June 1982, the president of the FN is invited to make a TV appearance. It is a success, and the press report his words the next day (see Bresson and Lionet 1994: 406; Faux et al. 1994: 26–27; Fredet and de Saint Affrique 1998). In May 1982 the Socialist Prime Minister had announced 'changes to economic policy', and in March 1983 he puts an end to 'politics inked in the left'. The socialists become neo-liberals. Economic realism and the right's management become the quintessence of good politics.

The FN gets only 0.11 percent in the first round of the council elections of 1982, but having appeared on television Le Pen gets 11.3 percent in Paris, and candidates of the right and left adopt his slogans. A process of change begins, and the party, lead by Stirbois, gets 16.7 percent of votes in the partial local elections held in Dreux later that year. The FN enters the city council ousting the PS. The right agrees to combine lists with the extreme right, which thus infiltrates French political life. Stirbois, general secretary of the FN since 1980, reinforces his position in the bosom of the party and succeeds in expelling the neo-Nazi element. After radio appearances in January 1984, Le Pen enters the *Figaro-Sofres*' barometer, which measures the popularity of political personalities. In a poll, 9 percent declare that 'they would like him to play a more important role in the years to come' (cited by Perrineau 1996: 34). By order of Mitterrand (Meyer 2002: 71), in February 1984, Le Pen is invited to appear at prime time on 'L'Heure de vérité', the most popular political TV programme. The FN distributes 15,000 posters to publicise the show. The audience discovers Le Pen, and those who have already heard of him find that he is not an agitator but a responsible politician. About 1,000 people join the party in the hours immediately after the show and the voting intention increases to 7 percent.

The Socialist government tackles the private school issue[5] and in doing so opens a Pandora's box. In June 1984 between 1 million and 2 million go out onto the Paris streets to protest. The government retreats in the face of the most significant demonstrations ever known in the country (see Becker 2002: 301–5). Meanwhile it allows FN members to attend these demonstrations for a cause many average French people approve of, decorated with their three-coloured sashes, and, furthermore, gives them the chance to make contact with the most extremist supporters of private schools. Bernard Antony, the leader of the extreme traditional Catholics, joins the FN and brings his troops with him. Though candidates contribute according to their chances of being elected,[6] the party's financial situation leaves much to be desired until a sponsor arrives in the form of a Romanian exile and member of the Unification Church, or Moonies (Fredet and de Saint Affrique 1998: 34, 59; Plenel and Rollat 1992: 266), who takes fourth place in the list for 4 million francs. The FN gets 10.95 percent of the vote and ten candidates are elected in June 1984. At the European Parliament a group of the European right is established and for the first time the FN is awarded public funds.[7] The cantonal elections bring 8.67 percent of votes to the FN. With 1,521 candidates it gains around 6 percent of votes in about half of all French cantons. For the legislative elections the FN chooses a strategy of opening with a list including people who are not from the party.

After failure at the elections of 1981 le Rassemblement pour la République (RPR) launches numerous associations to recruit for the party. Bruno Mégret is in charge of the Comités d'action républicain (CAR), whose declared aim is 'to unite those French who wanted to take constructive action without being affiliated to a party' (Chatain 1987: 141). Considered an alternative to the extreme right, the Comités have little success as the troops leave to join the FN (Dély 1999: 40). During the summer of 1985 Mégret starts negotiations with Le Pen. He brings together FN and CAR members in exchange for candidatures for some CAR deputies. The FN brings together all elements of the extreme right – traditionalist Catholics, supporters of social-nationalist state control and right-wing nationalist liberals. Uniting forces is all the more attractive since Mitterrand introduced proportional representation intended to prevent the traditional right from obtaining a total majority (Attali 1996: 1,193, 1,198, 1,422; Plenel and Rollat 1992).

Le Pen reserves third place in the list for Pierre Ceyrac, a northern deputy, nephew of the ex-president of the CNPF (the employers' union) and, most importantly, leader of the Moonies in Europe (Bourseiller 2002: 83ff.). The sect finances and supports campaigns for the local and legislative elections held in March 1986. The FN gets 133 elected at the local level and thirty-five deputies. The right gets the majority by two seats and this leads to the cohabitation of a Socialist president with a right-wing prime minister and government.

Between the budgets of the Assembly group and the European Parliament the FN collects between 30 million and 40 million francs, which permits it to think seriously about running in the presidential elections of 1988. Le Pen announces his candidature in April 1987, and throws himself into battle by opposing nationalist liberals and social-nationalist supporters of state control. He nominates the pro-liberal Mégret as his campaign director (see Darmon 1999: 45). He comes back from travelling (Bresson and Lionet 1994: 446) in the U.S. with 'a new look' copied from TV evangelists. He is the first French politician to adopt this style.

With the slogan: 'France unites', Socialist Mitterrand builds a centrist campaign. In April 1988 he gets 34.1 percent in the first round. Le Pen gets 14.39 percent and Stirbois issues the order to vote for Mitterrand (see Bourseiller 2002; Faux et al. 1994; Fredet and de Saint Affrique 1998). Re-elected, the President of the Republic dissolves the National Assembly.

In charge of Le Pen's campaign, Mégret's 14 percent put him in a strong position and he demands new responsibilities. Le Pen creates the General Delegation for him when Stirbois dies in a car crash (Dély 1999: 61–62). The first round of the legislative elections, with the majority voting for the right, is held in June 1988. Le Pen gets 33 percent of votes in the district of Marseilles and threatens to stand again in the second round. Other FN candidates perform as well. The right hesitates at first, and then makes a deal for the southern Rhône and the Var regions. There, in eight cases a rightist candidate is beaten by and withdraws in favour of an FN candidate (Becker 2002: 460). On the evening of 12 June 1988 the FN retains only one deputy. Le Pen is beaten by a Socialist candidate. The backwards dynamic of the legislative elections is amplified during the cantonal elections in October 1988 during which the abstention rate reaches more than 50 percent. The party gets only 5.2 percent of votes and this apparent decline is confirmed at the council elections. Things come to a head with 11.73 percent at the European elections.

In March 1992 both cantonal and regional elections bring defeat for the PS following numerous mistakes. Subject to the law of 1991, the FN is eligible for public funds that finance political parties and therefore has the means to campaign. It overtakes the PS with 18.22 percent against 14.66 percent in Île de France (Paris district), and with 13.9 percent overall it is henceforth present in all regional assemblies. The French say 'yes' to Maastricht's treaty in September 1992. As during the Gulf War, the right/left opposition is once more blurred as members of every party oppose the treaty. On the national level, cohabitation returns after the right wins the legislative elections in March 1993. The right launches a party lead by a young traditionalist Catholic, Philippe de Villiers. His programme attracts those who did not like the FN president's scandalous anti-Semitic statement. Nevertheless Le Pen gains 12.4 percent of recorded votes but no deputy. The FN again finds itself in competition with the right's anti-European list and that of the populist left during the European elections in June 1994 in which it gets 10.5 percent. The extreme right does not manage to come to an agreement that would enable it to form a group and therefore does not qualify for a subsidy.

In this period of crisis Mégret wants an alliance with the classical right while Le Pen goes in a social-populist direction with slogans like 'Le Pen, the People' and 'No right, no left, the French first'. Instead of Mégret he appoints a representative of the fundamentalist Catholics as general secretary of the FN. After introducing the TV evangelist style he introduces another innovation by becoming the first presidential candidate to be photographed with his wife for the campaign posters. Being fourth with 15 percent in the first round, he does not go through to the second. Chirac beats Jospin on 7 May 1995. One month later during the council elections, which register a record rate of abstention, the FN wins three cities and so gets four councillors; the party now has 1,500 elected at the local level, 240 regional councillors, one deputy in parliament and ten European deputies. In search of respectability, in 1996 the FN starts proceedings against *Le Monde* to prevent it using the epithet 'extreme right' in reference to the party.

In search of a new legitimacy of his own after a series of strikes, President Chirac dissolves the National Assembly in April 1997. The elections give the FN 14.61 percent, thus maintaining its candidates in 133 districts. As a result, the left moves up from 99 to 320 seats, the right drops from 465 to 248. The FN gets only one representative. A cohabitation then starts that is symmetrical to the preceding one, with a president from the right (Chirac) and a prime minister from the left (Jospin). Mégret is not satisfied with the results and calls for Le Pen's retirement and for an alliance with the right. Le Pen makes the latter impossible by repeating his declarations on the *Shoah*.

The FN gets 15.27 percent at the local elections in 1998 and Le Pen is once again arbiter for the elections of the regional president. Eight candidates from the classical right are elected with the FN vote. Recalled by their party, five of them resign but three others hold their positions. They are thus excluded from their party. During the campaign for the legislative elections, however, Le Pen, having lost his temper, attacks a Socialist councillor who had argued with Le Pen's daughter, and the court sentences him to two years' deprivation of civil rights. With the European elections imminent, Mégret wants to lead the FN list but Le Pen decides to entrust it to his wife, Jany Le Pen; she becomes a favourite of popular magazines, which praise her simplicity and love for animals. The sentence being reduced on appeal to a year, Le Pen heads a list that keeps only one Mégretist, at tenth place. The FN implodes. Competing with the anti-European lists of Villiers-Pasqua (12 percent) and of the CPNT (Chasse, Pêche, Nature et Tradition, 5 percent), the FN (Le Pen) and the FN-MN (Mégret) respectively get 5.75 and 3.31 percent of votes. The combined scores of the two extreme-right parties are approximately 10 percent until the presidential elections in 2002.

Presidential Elections – 2002

The candidates must have 500 signatures by the 2 April. Soon Le Pen claims that he is eighty signatures short. The political staffs of the right and left are concerned at the implications that Le Pen's not being able to run will have for democracy, and therefore the FN is admitted as a legitimate party. Chirac gets 19.88, Le Pen 19.5

and Jospin 16.12 percent. With Jospin out of the running, Le Pen presents as the sole alternative to Chirac at the second round. The country is flooded with demonstrations. The demonisation of him by the media is total. Chirac even refuses the ritual of a television debate and is re-elected with 82.1 percent of recorded votes. After the new President dissolves the Assembly, the right wins 365 out of the 577 seats in the next national elections. But despite general moral disapproval, 17.79 percent vote for Le Pen whose candidature gathers the largest proportion among the unemployed, workers and even those under twenty-five. At the end of that electoral period, Mégret's faction has disappeared, whereas inside the FN Bernard Antony and Bruno Gollnisch's more or less Catholic fundamentalist faction clashes with Marine Le Pen's modernist one.

The Right and the Extreme Right

Success of the Front National

It is striking to see how the rise of the FN runs parallel to the decline of the Parti Communiste (PC), which fell from 15.3 percent in 1981 to 3.3 percent in 2002. If we explain this fall by that of 'the Wall' and the PC's unsuccessful participation in the Socialist government of the 1980s, we must also add another factor: successive generations did not recognise themselves in the totalising culture of the PC. For a long time, it had denounced rock music, long-haired joint smokers as well as divorce and the sexual revolution, while it remained ignorant of developments in the media and elsewhere. Those generations either depoliticised massively or joined the Lutte Ouvrière and other Trotskyist groups that proposed more varied and fluctuating identities. To determine the scale of this shift it would be necessary to match workers' votes with the voters who identify themselves as left-wing, but it is possible that the PC and particularly the CGT (a union very close to it) facilitated the workers' transition to the FN by encouraging the worldview of its members who opposed immigrants.

Different studies divide FN voters into a hard core of 'repressive conservatives' and 'the reactives', the latter being divided into three groups according to motivation. The first group includes the economically and socially marginalised who express their hatred of the system by means of their vote. Commentators explain that in governing for the middle classes, the left and the right are commonly rejected by those sacrificed to the sociological majority. The second group would be made up of the right's disappointed supporters, who would protest and sanction by means of their votes to call their party to order, but they would not want Le Pen to be president or prime minister, although they might want to have some FN ministers in government. Finally, there are those straightforward republicans who would like to frighten those in power but who, for the benefit of the uniformity of the nation, also reject the idea of ethnic communitarianism.

Other texts insist that it is the reduction of politics to management, where institutions alone have the power, which persuades voters to desire such leaders who are then provided by extreme parties (Gaillard 1998; Geffray 2001; Pommier 1990). For the majority of voters the right and left govern identically, whilst admitting that in fact the world economy is governing, not them, and in these circumstances to be in government can only mean serving oneself. Never having been in power, the FN stresses that whether right or left: 'they are both rotten'. Manière writes that Chirac, like Jospin, gives the impression of there being a discrepancy between what he is and what he appears to be; he seems to have something to hide. He adds that in contrast: 'Le Pen has drawbacks but hides them badly' (Manière 2002: 56). His speeches start with: 'Frenchmen, Frenchwomen, I love you'.[8] However hard communication advisors try to train them, the mainstream parties' leaders would not be able to profess such love, and if they did, they would not be believed. The reason is that the elite's dominance in a parliamentary democratic capitalist regime is legitimised by means of an independent law to which love is irrelevant.

In addition, for many citizens today there appears to be a rather brutal contrast between the egalitarian imagination derived from the French Revolution (liberty, equality, fraternity) and the actual representations of the hierarchic scale of purchasing power. Incapable of satisfying their narcissistic libido through consumption these people continuously encounter disdain. They then search for a figure in whom to satisfy their narcissism. The FN offers such a master to revive the decadent nation. Rather than projecting it into the future however, the FN proposes that the nation has to resort to a fantasised authenticity, including various founding elements such as Jeanne d'Arc or Clovis. 'More reasonably', other politicians present themselves as managers of a law that does not belong to them. Thus populism can very precisely be defined as calling into question the separation of the law and those in power into a fusion dissolving the State of Right (see again Geffray 2001).

The Fight Against the Front National

The principal 'strategy' for controlling the rise of the FN seems to have consisted of 'demonisation' and 'cordon sanitaire'. Demonisation was successively encouraged by all political camps: the left used it as much to divide the right, as to convince the public; the right employed demonisation as much to keep its core electorate whilst proving the impossibility of an a'liance with the far right; and Le Pen used it to prevent such an agreement. Demonisation can thus, in the long run, be judged to be an inefficient, if not dangerous, strategy: inefficient because whilst the mainstream condemned the FN, the latter's popularity never stopped growing; dangerous because, as the boundary of the acceptable is subjective, lines become blurred and consequently certain taboos are relativised.

The strategy of creating a cordon sanitaire is political in the sense that, with voting on the basis of a majority over two rounds, it prevents the minority parties, or those not part of an alliance, from participating in government. It also features the so-called tactics of 'the republican front': a mutually agreed reciprocal withdrawal by right or left when the FN seems likely to win. Furthermore, a media cordon is based on the idea that the media 'fabricated' Le Pen by foregrounding him, and the FN, by vaguely linking immigration, insecurity, Islamism, suburbs, etc. The panic-stricken electorate then turns to the person and party, constructed by the media, that offer a solution to the threats and problems also supposedly produced by the media.

The FN's rise undeniably corresponds to Le Pen's television presence. Le Pen had been overexposed in the media for years. Of course certain sections of the press could not help but denounce the FN's neo-fascist ways, but in doing so they relaunched the FN's agenda: the poor state of law and order, the danger of immigration, the political monopoly by the same old parties, etc. The resulting ambiguous image was undoubtedly worse. The FN was presented as 'the deepest expression of France' and its militants as 'average Frenchmen'. Another section of the press created the Le Pen 'soap opera'. This was the case with *France-Soir* and *Paris Match*, which regularly featured some news about the Le Pens, for example, generating a drama in the summer of 1995 around the candidature of Madame Le Pen as the head of the list, and for the European elections (Darmon 1999: 29). The social influence (and the circulation) of such publications outweighs that of innumerable pamphlets, essays and studies explaining the (good) reasons for not voting for the FN. Given the partisan participation of the media, the strategy of cordon sanitaire is an appeal to them to stop discussing the FN and its president, and to greet them instead with a wall of silence.

The Question of Alliance

In spite of being divided, the right nevertheless consolidated its rejection of the FN in the early 1990s. Several factors should be taken into account in this respect. They include the coarseness of the president of the FN, and the fact that the right would lose votes by uniting with the FN but that it gains votes simply by adopting some of its slogans. Finally, the right's leaders, afraid of extremist outbursts, would find demonising the FN difficult once they had appointed FN ministers. As we have seen, the FN had itself been divided until the hard Lepenist wave of the late 1990s. Since then the right has been perceived as an enemy with whom there is no possibility of alliance.

What separates the classical from the extreme right is, first of all, a style of which we have endless examples: 'Communism triumphed because it knocked up the Church, an old naïve virgin' (cited by Warin 1995: 68); 'a liberal is an old woman who at the moment of being raped is starting to fold her skirt' (ibid.). The tone and manner softened, especially during the 2002 campaign, but the memory cannot be erased. The legitimate right cannot integrate such a style: it has the *habitus* of another world, but furthermore the people demand that its representatives present themselves differently. This style is a symptom of the underlying difference between the FN and other parties.

A style can be worked on however, so we must determine whether any aspects of the FN's programme are, or could become, acceptable to the mainstream.[9] Much of it is simple propaganda. The most important economic proposals include the lowering of taxes on direct inheritance, income tax and tax for small and medium-sized enterprises with the loss of income for the state being partially balanced by the increase in indirect taxes such as VAT. This measure presupposes a relatively closed market and thus the abrogation of European treaties. The most important political measures include closing L'Ecole de la Magistrature (which is considered too politicised), the repeal of laws repressing racist and revisionist statements, restrictions on the power of the Constitutional Council, and the promotion of the referendum initiated by the people 'as a restoration of democracy'. For an economy based on exports within Europe, any return to the franc and any exit strategy from the European Union would be nonsense. These radical propositions are not acceptable in their current form, but if modified they could be; the same goes for *la préférence nationale*.

For all that, the FN's programme heralds a real revolutionary party and one that considers itself omniscient. This is revealed where the party manifests its power, that is to say, in the towns it governs: businesses that take on the local unemployed receive municipal subsidies, school canteens are reserved only for children with two working parents and markets must sell regional products. More striking still is that streets are renamed, and public libraries' subscriptions to daily newspapers and weekly magazines are cancelled and replaced with subscriptions to Frontist publications. This is the heart of the FN's project, which combines its socio-economic programme with a project of pedagogical and identity inculcation, something the mainstream right has every reason to fear.

In the long run it will be difficult for the leading figures of the mainstream right to maintain 'the republican pact' and to ban any agreement amongst young troops from both sides. These young wolves, from RPR or FN, may prefer an alliance rather than see their parties pushed aside in favour of their adversaries on the left. If the FN, which is made up of these heterogeneous groups who only have the *préférence nationale* project in common, initiates an alliance, how could it remain united? In fact, it is still possible that the current parties could be reorganised into a new two-party system in which the mainstream right incorporates the FN, while its left wing would thereby become the right wing of a new political group known as the 'left'. This political model (American and English), which may correspond to a particular stage in the evolution of industrial societies, would be the end of the distinct French and continental European political tradition.

The End of the French Exception?

The working class constituted the core electorate of the FN at the presidential election on 21 April 2002, when abstention reached 30 percent: in Paris, with an openly homosexual Socialist mayor, the FN got 27 percent, and 60 percent in the working-class suburbs of Seine-Saint Denis. The FN thus apparently tapped an unexploited potential. Is it necessary to restore a censitary suffrage system so that 'social losers' do not express themselves dangerously? Since the results of 21 April, however, commentators have not been asking this question. On the contrary, they have been speaking of the reconciliation of the people with institutional politics. Generally it is also noted that as the political horizon becomes limited to the science of management, including the expertise of balancing the budget, citizens become reluctant to vote. Again and again, it has been said that a political space defined by ideology and a system of beliefs needs rebuilding.

One could simply say that in being more and more reluctant to vote the French follow, albeit with a delay, the political sociology of other nations. This abstention may express a criticism that the extremes then exploit, but during a time of management and *la fin de grands recits* it can also be interpreted as the sign of a kind of maturity. In complex societies, specifically in a France that is no longer organised along the lines of homogeneous group interests, but instead consists of an individualised society, the state is unable to fulfil the wishes of groups of citizens to such an extent that they are aware of their competition with other groups of citizens, even politically close ones. It is important to emphasise that, with the exception of the FN, all parties gave up a programming politics, arguably no longer consistent with actual conditions in Western societies, for a pragmatism responsive to pressures from and successive demands of various groups. On the one hand, these abstentionists thus knowingly relinquish the management of the country to a political universe in which the rules of careerism thrive. On the other hand, and paradoxically, the same people increasingly require politicians (more and more closely controlled by the law) to fulfil their logistical role, and to improve management. Given this, the only citizens who move to the ballot boxes are, for example, those who are part of a network of interests or are the specific customers of one party. Are politically inactive citizens unpatriotic or simply completely depoliticised?

High rates of abstention in the U.S.A. are sometimes said to lend little legitimacy to the governments elected, but few nations are at the same time so passionately civil and nationalistic. Many citizens consider that the management of the state is the business of a class of professionals from whom they simply expect some guarantees and a certain standard of living. There were thousands of people on the streets when on the evening of 21 April 2002 the threat of the extreme right became apparent. Abstentionists, preferring to leave affairs to a 'professional management', will only move for an issue of critical importance.

As already noted by *Socialisme et barbarie* in 1965,[10] Western peoples gradually seem to become satisfied with management politics and only mobilise (often tardily) when they consider something to be intolerable: the Vietnam War, the Belgium of the 'white walk' or Chirac's 82 percent ... After having applauded 'the awakening of youth to politics' the right, and the left, lamented: 'it was only a humanist reaction and not a political one'. Why should politics be so intrinsically good when all of human history teaches us the opposite? One can dream of another kind of politics, but one may as well accept that large meetings, such as football matches and rock concerts, now satisfy the instinctive urge to 'be together' – a role previously played by political or religious activity.

Today, scientific calculations of cost–benefit or the economic contribution of immigration are part of the process of defining 'what it is to be French'. In addition to adopting a 'minimum French identity' inevitably under threat, some resort to a version of 'maximum French identity'. These people adopt all possible features of such an ethnic and national identity. Defending themselves against the accusation of promoting a fascist state, they thank the FN for giving them a French identity defined around a community of blood, of language and of cultural features focused on the rejection of universalism and cosmopolitanism.

In contrast to this image and presence of a France of solidified identities, there is another one that acknowledges that the country is built on immigration: this part of France hesitates between the multicultural communitarian society conforming to the general model of developed nations, and a standardised republican hybridisation more suited to the country's own history. What could be more French than the songs of Yves Montand, the son of an Italian immigrant; or of Charles Aznavour, an Armenian immigrant; or the image of Isabelle Adjani with an Algerian father?

This tolerant France continues to grow, even while at the same time the FN gains in popularity. Research in 2002 concluded that between 1987 and 2002 the number of French people claiming that 'I would not be upset if I discovered that my son were homosexual' went from 4 to 17 percent among those declaring themselves to be right-wing, and from 10 to 23 percent among those declaring themselves left-wing. The number of those opposed to the death penalty and identifying themselves as right-wing grew from 32 percent in 1992 to 42 percent in 2002. There has also been a change in the number of people wanting a significant number of immigrants to leave – from 67 percent in 1991 to 51 percent in 2002 (*Le Nouvel Observateur*, 14 February 2002: 53–56).

An egalitarian nation in love with hierarchy; revolutionary but in love with institutions; a nation whose powers transform only by keeping what already exists. France seems to be periodically renewed only by revolution: only a new paradigm resolves inextricable situations. France required a revolution to leave feudalism, it needed Napoleon to establish a 'civil code' and May 1968 was essential to make the leap forward into late modernity. This France is still alive today. The contradiction is undoubtedly as old as the nation. One of its faces is described as 'deep'– its representatives often vote for the FN, it is endowed with a retrogressive imaginary and opposes the idea of a nation always under construction. Today, tolerant and progressive France is being challenged by it.

One of the cultural features of the country is that a large part of the population, including the middle classes, is dependent on the state, which itself results from the notion of a social world in which people are guided by an omniscient elite that is, to some extent, the quintessence of the people or the nation. The nation confers on the state, thus conceived, all powers. Since 1945 the state has gradually given itself the task of establishing a real, rather than a simply formal, equity. It has therefore transformed from defender of the right to freedom to defender of the right to welfare and funds. But the welfare state can no longer ignore the fact that given international capitalist competition the coffers are empty. Furthermore, whilst nobody wants additional taxes, it is to the state that everyone nevertheless turns when times are hard.

Like its enemy sister, tolerant and progressive France rebukes an allegedly inefficient administration, a slow postal service, public transport 'always' on strike, etc. without acknowledging the poor quality of these services inherent in liberal models. It wants an end to the *Grandes Ecoles*, which it denounces as too elitist and undemocratic, whilst praising American Ivy League universities without recognising that their fees are equivalent to the average managerial wage. It complains about the state's capital levy on the gross national product reaching 46 percent (in 2002) whilst ignoring that, except for in the U.S.A. (where, for reasons impossible to go into here, it approaches 30 percent), today it is more or less the same in all modern, industrialised countries. One of the striking features of French society is thus a deep ignorance of how various services, institutions, social mechanisms, etc. actually function in other countries, inside or outside the EU. Embracing such true cosmopolitan liberalism would require an effort that the average citizen cannot even imagine. The problem lies in the growing contradiction between negative representations of, for example, quality of services, level of tax, social contributions, and what citizens consider as appropriate to expect from their society via the state. How will progressive and tolerant France manage these demands that will cost it so dear?

I support the thesis that one of the essential reasons for the FN's success is the specific configuration of republican ideals organising social relations in France. Broad aspects of the FN's programme are in fact already (traditionally) included in the socio-politics of the right, as well as the left, in other countries. Let us look at Le Pen's famous statement: 'I love my daughters more than my cousins, my cousins more than my neighbours, my neighbours more than strangers and strangers more than my enemies. It is the same in politics: I love the French more' (*National Hebdo*, 5 June 1986, quoted by Chatain 1987: 6). Commentators were right to read praise for endogamy in this, but to speak of 'racism' is to misuse the word. A similar remark might not be qualified in that manner were it to come from a U.S. American or West African politician. In the case of Le Pen's statement it is sufficient to recall that public space is not the same as private space. But the public exists only relatively and only in correlation to the state of the common will. It is always the public sphere of a group (of a family, of a society, of an ethnic community, of the nation, of humanity). This is not a true 'public sphere', as it implies a whole series of exclusions of others. In a time of shared neo-liberal recomposition affecting all levels of society and corroding any transcendence, individualism develops, simultaneously privatising and ethnicising the public universe.

The first stages of multicultural policy were initiated about thirty years ago in the U.S.A., which has since passed from melting pot to multiculturalism. If the principle of religious or sexual tolerance opens the door to diverse communities, France is far from communitarianism, but various facts suggest that it is not impossible in the future. The first positive discrimination initiatives, such as priority zones in education, Islamic secondary schools, financial penalties for political parties whose membership does not include a given quota of women, have created a logic previously unknown in France. Furthermore, there is the process of regionalisation together with a promotion of regional ethnic identities that include linguistic elements (Catalan, Breton, Corsican, Alsatian). More remarkable still is the tendency towards the reinforcement of cultural differences.

Since the introduction of changes to broadcasting laws in October 1981, and the installation of independent radio stations (such as NRJ, Radio Shalom, Radio Beur), the French have been listening to programmes that are sometimes broadcast in Mandarin or Arabic, and which therefore represent different cultures in the anthropological sense of the word. 'High culture' is shared between France Culture, a national left-wing station, and Radio Courtoisie, which promotes a very traditionalist Catholicism and is close to the extreme right. The musical genres more or less shared by all (Aznavour, Beatles, Johnny Hallyday, Albinoni…) are losing ground to radically distinct genres corresponding to specific social groups.

If the nation is not yet made up of 'free and equal communities' rather than 'free and equal individuals', the whole 'system', that is to say, the social as well as economic logic with which everyone struggles, tends to be reduced to the addition of lobbies within a republican social model that is never fixed. The FN propaganda that came through my letterbox during the presidential elections in 2002 was entitled 'France and the French first'. It is clear that Le Pen is not Hamelin's flute player: his voters are not hypnotised by his music, but some choose it because 'Let's legalise statutory inequality' is its refrain. Why would/should people be generous, tolerant, anti-racist and so on when history shows, on the contrary, that people can be perfectly xenophobic and racist? As a simple observer, as well as a social anthropologist, I would say that for various contextual reasons the subjective state of humanity is closer to the ideology of the FN than to that of 'the progressivism' of the French parliamentary right, despite all the latter's defects. While many governments do not even try to establish democracy (even as the FN understands it), others more or less recognised as democratic (because their government results from multi-party elections) stay in power by repeating Bongo slogans.[11] Rather than risk losing power, they prefer to let their compatriots massacre and drive out foreigners, as in the Ivory Coast or Senegal regarding the Burkinabians and the Mauritanians.

Singapore applies ethnic quotas to residency; it is difficult for an economic migrant to live in the U.S.A.; and it seems almost impossible for someone with a black skin to migrate to Australia. Logically the entry into legality (green card and work permit) should be less difficult when the advantages it confers are weak in law and in fact.

During the twentieth century an influx of North African (then sub-Saharan and Asiatic) migrants followed the Polish, Italian, Spanish and Portuguese waves; at the third generation 30 percent of the contemporary French population is immigrant. Until the early 1970s two-thirds of immigrant workers were illegally recruited with official paperwork being completed retrospectively only after immigration had taken place. Public opinion then may have been that immigrant workers were useful for the country (but there were also 110 racist murders between 1969 and 1972). As with those who preceded them, North African immigrants were to remain in France, and in 1974 Giscard d'Estaing authorised family reunification. This measure is often overlooked in the majority of articles and books on the history under review here. It was, however, a significant event. In 1974, at the end of three glorious decades of economic boom and at the beginning of the growth of unemployment, the arrival of immigrant workers' families was a time bomb for the social morphology of the suburbs that was to explode ten years later. After 1976 and 1977, with unemployment spreading, the government put an end to the automatic issuing of employment cards to all foreigners who had entered illegally, and proposed to improve living conditions, initiating the first anti-racist campaigns. It also established a 10,000 franc assistance fund for voluntary repatriation cases, but the only ones to benefit were some Portuguese migrants who had always planned to return anyway after the 1975 Portuguese Revolution had taken place.

A new law for increasing state powers of deportation was passed in 1980, but was repealed in 1981 when the left came to power. During the following two years the left maintained a relatively tolerant policy on immigration. From 1983 an emergency law regarding illegal immigrants was put in place. Family reunification became more difficult and financial assistance for repatriation was renewed. At that time Prime Minister Rocard stated that 'France cannot accommodate all the misery of the world'; Fabius who succeeded him said '[France] can no longer receive foreigners'. The social elevator stopped and the fear of a downturn slowly brought about a popular rejection of immigrants.

In 1983 and 1984 protest movements emerged amongst workers of North African origin 'on whose broad back' and passivity a relative agreement was established for years between the leadership and the trade unions. It was also during these years that the generation called the 'Beurs' appeared, i.e., the offspring of migrant families of Arabic origin (Lemière 1997). Unlike their exploited parents, who had a place because of the substantial wealth they brought to the country, these young people, whether or not they are born French, find themselves in an economy that does not need them and a world that seems to offer them a system of social dependence and welfare as a future. Long before 2005, the first Beur riot erupted in the suburbs of Lyons in October 1990. A few months later, Giscard d'Estaing spoke of 'the invasion of France' and Chirac of 'the overdose on immigration'.

If from then on the politicians of the mainstream right paid great attention to what they said and new laws were passed banning all discriminatory and racist remarks, the topic of anti-immigration gradually established a social link in itself and by itself. The expression 'enough of immigrants' became a motto in certain social groups and surroundings (Tristan 1987). A community calling for complicity was established. Other citizens who, according to education, conviction or socio-professional situation, abhor this complicity often have to deal with obliging offers from plumbers, waiters, mechanics who, in the name of a 'French ethnic group', invite them to share in the expression of all possible variations of this motto. Thus a new politico-cultural ideological space established itself within the republic. As stated by Brigitta Orfali: 'The influence of the FN is not measured by the two million voters it got, but by the progressive and imperceptible change which it makes in the mentality of the French' (1990: 195).

Nevertheless, it is not clear whether the party imposed the topic of immigration on public discourse primarily as a result of its own strategic agency, or whether it was mainly exploiting a question raised as a by-product of systemic structure. The FN's rise could itself be seen as a symptom of a more powerful ideological wave: this thesis is supported by the development of neo-populism observable across Europe. That 'the FN is the result of the crisis' (Lecoeur 2002: 184) does not account for society's continuous economic and social reconstruction in a neo-liberal direction. It is reconstruction not crisis when profitable companies dismiss employees, and it is clear that the foreigner is just a scapegoat in such a situation when his or her absence would not change anything. To refuse others the right to enter, with equal rights, into the social structure is nevertheless a strategy for temporarily preserving one's own place. Actors are first of all rational and it is rational that they should vote for the FN, which says to them: 'You first'. This is not to suggest that they simply follow their own interests but rather that their decisions are made rationally on the basis of the information, knowledge and representations they have of the world and the symbolic system in which they live. Certainly the hypothesis of the loss of a French symbolic structural environment is not wrong, but the lost 'we' some people search for is, first of all, a mirror of a new imperialist/segregationist 'we'.

The FN programme is not representative of the fusty and backward France but instead it masks the populist and multicultural modernity of tomorrow. Designing the future is much more a question of politico-axiomatic decision making than anthropologico-intellectual argumentation. The Musée de l'Homme exhibition 'All kin and all different' has shown that, contrary to what everyone perceives in the streets, races are a myth. There is nothing obvious in this to contradict the rejection of the Other or *préférence nationale*. Humans create meaning and some choose the principle of equality and others do not. Such meaning is transient with no objective status. It is only an axiomatic gesture; principles do not exist before they have been laid down.

Notes

1. The Minister of the Interior under Giscard d'Estaing is Michel Poniatowski. The club is conceived as a 'Jean-Moulin Club de droite' (Duranton-Crabol 1996c: 273) or an 'American think tank' (Dély 1999: 21). Its creators are Yvan Blot (from RPR) and Jean-Yves le Gallon (from the Republican Party). It is widely believed that the club was named by chance because a clock decorated the room where its founders were meeting. However, the name allows the denomination 'horlogers' (those who set clocks right).
2. His car explodes during the time he is working on a book devoted to the financing of the parties. His files have yet to be found (Chatain 1987: 97–98).
3. In 1979 the Front National reinstates the annual holiday of Saint-Jeanne d'Arc that is held on 8 May in Pyramides Square (Paris) in front of her statue. All French schoolchildren learn that Jeanne 'sacked the English from France' (see Winock 1997 on the use of Jeanne d'Arc). It is an occasion for discussion of various topics from jobs being taken from the French to the disappearance of the nation: 'We see a real invasion that within 20 years will make the French nation disappear' (cited by Cuminal et al. 1997).
4. Since 1976 the law has dictated that to be eligible, potential candidates must submit a list of 500 signatures from higher representatives (46,000 deputies, senators, city and regional councillors …) to the Constitutional Council, each of whom can only back one candidate. Le Pen contacts Giscard d'Estaing through Le Chevalier (a member of the UDF) to propose a transfer of his poll after the first round. Giscard d'Estaing does not respond to this proposition.
5. To put it simply, according to public opinion, democracy in France is based on the school issue. The French school system dictates that parents put their children into schools corresponding to their home address. Given that school is a true means of social promotion, the system is very selective and the differences between establishments are considerable. The value of property correlates exactly with 'the school map' and parental strategies for placing their children in good schools are numerous – the easiest of which is to register with a private establishment. Paradoxically, these are practically free, being funded by the state.
6. This measure prevents numerous militants from applying. At a later stage candidates are also asked to sign an agreement to pay a third of their allowance during their term of office to the party (Bresson and Lionet 1994: 414; Fredet and de Saint Affrique 1998: 203; Konopnicki 2002a: 65).
7. Concerning the FN at the European Parliament see Bresson and Lionet (1994: 416–20) and McDonald this volume.
8. From 3 May 1984 in Balard cited by Cuminal et al. (1997: 23). No one since De Gaulle has spoken to the French in this way.
9. I refer to both the rather concise proposals of Le Pen whilst he was running in the presidential elections (2002) and to *Pour un avenir Français. Le programme de gouvernement du FN* – 435 pages including 300 proposals divided into 6 chapters and 16 columns ranging from the family to culture and citizenship, through justice and agriculture, which is accessible on the party's website where the quantitative data are regularly updated.
10. In 1965 the prestigious periodical *Socialisme et barbarie* (Axelos, Morin, Castoriadis) published its last copy (N°40) with the following editorial: 'in modern capitalist societies political activity tends to disappear'. *Socialisme et barbarie* together with *Les Temps Modernes, La Pensée et Esprit*, was one of the important left-wing journals of that time.
11. Bongo, President of Gabon, used the slogan 'Gabonaise first' in a presidential campaign.

Bibliography

Attali, J. 1996 [1993]. *Verbatim I, Deuxième partie 1983–1986*. Paris: Fayard.

Becker, J.-J. 2002. *Crises et alternances 1974–2000*. Nouvelle histoire de la France contemporaine, vol. 19. Paris: Le Seuil.

Bourseiller, C. 2002. *La nouvelle Extrême Droite*. Paris: Edition du Rocher.

Bresson, G. and Lionet, C. 1994. *Le Pen, biographie*. Paris: Le Seuil.

Chatain, J. 1987. *Les Affaires de M. Le Pen*. Paris: Messidor.

Cuminal, I., Souchard, M., Wahnich, S., Wathier, V. 1997. *Le Pen, les mots: Analyse d'un discours d'extrême–droite*. Paris: Le Monde-La Découverte.

Darmon, M. 1999. *Front contre Front*. Paris: Le Seuil.

Dély, R. 1999. *Histoire secrète du Front national*. Paris: Grasset.

Duranton-Crabol, A.-M. 1996a. 'Figaro Magazine (Le)', in J. Julliard and M. Winock eds *Dictionnaire des intellectuels français: Les personnes, Les lieux, Les moments*. Paris: Le Seuil, pp. 492–93.

—— 1996b. 'Groupement de recherches et d'études pour la civilisation européenne (GRECE)', in J. Julliard and M. Winock eds *Dictionnaire des intellectuels français: Les personnes, Les lieux, Les moments*. Paris: Le Seuil, pp. 562–63.

—— 1996c. 'Club de l'horloge', in J. Julliard and M. Winock eds *Dictionnaire des intellectuels français: Les personnes, Les lieux, Les moments*. Paris: Le Seuil, pp. 272–73.

Faux, E., Legrand, T. and Perez, G. 1994. *La main droite de Dieu, enquête sur François Mitterand et l'extrême droite*. Paris: Le Seuil.

Fredet, J.-G. and de Saint Affrique, L. 1998. *Dans l'ombre de Le Pen*. Paris: Hachette.

Gaillard, G. 1998. 'À propos du lien social et de l'activité économique: un regard clinique', in B. Schlemmer ed. *Sur les terrains de Claude Meillassoux*. Paris: Editions Karthala, pp. 325–41.

Geffray, C. 2001. *Trésor: Anthropologie analytique de la valeur*. Paris: Arcanes.

Konopnicki, G. 2002a [1998]. *Manuel de survie au front*. Paris: Mille et une nuits.

—— 2002b. *Les cent jours (5 mai–4 août 2002)*. Paris: Daniel Radford.

Lecoeur, E. 2002. 'Le Front National: sens et symboles. La construction d'un replis identitaire "ethnico-religieux" dans la France de la fin du XXème siècle', unpublished thesis. L'Université de Tours, 3 vols.

Lemière, J. 1997. 'Le mode de désignation des étrangers en France à l'épreuve du mouvement des sans-papiers de 1996–1997, proposition d'analyse à partir de la situation de Lille', in G. Gosselin and J.-P. Lavaud eds *Constructions et mobilisations identitaires*. Lille: Clersé.

Manière, P. 2002. *La vengence du peuple: Les élites, Le Pen et les Français*. Paris: Plon.

Meyer, P. 2002. *Démolition avant travaux*. Paris: Robert Laffont.

Milza, P. 1987. *Fascisme français, passé et présent*. Paris: Flammarion.

Orfali. B. 1990. *L'Adhésion au Front national: de la minorité active au mouvement social*. Paris: Kimé.

—— 2001. 'L'adhésion paradoxale: juifs, Antillais et ouvriers membres du Front national', in P. Perrineau ed. *Les Croisés de la société fermé. L'Europe des extrêmes droites*. Paris: Editions de l'Aube, pp. 185–99.

Perrineau, P. 1996. *Le Front national à découvert*. Paris: Presses de la Fondation nationale de Sciences politiques.

Plenel, E. and Rollat, A. 1992 [1984]. *La République menacée, dix ans d'effet Le Pen*. Paris: Le Monde-La Découverte.

Pommier, G. 1990. *Libido illimited. Freud apolitique?* Paris: Point hors ligne.

Tristan, A. 1987. *Au Front*. Paris: Gallimard.

Warin, O. 1995. *Le Pen de a à z*. Paris: Albin Michel.

Winock, M. 1997. 'Jeanne d'Arc', in P. Nora ed. *Les lieux de mémoire*, vol. 3. Paris: Gallimard, pp. 4,427–73.

PART III
European Perspectives

Chapter 10

'Healthy Native Soil' Versus Common Agricultural Policy

Neo-nationalism and Farmers in the EU, the Example of Austria

Gertraud Seiser

In discussion with colleagues in Vienna one striking assumption comes up again and again: that farmers, of course, are staunch supporters of nationalist and right-wing populist thought. Being rooted in their soil and tradition, particularly those living in mountainous areas, are they not the markers of locality in a globalising world and the very symbol of territoriality?

In Austria we all know the pictures showing Jörg Haider talking to a mass of sweaty, bawling figures dressed in traditional rural costumes, and letting himself get carried away with highly oversimplifying and polemic rhetoric. Or, standing on a platform, dressed in brown *loden* cloth, watching processions of folk-dance groups and veterans' associations marching by. All this makes 'the farmers' into a category, and it makes them suspect. Urban left-wing intellectuals picture them as a cliché: rural costumes, pilgrimages, brass bands and tractor roadblocks. Furthermore, the Freedom Party (FPÖ) is clearly anti-intellectual, and (another assumption) so are the farmers.

This raises the question of whether there is any kind of right-wing nationalist position concerning farmers, or are these parties instead preoccupied with immigration, hostile attitudes towards foreigners and populist attacks against the 'big shots'. A cursory look at some party programmes reveals that all are particularly concerned with farmers and agriculture. A comparison of the agricultural programmes of right-wing populist and nationalist European parties[1] shows fundamental common features: the number one priority is a renationalisation of agricultural policies and subsidies. This demand is always accompanied by a call for 'healthy' food for 'our native' population; such food, the programmes say, can only be guaranteed by family farms in contradistinction to industrial agriculture. For example, in an article entitled 'La mort programmée', the French Front National discusses in great detail the necessity of restoring a national, sound and self-sufficient agriculture for the 'Grande Nation' (Front National n.d.). The world of farmers and rural life is thus the epitome of the 'valeurs traditionnelles indispensables à la stabilité de notre pays' (ibid.: 139). Here are some further examples:

> The British National Party calls for the abolition of the CAP (Common Agricultural Policy). The present policy of encouraging production at any price by agri-business giants should be changed to support for the family farms which are the backbone of both healthy agriculture and vibrant rural communities. (British National Party 1999: 1)

> A self-reliant national agriculture is an indispensable element of a sound national economy. It is the only way to safeguard the basic supply with healthy foods for our population. This objective is being jeopardised by a European agricultural policy which subsidises over-production in other countries and forces German farmers to participate in an unfair competition causing an increasing number of farms to go under. This can be remedied only by a renationalisation of agriculture: German taxes for German farmers; support for the marketing of domestic produce; preservation of family farms... (Die Republikaner 2002: 33)

> The agricultural policy of the EU is opposed to these declared aims of maintaining traditional rural structures and extensive non-artificial production methods. To save Austrian agriculture from financial collapse, which can be anticipated by the planned eastwards expansion of the EU, we must urgently aim for a renationalisation of agricultural policy. The farmhouse as a place of work must be preserved. The structure of the family-owned and run rural business must be specially protected as a full-time occupation, without putting farmers with additional jobs at a disadvantage. (Austrian Freedom Party 1997: 29)

Many, but not all, of these parties obviously have no problem in juxtaposing these extremely protectionist positions with a declared belief in the neo-liberal market economy when it comes to the economy as a whole. The farmers and, in particular, the family farm are the embodiment of the national substratum and the backbone of the traditional values of the various nationalisms in Europe. If these family farms are protected and cared for at the level of the nation state they will produce sufficient quantities of healthy food, free from any chemical additives. At the moral level they reproduce the culture of the people and thus are a source that nationalist renewal can always draw upon. This ascription is by no means limited to right-wing populist or nationalist parties. There are, however, two distinctive features shared by these right-wing parties that distinguish them from almost all other political parties: the demand to renationalise agricultural policies and a negative attitude towards the Common Agricultural Policy (CAP) of the European Union.

The chapter tries to approach the following issues: What is the essence of CAP so fiercely rejected by right-wing populist and nationalist parties? What does the EU policy of subsidising look like from the perspective of the affected farmers? Are there developments in European agriculture and agricultural politics that make farmers particularly susceptible to neo-nationalist policies? Using the example of Austria I will then look at the political decisions that farmers make at the ballot box. Are the assumptions that the left or the right make about farmers founded? Is it actually true that a disproportionately high percentage of farmers vote for the FPÖ? I come to the conclusion that they do not, but why not? Is it on account of the FPÖ's agricultural policy? Or maybe because farmers are not what they should or seem to be? This raises another question: do neo-nationalist agricultural policies really address farmers themselves, that is, an electorate that constitutes only 4 percent of voters on an EU scale (prior to enlargement) and that continues to decline? I would like to conclude with some hypotheses that might illuminate (possible) routes along which social anthropology can further explore the relationship between farmers and neo-nationalism.

European Agricultural Policy

The Common Agricultural Policy (CAP) goes back to the founding of the European Economic Area at the end of the 1950s. Given the food shortages of the post-war period, the initial phase of this policy concentrated on increasing productivity in agriculture. This was to be achieved by subsidising producer prices (Schmeißer and Teufel 1999: 165). This strategy was by no means peculiar to Western Europe but was a common feature in all OECD countries at the time. This policy, of course, above all benefited the big farms in agriculturally favourable areas and thus increased the gap between rich and poor farmers. Farmers in large regions specialise in products they can supply at a very low price. In economically unviable mountainous regions cultivation had been abandoned altogether (Reiterer 1998: 180). CAP made the European Union independent of imports in the foodstuff sector; the individual member states with their specialised large areas, however, grew more dependent on each other.

In the main production areas this policy caused a massive increase in productivity within a very short time and, ultimately, production surpluses, which entailed major problems for governments in the early 1970s. In spite of the tremendous costs of subsidising surplus production, the EC countries, as well as Austria, did not attempt substantial reforms until the mid 1980s, and then again, in a more systematic attempt, in the 1990s (Schmeißer and Teufel 1999: 169). These reforms brought a diversification of the objectives of subsidising and an enormous number of increasingly detailed programmes: cutting back, but not entirely abolishing, subsidisation of producer prices; introduction of quotas, the best-known being the milk quota that aimed to reduce the butter mountains and milk lakes; premiums for the set-aside of agricultural land; compensatory premiums for 'less favoured areas' and for mountain farmers, in order to preserve the 'cultural landscape' in these regions; special subsidies for compliance with environmental standards, extensive cultivation and special crops, etc.[2]

So far, CAP has been the only field of EU policy involving the raising and (re-)distribution of funds at the level of the European Union. Some 50 percent of the overall EU budget is allocated to the agricultural sector each year. The mere fact that about half of the total budget of this supranational organisation is reserved for an ever-diminishing group that, meanwhile, constitutes only 4 percent of the population in the member countries puts agricultural policy at the centre of political and public interest alike.

The system of financial incentives, which for decades had aimed to increase productivity by maximising output whilst minimising input and with little concern for adverse consequences, entailed crisis-prone changes in production processes, especially in the main production areas. The BSE crisis is a good example: herbivorous animals were fed cheap animal protein to accelerate meat production, thus modifying the meat production process without taking into account possible consequences. Nitrate-polluted groundwater, foodstuffs contaminated with pesticides and, last but not least, BSE are, in addition to the EU enlargement process, at the centre of the current acceleration of CAP reform. I use the term 'acceleration' because since 1997 Agenda 2000 has already aimed at a reorientation of CAP towards reducing overproduction and towards environmentally sound forms of production;[3] however, a mid-term review of the programme already demonstrated that the measures taken had been insufficient.

At its Gothenburg meeting in 2001 the European Council agreed, 'that the CAP should continue to contribute to achieving sustainable development by increasing its emphasis on encouraging healthy, high-quality products and environmentally sustainable production methods' (European Communities 2003: 1). A completely new system of subsidies based, for the first time, on decoupling production and direct payments is currently being negotiated.

EU Policy of Subsidising
From the Perspective of Affected Farmers

Since the implementation of Agenda 2000 the motto of the EU has seemed to be: 'farmer, you choose; it's up to you! However, if you want subsidies or the purchase of your products guaranteed you have to do this or that at precisely the time we prescribe.' Filling in an application for subsidies alone requires the farmer to make a great number of economic decisions. These decisions, in turn, entail a cascade of further, more detailed decisions. This process usually results in long-term investments by farmers, encouraged by the subsidy programme. For example, automatic milking machines are very expensive and the EU subsidises up to 40 percent (in some cases even more) of the sum total for purchase and installation of such equipment. This causes farmers to make investments that, in fact, far exceed the financial capacities of medium-sized enterprises; even with these subsidies the farmer has to take out a sizeable loan with a period of twenty or thirty years. However, the subsidy programme itself is planned for a maximum period of five years and does not offer any guarantees beyond this. The necessary technological expertise and agricultural policy know-how is supplied by specialised advisors; this causes new dependencies.

Bourdieu found a very convincing metaphor when he described the situation of EU-subsidised farmers in France: 'All of a sudden, their situation seemed to me like that of workers on a kolkhoz who finance their own kolkhoz' (Bourdieu et al. 1997: 458). The imponderables of decisions made by governments or authorities at the EU level have a direct bearing on farmers' incomes and often also on their decisions concerning investments. These have far-reaching consequences and come as unexpectedly as a change in the weather.

The situation is further compounded by crises of identity caused by the massive infringement of a supranational modernity on the firmly established traditional rights of a population that is attached to its land through the obligations of inheritance.[4]

Farmers had no major problems in identifying with the first long phase of agricultural subsidies. The image of the independent producer remained intact as long as the difference between locally negotiated, fictitious costs of production and the world market price was covered by national or supranational subsidies. The shift away from productivity enhancing incentives in the objectives of agricultural policies constituted a blow to the economic self-image of farmers (Bel et al. 2001: 174). Accordingly, the meeting of the EU Ministers for Agriculture in the summer of 1998 in the Tyrol was accompanied by fierce protests from farmers who expressed their disapproval at being patronised by using the slogan 'We are independent producers, not charity cases.'

If one browses through the journals that Austrian farmers (automatically) receive each week on account of compulsory membership of their professional organisation, one gets the impression that Austrian farmers are helpless in the face of the ups and downs of world market prices if they have no state and EU subsidies. This situation results in farmers giving up agricultural activity (entailing the inevitable decline of the farming community), plummeting prices for agricultural stock products causing loss of farming income, radical changes of status with loss of prestige for farmers, and status gains for workers and employees.

To come back to the original question of whether there are developments, at the European level, that could make farmers particularly susceptible to neo-nationalist policies: EU agricultural policies have so far been anything but consistent and have often given cause for criticism from various directions. The same is true of national agricultural policies in the individual member states: 'It is difficult to identify any long-term consistent line of action', on the contrary, it is, 'considerably influenced by national agriculture ministers and their party programmes, together with – from the beginning of the sixties – an increasing link with EC-developments' (Bel et al. 2001: 170). Given this political background and the ensuing difficulty for the individual farmer in developing long-term strategies, a positive response by farmers to simplistic, popular solutions would not come as a surprise; especially if these solutions were supported by appropriate identity policies. As shown by scientific analyses, profound insecurity concerning their existence, fear of losing income and status, self-assessment as the losers of modernisation and globalisation, a tendency to foster dichotomous views of life such as 'good/bad', 'respectable, hard-working citizens' versus 'social parasites', etc. are characteristic attitudes shared by the Freedom Party's followers and voters (Berghold and Ottomeyer 1995; Pelinka 2000: 59). This corresponds to the sociological profile of those who have sympathised with the populist right in Europe since the late 1980s (Camus 2002: 44; Fleissner 2002: 30).

Using the example of Austria I will try to look more closely at farmers' attitudes towards the Freedom Party.

Farmers at the Ballot Box

The results of exit polls from 1986 to 2002 show us two things: first, farmers are the profession that least approves of the FPÖ. Only 10 percent of farmers voted for the Freedom Party in 1999 and only 1 percent in 2002. Secondly, farmers' approval of the Freedom Party was highest in 1995 when Austria acceded to the EU.

Given the fact that farmers account for only a small proportion of the total population there was a possibility that the results were slightly distorted; so I cross-checked the exit poll results with the results of the elections to the Chambers of Agriculture. These statutory bodies represent the interests of farmers and are

Table 1: *Exit poll results for Freedom Party by profession (%)*

Profession	1986	1990	1994	1995	1999	2002
Farmers	5	9	15	18	10	1
Self-employed	15	21	30	28	33	17
Civil servants	9	14	14	17	20	7
Employed	13	16	22	22	22	11
Workers	10	21	29	34	47	16
Retired	8	16	24	16	24	7

Source: Fessel-GfK, Exit Polls 1986–2002 (Plasser and Ulram 2003: 217). Reproduced by permission of WUV-Universitätsverlag.

organised at the level of provinces. Elections to the Chamber of Agriculture in the province of Carinthia, a stronghold of the Freedom Party, took place on 11 November 2001. Haider, governor of this province, won 42 percent of the votes in the elections to the regional government in 1999. In the elections to the Chamber of Agriculture, the Freiheitliche Bauernschaft (a subsidiary organisation of the FPÖ) got 27.5 percent of votes cast, losing 4.2 percent compared to the previous election, despite Haider's very committed election campaign (Wiener Nachrichten Online 2001). After that he had this message for his electorate, 'In the future, I will not commit myself to farmers' concerns in the same way as I have done so far' (Silber 2001: 2).

The proportion of voters for the Freiheitliche Bauernschaft was considerably lower in the other provinces of Austria. In the elections to the Chamber of Agriculture of Styria on 28 January 2001, for instance, this organisation got 7.6 percent of the vote. At the time of writing, the most recent Chamber of Agriculture election was held in Upper Austria on 26 January 2003. The Freiheitliche Bauernschaft lost 6.59 percent and got only 7.41 percent of votes. These statistical data suggest that the results of the exit polls after the parliamentary elections in 1999 were not a statistical outlier.

The Freedom Party's Agricultural Policy

Since the early 1990s the party's main topic in election campaigns has been its decidedly hostile attitude towards aliens and foreigners (Ottomeyer 2000: 79; Reinfeldt 2000; Scharsach and Kuch 2000: 74). In the field of agricultural policy this is reflected by the motto 'Austria first', which is used in the context of the eastwards enlargement of the European Union. In its present manifesto the FPÖ demands a renationalisation of agricultural policy, arguing that EU policies would destroy traditional rural structures and that EU enlargement would cause the financial collapse of Austrian agriculture. In their campaign prior to the 2001 elections to the Chamber of Agriculture in Carinthia, the Freiheitliche Bauernschaft went a step further: 'Enlargement of the EU is the end of Carinthian agriculture' (Freiheitliche Bauernschaft Kärnten 2001). It is obvious that this is likely to create fears among farmers: when eastern enlargement is being realised, you will lose the basis of your existence. The fact is, however, that Austria has a considerable surplus of exports to Central and Eastern European countries in the agricultural sector.[5] What is more, enterprises in the eastern parts of Austria with seasonal peak demands for labour almost completely rely on illegal and legal workers from the Czech Republic, Poland, Slovakia and Hungary.[6]

The agricultural policy of the Freedom Party largely follows the pattern of its other policies of the 1990s and shows the same elements as those identified by scientific analyses of these policies.[7] First, a nationalist and anti-European attitude runs through all political fields. However, this basic attitude does not express itself in factual political consistency and this often results in contradictory populist demands. The party, for example, denounces abuse of subsidies in agriculture and, at the same time, opposes a control of 'our farmers' (Freiheitliche Bauernschaft Kärnten 2001). This insinuates that only farmers in other EU countries obtain subsidies under false pretences. Secondly, the endeavour to appeal to each and any group of voters entails contradictions in the contents of the various policies. The present FPÖ programme, for example, juxtaposes a neo-liberal economic policy with a very protectionist agricultural policy. Some of the subsidiary organisations explicitly demand basic subsidies for each job in agriculture (FPÖ-Vorarlberg 2000; Freiheitliche Bauernschaft Kärnten 2001; Freiheitliche Bauernschaft Tirol 2001). In other contexts, the Freedom Party repeatedly denounced the concept of basic income as promoting 'social parasites' (e.g., Scharsach and Kuch 2000: 121f). Finally, Haider carefully cultivates his 'Robin Hood image' (Gingrich 2002; Ottomeyer 2000), verbally attacking the 'big shots', and there is even a photo showing him in a Robin Hood costume (Ottomeyer 2000: 13, fig. 1); nor does he tire of decrying the 'privileges' of the leaders in politics, administration and state-owned enterprises. The Freiheitliche Bauernschaft emulates his example using slogans such as 'Down with bureaucracy in agriculture' (FPÖ-Vorarlberg 2000) or 'Stop manipulation by agri-business and the food-processing industry' (Freiheitliche Bauernschaft Kärnten 2001).

Again, the parallels with programmes of right-wing nationalist parties such as the British National Party, the German Republicans or the Front National are clearly visible. The fact is that Austrian farmers do not respond positively to this policy. There are various possible reasons. An important one could be that the farmers are not as homogeneous as they are seen to be.

Some Remarks on Austrian Farmers

At the administrative level the term 'farmer' refers to rather disparate groups with varying economic capacity, income, modes of production and social structure. The lowest common denominator is their involvement in the production of agricultural and forestry products and/or animal husbandry. In addition, farmers, as opposed to agricultural workers, manage their own enterprises. Outside observers often ascribe characteristics such as homogeneity, stability and continuity to the group.[8] In reality, however, farmers have, during the past fifty years, experienced far-reaching processes of restructuring, concentration and change. In 1951, 30.3 percent of the working population earned their income in agriculture and forestry; in 2000 this figure was only 3.9 percent. In spite of this enormous structural change, most of which happened between 1950 and 1980, and which in many parts of Western Europe has brought about processes of massive concentration resulting in a number of very large farms, Austrian agriculture is still extremely small-scale: 41 percent of farms comprise less than ten hectares of land.

In Austria the average annual income from agricultural activity was €12,430 in the year 2000. The richest 10 percent of farms yielded an average annual income of €36,530 for each working family member. On the poorest 10 percent of farms, however, each working family member had to *invest* an average of €2,278 from other sources of income into the farm. Small-scale farms account for 55 percent of all enterprises and they do not provide a sufficient livelihood without further income from non-agricultural activities (Bundesministerium für Land- und Forstwirtschaft 2001: 57, 228).

Thus, 'farmers' constitute a social group that is characterised by 'marked regional and structural inhomogeneity' (Bundesministerium für Land- und Forstwirtschaft 2001: 115). The farmers themselves know this. Awareness of the differences from farm to farm and between the various regions is an essential element of their self-definition. They focus on the differences among themselves rather than between 'farmers' and other groups (Krammer 1995: 577). Above all, the high percentage of part-time farms means that we have to expect highly complex identities in this context. Part-time farming often involves various forms of migration to more or less distant places of work, in combination with employed or self-employed work in non-agricultural sectors. Furthermore, the usual class-based forms of social classification, often used as a reference system in politics and the social sciences (Kearney 1996: 115), are inadequate in this context.

My empirical material from field research among farmers in the Mühlviertel region also shows considerable differences both within the region and in comparison with other regions. The Mühlviertel claims, like many other regions in Austria, to be very special. This being special finds its expression not only in an intensively celebrated regional identity – formulated as belonging – but also in many ecological, social and demographic deviations from the statistical average in Austria. My research area, called 'Mühlviertler Alm', is a hilly region located between 600 m and 1,100 m above sea level.[9] Barrenness, poverty until the 1960s,[10] a relatively high percentage of people working in agriculture, many forms of pluriactivity,[11] a decreasing population due to migration in spite of a birthrate far above the Austrian average, above-average unemployment and below-average income are the statistical markers of the area. These characteristics show a surprising continuity throughout the twentieth century.[12] Many of the statistical data show record levels: since Austria's accession to the EU almost a third of its farms have given up farming activities, while in the village of Kaltenberg, which is one of the most climatically disadvantaged of the region, not a single farm has been abandoned. Considering these facts, the Mühlviertel region does not create a cheerless impression: houses and entrances are carefully well kept, the countryside looks tidy, decaying farmyards are rare. These differences to neighbouring regions, such as the Innviertel in Upper Austria and the Waldviertel in Lower Austria, are obvious and are a favourite topic of discussion among farmers.

While most of the farms continue their agricultural activity, many things have changed in the region: the number of statistically registered full-time farms has dramatically decreased, and traditional forms of agricultural activity have only been maintained on a small number of farms. Almost all farms appearing in official statistics as full-time have to rely on a broad spectrum of additional income apart from primary production. These activities include refinement of produce (such as the production of schnapps and home-made pasta), direct marketing of home-grown produce, renting rooms to tourists, supplying equipment for other farms, counselling and supervision in agricultural organisations and other sources of income one might define euphemistically as 'informal'. I have carried out field research in the region in the 1980s and 1990s (Seiser 1995; 2000). Looking at the situation ten years later, what strikes me as particularly remarkable is the high degree of networking between individual farms and between farms and non-farming people, institutions and businesses, which brought about further connectedness, new forms of cooperation and enormous technological progress in farming. Another impression ten years on is of the more optimistic outlook of farmers concerning the future of their agricultural activities. One of the main reasons for this certainly lies in the reorientation of EU support and the national environmental ÖPUL 2000 scheme, which benefits the region to an above-average degree by classifying it as a 'less favoured area' and a 'mountain region'.[13]

Living standards and quality of life – with some dramatic exceptions – are considerably higher than might be expected from official incomes. This fact finds its visible expression in high-quality furnishings and the size of homes in the area. These homes were built, or renovated and decorated, with a minimum of expenditure on labour bought on the market at the usual prices. Support among neighbours, exchange among relatives, and a high level of individual work leave the financial means for the purchase of prestigious goods like widescreen TVs, satellite dishes and leather couches for the living room. Thus, being embedded in social networks can compensate for an annual income far below the average.

This exchange of mutual support by far exceeds what may be called 'economic reciprocity' in the strict sense. It also involves the revival or maintenance of customs that accompany different stages of the life cycle and 'traditional' celebrations during the year. Being part of such networks also means being exposed to a higher degree of normative social control. The decision not to marry in church, for instance, may entail a collapse in this system of reciprocity; in practical terms this simply means that building a new stable will swallow up considerably more financial means for the 'nonconformists'. A 'genuine traditional' wedding involves a great deal of festive work for neighbours and relatives: decorating rooms and the farm entrance, organising pre-wedding parties and finally the sumptuous wedding celebration itself. These are the indispensable ingredients of a 'correct' peasant wedding initiated by 'correct' formal invitations. People helping in the often secretly conducted preparations for the wedding are rewarded with lavish banquets, music and dance. As many newly wed couples start renovating or extending the farm buildings soon after the wedding – encouraged by special aid for young farmers and start-up premiums[14] – marriage may be considered a strategy involving more than just the bond between two people.

Non-acceptance of the social dimension of this networking is, of course, possible, but inevitably has negative consequences. Even within the new, purely economic networks encouraged by EU subsidies one of the participants involved will sooner or later initiate the cycle of gifts and counter-gifts, well known to anthropologists.

Many of the social events performed in the name of 'old' traditions show strong links to the Catholic Church and Christian organisations. The Catholic Youth, which is very active in mobilising people for events in the community, the youth organisation of the conservative ÖVP (Austrian People's Party) and the Farmers' Association are closely linked and membership is a logical step in the careers of young people in the area. The informalisation of the economy, on the one hand, and the subsidising programmes of the EU, on the other, cause an intensification of social networks and these, in turn, reinforce normative social control, albeit in clearly new forms that refer to different values than those of the past. Local Christian-social structures, which seemed to be on the decline at the beginning of the 1990s, are currently being revived.[15] Results of the 2003 elections to the Chamber of Agriculture, with some 90 percent of votes for the ÖVP-dominated Bauernbund in some communities of the Mühlviertler Alm region, can hardly be explained without considering that Catholic and conservative organisations are strongly embedded among farmers in the area.

The situation of the 'typical' part-time farmer who has a full-time job in industry or a trade in Linz (the closest urban centre some 60 km from the Mühlviertler Alm area), and who continues to operate the farm together with members of the family, is altogether different. These farms usually have more financial means at their disposal but lack the time to participate in the socio-economic networks described above. Therefore they rely on strategies other than those of people who official statistics register as full-time farmers, and they also have multiple identities in their professional lives.

This group's circumstances have also undergone considerable changes during recent decades. State-owned industries such as VOEST, Chemie Linz and Steyr, which for a long time had been the main employers of the region, were particularly affected by privatisation, rationalisation programmes and layoffs during the 1980s and 1990s; this brought about changes that caused part-time farmers to engage in a greater variety of non-agricultural jobs. The classic combination of the husband working shifts at the blast furnace and the wife looking after the children and the animals on the farm has become a rare exception. Today it is often the wife who has a qualified job while the husband works on the farm, or one of them works in the trading or service sectors (as a bank clerk, teacher or in the caring professions, for example). Part-time jobs and new forms of self-employment are also on the increase. The classification of the working world into different sectors, which in Austria have also been associated with a rather stable affiliation to certain political parties, is disintegrating and gradually changing into a great diversity of combinations of pluriactivity and strategies. The heterogeneous image of the category 'farmer' differs within one region as well as between different regions and is further compounded by a multitude of non-agricultural professions and their peculiarities. Who defines him- or herself as a farmer on account of which criteria strongly depends on the context. So, one and the same person might present himself as an eloquent banker talking to the honoraries of the village over the Sunday morning early pint, whilst at another table he is a committed bio-farmer. He is both, and he is mayor of the community too.

Austrian political scientists give the following prerequisites for the Freedom Party's success: since the mid 1980s Austria has seen the gradual breaking up of traditional patterns of party adherence and camp mentality (blue-collar workers vote Socialist, the self-employed, farmers and civil servants vote Conservative) as a consequence of the progressive disintegration of a sectoral working world (Plasser et al. 2003: 103, 145). According to the authors, increasing flexibility in the working world also caused a more flexible behaviour at the polls (ibid.: 103, 125). Growing flexibility of the working world as a result of a globalising economy and neo-liberal transformation of welfare systems in Western European countries causes rising unemployment, frequent changes of job and cuts in welfare expenditure (Aiginger 1995), which in turn result in disconcertion and fear of losing income and status. Deteriorating living conditions make voters, freed now from traditional party ties, susceptible to nationalist and right-wing populist catchphrases (ibid.: 128).

Using my regional example, I have tried to show that ever more flexible and informal working conditions resulting from far-reaching structural changes can be found in the field of agriculture too. However, here this development has so far not brought about the disintegration of traditional party ties. As far as full-time farmers are concerned, increasing pluriactivity and informal labour are even accompanied by a revival of Catholic and political subsidiary organisations with close ties to the People's Party. The intrusion of a globalising outside world is being countered, as it were, by intensified networking at a local level. This in turn strengthens the community in the sense of shared experiences, activities, places and histories (Amit 2002: 18), a community in which part-time farmers are deeply rooted as well. This may explain the fact that both these groups overwhelmingly voted for the ÖVP again at the 1999 and 2002 elections.[16]

Another decisive factor for their lack of support for the FPÖ consists – at least in the area where I conducted my survey – in the enormous popularity of (former) EU Agriculture Commissioner Franz Fischler (who is Austrian and a member of the People's Party). My interviewees unanimously considered Franz Fischler *their* man in politics. Not a certain party, not the Conservative People's Party, and certainly not Federal Chancellor Wolfgang Schüssel, but Franz Fischler in Brussels. In order to put these statements into perspective I have to say that these interviews were carried out in a region that was among the winners of the EU subsidising system and where the administration of subsidies usually worked well.

Since Austria joined the European Union in 1995, the concentration processes in agriculture have accelerated further. Almost one third of people working in this sector in 1995 have since left their farms. This benefits those who have stayed as now they find cheap land for cultivation and better income. There are no studies of the political attitudes of those who no longer belong to the category 'farmers'. It might well be that this group sympathises with the Freedom Party. I am rather sceptical though because not all of them are really 'losers'. Many of them simply feel relieved and freed from the burden of their inheritance.

As a matter of fact I have no simple answer to the question of why farmers seem to be rather immune to Haider's temptations, but I have a story. Ten years ago the majority of part-time farmers commuted daily between the region where I conducted my studies to Linz, the capital of the province, and worked shifts in the steel and chemical industries there. In an interview in 1993, dealing with inheritance and modes of transferring property, one farmer told me about his political attitudes: 'You know, it's like this: from here to Gallneukirchen [15 km from Linz, and the beginning of a more densely built-up urban area], I am a Conservative; from there up to the gate of the steel works, I am a Social Democrat; the moment I pass the gate, I am a Communist.' At the time I was outraged at this blatant opportunism and lack of positioning. Today I rather admire his clear perception of the various interests and who will best represent these in different situations.

Furthermore this attitude is clearly distinguishable from the Freedom Party's concept of *soziale Volksgemeinschaft* (social community of the people): in this model some monocratic, authoritarian and lean state leadership would balance out conflicts of interest between the different groups in a top-down approach. This would allegedly benefit all involved and, finally, make obsolete all institutions of the system of 'social partnership', professional associations and various chambers, and, ultimately, even if not yet clearly articulated, the multi-party democracy (Scharsach and Kuch 2000: 132–56). The part-time farmer is not without identity. He lives in various different worlds and he is aware of this: in his farming environment he appreciates the support of a conservative agricultural policy that is protectionist and preserving, while in an urban environment he relies on a Social Democrat policy that strives for modernisation and equal opportunities. In the factory, however, he prefers the uncompromising, class-based positioning of the Communists to the manager capitalism of the Social Democrats.

Thus, 'the farmers' cannot be simply characterised as nationalist, rooted in their soil and traditions. A modernised reincarnation of old, categorising ascriptions – like 'conservative camp mentality' – would also be wrong. Approaches used in social anthropology that depart from a situated and positioned subject in a globalised world of local communities seem to be more appropriate to reflect the complexities of, and perpetual change in, the environment farmers inhabit.

Conclusion

The images of farmers passed around in urban milieus, which are also being used by representatives of the Austrian Freedom Party in their public performances, suggest a close connection between (neo-) nationalist ideologies and the professional group of farmers. Departing from these images I looked at the party programmes of four right-wing populist and nationalist parties in Europe. While only 4 percent of the EU labour force work in agriculture, all these parties explicitly express their concern for farmers. One common denominator in the agricultural programmes of the British National Party, Die Republikaner, Le Front National and the Austrian Freedom Party is the demand for 'healthy food for our own population'. Consequently, these parties call vehemently for a renationalisation of agricultural policies.

My first question was whether there were elements in European agricultural politics that would make farmers particularly susceptible to neo-nationalist policies. The original main objective of CAP, i.e., to ensure a sufficient supply of food for the European population at reasonable prices, had been achieved within a relatively short time. The price Europe had to pay for the realisation of this goal consisted of tremendous expenditure, regional specialisation and, as a consequence, mutual dependence of the EU member states, and health-related and environmental problems on account of an uncompromising increase in productivity in industrial agriculture. The number of persons working in agriculture has rapidly decreased and the remaining farmers have to cope with a highly complex, often unfathomable supra-national agricultural policy, which interferes with their economic decisions and professional identity. Given this situation it would not come as a surprise if a larger number of farmers were to support right-wing populist parties, which denounce this kind of policy.

Taking Austria as an example, one has to face the fact that this support – in spite of considerable efforts on the part of FPÖ farmers' representatives – simply does not exist. In a next step I focused on farmers as a group, to question assumptions of homogeneity and continuity. Even a quick glance revealed enormous differences within this professional group. A look at the details of the Mühlviertel region showed that recent processes of global agricultural development are being countered locally by intense economic networking with an impact on social, cultural and political spheres. It was possible to identify some reasons for the current realignment of farmers to the People's Party.

Now we are left with the last question I raised at the beginning: do neo-nationalist agricultural policies really address farmers themselves? To put it differently: why do these parties care so much about a professional group that is hardly inclined to vote for them?

For the Austrian case I would propose some ideas worthy of further research: peasants are not interesting as potential voters for the Freedom Party; there are too few of them (not only in Austria); and they have strong ties to the Catholic Church (in Austria). There are, however, two points that make them seem interesting.

The first relates to ideas of purity and order, which can be traced back to a biologistic, racist core. Neo-national parties are afraid of mixing, of interbreeding (they all oppose genetic engineering and show a pronounced predilection for organic farming). The key themes are the original, genuine and unmixed. Only unmixed and pure things are healthy. Only unmixed and healthy food should be ingested into the body. Foreign cultures change and destroy the body of the people;[17] foreign, adulterated food causes individuals to fall ill. The most explicit formulation of this idea can be found in the party manifesto of the Front National (n.d.: 131–43, 139). Thus, agricultural policy is not an issue concerning economics, but rather one with a strong bearing on public (national) health. Here, the tendency to play with fears becomes visible again. This kind of policy is not addressed to the farmer, but to the consumer who wants to be sure that the food he or she buys at the supermarket is unadulterated, free of BSE and GMOs.

Secondly, at the level of culture, the genuine, original and unadulterated are represented by folk culture. Here, again, farmers are seen as the source and the guardians of this (genuine) form of culture: while 'foreigners' are the constructed 'Other', farmers are the preferred surface for the projection of 'self'. They are a symbol of the 'essence of the people' and, by virtue of their property, they are inextricably bound to their soil. Folk song, folk costume, folk culture, what is special and genuine about 'national' culture are the associations that farmers tend to evoke. Haider himself said, 'Any form of culture in Europe has its roots in peasant culture' (Czernin 2000: 46). This view has some tradition. Wilhelm H. Riehl, founding father of the German *Volkskunde* (folklore studies) in the nineteenth century, considered peasants the unwavering core, the germ cell of the future of the nation (Weber-Kellermann and Bimmer 1985: 43). Bausinger has shown how, during the Nazi regime, this perspective consequently developed into the extreme of *Völkische Wissenschaft*, which restricted folklore studies to *Deutsche Bauernkunde* (German Peasant Studies; Bausinger 1971: 61).[18]

At the social level this ideology finds its expression in a strong emphasis on the family farm, and runs through all party manifestos. What are the constituent elements of this family farm? What makes it 'better' or what are the associations this image evokes? The following belong to the realm of ascriptions rather than empirical fact: abundance of children; low divorce rate; group and local endogamy; unity of production and consumption (what the peasant eats has to be healthy for all others); territorial boundedness; freedom, autonomy and self-sufficiency within a limited, controllable frame; safeguarding of the *Kulturraum*, the naturally grown structure of the countryside (not for him/herself, but for the population in general). Neo-nationalist parties are against globalisation, and the imagined features mentioned above represent quite the opposite of globalisation at a social level.

The point on neo-nationalism I want to bring into discussion is that 'the farmers' are being used by neo-nationalist and right-wing populist parties as a romanticising metaphor for the genuine, unadulterated, special and the typically national. They serve as a counter-image of deterritorialising globalisation and stand for territorial boundedness of the nation state. Somehow 'the peasants' (all the party manifestos mentioned have a 'peasantising' view of farmers) represent the core of the 'hard-working, decent, honest, territorially rooted people' threatened by extinction, as is the national culture as a whole. Farmers seem particularly suited to emphasising the cornerstones of neo-nationalist policies: purity, separateness and stirring anxiety.

Notes

I am especially grateful to Julene Knox for her intensive and sensitive editorial assistance. I want to thank Sabine Strasser and Wolf Zemina for in-depth discussion and critical comments on earlier drafts.

1. The comparison relies on the online programmes of the British National Party, the Republican Party in Germany, the Front National in France and the Austrian Freedom Party. For a classification of these parties as right-wing populist, nationalist, right-wing nationalist, etc. see Betz (2002), Camus (2002), Pelinka (2002).

2. See the representation of programme structures and subsidies in Bundesministerium für Land- und Forstwirtschaft, Umwelt und Wasserwirtschaft (2001: 23), the report of the Federal Ministry of Agriculture, Forestry, Environment and Water Management.

3. Agenda 2000 is a programme for the further development of the European Union submitted by the Commission in 1997 and adopted in 1999. One of the four parts of the Agenda deals with the reform of EU agricultural and regional policies for the period 2000 to 2006 (Krammer 2002: 88).

4. See interviews with farmers in Bourdieu et al. (1997) or Krammer (1995) and Burger-Scheidlin (2002). Interestingly, some of the farmers interviewed by Bourdieu openly show a leaning towards the Front National.

5. Austria's export surplus to these countries amounted to €72.67 million in 2000 (Bundesministerium für Land- und Forstwirtschaft, Umwelt und Wasserwirtschaft 2001: 38).

6. See various parliamentary debates on quotas for harvesters and migrant workers in agriculture on the homepage of the Austrian Parliament (http://www.parlinkom.gv.at).

7. FPÖ policies have been analysed by various disciplines (e.g., interdisciplinary: Eismann [2002]; political sciences: Betz [2002], Pelinka [2000], Plasser and Ulram [2000]; psychology: Ottomeyer [2000]; linguistics: Reinfeldt [2000]; anthropology: Gingrich [2002], Fillitz [this volume]). My assertion that agricultural policy follows the same patterns is based on an analysis of the homepages of several FPÖ subsidiary organisations, in particular those of regional organisations of the Freiheitliche Bauernschaft (FPÖ-Vorarlberg 2000; Freiheitliche Bauernschaft Kärnten 2001; Freiheitliche Bauernschaft Tirol 2001).

8. See Krammer (1976) for an excellent analysis of the historical construction of homogeneity and continuity of Austrian farmers.

9. The Mühlviertler Alm is a regional association, founded in 1993, and consisting of eight communities with around 13,500 inhabitants in an area of 360 sq. km. The main objective of the association is to promote the region and its products with a newly established corporate identity.

10. Until 1955 the Mühlviertel was in the Soviet occupied zone, and these areas lagged a good ten years behind in terms of development when compared with other occupation zones. Special reconstruction programmes promoting modernisation of the region were introduced as late as 1961.

11. Pluriactivity is a more general term than part-time farming. It is defined as the involvement of household members of a farm in 'other gainful activities' irrespective of the type, level, regularity or extent of these activities (Brun and Fuller 2001: 101).

12. For a detailed description of the economic and social development of the region between 1920 and 1994 see Seiser (1995).

13. In the fields of environment and rural development the EU lays down a framework of guidelines, while the management and concrete implementation of such programmes rests with the individual member states. ÖPUL 2000 is an Austrian programme for a sustainable, extensive agriculture and the conservation of the natural landscape initiated in order to implement EU Council Regulation (EC) No. 1257/99 at the national level. Almost 60 percent of the budget earmarked for rural development in Austria is being channelled through this agri-environment programme (Krammer 2002: 126).

14. In the Mühlviertel area farms are traditionally transferred to the next generation at the time of the marriage of the son or daughter who is prepared to 'take over' the farm. The EU subsidises investments by young farmers if they are not over forty years old, have been operating the farm for a maximum of ten months and have completed officially recognised agricultural training. In less favoured areas these premiums can reach up to 40 percent of investment costs. It is possible to include the costs for the work input of the farmers' household into the calculation of overall investment cost for the application form.

15. These developments can only be briefly mentioned here. I am currently working on a doctoral thesis focusing on the economic self-image of farmers in areas highly subsidised by the EU, which proposes to discuss these developments and interactions in greater detail.

16. Plasser and Ulram (2003: 216) published the following exit poll results for farmers voting for the ÖVP: 1986: 93%; 1990: 85%; 1994: 73%; 1995: 72%; 1999: 87%; 2002: 95%.

17. See the chapter by Thomas Fillitz in this collection.

18. In German-speaking countries, a reassessment of these rather twisted projections was performed by European ethnology during the past twenty to twenty-five years (Jacobeit et al. 1994).

Bibliography

Aiginger, K. 1995. 'Von der Mitte aus, auf dem Weg nach vorne. Österreichs Wirtschaft in den 1980er und 1990er Jahren', in R. Sieder, H. Steinert and E. Tálos eds *Österreich 1945–1995*. Vienna: Verlag für Gesellschaftskritik, pp. 268–78.

Amit, V. 2002. 'Reconceptualizing Community', in V. Amit ed. *Realizing Community: Concepts, Social Relationships, and Sentiments*. London: Routledge, pp. 1–20.

Austrian Freedom Party. 1997. Program of the Austrian Freedom Party, www.fpoe.at/bundneu/programm/partieprogramm_eng.pdf, 34pp (consulted 25 January 2003).

Bausinger, H. 1971. *Volkskunde. Von der Altertumsforschung zur Kulturanalyse*. Vienna: Carl Habel Verlagsbuchhandlung.

Bel, F., Dax, T., Herrmann, V., Knickel, K., Niessler, R., Saraceno, E., Seibert, O., Shucksmith, M., Uttitz, P. and Veuthy, F. 2001. 'The Role of Policy in Influencing Farm Households' Behaviour in European Mountain Areas', in T. Dax, E. Loibl and T. Oedl-Wieser eds *Pluriactivity and Rural Development: Theoretical Framework*, Forschungsbericht No. 34. Vienna: Bundesanstalt für Bergbauernfragen, pp. 168–91.

Berghold, J. and Ottomeyer, K. 1995. 'Populismus und neuer Rechtsruck in Österreich im Vergleich mit Italien', in R. Sieder, H. Steinert and E. Tálos eds *Österreich 1945–1995*. Vienna: Verlag für Gesellschaftskritik, pp. 314–30.

Betz, H.-G. 2002. 'Rechtspopulismus in Westeuropa: Aktuelle Entwicklungen und politische Bedeutung', *Österreichische Zeitschrift für Politikwissenschaft* 31(3): 251–64.

Bourdieu, P., Accardo, A., Balazs, G., Beaud, S., Bourdieu, E., Broccolichi, S., Champagne, P., Christin, R., Faguer, J.-P., Garcia, S., Lenoir, R., Oeuvrard, F., Pialoux, M., Pinto, L., Podalydès, D., Sayad, A., Solié, C. and Wacquant, J.D.L. eds. 1997. *Das Elend der Welt*.

Zeugnisse und Diagnosen alltäglichen Leidens an der Gesellschaft. Constance: UVK Universitätsverlag Konstanz.

British National Party. 1999. European Election Manifesto. 'Freedom to Protect Rural Britain', http://www.bnp.org.uk/euroeconomy.html, 2pp. (consulted 18 September 2002).

Brun, A.H. and Fuller, A.M. 2001. 'Farm Family Pluriactivity in Western Europe', in T. Dax, E. Loibl and T. Oedl-Wieser eds *Pluriactivity and Rural Development: Theoretical Framework,* Forschungsbericht No. 34. Vienna: Bundesanstalt für Bergbauernfragen, pp. 97–111.

Bundesministerium für Land- und Forstwirtschaft, Umwelt und Wasserwirtschaft. 2001. *Grüner Bericht 2000. Bericht über die Lage der österreichischen Landwirtschaft 2000.* Vienna.

Burger-Scheidlin, H. 2002. 'Kultur-Landschaft(s)-Pfleger. Selbstverständnis, Image und Identität der österreichischen Bergbauern', unpublished MA thesis, University of Vienna.

Camus, J.-Y. 2002. 'Die radikale Rechte in Westeuropa. Vom nostalgischen Aktionismus zum fremdenfeindlichen Populismus', in W. Eismann ed. *Rechtspopulismus. Österreichische Krankheit oder europäische Normalität.* Vienna: Czernin Verlag, pp. 40–55.

Czernin, H. ed. 2000. *Der Westentaschen-Haider.* Vienna: Czernin Verlag.

Die Republikaner. 2002. Bundesparteiprogramm der Republikaner, http://www.rep.de/parteiprogramm, 38pp. (consulted 30 January 2003).

Eismann, W. ed. 2002. *Rechtspopulismus. Österreichische Krankheit oder Europäische Normalität.* Vienna: Czernin Verlag.

European Communities. 2003. 'CAP Reforms – A Long Term Perspective for Sustainable Agriculture', *EU Institutions press releases* MEMO/03/10, 22 January 2003, http://europa.eu.int/rapid/start/cgi/guesten.ksh?p_action.gettxt=gt&doc=MEMO/03/10/AGED&lg=EN&display=, 6pp. (consulted 7 May 2003).

Fleissner, P. 2002. 'Einstellungen gegenüber Minderheiten in der Europäischen Union', in W. Eismann ed. *Rechtspopulismus. Österreichische Krankheit oder europäische Normalität.* Vienna: Czernin Verlag, pp. 22–39.

FPÖ-Vorarlberg. 2000. *Ländle 2000 Plus.* Landwirtschaft, http://www.fpoe-vlbg.at/ (consulted 13 December 2001).

Freiheitliche Bauernschaft Kärnten. 2001. *Starke Bauern, starkes Kärnten,* http://www.bauernbefreiung.at/kampagne.htm (consulted 13 December 2001).

Freiheitliche Bauernschaft Tirol. 2001. *Anträge an die Vollversammlung der Landeslandwirtschaftskammer für Tirol am 14.5.2001,* http://www.fpoe-vlbg.at/bundeslaender/tirol/organisationen/fbt.htm (consulted 13 December 2001).

Front National. n.d.'La mort programmée', in Front National ed. *Le Programme du Front National,* pp. 131–43, http://www.frontnational.com/pdf/programme.pdf (consulted 18 September 2002).

Gingrich, A. 2002. 'A Man for All Seasons: An Anthropological Perspective on Public Representation and Cultural Politics of the Austrian Freedom Party', in A. Pelinka and R. Wodak eds *The Haider Phenomenon in Austria.* New Brunswick: Transaction Press, pp. 67–91.

Jacobeit, W., Lixfeld, H. and Bockhorn, O. eds. 1994. *Völkische Wissenschaft. Gestalten und Tendenzen der deutschen und österreichischen Volkskunde in der ersten Hälfte des 20. Jahrhunderts.* Vienna: Böhlau.

Kearney, M. 1996. *Reconceptualizing the Peasantry: Anthropology in Global Perspective.* Boulder: Westview Press.

Krammer, J. 1976. 'Analyse einer Ausbeutung I. Geschichte der Bauern in Österreich', *Sachen* 2(1–2): 4–98.

——— 1995. 'Von "Blut und Boden" zur "Eurofitness". Die Entwicklung der Landwirtschaft seit 1945', in R. Sieder, H. Steinert and E. Tálos eds *Österreich 1945–1995.* Vienna: Verlag für Gesellschaftskritik, pp. 567–80.

——— 2002. *Landwirtschaftliches Organisations- und Förderungswesen. Lernbehelf.* Vienna: Bundesanst für Bergbauernfragen.

Ottomeyer, K. 2000. *Die Haider-Show. Zur Psychopolitik der FPÖ.* Klagenfurt: Drava.

Pelinka, A. 2002. 'Die FPÖ in der vergleichenden Parteienforschung. Zur typologischen Einordnung der freiheitlichen Partei Österreichs', *Österreichische Zeitschrift für Politikwissenschaft* 31(3): 281–90.

Pelinka, P. 2000. 'Die rechte Versuchung. SPÖ, ÖVP und die Folgen eines falschen Tabus', in H.-H. Scharsach ed. *Haider. Österreich und die rechte Versuchung.* Reinbek bei Hamburg: Rowohlt Taschenbuch Verlag, pp. 46–66.

Plasser, F. and Ulram, P.A. 2000. 'Protest ohne Parteibindung. Die Wählerschaft der FPÖ', in H.-H. Scharsach ed., *Haider. Österreich und die rechte Versuchung,* pp. 128–43. Reinbek bei Hamburg: Rowohlt Taschenbuch Verlag.

——— eds. 2003. *Wahlverhalten in Bewegung. Analysen zur Nationalratswahl 2002,* vol. 28, Schriftenreihe des Zentrums für angewandte Politikforschung. Vienna: WUV-Universitätsverlag.

Plasser, F., Ulram, P.A. and Seeber, G. 2003. 'Erdrutschwahlen: Momentum, Motive und neue Muster im Wahlverhalten', in F. Plasser and P.A. Ulram eds *Wahlverhalten in Bewegung. Analysen zur Nationalratswahl 2002,* vol. 28, Schriftenreihe des Zentrums für angewandte Politikforschung. Vienna: WUV-Universitätsverlag, pp. 97–157.

Reinfeldt, S. 2000. *Nicht-wir und Die-da. Studien zum rechten Populismus. Studien zur politischen Wirklichkeit,* Schriftenreihe des Instituts für Politikwissenschaft der Universität Innsbruck vol. 8, series ed. Anton Pelinka. Vienna: Braumüller.

Reiterer, A.F. 1998. *Moderne Gesellschaften. Sozialstruktur und Sozialer Wandel in Österreich.* Vienna: WUV Universitätsverlag.

Scharsach, H.-H. and Kuch, K. 2000. *Haider. Schatten über Europa.* Cologne: Kiepenheuer & Witsch.

Schmeißer, M. and Teufel, K. 1999. 'Die Gemeinschaftspolitiken', in D. Herz ed. *Die Europäische Union. Politik. Recht. Wirtschaft.* Frankfurt/Main: Fischer, pp. 145–91.

Seiser, G. 1995. '"Schniddan" – zum Roggenanbau im Mühlviertel. Arbeitsabläufe und Arbeitsorganisation 1920–1994 im Kontext einer lokalen bäuerlichen Gesellschaft', unpublished MA thesis, University of Vienna.

——— 2000. 'On the Importance of Being the Last One: Inheritance and Marriage in an Austrian Peasant Community', in P.P. Schweitzer ed. *Dividends of Kinship: Meanings and Uses of Social Relatedness.* London: Routledge, pp. 92–123.

Silber, W. 2001. 'Marktschreier haben keine Chance in der Agrarpolitik', in *Österreichische Bauernzeitung* 6 December: 2.

Weber-Kellermann, I. and Bimmer, A.C. 1985. *Einführung in die Volkskunde/ Europäische Ethnologie,* 2nd edn. Stuttgart: Metzler.

Wiener Nachrichten Online. 2001. *Landwirtschaftskammerwahlen in Kärnten,* http://www.wno.org/newpages/par67.html (consulted 13 December 2001).

Chapter 11

New Nationalisms in the EU

Occupying the Available Space
Maryon McDonald

Introduction

I recall my early days of fieldwork in European institutions in the 1990s. I tried to make a joke but it did not go down well. I was discussing the visit of the British Queen to the Parliament with European Parliament officials, one of whom is now an MEP. There was some deliberation about what might be a good metaphor in a speech to convey the unity of the Parliament, Europe and this sovereign. Perhaps the 'family', it was suggested. 'Divorce', I retorted cheerily, and then added feebly that, of course, I did not really mean that member states should part company. But it was too late. All eyes were on me in pity and disapproval. 'There is no divorce in this family', a sober voice responded.

I soon came to realise that Europe was no joking matter in these circles. I was sharply asked on a consonant occasion if I approved of the blood of the battlefields of Flanders. By including these details here, I do not wish to suggest either an insensitive flippancy on my part or a tedious seriousness on the part of others, for neither would, I think, be at all accurate. Indeed, inside the European Commission a particular form of cynicism is pervasive.[1] The point I wish to make here is that criticism of the EU is not easy. Indeed, persuasive metaphors elide in the way Europe has been constructed such that they often seem to leave no easy ground for any critique outside an apparently zero-sum game of nasty nationalism, on the one hand, or the EU, on the other. This is a problem that I will be expanding on.

This chapter touches on three main points. First, there have been some key historical moments at which the legitimacy of the EU has been questioned, and these together mean that older discourses of belonging have been delegitimated and that allegiance to the nation state has been moved to the far right politically.

Secondly, within the institutional structures of the EU, opposition to European integration has been muted in the past, as it has been outside the EU's institutional structures, other than through the space of the far right. This opposition can make use of a persuasiveness that Europe supplies, but that can carry its own diminution; the EU, I suggest, has both produced neo-nationalisms and re-empowered itself through them. Thirdly, and we will see this throughout, I argue that there is a pervasive metaphoric supplied by dominant models of rationality and their alterities – a complex of ideas that we can refer to as the discourse of positivism, on the one hand, and romanticism, on the other – which organises our understandings of Europe and its opponents, in an internal debate of Europe with itself.

Europe Against Nationalism

The European Union now seems to be an established fact. Within the metaphors of space and time that its most fervent adherents use, it is a building that we are all constructing, or it is a train that must move ever forwards. In legal terms – and it is a profoundly legalistic enterprise – there has been no easy way out. Moreover, the very notion of 'Europe' has been appropriated by the EU, in synonymy with the moral high ground. The nature of this moral high ground has become a matter of argument productive of manifestly 'political' discussion within what are known as 'the member states'. But the high ground of a united Europe was never meant, at its inception, to be consonant with any particular party politics; it was always meant to be above that rough and tumble – to be, in an important sense, unaccountable – and thereby able to go forwards unimpeded by the intrusion of private and nationalist influence alike. In retrospect, we might be tempted to say that there were always going to be problems with such a vision. At the same time, it is a vision that has been resoundingly successful, whatever its problems, in that it has been empirically embodied in twenty-five states across the European continent.

Picture an agglomerative space that is an abstract but knowable space of planning and governmental intervention: this is what we have been enabled to do theoretically by the work of Foucauldian writers such as Rabinow (1989) and Rose (e.g., 1999). It is the context of France, in turn, that enabled these writers, including Foucault himself, to imagine and get hold of that space – that *agglomération* and *espace* of French planning discourse – and it was largely French thinkers who invented the whole EU edifice. This chapter will make frequent reference to France for this reason, and for other reasons that will become apparent. In the invention of this Europe, the ideas of the Enlightenment and versions of a post-Napoleonic *espace publique* conjoined, at the EEC's inception, with the fact that France had been invaded, by enemies and allies, four times over the last 200 years. After the Second World War, reconstruction could be imagined and empirically practised on a different scale and with different commitments. The *espace publique* became Europe, and a technocratic exercise began that was to take European nations beyond what were seen as 'egotistical' and dangerous investments in their own self-definition. The moral language of 'egotism' has been common. Europe was supposed to signify going beyond nationalism and all nationalism's attendant horrors as witnessed in the Second World War. Nationalism, in this scenario, has been something to battle against. For half a century now there has been no easy space in which to debate this issue. The terms are all prejudged.

In saying this, I do not mean that there has been no opposition to the EEC/EC/EU or their policies. Not at all, and I shall come to that in a moment. What I mean is that the inevitability of the construction of Europe is not just – as one might see in the usual analyses – a question of business interests, or the *engrenage* of Brussels, or the result of the clever or devious dealings of ministers, and so on. Rather, there are important discursive automatisms at play here. I carried out fieldwork in EU institutions in the early and late 1990s. I discovered very early on that it is not easy to question 'Europe' fundamentally without seeming to relish war, or without appearing to be part of some apparently dangerous or lunatic right wing. This is not the case solely within these EU institutions, where it is merely the crystallisation of a problem that exists more widely. When an apparently lunatic or dangerous right wing emerges – as some would argue it now has, in what are broadly being called 'neo-nationalisms' – we should not look to that phenomenon itself for the casting of blame but rather to 'Europe' and to the very terms in which we have allowed the EU to take shape.

Europe in Question

Taking some licence in the use of historical pivots, we might say that prior to the Constitution referendums in 2005 there have been two broad periods in the past in which the legitimacy of the European Economic Communities (or EEC, later the EC and then the EU) has been in question: in the 1960s and then in the 1980s and 1990s. These have important implications for the subject at hand.

First, there was the period of the 1960s when many of the assumptions and implicit aspirations that had helped to found the EEC began to be seriously and openly challenged (see McDonald 1996; 1997; 2000). The top-down technocratic planning regime, exported from post-war France, was shaken. Modernisation gave way to alternative realities. Cross-cutting and challenging the old temporal and spatial assumptions of modernisation, new political objects such as the 'environment' emerged, along with associated 'Green' ambitions, and rethinkings of 'development'. This was a period of strong criticism of the French social modernism of which Rabinow has written (1989), and which has been seen to be inherent in the European project (Holmes 2000a; 2000b). One important counter-invention of this period was cultural diversity as we now understand it, as something to be celebrated and promoted. Positivism, as modernity, found at its boundaries radical forms of cultural diversity as its romantic opponent. As top-down gave way to bottom-up or the 'grass roots' and the imperatives of 'participation', another important counter-invention was a new populism, the reinvention of the 'people' as a metaphor of accountability. The 1960s was famously a period of dissent, and a time when ethnic nationalisms, regionalisms and minority identities grew in opposition to the nation state; they often took over, for the purpose, the do-it-yourself kit of items such as language, culture, people, history and territory that had been so important for the creation in Europe of the old nation-state nationalisms themselves. These new ethnic and regional identities situated themselves in the language of the radical political left, and formed a powerfully attractive metaphor of dissent and opposition; it was barely noticed that some of these new identities ominously marched culture, language and blood-kin back together into history (McDonald 1986b; 1999). It was also barely noticed that 'class' was beginning to be eclipsed in favour of nation, region or ethnic group, and some of the leaders of these new social movements still struggled in the 1960s and 1970s to elide the two languages (McDonald 1989). The alternative realities of these new ethnic and regional self-definitions challenged the old positivist-derived realities of the EEC. The EEC tried briefly in the 1980s to fight back and get in on the same identity act with the 'People's Europe' programme (Shore 2000), but this was doomed to fail. The EEC did not have any singularity of people, culture or language, for example, and Europe had already been defined in the plural. The space was already occupied, by old and new nationalisms alike (McDonald 1994b).

This 'People's Europe' programme came during a period, in the 1980s and 1990s, when the legitimacy of the EEC was again quite forcefully questioned. In this second period, two events can be highlighted. First, the fall of the Berlin Wall in 1989 served to discredit further an older idiom of belonging – that of class. At the same time, with the collapse of the East, the clarity of Europe's own self-definition was in question. Secondly, the EEC's internal market was under construction, with nearly 300 directives in a short space of time. By the time of the Maastricht Treaty referendums, a perceived interference from Brussels was already an established fact. Going beyond nationalism had once seemed self-evidently right but 'Europe' was now met with nationalist reactions in which a discourse of nations, cultures and peoples was reinvigorated, if only momentarily. The European Community nevertheless thrived by placing itself within an important internationalist legacy, bolstered by growing talk of 'globalisation', and a now long-standing distrust of the nation state as a vehicle to define economic interests and achieve political ends. All this, together with the proliferation of ethnicities, seemed to move the nation state and its defenders to the right politically.

In general, by the late twentieth century, the space of the political left was occupied by the EU or by ethnic minorities. And therein lies the rub. To try to criticise the EU (as I shall refer to it hereafter) in any fundamental way could now readily feel like a right-wing criticism of ethnic minorities. It has been difficult for any parties in Europe to establish a radically critical stand without appearing to be either 'egotistical' or 'racist' or both, or at some time being accused of such qualities in the European Parliament. Similarly, and importantly here, this same space has conjured up its own realities. Joining an anti-EU party seems to mean risking having racists as fellow travellers. For example, the U.K. Independence Party (UKIP), the only party in the U.K. that has offered, at European elections, a serious voice of radical criticism of the EU – to the point of advocating withdrawal – has also felt the need to add into its manifesto the claim to a 'strong line on immigration'.[2] The British National Party goes very much further in this anti-immigration vein, of course, as do other parties of the far right in Europe, including Le Pen's Front National in France. It is worth bearing in mind that it was elections to the European Parliament in 1984 that brought Le Pen and his party into the limelight on the international political stage, on a manifesto openly and radically critical of the European Community. In an important sense Le Pen was invented by Europe. Once this had happened, empirical confirmation of what could happen was available. With a single stroke, the space of criticism of the EU was occupied.

By the turn of the century, as we have seen, the EU and ethnic minorities had generally come to occupy the space of the political left; with few exceptions (such as Greece, or Sweden's welfarist nationalism, for example), nationalism in the name of the old nation states was left to inhabit the space of the political right. We could say that this was, in EU terms, to be expected. The EU had been ready for opposition from right-wing nationalism and has generally been given new life, and new clarity of definition, by it. The stage was set for the EU to redeclare itself the opponent of nationalism, and to claim a historicist rectitude in doing so. New nationalisms have had the capacity merely to reinvigorate the EU. The material of the report of the MEP, Glyn Ford, on racism and immigration issues, which condemned the xenophobia of the old nation states, was produced to great acclaim from parliamentary committee discussions in the late 1980s and at the beginning of the 1990s (and then published as Ford 1992). The committee's topic of xenophobia and racism was still a hot favourite in EU institutions, in the self-descriptions of what it meant to be in 'Europe', when I began my first round of full-time fieldwork in Brussels and Strasbourg nearly two years after the committee discussions ended. It was an important subject that could and did rally all sides and parties, with the exception of the far right, and it did so in spite of the fact that the EU at that time had no specific legislative competence in matters of racial discrimination. A decade later, Haider's victory in Austria saw the EU spring into self-definitional life again, and it did so this time with even greater vigour from some of the member states than from that self-perceived 'motor and conscience' of Europe, the European Commission. Romano Prodi, the President of the Commission, had to remind member states at one stage that a boycott of Austria could be an infringement of the EU's own legislation.

The Real Movers and Shakers

The net result of all this might seem to be a simple story: we have the EU on the one hand, and a nasty racism and fascism evoking the worst of nationalism's excesses on the other. That apparent racism and fascism bring the EU to life again. It is partly in the beguiling simplicity of this story that its effectiveness resides.

One effect is that credible, middle-ground opposition to European integration is effectively silenced. It is silenced in part by the historicist rectitude I have indicated already, which inhibits radical questioning for fear of a tacit or overt discursive collapse of such opposition into an affinity with the horrors of the past (a past in which the Second World War still dominates, but in which the First World War, for example, or dictatorships can be contextually rolled into that same single spectre). In saying this, I must stress again that I do not mean that there has been no opposition to the EU, for I have already made clear that there has been, even if this opposition has not always been easy to sustain. Similarly, I do not mean that no 'alternative' Europe is morally permitted within EU institutions, for such has been very much the ambition of various parties born of the periods of dissent that I have mentioned; with few and passing exceptions, however, such movements have largely participated in, or been drawn into, a vision of a reformed Europe rather than any radical opposition to it. Radical opposition to the EU tends to be silenced because the racism against which Europe defines itself most clearly has penetrated the decision-making arenas of the EU itself and has occupied the space of that opposition. It has penetrated most noisily in the form of far-right parties in the European Parliament – an arena in which self-definition is naturally sought and found in opposition to such parties, and where no one who wants to be effective in the Parliament wishes to be tainted by them.

The European Parliament has gradually increased its power in the decision-making process of the EU, but its formal effectiveness in amending directives has depended on getting an absolute majority of votes.[3] Deals have had to be done across party lines and across the left/right divide that has long defined European understandings of 'politics'; this has shocked some new MEPs at first, and especially those unused to a tradition of coalition government. Such open deals across political groups and across left/right boundaries have nevertheless been regarded as a necessity, if only for the sake of 'Europe'. Even anti-mainstream and self-consciously 'alternative' groups and movements born of the periods of dissent I have outlined (e.g., the 'Greens') – groups committed to reforming Europe from within rather than to any more radical contestation of what is commonly known as 'the European project' – have found themselves having to do deals with majority parties and mainstream political groups in the interests of effectiveness. Such deals are important, and the notion of 'compromise' has a special life in these institutions. Even so, no political group in the European Parliament has done deals with those perceived to be of the far right. In the Council, there is a different scenario, albeit one that is not easily available to public scrutiny.[4] When Berlusconi came to power in the Italian elections in 2001, the U.K. Prime Minister, Tony Blair, seemed to lose no time in visiting him. Commentaries from old hands in Brussels pointed out that there was not meant to be any self-evident meeting of minds in this visit, but rather preparation for the deals and alliances forged in 'Council *realpolitik*'. Blair gained a potential ally as did Berlusconi, but within this, Berlusconi, it was said, would have to learn to tone down his more extreme statements of nationalism and any apparent racism. It is accepted that council ministers, prime ministers or presidents will claim, when facing their own electorate, to be fighting for, or to have fought for, their own 'national interests'. Once subject to the EU decision-making realities in Brussels and Strasbourg, however, all such figures are said to become interestingly 'sucked in' and, for better or for worse, are expected to be so. Without major allies it has been difficult to have any real effect in any of the EU institutions. It is not always easy to get it right, however. Attacks on racism are fine and exemplary, but attacks that themselves rely on nationalistic, discriminatory commentary are not. When, in a speech in the European Parliament in July 2003, Berlusconi made what appeared to be a nationalistic, stereotypical attack on a self-consciously 'European' MEP from Germany, in which he appeared to liken the German MEP to a Nazi concentration camp guard, he was loudly condemned – something that seemed to surprise him. Of even greater surprise to some was the fact that it was the European Parliament's Alleanza Nazionale, an Italian party of the far right (see Stacul, this volume), itself perceived to be nationalistic and racist, that condemned him most loudly. The Alleanza Nazionale had been trying to 'reposition' itself away from the far-right taint and towards higher ground in order to be 'taken seriously' within the European Parliament and to win allies and do deals, and all that the 'political' demands in this arena. Condemnation of racism, and of figures such as Berlusconi, was the obvious way in this context to voice one's own 'European' respectability.[5]

There are some interesting conundrums here. The EU is founded in opposition to racism and nationalism alike but is also revivified by neo-nationalisms, achieving a clarity of definition that may otherwise be elusive. At the same time, the EU could be said to breed nationalism and racism in that, for many in Europe who are critical of the EU, these may appear to be the only spaces that are left in which a radically critical dissent can forcefully be voiced. In the 2004 European Parliament elections, the far right increased its overall share of seats. Contributing to this result, there had no doubt been an added, knock-on effect from the racialised perceptions and fears of September 11th, and the subsequent near-success and national respectability the following year of Le Pen, who had come second in France in the first round of the presidential elections.[6] Whatever the case, these neo-nationalist far-right parties have been finding themselves present in the new European Parliament in sufficient numbers to consider founding their own formal political group, which would give them more speaking time and resources.[7] Whilst some outside the European Parliament may worry about this, MEPs from other persuasions generally do not: there has been some self-consciously

'European' self-satisfaction and mirth amongst the larger political groups about the history of such alliances or attempted alliances between far-right parties, which have generally split apart again on nationalist grounds, or in arguments over the historiography or legacy of the Second World War. They have also, on occasion, accused each other of 'racism' and of 'fascism'.

If we return to Le Pen for a moment, one can see that in some ways he and his party have been invented by the EU, and they thrive in opposition to it. The Front National (FN) founder himself is no longer in the European Parliament. When I did fieldwork in the Parliament in the 1990s, however, he was present and I attended some of the meetings of his party and followers.[8] My presence was permitted only for part of the time and only after some discussion, and because I had been attending the meetings of other groups and national delegations within them. There was also some manifest pleasure, from the FN aides who let me in, at the fact that I eschewed English-language interpretation. Away from the plenary 'hemicycle', and away from other formal meetings, the main focus of discussions of the FN was generally France and French affairs. They were not in the Parliament to further European legislation or policy, or to discuss it in any great detail. The rhetoric used by the FN and other similar parties was persuasive, explicit for the visitor or newcomer and familiar to the anthropologist. The European Community was 'elitist', but the FN was apparently mainly concerned with *le peuple*. It believed in the community, family, nation and domestic hearth. The EU was singular; the FN believed in diversity. The EU stood for 'rationalism' and 'the market', it was claimed, whilst the FN was concerned with 'popular feelings' and 'culture'. Moreover, the FN was concerned about 'different cultures', with difference being so important to the peoples of Europe. We slipped persuasively into naturality: there were fundamental differences between people. It was natural – 'as the anthropologist will tell us, perhaps?' – to fear difference and to want to preserve one's own culture. Besides which, the EC was 'corrupt', thoroughly 'rotten' (*pourrie*). Within this discourse at least – although not in the one outside that encompassed it and condemned it as fascism – the moral tables were turned. In Le Pen, and others like him, we see a critical and familiar juncture. This is where certain traditions of romanticism happily take in the Enlightenment's dirty washing.

These men were happy to take on what 'Europe' might devalue or ignore, and turn it to virtue. Anthropologists have colluded in divisions of the world that positivism and romanticism have supplied, and have structured them into a variety of moral geographies. Some of the recensions of the North/South division of Europe were embodied in the meetings I attended. Europe claimed the Enlightenment heritage. It apparently thought it had real politics and rationality while these southern men of the people were left behind in a web of personal patron–client relations.[9] Some of the FN members or their aides, and others from far-right parties sitting with them, wore dark glasses throughout along with smooth suits and shiny patent shoes. This was where it all happened. Europe was lost; these were the real movers and shakers. These were the men who were really connected and 'in touch'. They had the very legitimacy that the EU, apparently, did not.

In effect, it could be argued that the FN and its fellow travellers were 'connected' to no one, shunned for their racism, and this certainly appeared to be the case in the European Parliament context for much of the time. However, their discursive appropriation of all the metaphorical antitheses of modernity, which that modernity requires for its own definition, connects them to all that the modern world both threatens and holds dear: a world of emotions, community, culture and tradition. They are in that ambiguous *Gemeinschaft* evocative of the wild Mediterranean, or of the Scottish Highlander and the Breton Celt (Chapman 1978; McDonald 1986a, 1986b, 1989). They are in a world that has brought anthropologists running, but which also causes the same anthropologists to skid to a reflexive halt when they find they have been tricked (see Holmes 2000b).

Positivism and Romanticism: Some Metaphors We Live By

When, in the social sciences, we use such terms as the 'West', 'Euro-America' or even 'the modern world', what are often tacitly designated are the twin discourses that we might very loosely characterise as positivism and romanticism. These discourses took their definitive shape in the eighteenth and nineteenth centuries. The one has fed off the other, from Enlightenment and Counter-Enlightenment, the French Revolution and counter-Revolution and all their partisans, and right on to modernity and new ageism and so on; the recensions are numerous and reach into common folk psychologies of 'rationality' and 'emotions', and more (Chapman 1978; McDonald 1989).[10] I have shown in previous studies how different versions of these same discourses of positivism and romanticism have been rolled together into ideal gender constructs of man and woman, or ethnic categories such as Anglo-Saxon and Celt (see, for example, McDonald 1987; 1989; 1994a; 1994b; 1999). Within France, where a congruent left/right politics was born and where majority France has similarly constructed its own internal minorities, the space of those minorities has always been a source of greater fear and one that is powerful to appropriate. The same metaphorical elisions that have formed ethnic minority categorisations such as the 'Celt' have also forged the rhetoric of the far right, both within France and elsewhere in Europe. The potential was, we might say, always there, but it was a point that could not easily be made in the relatively recent past – including within anthropology – without finding oneself classified as somehow right-wing, anti-ethnic or fascist (see McDonald 1986b; 1999). Unsurprisingly perhaps, the same hostility to, and muting of, any commentary that points out commonalities between the discourse of those who 'protect' minorities and the discourse of those who are seen to oppose them was and is present and effective in EU institutions.

One metaphor that has been important to anthropology, ethnic minorities in Europe and the far right alike is that of 'culture'. Whilst some might find it difficult to imagine rescuing this term analytically, it is significant that many in anthropology have felt compelled to make efforts to do so (e.g., Baumann 1996; Kuper 1999). More important for our purposes here, perhaps, is to glimpse its persuasiveness and its problems. 'Culture' has taken its shape in contradistinction to something material – from the attributed materialism of the French that defined German *Kultur* oppositionally in the eighteenth and nineteenth centuries, to the industrial back-to-backs that gave 'culture' its elevating shape in the nineteenth-century England of Matthew Arnold, and on to post-1960s aspirations in Europe to alternative worlds of different 'cultures', in flight from the nastiness of capitalist materialism (for some of the history of 'culture', see Kuper 1999). Put another way, in a world of mind/body dualities, culture has elided with the mind, or in the face of a dominant rationality, culture has readily become that rationality's alterities. Whilst this has had its attractions, appearing to offer all that baser nature and material mundanities do not, 'culture' has also been self-limiting. Anthropologists have long had to fight against an image of their subject matter as ephemeral, and know well, for instance, the problems of appearing to deal in mere 'ideas'.

The history of 'culture' is obviously more complicated than this brief glimpse can offer, but it is nevertheless clear that something more 'real' was always lurking in the definitional wings. Culture was the property of romanticism, but reality was that of the positive reasoning of the Enlightenment and its expressions in natural science and the economy. At the opposite conceptual pole to 'culture', the two main models of rationality that have laid claim to a privileged grasp of reality in Europe were developing: the rationality of natural science and then that of economics.

In the eighteenth century, the ponderings of Adam Smith and his friend Adam Ferguson (who was active in the invention of the 'Celt') crystallised questions that had been posed in various forms and for some time. How can people get on with each other? In other words, how is 'civil' society possible? Or simply, how is society possible? At various points in the work of these men, these questions merged and separated. One classic set of answers had involved a Hobbesian strong hand, and a 'contract' that gave power to a sovereign state to effect an ordered social life. Another set of answers now began to take shape, however: men (for such was the term) were already 'social'. This much we knew from Montesquieu, but the theory now went further. 'Society' already existed, and it was possible because of a natural disposition to exchange. At the base of the social was the market. Natural dispositions effected a guiding self-interest that helped to effect the 'invisible hand'. Much of this has, of course, been hotly debated analytically and politically, and the 'market' metaphor no longer stands unchallenged in anthropology any more than would culture (Carrier 1997; Dilley 1992). However, the 'reality' of the market is an everyday affair and we know that 'culture' can get in the way. This is very much the rationality driving the EU's own internal market.

It was out of romanticism that 'culture' (and femininity, and the minority 'Celt' alike) was forged. It is out of the Enlightenment's positive reasoning (later positivism) and its children that the EU – in its own priority of the market – has been created. In between the market and culture, in a collusion of the political and the epistemological, sits the social. Since the nineteenth century, this has been a space of intervention, initially intended to palliate the depredations wrought by the market (see Rose 1999). In France, Catholicism informed many of the efforts of intervention, and theories developed that sought to vitiate the effects of the rationality of the market through ideals that ranged from 'solidarity' to an 'unseen hand' of social decency. In the EEC, this was turned into the integrating method of 'convergent action' (Monnet 1978; see also Holmes 2000a, 2000b). It is in this context that a moral criticism such as 'egotism' can feel particularly apt against those who try to stand firm before the apparent inevitabilities of EU integration.

Against the rationalism of the EU's construction – which, in the EU's own institutions, can incorporate the ideal 'society' of welfare as the market's 'flanking measures' – sits the world of 'culture'. It is not difficult to find scenarios in the modern world, or in the West or Euro-America, in which culture appears as a romanticism that a more rigorous science might dispel. We apparently live in a large spatio-temporal building project in which epistemological and political priorities collude: the foundations are the market or the economic, on which rests society or the social, and on the upper floors, where clouds float past the windows, is culture.[11] At the same time, for better or for worse, there has been no easy turning back from the post-1960s world of multiculturalism (see Kuper 1999; Rose 1999). Culture has been taken on by ethnic minority activists and by sensitive governments alike. Politically, anyone criticising multiculturalism, like anyone wishing to question the EU, can easily find him- or herself dubbed a fascist of some kind.

It feels then as if we are roughly back where we started. Ethnic minorities and the EU occupy the space of the political left. But something else has happened. The far right has also taken over 'culture'.[12] We have seen this in some of the comments of the far right already cited. The far right has appropriated 'culture' along with all the slippages of metaphorical persuasiveness and of ethnic and populist accountability that it offers, and leaves to the EU the space of the material, not in the guise of progress and rationality but instead of a nasty, insensitive, elitist, corrupt materialism. From the work of *Kultur* in German condemnations of a French materialist *civilisation* in the eighteenth century, right through to a common experiential imagery of the modern run-down inner city of 'racial tension' that a condemnation of the materialist world can now evoke, and on to the 1999 'corruption' scandals in the European Commission, we feel we know what Le Pen and the rest of the far right mean. It is all clever stuff, feels real and is difficult to contest.

Le roi est mort ...

The metaphorical elisions of positivism and romanticism that neo-nationalist politicians such as Le Pen employ are difficult to contest in their own terms. Because of their multiple elisions, their seepage from one context to another, they seem to describe a world that feels real and true (cf. Chapman 1978).

Accusations of 'racism' would generally, within EU institutions, place the accuser in a line of continuity with those who stand against the horrors of the Second World War. 'Racism' is an accusation that MEPs regularly throw at the far right, and one that tends to define the very category of the 'far right' for the majority parties. Racism is also an accusation that anyone daring to criticise 'Europe' risks courting. The space of criticism is occupied, but it is occupied by a discourse that can also profit from the languages of self-conscious tolerance and difference that developed after the Second World War and produced cultural relativisms. Le Pen can claim, and has claimed, to be within that camp – not to be a 'racist' but to be a cultural relativist, to be a supporter of cultural difference. The 'far right' of majority perception can choose to claim, in other words, the full space of conceptual opposition to the Enlightenment heritage, a space that is simultaneously inherent to the self-definition of that heritage, and part of it. French intellectuals have struggled to deal with this capacity of the far right to appropriate the discourse of their opponents, to appropriate the language of 'culture' born of romanticism, which, as multicultural sensibilities, has generally become the property of the political left. The Enlightenment produced a universalising mission, it is argued, a civilising mission for France and for Europe, which fed into a colonial 'discriminatory' racism. That much is clear. A postmodern world without universals, however, is one in which bounded 'cultures' can be made to appear to collide with each other without being able to communicate; the solution, for opponents of the far right, has been to see this as a 'culturalist racism' or a 'differentialist racism' (e.g., Policar 1990; Taguieff 1988, 1990; see Candea 2004). We are still within the same idiom of accusation, therefore, and we are still within those giant twin discourses. Indeed, such discussions are evocative, within social anthropology, of what used to be called the 'rationality debates', in which the dominant models of rationality were titillated, particularly from the 1960s to the 1980s, by cultural relativism.[13] These debates constructed a world of rationality on the one hand, and then imaginary people and cultures on the other that were rationality's 'Other' and through which its points, about a necessary universality or no communication at all, could be made. Such debates are recensions of the debates of Enlightenment's rationality with itself. The West lives on. Europe is intact.

The events of 11 September 2001 and their aftermath, along with further 'marketisation', the 2003–2004 war in Iraq, the enlargement of the EU and a looming European Constitution constructed by appointed luminaries and agreed by European leaders without proper reference to their 'people' all helped to bring new and strongly 'Euro-sceptic' and 'Euro-critical' parties into the European Parliament after the 2004 elections. A new space of radical criticism seemed to be opening up (Banks 2004). The tarnish of far-right racism is ever threatening, however. Difficulties of reputation that UKIP, which achieved twelve seats in the European Parliament, and similar parties (e.g., Sweden's 'June Movement') have already had would suggest that creating and occupying a serious space of criticism of the EU, without being ridiculed as cranks, emotional or irrational, or without being accused of fascism or racism, is not easy. It will take very little for such images to be empirically confirmed, and the very presence of these parties will again reinvigorate an unassailable 'Europe'. The proposed Constitution may generate different visions of Europe more generally but these can find shape in, and be contained within, conflicts of the market and the social. Nationalism cannot easily be rehabilitated; the political left has no constructive theory of it, and no new languages of identity, belonging and opposition are easily available. Within weeks of the 2004 election, with the presence of the new nationalist parties as well as an increase in the far right, a European Parliament was being envisaged that might be newly and radically divided along EU/anti-EU lines. It will be interesting to see what eventually fills these categories, but one can already guess at some of the further seepage that will take place. Against the EU's critics stand the serried ranks of high-minded Europeans, over 200 years of Enlightenment and Counter-Enlightenment thinking, and an ongoing debate of rationality with itself. We will, it seems, be Western and European for some time yet.

Notes

1. This cynicism was the subject of one of several internal studies of the European Commission that I have carried out, at the Commission's request, following the first internal ethnographic study of the European Commission by an anthropological team in 1993 (Abélès, Bellier and McDonald 1993). Different forms of cynicism have been commented on for very different contexts elsewhere – see Sloterdijk (1988); Zizek (1995); Navaro-Yashin (2002).
2. See the party's website: www.UKIP.org.
3. For the fullest account of the workings of the European Parliament, see Corbett (1998).
4. On some aspects of the workings of the Council, see Westlake (1999).
5. The Alleanza Nazionale, along with the Italian Lega Nord, has offered the peculiarity for neo-nationalist groups of claiming to be pro-European. The Alleanza Nazionale, which has suffered its own internal divisions, formally declared itself 'post-Fascist' in order to join the 'Union for Europe of the Nations' (UEN) group, which it managed to do in 1999. This broader group, in which the Irish Fianna Fáil, dissident French Gaullists and the Danish People's Party have figured, is felt to be dominated by its French origins. It ostensibly transposes France's 'liberty, equality, fraternity' into a manifesto for the exercise of sovereign 'national wills' in the name of 'diversity', democracy and 'the identity of European peoples'. It supports, however, a European common foreign and security policy, and European aid to developing countries. Alleanza Nazionale has had to work hard at its public repositioning to stay within this group. At the same time, the UEN itself is necessarily vulnerable: it is not generally 'taken seriously' by other groups and has needed to maintain its own numbers. It is sometimes seen as distinct from the 'far right' (although then explicitly tainted with it again as the occasion demands) and the Irish presence in particular has meant that it has been

viewed with ambivalence. It is said to uphold a 'soft nationalism' and has some respected members who have associations with established parties of government (see Fieschi 2000b). An anti-immigration stance has emerged in national manifestos whilst some claim proudly, in the European Parliament context, to have drawn Alleanza Nazionale away from racism; the group's own image was certainly not helped in the Parliament, however, by that party's presence.

6. Le Pen and the Front National had been actively working, since 1995, to improve their image by, for example, winning over women and 'youth', who could also be made to share the platform of 'victimisation' that Le Pen was by then claiming at the hands of majority parties. For discussion of Le Pen, the Front National and their place in the European Parliament, I am indebted to members of that party and of the EP administration, and more recently to Catherine Fieschi of the School of Politics, Nottingham University, U.K., and Giacomo Benedetto of the London School of Economics, U.K. The brief and summary comments presented in this short chapter cannot do justice to the range and richness of our discussions, and any errors are my own. For more general details on Le Pen and the far right, see, for example, Fieschi (1996; 2000a; 2000b); Fieschi, Shields and Woods (1996); Cronin (2004); and Gaillard-Starzmann (this volume).

7. Political 'groups' in the Parliament now require a minimum of nineteen MEPs from at least five member states in order to be formally constituted – and to qualify for more money, more secretarial resources, more committee seats, more speaking time in debates and representation on the 'Conference of Presidents' (of the groups). At the time of writing, four far-right parties were said to be seeking to form a group – the Flemish Vlaams Blok (three MEPs), the French Front National (seven MEPs), the Italian Lega Nord (four MEPs) and Austria's Freedom Party (one MEP). It was hoped that others might join too: e.g., Movement for a Democratic Slovakia (of ex-Prime Minister Vladimir Meciar; three MEPs), and the Polish Self-Defence Party (six MEPs) of Andrzej Lepper. Lepper had already made headlines by comparing the EU enlargement to the 1939 Nazi invasion of Poland (see *European Voice* 8–14 July 2004, vol. 10[25]: 15). It is not clear that a common platform will be easy amongst these parties, however; but it is significant that some nationalist and anti-EU parties from the former Eastern Europe are drawn into apparent consonance with the racist discourses of the existing far right. (Others have been attracted to the UEN outlined in note 5, above, or to join an independent group with UKIP, for example; none has thereby necessarily escaped the far-right taint.) If a distinct political group is not formed, the far right will remain part of a general category of 'Non-attached' (known as 'NI' or *Non-inscrits*).

Some of the development of groups in the Parliament (although only those aspects made visible as 'data' for public consumption and with gaps and a time lag) can be followed on the European Parliament's website: www.europarl.eu.int.

8. After a legal process lasting six years, Le Pen was suspended from the European Parliament in 2003 in keeping with a European Court of Justice ruling following an assault on a woman from the French Socialist Party in 1997. At the time of my own study, prior to this assault and the subsequent (temporary) suspension of its founding leader, Le Pen's FN was part of a small 'Technical Group of the European Right' in the European Parliament, a group already split by internal disagreement. They had called themselves a 'group' in order to have access to group resources, but only a 'technical' group because they did not want to have regular formal meetings or necessarily to agree on a common platform or policy. The rules on group formation subsequently changed (requiring more MEPs from different member states, for example, and explicitly requiring political affinity in the place of technical convenience), which made such an arrangement more difficult. The subsequent increase in far-right MEPs after the 2004 elections placed a far-right, fully constituted 'group' on the horizon again (see footnote 7 above).

9. For a list of the major relevant ethnographies that confirmed a North/South divide, and some of the implications of this within the European Commission, see McDonald (1997).

10. This seems a convenient point at which to try to clarify two things. First, I am not claiming here any conspiracy or any exhaustive hegemony of these dualities; nor am I indulging in structuralist binary oppositions, that analytical model itself being a product of the world I am describing here. Rather, I am trying to point to a pervasive complex of metaphors that appear to constitute a

recognisable world of Europe or the West, and in which its realities so often appear to be shaped, steeped and prejudged. Secondly, I do not wish to appear to oversimplify the phenomena of 'nationalism' or 'neo-nationalism', which receive fuller analytical treatment elsewhere both in this volume and beyond it. In order to make my points, some simplification all round is inevitable, however. In discussions within the social sciences about the component features of nationalisms in Europe, it is often these same strands of thought – in the shorthand of 'the Enlightenment' and 'romanticism' – that analyses have invoked, implicitly or explicitly, with some debate about how much one or the other has contributed. It does not seem possible to have one without the other, however, and it is a particular conjunction of specific aspects of both romanticism and Enlightenment rationalities that is generally felt to have enabled the most frightening nationalist excesses, in Nazi Germany (Adorno and Horkheimer 1979). These excesses, in turn, would seem to have reproduced a Europe stalked by some of the same discursive dualities, in which opposition is incorporated.

11. For some of the empirical implications, see McDonald (1997).
12. For another warning about this possibility from within anthropology, see Stolcke (1995).
13. A taste of these debates can be found in, for example, Hollis and Lukes (1982).

Bibliography

Abélès, M., Bellier, I. and McDonald, M. 1993. *Approche Anthropologique de la Commission Européenne*. Brussels: European Commission unpublished report.

Adorno, T. and Horkheimer, M. 1979. *Dialectic of Enlightenment*. London: Verso.

Banks, M. 2004. 'Lowest-ever Turnout and an Upturn for the Eurosceptics', *European Voice* 10.

Baumann, G. 1996. *Contesting Culture*. Cambridge: Cambridge University Press.

Candea, M. 2004. '"More Racist Than Us": North Africans and Racism Accusations in Corsica', Unpublished Seminar Paper, Department of Social Anthropology, Cambridge, U.K.

Carrier, J.G. ed. 1997. *Meanings of the Market: The Free Market in Western Culture*. Oxford: Berg.

Chapman, M. 1978. *The Gaelic Vision in Scottish Culture*. London: Croom Helm.

Corbett, R. 1998. *The European Parliament's Role in Closer Integration*. Basingstoke: Macmillan.

Cronin, D. 2004. 'Is Le Pen Mightier than the Sword?', *European Voice* 10(21), European Election Special, p. 6.

Dilley, R. ed. 1992. *Contesting Markets: Analyses of Ideology, Discourse and Practice*. Edinburgh: Edinburgh University Press.

Fieschi, C. 1996. 'Jean-Marie Le Pen and the Discourse of Ambiguity', in J. Gaffney and H. Drake eds *The Language of Leadership in Contemporary France*. Aldershot: Dartmouth.

——— 2000a. 'Rally Politics and Political Organization: An Institutionalist Perspective on the French Far Right', *Modern and Contemporary France* 8(1): 71–89.

——— 2000b. 'European Institutions: the Far-Right and Illiberal Politics in a Liberal Context', *Parliamentary Affairs* 53: 517–31.

Fieschi, C., Shields, J. and Woods, R. 1996. 'Extreme Right-wing Parties in Europe', in J. Gaffney ed. *Political Parties and the European Union*. London: Routledge.

Ford, G. ed.1992. *Fascist Europe: The Rise of Racism and Xenophobia*. London: Pluto Press.

Hollis, M. and Lukes, S. eds. 1982. *Rationality and Relativism*. Oxford: Blackwell.

Holmes, D. 2000a. *Integral Europe: Fast-capitalism, Multiculturalism, Neo-fascism.* Princeton: Princeton University Press.

———— 2000b. 'Surrogate Discourses of Power', in I. Bellier and T. Wilson eds *An Anthropology of the European Union.* Oxford: Berg.

Kuper. A. 1999. *Culture: The Anthropologists' Account.* Cambridge, MA: Harvard University Press.

McDonald, M. 1986a. 'Brittany: Politics and Women in a Minority World', in R. Ridd and H. Callaway eds *Caught Up in Conflict: Women's Responses to Political Strife.* London: Macmillan.

———— 1986b. 'Celtic Ethnic Kinship and the Problem of Being English', *Current Anthropology* (with comments and reply) 27(4): 333–47.

———— 1987. 'Tourism: Chasing Culture and Tradition in Brittany', in M. Winter and M. Bouquet eds *'Who from their labours Rest?' Conflict and Practice in Rural Tourism.* London: Gower.

———— 1989. *'We Are Not French!' Language, Culture and Identity in Brittany.* London and New York: Routledge.

———— 1994a. 'Drinking and Social Identity in the West of France', in M. McDonald ed. *Gender, Drink and Drugs.* Oxford: Berg.

———— ed. 1994b. *Towards an Anthropology of the European Union.* Brussels: European Commission unpublished report.

———— 1996. '"Unity in Diversity": Some Tensions in the Construction of Europe', *Social Anthropology* 4(1): 47–60.

———— 1997. 'Identities in the European Commission', in N. Nugent ed. *At the Heart of the Union: Studies of the European Commission.* Basingstoke: Macmillan.

———— 1999. 'A Deadly Linguistics? Tales from the Celtic Fringe', in T. Allen and J. Eade eds *Divided Europeans: Understanding Ethnicities in Conflict.* Dordrecht: Kluwer.

———— 2000. 'Accountability, Anthropology and the EC', in M. Strathern ed. *Audit Cultures: Anthropological Studies in Accountability, Ethics and the Academy.* London: Routledge.

Monnet, J. 1978. *Jean Monnet: Memoirs.* London: Collins.

Navaro-Yashin, Y. 2002. *Faces of the State: Secularism and Public Life in Turkey.* Princeton: Princeton University Press.

Policar, A. 1990. 'Racism and its Mirror Image', *Telos* 83: 99–108.

Rabinow, P. 1989. *French Modern: Norms and Forms of the Social Environment.* Cambridge, MA: MIT Press.

Rose, N. 1999. *Powers of Freedom: Reframing Political Thought.* Cambridge: Cambridge University Press.

Shore, C. 2000. *Building Europe: The Cultural Politics of European Integration.* London: Routledge.

Sloterdijk, P. 1988. *Critique of Cynical Reason.* London: Verso.

Stolcke, V. 1995. 'Talking Culture: New Boundaries, New Rhetorics of Exclusion in Europe', *Current Anthropology* 36(1): 1–24.

Taguieff, P.-A. 1988. *La Force du Préjugé.* Paris: Editions la Découverte.

———— 1990. 'The New Cultural Racism in France', *Telos* 83: 109–22.

Westlake, M. 1999. *The Council of the European Union.* London: John Harper Publishing.

Zizek, S. 1995. *The Sublime Object of Ideology.* London: Verso.

PART IV
Global Perspectives

Chapter 12

Neo-nationalism in India

A Comparative Counterpoint
Mukulika Banerjee

Introduction

Aggressive nationalism, expressed through mainly religious (Hindu) discourse, is now a well-established political phenomenon in India. In one incarnation (the parliamentary Bharatiya Janata Party) it has captured control of the federal government, ruling from 1998 until May 2004. In this chapter I outline its main ideas and organisational forms before considering whether it is really 'neo' and how it compares with the European experience. These comments, I hope, usefully counterpoint the other examples in this volume.

Historical and Ideological Antecedents

The intellectual origins of the Hindu right wing lie in the early twentieth century.[1] Its ancestral ideologue, V.D. Savarkar, sought an oppositional response to the Raj that was grounded in 'indigenous virtues', and he saw religion as offering a radical alternative to a British rule grounded in the European Enlightenment. However, he also recognised that the extremely diffuse and varied nature of Hindu thought and practice made it ill suited to the kind of focused militancy he desired. So he drew on the thinking of various older Hindu revivalist movements that, for much the same reasons, had been seeking to move Hinduism away from what they saw as its excessive fatalism, otherworldly view, localism and effeminacy towards a more assertive, politicised, monotheistic and 'muscular' spirit that closely resembled the colonial Protestantism it sought to combat. Savarkar founded a secret society, Abhinav Bharat (Modern India), in 1904 and was arrested several times on charges of terrorism and illegal activities, spending time in prison.

From 1906 to 1910 he lived in Britain, where he discovered the writings of the Italian nationalist Giuseppe Mazzini. Savarkar appreciated Mazzini's cultural pride, nationalist self-assertion, modernist outlook and vision of a strong, culturally homogeneous nation embodied in a unitary state. The prime lesson he drew was of the desirable congruence of territoriality and culture as a basis for nationhood. Transposing Mazzini to India, Savarkar claimed common emotional attachment to the name of the (Hindu) nation; a coherence and unity of language as the central carrier of cultural essence and feeling (Sanskrit in the past, later modern Hindi); a physical underpinning of culture by blood and race (with caste endogamy approved as a mechanism for keeping the blood of the whole nation pure); and imaginative ties centred around the 'holy land' and its sacred topography of shrines and myths. He thus elaborated the idea of a deeper and ancient unity beneath the superficial diversity of modern Hinduism. He called this *Hindutva*, an ethnic 'Hindu-ness' that he ascribed to all Hindus: 'Hindutva is not a word but a history. Hinduism is only a derivative, a fraction, a part of Hindutva ... [which] embraces all the departments of thought and activity of the being of our Hindu race' (Savarkar 1969: 3–4).[2] Through Hindutva, Savarkar hoped to develop and instil a pride that would inspire opposition to the colonial power. To this end he supported the founding of the Rashtriya Swayamsevak Sangh (RSS, Organisation of National Volunteers) in 1925 by a fellow Maharashtrian Brahmin, K.B. Hedgewar. This survives today as the oldest element of the Hindu right, with more than 2 million activists, and it still conducts daily parades modelled on the military drills of the Italian Fascist movement of the 1920s.

Hindu nationalist discourse was developed in the next generation by M.S. Golwalkar, the leading ideologue of the RSS; his book *We, or Our Nationhood Defined* (1939) expressed an obvious admiration for Nazism and what he called the 'German Race Spirit'. His key preoccupation was how to control the fragmenting impulses of modernity by constructing cultural holism and national strength, and he explored what he called the five 'unities' defining nationhood: geographical, racial, religious, cultural and linguistic. Through discussion of the major European nations, plus Turkey, Russia and the U.S., he sought to show that cultural unity was a precondition for the viability of a state: 'Like Herder and Fichte, who wished to recruit culture and nation on a unique German road to modernity, Golwalkar wished to recruit Indian spirituality and culture in order to arrive at modernity as a strong, unitary and coherent society' (Hansen 1999: 84).

The fundamental effect of the thought of Savarkar and Golwalkar was to provoke two conceptual leaps. First, in order to serve the purpose of providing the common sentiment of 'belonging to the nation', Hinduism had to be detached from its natural, polytheistic and sectarian form and projected as a more rigid and unitary religion than it was. As Ashis Nandy has argued, this was less a matter of 'reviving' Hinduism than of building the national spirit (Nandy 2002). The second leap was the re-imagining of the relationship of Hinduism to the other religions of India. Rather than being merely the religion of the majority, it was now essentialised as the *only* religion of India, with all others, notably Islam (which a quarter of the population followed), described as alien and as enemies of Hinduism.[3] Given the new identification of the Hindu religion with the nation, non-Hindus were now marked out as clearly inferior members of the Indian nation at best, or at worst as not being members at all.

There were, of course, other major approaches at this time to defining the nature of 'Indian-ness'. For Gandhi, religion was important but rather than the chauvinism of any one religion it was the importance of all religions in providing an ethical code for public life that he deemed particularly Indian. Thus, while for himself Hinduism provided a suitable moral framework, others who wished to follow his political ideology of *satyagraha*, Muslims such as Gaffar Khan and Maulana Azad, could choose to locate their spiritual resources in Islam, as did the Akalis in Sikhism.

A different response, associated with Nehru, eschewed the place of religion in political matters. For him the notion of 'Indian-ness' could be forged mainly on the basis of a syncretic historical Indian past and a future idea of India, a shared common project of modernist nationhood. He stressed the importance of the state in forging this new identity, with the army and civil service helping to create this new Indian cosmopolitanism and cohesion. No attempt was made to impose a single or uniform 'Indian' identity, which he viewed as a weakness of Western theories of nationalism, and citizenship (imparted by democracy) was to be defined by a universalistic and civic criterion. Laws on religion formulated under Nehru's regime were thus treated similarly to policies about the language issue, where a pluralistic model was adopted; 'secularism' was thus a pragmatic way of reconciling differences for the sake of good governance in independent India.

During the nationalist struggle the Hindu right was marginalised because of the success of Gandhi and Nehru. Savarkar's cultural nationalism was masculine, elitist, rationalist and in favour of rapid modernisation, and his religion was instrumental (he had no personal faith), essentialist, exclusionary and violent. In contrast, Gandhi's nationalism was populist, feminine, spiritual, anti-modern and anti-Western; his religion was an intense personal faith that did not merely express his politics but thoroughly shaped them, while his view of Hinduism was syncretic and tolerant. It was Gandhi's politics that won out; however, he paid for this success with his life, gunned down by Hindu extremists who were determined to ensure that the non-Gandhian alternative would remain alive.

Contemporary Developments

In the first four decades after Independence the RSS was banned for long periods and went underground for a number of years, but Hindutva ideology continued to develop. A complex web of related organisations grew up, which came to be known as the Sangh Parivar (Family). Its main contemporary elements besides the RSS are: the Vishwa Hindu Parishad (World Council of Hindu Churches, VHP), which is dominated by Hindu abbots and works as an extremist branch of the RSS; the Shiv Sena (a regional offshoot in Maharashtra that glorifies the Hindu warrior Shivaji of Western India); Bajrang Dal (named after the Monkey-god Bajrang) and whose cadres provide the local organisational base and rank-and-file members in various parts of the country; and the Bharatiya Janata Party (BJP), founded in 1980, which pursued increasingly militant campaigns as Congress authority gradually eroded following Mrs Gandhi's abuses of power in the 1970s and subsequent electoral failure, which eroded the confidence people had in the Congress Party.

These campaigns were explicitly religious and focused on the 'sacred geography' of the Hindu nation. Chief among them was the campaign against the sixteenth-century Babri Masjid mosque at Ayodhya (100 miles east of Lucknow, the state capital of Uttar Pradesh), which was alleged to have been built over an older temple marking the birthplace of the Hindu god-king Ram. The Ram Janmabhumi Movement, nurtured by BJP publicists, called for the replacement of the mosque with a magnificent 'restored' temple. This was the key BJP agenda throughout the election campaigns of the late 1980s and early 1990s and its manifesto promised that on coming to power a BJP government would build the temple: 'This dream moves millions of people in our land; the concept of Rama lies at the core of their consciousness' (BJP Manifesto).

Ayodhya was used to evoke a sense of common attachment to the idea of the nation. More specifically, the (re-)creation of Ram and his birthplace was a calculated practical effort to address the fact that Hinduism, unlike the great monotheistic religions, could not be identified with a single place and deity. The temple would be a tribute to Ram, and through him to *Bharat mata* (Mother India) and was meant to signal that Hindus would no longer tolerate being an 'oppressed majority', denied their rightful status by politicians pandering to minority (Muslim) voters. The right wing stressed the need for vigilance against the threats of Muslim treachery, of further separation, of the conversion of Hindus and of other anti-national activities, and issued constant reminders of the gruesome events of Partition that had cost over a million lives.

This message was fortuitously bolstered by the telecast at the time of the serialised epic *Ramayana*, which ran from January 1987 to September 1990. This reached a mass audience and facilitated the collective sharing of an idealised past and a utopian ideal of life under the governance of Ram. That the epic was a story with no claims to historical veracity seemed in time to be less important than its ubiquitous 'recognition' and discussion by the vast audience, which anointed it as a kind of de facto and indelible truth. As Rajagopal comments, such television was unwittingly a means of 'retailing' Hindutva, and it was against the perceived truth of a golden Hindu past, declared week after week, that the 'opportunity of religious nationalist mobilization was eventually seized' (Rajagopal 2001).

During the elections of 1991, Lal Krishna Advani, a prominent leader of the BJP, was photographed with bow and arrow in hand and vermilion on his forehead. His pose was immediately recognisable as that of the icon of *kodanda* Ram, the god Ram with bows and arrows. But the image of Ram has itself been radically altered since its appropriation by the proponents of Hindutva (Kapur 1993). Earlier he had mainly been depicted in his *shanti* state, kind and benevolent, invariably flanked by his wife Sita and brother Lakshman, who had accompanied him to his exile to the forest in the epic *Ramayana*. But this incarnation of Ram was considered too effeminate to adorn the walls of RSS offices (Nandy 2002: 133–34) and so the iconography of Ram was altered to suit the message of militancy. The Ram of Hindutva is thus the one in Advani's pose: armed, muscular and alone.

It was this image that was paraded on a chariot throughout the length and breadth of India, spreading the message of Ayodhya, collecting bricks for the promised temple and mobilising supporters to join the pilgrimage (*yatra*) there. The symbolism of the temple chariot was partly that of a god riding through his domain, confirming his territorial sovereignty and extending his blessings to the faithful, but it also perpetuated the militant symbolism of the war chariot of Arjuna in the *Gita*, which emphasised the duty of the warrior to fight when war is inevitable.[4] The *yatras* were joined by numerous minor processions on the way, and were headed by 'chariots' – decorated trucks – carrying huge pots (*kalashas*) of water from the Ganga, which was sold to devotees en route. The routes of the *yatras* were chosen with care to cover the entire sacred Hindu geography of the sub-continent, some proceeding from north to south and east to west, others weaving more idiosyncratically to link up especially sacred sites.[5] They converged on Nagpur, the geographical centre of India and the headquarters of the RSS, to symbolise the essential unity of India and the centrality of the RSS in upholding it. The *yatras* consciously echoed traditional Hindu pilgrimages and played on the fact that pilgrimage has become more popular in the colonial and post-colonial periods with improvement in the infrastructure of travel and accommodation (Van der Veer 1994).[6] It is considered particularly pious to have visited all four *dhams*, the four cardinal points of the sacred geography, during the course of one's lifetime as a Hindu. Utilising this traditional model of pilgrimage, the BJP thus combined Western-derived discourse of the nation as a territorially based community with religious discourse on sacred space to create a powerful political ritual.

The Ayodhya story and political strategy struck an undoubtedly popular chord (for reasons I discuss below) and brought significant electoral gains. In the national elections of 1991, the BJP won 20 percent of the vote and 119 seats out of 511 in the National Parliament, thus making it the largest opposition party to the Congress Government. It also won the state election and formed a government in Uttar Pradesh, India's most populous state, where Ayodhya is located. However, in December 1992 Babri Masjid was illegally destroyed by the 'spontaneous' actions of 'volunteers' (with the VHP in fact playing a central role), and this act of violence and extremism worried many sympathisers and negatively affected the BJP's profile. In addition, intensifying caste tensions led to significant successes for new lower-caste-based parties. With its high-caste perspective on Hinduism and history, the BJP message was not naturally positioned to appeal to this growing self-assertion of the lower castes, and in the 1993 state elections the BJP lost Uttar Pradesh.

The BJP now faced a dilemma. On the one hand, electoral success required a broadening of its appeal beyond its core zealots, which suggested a softening and widening of its political message. However, on the other, it was also concerned that such a move would cede leadership of the right to more extremist forces such as the VHP. The policy and presentational task was thus to develop a platform that would retain the religious integrity and undoubted mobilisational potency and style of the Ayodhya campaign but within a less shrill and more pragmatic manifesto that could appeal to centrist voters.

A further dynamic that had to be taken into account was the growing regionalisation in Indian politics and the emergence of regional parties. The right had already participated in and benefited from this to some degree, especially in the state of Maharashtra, where the BJP ally Shiv Sena had purveyed a very locally specific rendition of Hindu nationalism, in the form of the local hero Shivaji. However, the proliferation of parties and the growing role of coalition politics was a further incentive to the BJP to moderate its message sufficiently to allow other parties to be able to tolerate cooperation with it.

In the 1996 election therefore, the manifesto combined ethno-nationalist themes with more pragmatic policies. It increased its attention to economic questions, in particular blending and balancing a revival of the independence era rhetoric of *swadeshi* (national production and self-reliance) with a pragmatic accommodation to the free market towards which Congress had already begun to move. Appealing to the business classes and seeking to pose as the party of economic growth, the BJP stressed the importance of the small-scale sector, 'which has been entirely ignored by the Congress and whose very existence is threatened by the present policy of economic liberalization' and which would receive 'all encouragement and help from a BJP government'. It also pledged to reduce the economic role of the state and confine the public sector 'only to sensitive areas where the nation's security is involved' (BJP Manifesto).

Such messages did not displace the core ideas however, but instead merely overlaid them. The manifesto still defined the Indian citizen as someone who considered India as his or her sacred motherland. It further stated: 'Hindutva, or cultural nationalism, shall be the rainbow which will bridge our present to our glorious past and pave the way for an equally glorious future ... Hindutva is a unifying principle which alone can preserve the unity and integrity of our nation. It is a collective endeavour to protect and re-energize the soul of India, to take us into the next millennium as a strong and prosperous nation' (BJP Manifesto).

The new approach was highly successful and found a growing constituency among upper-caste Hindus, urban middle classes and upwardly mobile groups in northern and western India. The BJP captured much of the upper-caste vote from the Congress through the north Indian Hindi-speaking belt and in the west, and became the largest single parliamentary party, putting together a coalition government of twenty-three political parties. That coalition was predictably unstable and short lived, and fell to a broad alliance of secular and left parties. But that group also had little to bind it together positively and gradually fragmented, such that the BJP returned to government in 1998. It called elections in 1999 and substantially strengthened its position, going on to rule over a stable coalition until early 2004. Key policy developments during that government included privatising public sector assets, active nuclear-testing programmes and radical changes in the writing of history in school textbooks.

The right also continued to increase its organisational base and communication skills. Clear expositions of the Hindutva agenda were carried in official publications, which were further simplified for wider consumption through election manifestos and carefully positioned propaganda in the print and electronic media. In the election campaign of 2004, the BJP message reached most of India's 30 million mobile phone users and email addresses. The political message continued to be subtly altered to suit parliamentary politics and the mood of the nation. This air of moderation was further helped by having the popular and relatively mellow figure of Atal Behari Vajpayee as leader and Prime Minister; he already has a long and respectable political career behind him. The party had thus learned to work within the democratic multi-party system.[7]

There are clear limits to this moderation however, and the elderly Vajpayee is in truth a velvet glove on an iron fist. The parliamentary leaders are ever mindful of their dependence on the local cadres of the grass-roots organisations and these people generally have a taste for stronger ideological fare. Vajpayee had been appalled by the massacres of Muslims during riots in Gujarat in February/March 2002 and sought to sack Narendra Modi as Chief Minister; but he was opposed in this by the BJP party leadership and Modi remained.

The BJP and its allies unexpectedly lost the national elections in May 2004. What was clear from the results of this election was that the vote share of the neo-nationalists was not significantly diminished, rather it was their complacence and lack of appeal to the lower political orders that cost them seats in parliament and hence power. It remains to be seen whether they are able to realign their message to appeal to these sections of society while in opposition.

Comparison with European Neo-nationalism

The first question I would pose is whether it is really accurate to view the BJP as a manifestation of *neo*-nationalism. Neo-nationalism, as one might talk of it in contemporary Italy, Germany or Serbia, seems to follow a particular historical trajectory. These are recently formed states (1857, 1870 and 1908 respectively) and nationalist ideology played an important role in their births. More fundamentally, that ideology went on to develop from a nation-building project that stressed who was or should be in the nation into a 'hyper-nationalism' (fascism) that was expansionist (extra-national in ambition) and exclusionary (laying more emphasis on who should *not* be in the nation). This hyper-nationalism was defeated and suppressed by external powers (U.K./U.S.A. and USSR), who replaced it with non-nationalist systems and regimes (liberal democracy or Soviet socialism). Several decades later, however, those systems have in turn become discredited either partially (Italy) or wholly (Serbia), and nationalist ideas have become resurgent.

It seems therefore that the designation of neo-nationalism properly depends first upon the experience of a significant historical hiatus and then second a reinvocation of the nationalist ideology that pre-dated that hiatus. It is not obvious that either of these circumstances are true of France or the U.K., so I would be inclined to view talk of *neo*-nationalism there as metaphorical, indicating little more than a loose affinity of tone and protesting intent with genuine neo-nationalisms elsewhere. What though of India?

India clearly did have a nationalist project that helped build the nation. Though this took place in an 'anti-colonial' context, it was not all that different from the experience of Italy in 1857 or Germany in 1870, where there were also fragmented territories and varied structures of rule (princely states, obscure duchies, church-owned territory) and external foreign interference (mainly from France and Austria). All such problems of territory, unity and independence had to be resolved by the Indian freedom fighters too.

Post-independence India did not however suffer the kind of humiliation and/or impoverishment experienced by Germany or Italy (in the First World War) that provided the breeding ground for their fascism.[8] Hyper-nationalism did not seize power in India and was not suppressed by external power. In short, India moved to nationhood and liberal democracy – in German terms achieving its '1870' and '1945' – at the same time, without the agony in between. So there was no hiatus comparable to that of the European countries (or Japan) where we might legitimately talk of neo-nationalism.

The second part of the typical 'neo' story does however seem applicable to India. Though not backed by any occupying power, the liberal democracy Nehru established did effectively suppress the (modestly influential) hyper-nationalist impulses in the country. This remained possible while the state and Congress Government was respected and authoritative, as it was for thirty years, until the Emergency in 1975. We might see that period as comparable to the similar period of calm and consensus in post-1945 Germany and Italy. Thereafter, however, there was growing scepticism about the authority of the state and the validity of what it said about the nature of the nation.

In European countries this process of dwindling authority typically reflected the growing sense that the vision purveyed by a centrist and bureaucratic ruling class was a complacent and self-serving one that was either oppressing the masses (from a leftist perspective) or failing the nation (in the eyes of the right). In Italy and Germany leftist terrorists attacked centrist governments as reactionary capitalist lackeys, while rightists violently counter-attacked the leftists but also attacked the centre as corrupt, weak and traitorous. In the socialist states, like Serbia, oppositionists viewed the Russian-backed and high-living *nomenklatura* elite as both oppressive and traitorous. These sentiments flourished among intensifying economic problems (capitalist stagnation in the 1970s; socialist stagnation in the 1980s).

Very broadly then, neo-nationalism in Europe has tended to be a Romantic vision offered as an alternative to a disgraced bureaucratic status quo. This characterisation would seem to apply well to India, in the context of the long, slow decline through the 1970s and 1980s of both Congress's political authority and India's economic vitality. This was the breeding ground for the various alternative visions of the nation we have already noted, including not only Hindutva but also caste struggles and a more assertive regionalism. All three trends have been given further impetus throughout the 1990s by the frustrations and inequalities caused by India's move from state capitalism to the free market. Again, this parallels developments in Eastern Europe particularly, where the pains of 'transition' to capitalism have pushed many people, especially an undermined and degraded proletariat, towards neo-nationalist sympathies. Likewise, the globalisation of consumption that accompanies such capitalism has brought foreign goods, images and habits to both India and Eastern Europe that disturb traditionalists and encourage perceptions of 'cultural threat'.

Against this backdrop, Hindutva skilfully plays on the sentiments and concerns of different categories of people: the aspiring lower middle classes and their sense of exclusion from the old political mainstream; the peasants and small farmers who respond to the call of the faithful; the upper castes who appreciate a conservative means of political assertion that does not challenge the caste hierarchy; the sections of the intelligentsia who find in the movement an echo of their own frustrated ambitions for national cultural greatness; the non-resident Indians overseas who sense that a strong nationalist party would bolster the country's reputation abroad and hence their own expatriate situation; and businesses that seek a strong nationalist party to replace the Congress and become what the Congress had never been, namely, an ideologically based party articulating a distinct and explicit consensus.

My second question is whether the explicitly religious rhetoric of Hindutva makes it radically different from European neo-nationalism. In one sense, perhaps. Certainly nineteenth-century nationalism in Europe tended to see nation building as the culmination of a secularising process that displaced religion and in particular the influence of the established (usually Catholic) Church. The same was true of hyper-nationalism, with Hitler and to a lesser extent Mussolini acting against the church as a centre of authority and purveyor of alternative ethics that could not be tolerated.

Looking at neo-nationalisms, however, the matter seems less clear-cut and in particular seems to depend on the place of religion in the discredited status quo. Where religion is not part of the status quo, for instance, because it was suppressed as in communist Eastern Europe, then hyper-nationalism does tend to draw upon it (e.g., the importance of Orthodoxy to Serbian identity and Catholicism to the Poles). In Italy, too, the right has seen post-war governments as irreligious and immoral and urged a greater role for the church. In that sense, for the BJP too religion has to some extent merely been a readily available stick with which to beat a secular status quo.

In any case, religion clearly often overlaps with wider 'ethnic' considerations. Croats and Serbs share a territory and language and most of a culture and history but are divided by their respective Catholicism and Orthodoxy. Ulster Independence and British neo-nationalism more generally are based on a Protestantism and anti-Catholicism that is no less religious for being vague. A common denominator in places with neo-nationalism is enmity against ethnic minorities who 'belong' to neighbouring states. This is most obvious in Eastern Europe – Serb nationalists hate their Albanians, Hungarian nationalists their Romanians, both substantial minorities who had lived in the same place for centuries but who suddenly found themselves stranded in the 'wrong country' following the creation of new national units and boundaries out of the collapse of the multi-ethnic Austrian Empire in 1918. In the Indian case, however, the neighbouring country, Pakistan, set itself up from the start on the basis of religious criteria as the Muslim 'land of the pure'. In this sense, Hindutva, at its crudest, is merely expressing banal enmity towards the 'Pakistanis' left stranded in Indian territory. This may be unfortunate, but it is hardly an unfamiliar scenario historically, and in the Balkans it was precisely such 'ethnic' tensions that were a major contributor to the emergent hyper-nationalism that afflicted nearly all the new states in the inter-war period. What is surprising therefore, especially given the three Indo-Pakistan wars, is not the current official antagonism towards Indian Muslims so much as the fact that it took four post-independence decades for such enmity to flourish, a delay which can only be seen as the great achievement of Gandhi and Nehru.

Overall then I would suggest that the religious nature of the BJP puts it at one end of a continuum of religious evocations by neo-nationalists elsewhere, rather than marking it out as something fundamentally different. Beneath the religious trappings is a sentiment and idea, shared more widely among neo-nationalists, of a golden age and imagined community that pre-dates some subsequent fall from grace.

Notes

I would like to thank all the participants at the workshop in Brussels where this material was first presented and especially the editors of this volume for their comments. My thanks also, as always, to Julian Watts.

1. There is a vast and excellent literature on different aspects of religious nationalism in India. Peter Van der Veer's *Religious Nationalism* (1994) was an early leader in the field. Since then several others have followed. Hansen (1999) and Jaffrelot (1996) are particularly good at delineating the organisational aspects of the Sangh Parivar. Rajagopal (2001) discusses use of mass media in politics, and Kapur (1993) pays special attention to the changing iconography of the image of the deity Ram, the centrepiece of the Hindutva movement.
2. 'Hindu' denoted all those religions that had grown 'out of the soil of India'.
3. The Orientalist perceptions of religion in India, in which Hinduism was considered more feminine and spiritual than a martial Islam, especially preyed on the minds of the nationalist ideologues and further fuelled this opposition.
4. In the pamphlets of the VHP, Arjuna's chariot is a recurring symbol. The 'chariots' of the VHP also carried a symbol of *Bharat mata.*
5. One went from Kathmandu in Nepal to Rameshwaram in Tamil Nadu; another from Bengal in the east to the Somnath Temple in Gujarat in the west; a third from the holy city of Hardwar to Kanya Kumari.
6. A large part of the sub-continent is interconnected by clusters of pilgrimage centres such as Banaras, Kanti, Hardwar, Ayodhya, Dwarka, Mathura and Ujjain. Pilgrimages traditionally involved a journey from one's village or home town to a sacred centre and back, and its performance appears to reinforce the notion of a wider community of believers.
7. In December 2002, we witnessed its latest success in the state of Gujarat where the clinical instigation of violence between religious communities just before the elections ensured a resounding victory for the neo-nationalists.
8. If Bose had led an authoritarian post-independence India and then suffered severe territory loss to China, a similar humiliation might have occurred. Arguably this is what happened to Pakistan after its defeats in 1965 and 1971.

Bibliography

BJP Manifesto. Available online at http://www.bjp.org/manifes.

Golwalkar, M.S. 1939. *We, or Our Nationhood Defined.* Nagpur: Bharat Prakashanto.

Hansen, T. 1999. *The Saffron Wave.* Princeton: Princeton University Press.

Jaffrelot, C. 1996. *The Hindu Nationalist Movement.* New York: Columbia University Press.

Kapur, A. 1993. 'Deity to Crusader: The Changing Iconography of Ram', in G. Pandey ed. *Hindus and Others.* Delhi: Oxford University Press.

Nandy, A. 2002. 'Present State of Health of the Gods and Goddesses', in *Time Warps: Studies in the Politics of Silent or Evasive Pasts.* London: C. Hurst & Co.

Rajagopal, A. 2001. *Politics after Television.* Cambridge: Cambridge University Press.

Savarkar, V.D. 1969. *Hindutva: Who is a Hindu.* Bombay: S.S. Savarkar.

Van der Veer, P. 1994. *Religious Nationalism.* Berkeley: University of California Press.

Chapter 13

Nationalism and Neo-populism in Australia

Hansonism and the Politics of the New Right in Australia
Bruce Kapferer and Barry Morris

Introduction

On 20 August 2003, Pauline Hanson was sentenced to a three-year jail term for the fraudulent registration of the One Nation Party in Queensland. This appears as the final chapter in a rake's progress in which the astonishing, if brief, rise of a political unknown of modest background, which threatened the political hegemony of the ruling parties and gave vent in public discourse to values that contradicted a postmodern, multicultural image of post-colonial Australia, ended in disgrace, criminal conviction and imprisonment. Hanson was convicted of the kind of dishonest practice of which she and her followers routinely accused the ruling parties and which refused a popular demand for openness and transparency and subordinated public morality and law to private political and economic gain. She was accused of electoral fraud: of rigging the party membership numbers to meet the legal requirements for political registration and government funding. This irony was compounded in the manner of her punishment. Hanson was jailed in an institution many of whose inmates are from the very communities (Aboriginal and Asian) that were the targets of her often stigmatising rhetoric, which was fuelled by an all too familiar possibility of an egalitarian ethos. To many Pauline Hanson's fall was poetic justice. Her popularity had been seen as deeply embarrassing to progressivist representations of postmodern Australia. Pauline Hanson and her One Nation Party were seen as resurrecting better-buried memories and values of Australia's racist past that involved in particular the destruction and dispossession of the Aboriginal people of Australia and a history of bigotry towards non-Anglo-Saxon immigrants.

Of course, few events are as simple as they seem and fail to take a determined or expected course. Hanson's imprisonment occurred at a moment when she and One Nation were all but dead as a social and political phenomena. Her prosecution and conviction became a focus for popular criticism and disaffection with the state, its system of justice, the practice of politicians and what was seen as the victimisation of the ordinary Australian, i.e., middle- and lower-income groups of largely white settler Australians usually of Anglo-Saxon or Celtic background, though not exclusively so by any means. The media revealed a cloak-and-dagger story of behind-the-scenes political and economic deals coordinated by a key agent of the ruling National Liberal Party (whose interests had been seriously affected by Hanson's rise). The aim had been to fund the personal vendetta of a rejected One Nation contender through the courts. Hanson's demise was depicted as yet another instance of the little person suffering at the hands of a justice system manipulated by the powerful, and of the common man as the victim of state excess. Her sentence was presented as out of all proportion to the crime. Widespread moral outrage was expressed to the effect that murderers and rapists could be expected to receive lighter sentences. The social constructions surrounding the event threatened, perhaps momentarily, the reinvention of Pauline Hanson as a victim hero of the same order as other Australian heroes of its recent and not so recent past: the developing narratives of this event resonated with the almost Nietzschean thematic of former individualist battlers who, like the infamous Ned Kelly, were able to fend off the powers of authority and order for a while only to succumb eventually to the overwhelming and iniquitous forces of the state.

In the development of this discourse Hanson as a catalyst of populist antagonism to minority groups, from Aborigines, to immigrants and especially refugees from the Middle East and from Asia, took backstage. Perhaps one reason for this was that at the time of Hanson's imprisonment the message of her initial apotheosis had long since been appropriated by ruling interests. Her racism had disguised a neo-conservatism that was now in full flower. The Liberal National Party Coalition under Prime Minister John Howard had successfully pursued a series of populist policies – inspired by the political shock of the Hanson phenomenon. This had included an aggressive anti-refugee policy and a radical reconsideration of social and economic reforms concerning indigenous Australians in line with a restructuring of state and society with reference to the objectives of neo-liberalism. The whole thing was topped off by the avid support of Australia's Prime Minister, a George Bush in minor key, for the invasion of Iraq.

Our concern here is to demonstrate the close affiliation in the Australian context between what can be described as the exclusionary, often racist, discourse of Hansonism, on the one hand, and the development of neo-liberal ideological practices in the context of the restructuring of the post-colonial, postmodern state of Australia, on the other. It is our thesis that Hansonism was at once a continuation of and a radical reorientation within Australian egalitarian thought and practice. The discursive practice of egalitarianism, what we refer to as egalitarian individualism, had its roots in the modernist and post-colonial state but took new direction in the post-Fordist circumstances of what we refer to as Australia's society of the state. In effect, the restructuring of the state and of social formations within its frame in the course of contemporary conditions of globalisation reinvented and in some ways intensified egalitarian discourse but in novel directions, simultaneously giving it renewed agency in the reformations taking place. We address egalitarian discourse as manifesting the distinct crises of the state in modernity and postmodernity in its historical continuities and contemporary discontinuities. The Hanson phenomenon casts a particular accent on such processes.

The argument that we present starts by exploring some of the historical sources of Australian egalitarian thought and practice, and concentrates upon the relatively distinct context of the colonial formation of the state. It is against such a background that some of the significance of the perils of Pauline in relation to the postmodern ruptures of Australia's society of the state can be grasped. One theme in particular underlies the discussion as a whole and concerns what may be described as the inner tension of egalitarian practice and thought. We refer to what may be called the critical aporia of egalitarianism that Hansonism throws up: the paradox of a discourse whereby the powerful assertion of the rights of individual and community is effectively implicated in their radical denial. Bound within a virtually inescapable dialectic of difference and similarity, egalitarian discourse of the Australian kind has as its potential not only a socio-moral hierarchialising of peoples and their practices, but also a tension towards their systematic exclusion. This is particularly so, we suggest, in the contemporary circumstances of state crisis in the broader context of globalisation. Furthermore, our implication is that in her initial racist manifestation Hanson merely gave explicit recognition to forces that are deeply entrenched in the institutional and other processes whereby Australia's society of the state is continuously and always diversely reinvented. Hanson has two appearances, on the one hand, as a class and ethnic xenophobe and, on the other, as victim. The two are inseparably linked; their distinct appearance is mediated in the crisis of the contemporary state.

Hansonism in Historical Perspective: The Colonial State and the Anglo-Celtic Diaspora

Our attention to the Hanson phenomenon focuses on the ideological and related practices that have been at the centre of the Australian nationalist imagination since before 1901, when the several colonies of the continent were federated as the independent Commonwealth of Australia. We gloss the ideology that we discuss in its several historical manifestations as 'egalitarian individualism'. It is vital in various populist and state-articulated developments. Australian egalitarian individualism is akin to that which has been variously described as integral to global modernities in Europe and North America (see, e.g., De Tocqueville 1968; Dumont 1980; Foucault 1977, 1979, 1991). We stress individualism *as a value* and not the trivial fact that it is individual human beings acting in concert or separately who continually make and remake their existential and historical realities. This, as Dumont and others have tirelessly emphasised, is true for all social contexts. However, individualism as value is a relatively modern phenomenon connected with the development of secularism (including its religious forms such as Protestantism) and the spread of capitalism and closely associated bureaucratic and managerial practice in state and non-state institutions.

Individualism *as an ideology* (i.e., a discursive system of value – our concern here) constructs the individual subject as the primordial and generative centre of all social and political realities. Egalitarian individualism insists on the fundamental equality of all human beings in nature and represents social inequality (often described as hierarchy) as the contradiction of egalitarian ideals. In Europe, of course, such an ideological vision was vital in the French Revolution and carried through as the characteristic ideal of the American Revolution. Many forms of such egalitarianism are apparent in pre- and post-Enlightenment discourse and were a force in anarchist and socialist movements worldwide. Such ideas were also vital to the pragmatic interests of power and control whose effects were the denial or restriction of pressures towards freedom and liberation. Foucault, referring to Bentham's individualist reformist pragmatism and orientation to a specular state (Bentham's panopticon was actually built in the penal colony of Van Diemen's Land, Tasmania), explores aspects of the individualism underlying the formation of the bio-power of the modern state (Foucault 1977; 1979; 1991). Individualism is an aspect of the inhabitation of the person by the state and part of what Foucault describes as governmentality, whereby modern citizens govern themselves on behalf of dominant state interests. Hardt and Negri (2001) have recently expanded Foucault's notion of bio-power and governmentality to discuss the forces of control in what they call Empire, or the political orders articulating globalisation. We make the reference to underscore the close affinity of individualism with state interest and, paradoxically, with hierarchialising and subordinating power relations that are very apparent in contemporary Australian populism and developments in citizen conformity and protest.

While the formation of Australian egalitarian practice shares much with other colonially formed settler states there are, nonetheless, important distinctions. An obvious feature of most colonial and post-colonial contexts is that their social and political realities were formed or reconfigured through the institutions and practices of the colonial state. The order of the state defined the social orders it encompassed and established the limits to the autonomy of those social formations already founded in the context of the colonial state. Australia is a particular but extremely radical instance of such a process. Although there was a sizeable indigenous population at the time of colonisation, the British colonial authorities declared the country to be *terra nullius*. This had disastrous consequences for the

Aboriginal population whose own institutions received virtually no government legitimacy. Their lack of legal and official recognition removed the capacity of Aborigines to negotiate the terms of their own existence in the context of the state. The situation of Aborigines emphasises the uncontested and totalistic character of the colonial state in Australia whereby it was able to determine, effectively unchallenged, the social and political conditions of its existence. This was further facilitated by the fact that major centres of population were initially established as penal settlements: colonial hells governed by particularly brutal military regimes (see Hughes 1996).

From the foundation of Australia the colonial state was an absolutist state and a disciplinary society, thus achieving from the outset what the modern state might have projected as its own future (see Lattas 1985). The state was the circumstance within which social relations and their subjectivities were constituted: the process of exploration and settlement being more or less completely mediated through its offices. We reiterate to strengthen the point. In Australia the modern state did not so much emerge from within an already established and diverse scattering of settlements and communities, rather these emerged from within and by means of the machinery of the state. Australian society was, through and through, a conception of the state – a complete construction of the state. The state did not become internal to the person so much as the person was already instituted as internal to the state. If the bio-power of the state, in the sense that Foucault has described for Europe, grew as a process of historical evolution, in Australia the state as bio-power was there from its inception.

From the start the all-embracing character of the Australian state (both in its federal and regional manifestations) was influential in the development of an internal discourse of opposition to the state. This is apparent in two early ideological developments in Australian nationalist imaginaries and practice, which are referred to as the 'pioneer legend' and the 'Australian tradition'. To a large extent these refracted the fact that while state power and the institutions for social control were concentrated in urban centres much of the population was distributed through rural areas, which, of course, were central to the economy and initially provided the major labour opportunities. Located in the 'pioneer legend' and 'Australian tradition' orientations is a state/people (also city/country, see J. Kapferer 1996) opposition that is strongly apparent in later ideological developments, especially that of Anzac (discussed below). Shades of these ideological positions are evident in Hansonism, particularly Hanson's popularity in the small town communities of rural Australia, and in broader social reactions to neo-liberal programmes, which might otherwise be distanced from Hanson's views.

The 'pioneer legend' and 'Australian tradition' visions privilege rural Australia (referred to as the 'bush') as the primal scene. In contemporary Australia they are reproduced to support values of mutual help in times of crisis, and notions of citizen service – an idea to which the Anzac tradition of post-colonial Australian nationalism was to lend particular poignancy. The 'pioneer legend' depicts the pastoral pioneer as the hero in a battle with nature in which individual perseverance and effort overcome hardship. As Hirst has put it, the pioneer legend is the core element in Australian nationalism as it deals, 'in an heroic way with the central experience of European settlement in Australia: the taming of the new environment to man's use ... Their enemies are drought, flood, fire, sometimes Aborigines ...' (1978: 316). Not only does the pioneer 'show the way for following generations', but also gives historical witness to the egalitarianism and camaraderie that emerged across class lines between owners and workers in collaboration against the hardships of an unfamiliar and hostile Australian environment. 'Pioneer' largely refers to the smallholder, who developed the land and shared the early hardships with his workers. The 'bush' is more than an escape from unsatisfying society: it is the ideal community central to the reproduction of a national subjectivity and differentiated from class- and conflict-ridden city and society.

The 'Australian tradition' also makes the bush vital in the national imaginary, and as with all imaginaries this did not arise *de novo*. The country regions were the sites for early workers' struggles. Some of the most important union and labour movements had their origins in the bush. The Australian socialist movements saw their early impetus in rural regions. The infamous 'White Australia' policy had its roots in a (largely rural) labour movement concerned to protect its interests and maintain what it perceived to be the homogeneity integral to its projection of class and egalitarian solidarity (see Hancock 1961; Turner 1982; Ward 1958).

The imaginaries of Australian nationalist ideologies we discuss combine senses of stoicism and fatalism (of the individual pitted against all odds and, in a Nietzschean way, who in all likelihood can be expected to succumb even despite superhuman efforts). There is an echo in such sentiment of the experience of the penal system. Many of the terms associated with rural life (e.g., station, muster) are derived from colonial prison practice.[1] The bush is an ambiguous and historically complex conceptual category. It does not fall into easy semiotic dualisms of nature/culture, but is the place where human beings were subjected to the harshness and vagaries of dominant elites and of government authority and regulation. Convicts were sent to the bush to work as virtual slave labour. It was a place to escape from authority and therefore was potentially as liberating as imprisoning. It was in the bush, following the end of transportation in 1868, that the intense ideological efforts to invert the master/servant relations took early form.[2] Overall the mix of optimism and pessimism still apparent in modern egalitarian ideologies in Australia might be seen as in some respects continuous with the earlier sentiments that we have described.

Generally, the bush continues to hold a place in the Australian nationalist imagination as the originating context for the production of generally valued ideals of self-regulating individual common sense and goodwill. These ideas were to flower in the Australian legend of Anzac (a voluntary army of largely rural men) and its ideology of 'mateship'. However, in Anzac a stronger communitarian idea was to develop, which was appropriate to the nationalist vision of Australia as a new and original kind of society in which bush ideologies, with their often dominant reveries of isolation and loneliness, had less place.

It should be clear from what we have said that the bush was no Arcadian realm in early nationalist imaginaries, although aspects of this have more recently emerged (in representations of traditional Aboriginal society, re-evaluations of desert wilderness, etc.). Furthermore, the ideas it spawned were through and through modernist urban visions of class struggle, excoriating conditions of work, general hardship and poverty. They were not so much idyllic romantic constructions as views that were thoroughly integral to the experiences born of modernism (of industrialism and urbanisation). This extends an understanding of why bush ideologies could continue to be relevant in the growing city contexts of Australia. It was not merely because country people migrated to the towns, but because the sensitivities of bush ideologies were already urban in the encompassing notion of modernism that we use here: for example, bush ideas of personal loneliness, of wilderness, translate into common urban characterisations of forms of individual alienation.

Australia as a modernist society from the very start, and one in which the state played the key mediating role, expands an understanding of the egalitarian ideas that developed over the nineteenth and twentieth centuries and their instrumentality as an agency of government and populist expression.

Australian egalitarianism is a continuing, if heterogeneous, construction of Australia as a modernist society of the state. We stress the particularity of this ethos, its historical specificity. While Australian egalitarianism resonates with other populist egalitarianisms elsewhere, contrary to other interpretations (see Davidson 1997), the history of its evolution as well as its circumstances is significantly distinct from overtly similar developments in Europe and America. Colonising forces are conventionally seen as a major mechanism of modernisation at metropolitan peripheries. Australia is certainly no exception, but we reiterate that there was no gradualist formation of modernism in Australia, it was modernist through and through from the very start. Moreover, it was virtually completely British in its modernist political, social and economic institutions. This was rather different from comparable political orders such as North America where colonial beginnings were far more diverse and where social formation took place beyond the regulatory reach of the state. In North America (especially the U.S.A.) there was a suspicion of British and other European-centred institutions (encouraged perhaps by strong nonconformist influences), and a powerful energy to start something new.

The egalitarian cultural and social conformity of Australian ideology and institutional practice relates to its greater social homogeneity as compared with other colonial situations. Largely British, the immigrant population brought with it social conflicts and other divisions that certainly had ideological and practical roots in Britain, but in the context of Australia these achieved an added dynamic and value. They became a force for a sense of unity despite conflict. More to the point, they were active in the institutional construction of modern Australia and vital in producing a taken-for-granted cultural hegemony: the assumed dominance of what are now termed Anglo-Celtic values or, more recently, the often hidden power of 'whiteness' in much Australian governmental and social practice (see Hage 1998).[3] It was such value that was influential in the White Australia Policy when sections of the population felt their interests and hegemony threatened and which has re-emerged in Hansonism and the unabated hostility towards refugees.

One general point should be restated at this stage. This relates to the internality of egalitarian thought and practice within the apparatuses of the state. The liberal historian, W.K. Hancock (incidentally an ambivalent supporter of the White Australia Policy), writing in 1930 asserted that the state had an essential role in the creation of Australian egalitarian society (1961: esp. chapter VII).[4] He recognised the identity of state interest with the promotion of individualist value. Hancock articulated the state formation of the individual subject as a self-governing entity as vital to government control and social coherence. For Hancock, the prevailing ideology of Australian democracy was simple – justice, rights and equality rested on the 'appeal to government as an instrument of self-realization' (ibid.: 57). It is Australia as a society of individual self-discipline (Australia as a disciplinary society) that aids an understanding of the ideological centrality or national fetishism of such practices as sport and the expanding importance of nationalist celebrations like Anzac Day and its traditions and even the ceremonialisation of recent national disasters such as the Bali bombing. Here too is located some understanding of contemporary discourses in Australia concerning citizenship and the construction of projections of what kind of society Australia should become and who may not be appropriate to it.

Egalitarian Individualism and the Anzac Tradition

A short account of the Anzac tradition brings our discussion into the centre of Australian nationalist discourse and the way it may bring together social and political elements that on the surface could be seen to be opposed.

Australian nationalism and the consciousness of Australian identity now and in the past had little purpose other than to mark Australian distinctiveness in an era of nationalism that still bears force. Unlike elsewhere, it did not grow out of social and political struggle with the colonial hegemon. Rather, what antagonisms there were were reconstituted as a resolution in an idealism in which erstwhile opponents were united in agreement. In effect the ideology of Australian national identity emerged as an imagined resolution of difference as sameness, or unity of project. In this sense it did, as its critics have complained, continue some of the logic inherent in the British ideology of Empire.

The foregoing considerations are underscored in the phenomenon of Australian nationalism and the consciousness of Australian identity. These were constructions of the society of the state having little purpose other than the creation of a sense of distinction appropriate in an age of nationalism. Perhaps, too, Australian nationalism as it developed enshrined those values born of division in the largely British society of the state, recreating them as principles of unity rather than of conflict. Australian nationalist ideology and discourses of Australian identity did not grow out of processes of social and political struggle. They developed after the fact of independence and were thoroughly representational – already, first and foremost, media events concerned to produce a popular sense of distinctive personal and collective identity relevant to the creation of the Federation of Australia in 1901, the union of hitherto separate colonies. The idea of Australian identity developed within discourses relevant to the dominant British population further embedding its values as integral to the hegemony of the state.

Australian political life was powerfully organised around issues of class and other related conflicts (e.g., Protestants versus Catholics) but these were suppressed or transmuted as part of Australian national presentation. An outstanding example is the legend of Ned Kelly, which expresses the mutual antipathy between Irish and English, between smallholder and large landowner, and between dominating urban capital and its authorities and labouring factions (see McQuilton 1979). The legend, in effect, achieves in numerous representations an uneasy resolution and unity of the competing interests engaged in the production of Australia and generates a national value of resigned acceptance, the 'Such is life', despairing, almost defeated, tone of so much that passes for Australian nationalist value.[5] In a major way the discourse of Australian identity engaged the language of class to draw distinctions between Australian forms of life and those of the 'homeland' and its erstwhile ruling system – Britain. Thus Australians were presented as egalitarian and classless whereas the English were typified as class-ridden and hierarchical. Effectively, class conflicts internal to the colonial and post-colonial social orders were both denied in Australian nationalism and reconfigured as a cultural distinction between Australia and its erstwhile colonial ruler.

Australian nationalism has its clearest (and most worshipped) representation in the Anzac tradition constructed around the legendary exploits of Australian and New Zealand volunteer servicemen (non-conscripted citizens) at Gallipoli in 1915, where they were defeated by Turkish troops. This tradition, consciously developed to epitomise the heroism of egalitarian Australian individualism against all manner of hardship and suffering (frequently conceived as caused by the ineptitude of hierarchical management), rather than the day of federation was established as the 'true' birthing event of the new nation. The egalitarian ideology of Anzac, one which has gone through numerous elaborations since, celebrated a community of individuals who expressed a fundamental unity in nature undifferentiated by the artifice of 'culture' or the legacy of civilisations premised on unnatural hierarchical distinctions. The Anzacs – as their hagiographer, C.E.W. Bean (the inspiration behind the Anzac ceremonial centre, the Australian War Memorial at Canberra) described – bore the heroic characteristics of those in the ancient cradles of civilisation (see B. Kapferer 1988). In effect, they were constructed as manifestations of ancient ideals, 'new men' who reinvented what intervening civilisations had debased. The society that they represented was a society of equals who possessed as inner qualities the capacity to govern themselves. Thus the need for hierarchical orders of power and control was made redundant.

Anzac Day, the annual event honouring Australia's servicemen and women and arguably still the most important national event (even more than Australia Day, marking the arrival of the First Fleet, which is growing in popularity), takes the form of a symbolic suspension of state authority. An interpretation of the practices associated with the Anzac rites on the day is that ordinary citizens, the people, are given over to the formation of their social relations independent of the authority and mediation of the state. The people are constituted as a community of individuals without internal distinction and bound by acts of mutual reciprocity and recognition of interpersonal equality (mateship). At the close of the rites the state is reaffirmed and presented as emergent from the body of the people. The people/state opposition and tension, which marks the dynamic of events on Anzac Day, is in many ways a ritual working out of the Hobbesian state/society dilemma at the heart of the modernist state. The autonomy of the People, it may be interpreted, is recognised by the State. The agents of the State acknowledged the potency of this autonomy even as it is yielded to the State in war as in peace in the interest of social and political continuity. Much of Anzac Day is, of course, centred upon the gift (sacrifice) of the autonomy of the People to the State.

There is a clear Christian resonance in this obdurately secular ceremony. Seen by many as largely Protestant in ethos it nonetheless carries themes that are present in all denominations, which enables people of vastly different religious backgrounds to participate. The argument of sacrifice is potentially trans-religious especially as it is clearly carried through in contemporary discourse and rhetoric, in Australia and elsewhere, of citizenship and human rights.

The Anzac tradition has frequently been interpreted as an artefact of days gone by. Whilst it is dismissed as a relic of Empire, masculinist and militarist, it has somehow survived such onslaughts even gathering strength in the imagination of new generations who have not experienced war. There are now efforts to get Anzac Cove in Gallipoli listed as a World Heritage site. There are numerous reasons why Anzac seems to go from strength to strength as the prime nationalist occasion, not least among these being media attention and the preparedness of the organisers to adapt its practice to shifts in social attitudes.

However, we consider that the egalitarian individualist logic of Anzac continues its relevance *because* of contemporary global processes and their particular local effects in Australia. In certain ways Anzac was already postmodern! Certain vital aspects of current realities – the structural shifts that have occurred because of globalisation – discover an import in Anzac and impel its reinvention or reissuing.

Not only was Anzac nationalism a thoroughly modernist idealism (in which real class conflicts and other social differences were suppressed) born, of course, in the first industrial war, but it virtually denied its own historicity. The anti-historical feature of the Anzac ideology marks it out from other nationalisms (which often revel in the falsity of their histories) and aggressively underpins its essentialism and universalism. It is this fact that enables it to have continuing force in what is an immigrant society. In certain respects Anzac ideology enables the erasure of different histories and their amalgamation in the expression of a foundational individuality. Paradoxically, it is relevant to current globalising realities that may be characterised as intensifying biological and technological determinisms of modernist times. Anzac is pre-adapted, as it were, for a postmodern society with its strong emphasis on individual agency and self-discipline. The occasion of the event, after the parades are over and frequently during them, manifests as loose and shifting gatherings (communities) of men (and now women) iconic in many ways with the porous and shifting boundaries of postmodern society. The 'communities' that take form have no internal structures of authority, in fact they actively resist them, and are expressly antagonistic to those forms of society that are coherent and ordered and which deny individual autonomy. The practice of Anzac seeks to achieve a resolution of any potential contradiction between individual and community interest (see B. Kapferer 1988).

This should not obscure its powerful modernist overtones, however. This is especially so as regards the relation of the people (the Anzacs) to the state. We stress the Hobbesian or contractarian idea of the state that Anzac projects that may be becoming sharply out of place in the neo-liberal retraction of the state in which the nature of the contract between people and state is in the throes of reform and often radical renegotiation.

Anzac is the most important practice of nationalist ideals, but it is accompanied by a growing number of other festivals that ritualise individualist value. Some of these, considered by many to be more appropriate to modernity, communicate comparable ideals. Thus major occasions of celebration in Australia, e.g., Australia Day and the Sydney Gay and Lesbian Mardi Gras (now advertised as among Australia's greatest tourist attractions) display similar egalitarian themes. Australia Day has recently received greater attention. This has some connection to recent patterns of immigration to Australia and the policy of multiculturalism. It is a state- and corporate-sponsored instrument of national ideological incorporation. It concentrates around the eating of different ethnic cuisines celebrating differences that can be ingested in a demonstration of essential oneness. The Gay and Lesbian Mardi Gras is, of course, presented as anti-masculinist and opposed to prejudices based on gender difference, which are seen as being at the root of conventional social hierarchies (Nicoll 2001). In a sense it is also anti-society though in a different way from Anzac. As with Anzac it celebrates individuality and expresses powerful ideals of self-discipline and control (even as these are given a sexual value loading). In recent performances, the organisers have provided their own marshals who, in partnership with the police, maintain the order of spectators and participants. In addition, sport, the national obsession, provides countless arenas for the observation of natural capacities, self-discipline and mutual camaraderie.

Hansonism and Neo-liberalism: An Anti-postmodern Postmodern Turn Within Egalitarianism

The emergence of Hanson and One Nation gave expression to prejudices that to many contradicted the progressive developments in thought and practice in Australia. It seemed to air attitudes that those in middle-class urban Australia had come to associate with the bush and what were often characterised as the narrow 'red-neck' ideas of its poorer communities.[6] Hanson and her followers were seen to profess a racism (especially views towards Aborigines and new immigrants, particularly from Asia) that many in Australia were attempting to distance themselves from. The Australia of the past dramatically demonstrated that it was still very much alive. Hansonism achieved a marked popularity in rural areas and towns, but also, even if more muted, in the cities. Hanson and One Nation were an embarrassment to those in Australia who saw the country as cosmopolitan and at last rid of its colonial, Crocodile Dundee, backwater image.

However, Hansonism was, of course, an expression of popular resistance to changes being wrought within the country as a result of globalisation. It was also an expression of possibilities of egalitarian individualist ideas and practices. This much was recognised by its opponents who associated it with what were regarded as the worst imperialist and racist views of 'old identity Australia'. These were the views of members of the Anglo-Celtic population who had not adapted to contemporary realities in which political and social power was shared with communities who had few if any ties to the Empire of the past. While there is much evidence to indicate that this was indeed the case, the criticism of Hanson was often from within similar egalitarian individualist perspectives. Both the criticism of Hanson and the criticism she and her followers constantly announced centred on the opinion that both sides, if in different ways, were fostering the growth of inequalities. (Pauline Pantsdown, who dressed in drag, was prominent among those who ridiculed Hanson's conservative attitudes and dogged her political progress, see Nicoll 2001.) Furthermore, as events were to demonstrate, those who may have opposed Hanson began to support programmes that she had initiated regarding Aborigines, refugees and certain immigrant groups. Many of Hanson's opinions were reissued as neo-liberal political, economic and social policy expressing similar lines of social and political exclusion and an apparent return to 'old values'.

If it was a return to past values, Hansonism and the neo-liberalism (both of the left and the right) that overcame her were produced in the structural conditions of the present. These conditions were manifested as a postmodern and post-colonial crisis that achieved especial significance through egalitarian individualist value.

What is most striking about the One Nation period (1996–1998) and after is the intensity of nationalist egalitarian individualist discourse. This took various forms, but particularly dominant was the revitalisation of the old egalitarian problematic, enshrined in Anzac, concerning the state/people relation. This expressed a consciousness of major changes in the order of the state and its social context. Hanson took the position that the agents of the state in coalition with old and new political and economic elites were subjecting the ordinary population (the taxpayer) to illegitimate hardships that defied egalitarian ideals. In Hanson's view it was a world of 'fat cats, bureaucrats and do-gooders' taking advantage of ordinary taxpayers who effectively lost their money to the support of 'Aborigines, multiculturalists and a host of minority groups', and funded the increase in the 'power and position' of already dominant groups (Hanson 1996). The state was in other words breaking its Hobbesian contract with the people. Hanson and One Nation engaged a class rhetoric, barely concealed in Australian egalitarianism, to argue that the ideals of equality in Australia were being smashed by government policy. The paradox of Hanson's pleas – in the eyes of many – was that she often attacked those who were the clear sites of disadvantage whose evident socio-economic inequality had to be rectified. Hanson's class and populist rhetoric were brought to ridicule as well as her self-presentation as the owner of a fish and chip shop, a person who was simply educated and a single mother. Ironically, this, in itself, indicates the emergence of a language of class opposition and subjugation (let alone sexism) now decentred from its location within a structure of class relations as a consequence of the atomisation and fragmentation of class in a post-Fordist era. Paradoxically, however, the engagement of class rhetoric in the subversion of Hansonism indicates the persistence of the forces of class (though taking new shape) behind the moral progressivism and egalitarianism of those who rejected Hansonism.

If the language of class was engaged to subvert Hanson's inegalitarian egalitarian (and cross-class) appeal, a further irony was the engagement of her nonconformism as a method of degradation. Hanson was represented as an inappropriate, nonconformist egalitarian, an individualist who was not egalitarian, i.e., did not subordinate herself to the collective moral will as well as manifesting a distinction from a communal uniformity. The ambiguities and contrary tensions germane within egalitarian thought and practice were exploited against her. Thus, the attack on One Nation often took the form that Hanson (and many of her followers) were not typical individuals. She was revealed as a divorcee on bad terms with her children and thus in contravention of 'ordinary' values. She was an unconventional exception, separate from the crowd – a kind of inverted 'tall poppy', which is a term of abuse in egalitarian Australia against those who stand out and effectively subvert its egalitarian ideals.[7] We referred to Pauline Pantsdown who shadowed Hanson. The one revealed the unconventional and the bizarre in the other. They were bonded in identity in their exceptionalism, as transgressive extremists, breakers of the norms, rather than as purveyors of accepted convention (Nicoll 2001). Irony built upon irony, for the debates surrounding Hanson offered the opportunity for Hanson and her opponents to invent new values even as they often seemed to repeat the old.

The more general point that the foregoing exemplifies is that the values of egalitarianism are capable of being pursued in a variety of, often contradictory, directions. The continual development of new import in its terms ensures the vitality of an egalitarian ethos: new meanings or re-evaluations are a potential of egalitarianism founded as it is on a dynamic of uneasy resolution and tension. Thus while individuality is valued it is potentially seen as subversive of the value of an undifferentiated essential sameness. Australian nationalist egalitarianism is able to take multiple directions, hence its routine political use as well as its risk, exploiting the tensions in its discursive orientations.

The historical context that gave rise to Hanson and eventually the incorporation of many of her ideas in contemporary mainstream politics was an era of liberalisation (from the late 1960s through to the present). This was spearheaded by the Australian Labor Party, which addressed a variety of internal social inequities. It instituted efforts to overcome social and economic disadvantage among Aborigines and in its advocacy of a policy of multiculturalism it aimed to ensure improved rights and recognition for ethnic minorities.[8] Australia opened its doors to immigrants from Asia and the Middle East who had hitherto been restricted in entry. Similarly, it was the Federal Government under Labor that instituted a programme of economic deregulation consistent with the globalising policies of the World Bank and the IMF. Between 1983 and 1985 the Federal Government deregulated Australia's financial institutions, 'floating the Australian dollar, removing capital controls, allowing entry to foreign banks' (Daly and Pritchard 2000: 174).[9] These changes, of course, influenced an intensification of notions of individual agency and potency already explicit in egalitarianism, but it also subverted the collectivist anti-difference (difference as the source of inequality) that is a vital value in Australian nationalism.

The momentary One Nation phenomenon and the more enduring neo-nationalist developments that have followed in its wake are in large measure a reaction and an effort both to restore long-term hegemonies and to reposition the upwardly mobile in the changing hierarchies of power and society. Egalitarian nationalism has discovered new impetus in the largely state-mediated changes.

Hansonism was one expression of critical shifts in the social order and a perceived threat to the dominance of the Anglo-Celtic population in whose interests an egalitarian nationalism had largely worked (as it still does). We stress, however, that more than an expression (in the sense of a reflection of what in fact was at base), it was a construction motivated through egalitarian thought and practice that attached specific significance to ongoing processes.

There is strong evidence that from the 1980s policies of deregulation had increasingly led to impoverishment in rural areas and small towns and growing migration from them to the cities.[10] Small business (of which Hanson and her followers were often representative), a powerful site of values of individual autonomy, was adversely affected along with the communities with which it was mutually dependent. This was exacerbated by a decline of public services to rural areas and small towns. That small business interests should take up the cudgels of egalitarianism was in itself relatively original. To some extent One Nation populism replaced what was once the more vocal egalitarianism of the labouring and lower middle classes (in the cities and the country) whose power had been reduced by the decline of industry and privatisation of government corporations. Many laid off from manufacturing industry had themselves entered small business and had been encouraged to become stakeholders in public floated companies. In a real sense One Nation stood for struggling local small business against the large private, usually foreign conglomerates.[11] The latter were frequently rocked by corruption scandals provoked by greed in the apparent opportunities created by deregulation, the breakup of government monopolies, etc. Although the egalitarian rhetoric of One Nation appeared to be a throwback to the past, the meaning of its discourse was thoroughly contemporary. The values of Anzac nationalism were given a new twist.

There was some realisation among politicians of the left and the right that One Nation was speaking to new fractures as well as the accompanying distress in large sections of the population. This is reflected in the way politicians sometimes hedged their bets in elections, giving their voting preferences to One Nation. It is our opinion that the leader of the ruling Liberal Party, John Howard, felt the pulse correctly. He initially wavered in his condemnation of the outright racist aspects of Hanson's appeal. Although he and his party members eventually rounded on One Nation and participated in its destruction, it was destruction more by incorporation than anything else. Prime Minister Howard refused, despite protests from some in his own party, to support officially the movement for Aboriginal Reconciliation mainly promoted by Aboriginal representatives and educated members of the urban middle class.[12] This is, at the least, in tacit agreement with the Hanson message. As with Hanson, he refuses to acknowledge the responsibility of his generation of white Australians for the destruction and dispossession suffered by Aborigines in the past. It is Howard's government that has brought in new controls over immigration and effectively closed Australia's borders to refugees, establishing the harsh camps for illegal immigrants that have been declared by the United Nations as infringing human rights. These policies are widely believed to have won him majorities in successive elections despite public corporate scandals and what some see as the introduction of a complicated and punitive goods and services tax. This last point indicates that if economic concerns are causes of the final instance, they are not necessarily first causes. These concerns, in the context of Australia at least, have much to do with the ideas through which the significance of reality is constructed and onto which responsibility for difficulty and hardship is often too easily deflected.

The One Nation phenomenon is of considerable interest because it triggered a revitalisation of an Australian nationalist egalitarianism. We have argued that if it continued old ideas it also gave them novel valence and direction. This has persisted and been elaborated in the neo-liberalism of Howard and his government. Howard himself has transformed from an earlier image of the careful accountant (during years of opposition to Labor) into a figure somewhere between the Australian sports fanatic and the swaggering, broad-brimmed-hat wearing hero of Australian folk caricature and bush legend.

There is one feature of the new nationalist intensity that demands closer consideration and this relates to the singling out of Aborigines and new immigrants (usually of Asian and Middle Eastern background) as well as refugees as objects against whom to assert Australian egalitarian difference and value. Undoubtedly, it is an aspect of what Sartre (1962) recognised long ago: the assertion of identity through an act of constructing and then negating an Other. The ideo-logic of egalitarian thought and practice in the past and in the present is also relevant, as we have discussed. Thus, implicit in egalitarianism is that the ideals of egalitarian unity are most likely to be achieved where there are similarities in essence, for example, in cultural orientations and practice, rather than where there are marked differences. It was with such an egalitarian argument that the well-known Australian historian Geoffrey Blainey vehemently criticised the multicultural policies of the 1980s through which a large number of immigrants from South-East Asia came and settled in Australia's cities. Blainey claimed their cultural differences would inhibit the formation of a coherent and harmonious Australian nation founded in the moral ideals of egalitarianism (see B. Kapferer 1988). His argument continued notions integral to the earlier White Australia Policy and has been reissued in the moral outrage of majority Australians against populations that appear to flout egalitarian value with their customs. Certainly, policies of major government funding for Aboriginal organisations and land rights legislation as well as for multiculturalism and encouragement of ethnic minority rights created a sense among the 'silent' and hitherto non-ethnically marked majority population that they were the victims of inegalitarian programmes.

Other factors are worth considering. To extend an earlier argument, Hansonism realised an inherent contradiction at the heart of Australian nationalism: that its egalitarianism underpinned the social and political dominance of the majority population. As we have said, the origins of Australian egalitarian ideologies were in an Anglo-Celtic population that assumed the superiority of its values. This assumption was problematised in the circumstances both of the new Aboriginal policies (especially after the Mabo and Wik High Court decisions that overruled the doctrine of *terra nullius*) and in the context of multiculturalism and increased immigration from Asia. The One Nation attack on these policies was a thoroughgoing reassertion of cultural orientations that were felt to be relatively and illegitimately reduced. In fact government policies were integral to the formation of a cultural self-awareness (of a cultural identity) that had not been so clearly formulated before.

As we have said, the Anzac ideology of the pre-Hanson years was, in a sense, not merely anti-society: it was anti-cultural. Its cult of natural equality valued an essential unity in humanity that was in fact threatened by cultural and social difference conceived to be unnatural. The events and developments surrounding One Nation marked a shift in egalitarian thought and practice that recognised it as, through and through, the cultural field shared by the majority population, who now consciously defined themselves as Anglo-Celtic in relation to an explicitly multicultural context.

The foregoing is strengthened in the context of other changes we have outlined: the collapse of small rural populations, increased rural migration to the cities, the fragmentation and dispersal of working populations centred on localised industry and so on created forms of social alienation that were counteracted through an intensified commitment to idealised values that buttressed a sense of community (albeit an imagined community of mutual interest and belonging).[13] This was heightened in consciousness by the fact of increased migration into Australia through the 1980s and 1990s. Immigrant populations, especially early in their experience, tend to be relatively coherent and mutually supportive. It is a well-recorded strategy of immigrant settlement worldwide. They often tend to closure and not merely because of the prejudice and rejection of host populations. In addition to government programmes of support, this exacerbated processes of greater cultural self-awareness among majority Australians and impelled further processes to cultural unity closure reflected in popular support for greater controls on immigration. The cultural turn among majority Australians was one influence on the displacement of difficulties driven in global political and economic transformations onto populations whose existence was conceived to subvert or threaten the social, moral and now consciously realised cultural hegemony of majority Australians.

Conclusion

The broad similarities linking Australia with other nations undoubtedly relate to political and economic processes produced by globalisation and the consequent crises it has produced in the political order of the state. What is evident to us in the One Nation Party's demands to return to protectionist policies of the past is the appeal to those who have been the major casualties of rapid economic change. Indeed, there is an admixture of century-old protectionism in both One Nation policies and the rising political tide of neo-liberalism and neo-conservatism that has engulfed Australia. Whether it be the response of 'Fortress Australia', the Howard government's remedy to refugees coming to Australian shores, or the demands of 'One Nation' to 'wind the clock back' and protect the community from international competition, the demand to protect Australia from foreign threats, be they refugees or cheap imported goods, is a consistent one in Australian nationalism. Yet, Hansonism says as much about the uneasy marriage between neo-liberalism and neo-conservatism in the Australian nationalist context. The crisis of the political order of the Australian state can be equated to the breakdown of pre-existing political and economic arrangements, but in acknowledging this we should not underestimate its contested and contradictory character.

The opposition to 'privileged' status of 'special interest groups', i.e., indigenous and migrant groups, and the winding back of state regulatory functions advocated by the Howard government has now more than ever forced the government to intensify egalitarian appeals seeking to minimise inner contradictions. The egalitarian state required the minimisation of racial and cultural difference. The Prime Minister has personally intervened and supported attacks on multiculturalism and the so-called 'Black Armband' history, which had sought to restore indigenous struggles against the processes of colonisation as part of Australian history, as divisive examples of political correctness. Ironically, attempts to separate the more controversial racist policies of One Nation from the impact of neo-liberal policies and economic deregulation ignore the deep historical roots of Hanson's appeal for more protectionist policies and a more interventionist government. We have contended that they are very much in keeping with an egalitarian ethos and logic that historically have been at the centre of Australian nationalism and remain so.

Yet, it is perhaps the structural changes and the ideological revisions of Anglo-Celtic Australia and the decline and discrediting of the Anglo-Celtic narratives of nation building that do much to explain Hansonism's contemporary relevance and the broader success of neo-conservative policy. Indeed, much of the attack by Hanson and Blainey on immigration and multiculturalism is directed at the ascendancy of 'white cosmopolites' (Hage 1998) to government, who implement policies accused of being unrepresentative of the people. For Howard and the neo-liberal/conservative right it is the progress and direction of social and historical research performed by a new class of 'intellectual elite' (Dixon 2000) that poses the direct threat to national identity and ideologically sustains the rejection and cutbacks in previous multicultural and indigenous policy. In addition, the new immigrant groups coming in under the conditions of state deregulation have been highly competitive and successful. The formation of relatively stable and well-integrated immigrant communities, real or imagined, based on ethnic or religious ties stands against the fragmentation of the dominant population. This is no more dramatically represented than in the accelerated breakup of rural communities and the massive drift to the cities in the latter decades of the twentieth century. Hansonism's appeal found resonance with those at the bottom of the socio-economic ladder: that is, those most directly affected by restructuring processes and particularly those in the more socially and economically peripheral rural areas. It emerged as a reaction to the set of historical forces that threatened the ideological terms of Anglo-Celtic dominance.

Hanson and One Nation were phenomena in large part generated in the crisis of the Australian society of the state. The public discourse that they provoked revealed many of the contradictions at the centre of Australian egalitarianism. It demonstrated both the continuing relevance of egalitarian thought and practice and its redirection in the changing social and political complexities of contemporary post-colonial Australia. We have stressed some of the distinctive aspects of Australian egalitarianism but acknowledge its affinity with modernist-becoming-postmodern discourses elsewhere. Refractively, the Hanson event may throw some light on the paradoxes contained generally in postmodern discourses of egalitarianism and their capacity to be agents in the production of human distress as well as its overcoming.

Notes

1. Words such as 'station', 'muster' and 'superintendent' were part of the vocabulary of the convict system and were subsequently used throughout the pastoral industry (Fromkin, Blair and Collins 1999: 405).
2. The transportation of convicts to Australia began and ended at different times in different colonies: New South Wales, 1788–1850, Van Diemen's Land (Tasmania), 1804–1853, Western Australia, 1850–1868.
3. Hage (1998) argues aspects of this point, but a serious failure in his analysis concerns his neglect of the historical factors engaged in the construction of the Australian situation, both its egalitarian ideas and the structure of instituted, often state-mediated practices (see B. Kapferer 2000). The argument concentrates on attitudes often seriously alienated from their social base. A major gap in his argument concerns serious reference to the White Australia Policy (it was vital in Labor Party policy until the Whitlam years of the late 1960s and early 1970s).
4. For Hancock, the White Australia Policy was an 'indispensable condition of every other Australian policy' (1961: 59). The egalitarian state required the minimisation of racial and cultural difference. Hancock cites Alfred Deakin, who drafted the foundational legislation of the new Australian Commonwealth:

> the unity of Australia means nothing if it does not imply a united race ... (where) its members can intermarry and associate without degradation on either side, but implies ... a people possessing the same general cast of character, tone of thought, the same constitutional training and traditions. (ibid.: 61)

5. Robert Hughes suggests that Kelly's last three words, 'Such is life', capture the stoicism and fatality that is 'the shrug that echoes through the nation's history' (cited Adams 1992).
6. The bitter rejection of these urban characterisations of regional Australia has been given eloquent expression in the work of Australia's leading poet, Les Murray, in *Subhuman Redneck Poems* (1996) and the work of historian, Miriam Dixon, *The Imaginary Australian* (2000).
7. The term 'tall poppy' was originally used by a premier (Lang) of the state of New South Wales in the period between the two World Wars to refer to the wealthy who were instrumental in depriving ordinary people of their way of life. Hanson, in fact, engaged tall poppy rhetoric in its original sense. By attacking the disadvantaged Hanson was, indeed, herself a tall poppy. Interestingly, within a new cultural climate of individualism, the idea of the tall poppy is being revalued. Rather than to be abused the tall poppy is to be admired as an exemplar of individualist ambition.
8. The Federal Labor Government officially adopted multiculturalism as policy in 1973.
9. The winding back of the functions of the nation state, which involved minimalising of developed welfare systems and the privatising of nationalised industries, occurred under the Howard government.
10. Thirty-three of the thirty-seven poorest electorates in Australia are now located in rural regions and 'the general health of rural people is, by urban standards, very poor ... (with) above average rates of premature mortality and death through heart disease, cancer, suicide and tuberculosis' (Lawrence 1996: 335).

11. The pressure on small rural communities/small business is evident in the research carried out in two rural seats (Barwon and Dubbo), where One Nation gained the highest primary vote in New South Wales (Howard 2001). The research revealed major concerns with economic rationalisation, service cuts to rail and roads, banks and health services and the decline of small businesses as the population drifted to major regional centres (ibid.).

12. Howard has reiterated this point on many occasions since he has been in government. Howard's position has been consistent in his response to what has been termed 'Black Armband History', the government commissioned responses to the 'Stolen Generations' Inquiry and the debate over the High Court's Wik decision on native title rights. Howard's confrontation with delegates at the Reconciliation Convention in Melbourne in 1997 was symptomatic of his opposition. As delegates stood up and turned their backs on him as he spoke, he stated that he was unwilling to accept that Australian history was 'little more than a disgraceful record of imperialism, exploitation and racism' and hence that contemporary Australians should not be held responsible for the sins of past generations (McKenna 1997: 10).

13. In metropolitan Sydney, for example, higher unemployment rates ensued from deindustrialisation, particularly for low-skilled or unskilled workers. In a decade, manufacturing declined from 20 percent to 15 percent of GDP (BIE 1994: 30). One quarter of the entire manufacturing sector workforce, or, in real terms, 123,000 jobs, disappeared from the low-skilled or unskilled sector (ibid.: 30).

Bibliography

Adams, B. 1992. *Sidney Nolan: Such is Life*. Sydney: Vintage.

Bureau of Industrial Economics. 1994. 'State Economic Performance, 1981–82 to 1991–92', Occasional Paper 19. Canberra: Australian Government Publishing Service.

Daly, M. and Pritchard, B. 2000. 'Sydney: Australia's Financial and Corporate Capital', in J. Connell ed. *Sydney: The Emergence of a World City*. Melbourne: Oxford University Press.

Davidson, A. 1997. *From Subject to Citizen: Australian Citizenship in the Twentieth Century*. Melbourne: Cambridge University Press.

de Tocqueville, A. 1968. *Democracy in America*, trans. by G. Lawrence, eds P. Mayer and M. Lerner. London: Collins.

Dixon, M. 2000. *The Imaginary Australian: Anglo-Celts and Identity*. Sydney: University of New South Wales.

Dumont, L. 1980. *Homo Hierarchicus*. Chicago: Chicago University Press.

Foucault, M. 1977. *Discipline and Punish: The Birth of the Prison*, trans. A. Sheridan. London: Allen Lane.

——— 1979. *The History of Sexuality: An Introduction*, trans. R. Hurley. London: Allen Lane.

——— 1991. 'Governmentality', in G. Burchell, C. Gordon and P. Miller eds *The Foucault Effect: Studies in Governmentality*. Hemel Hempstead: Harvester Wheatsheaf.

Fromkin, V., Blair, D. and Collins, P. 1999. *An Introduction to Language*. Marrickville: Harcourt Australia.

Hage, G. 1998. *White Nation: Fantasies of White Supremacy in a Multicultural Society*. London: Pluto Press.

Hancock, W.K. 1961 [1930]. *Australia*. Brisbane: Jacaranda Press.

Hanson, P. 1996. *Parliamentary Maiden Speech*, 10 September 1996, Parliament House, Canberra.

Hardt, M. and Negri, A. 2001. *Empire*. Cambridge, MA: Harvard University Press.

Hirst, J. 1978. 'The Pioneer Legend', *Historical Studies* XVIII: 316–37.

Howard, D. 2001. 'Understanding Racism Against Australian Aborigines in Contemporary Australian Society', paper delivered at 'Double Edged' conference, December 2001, Newcastle University, Newcastle, Australia.

Howard, J. 2000. *Perspectives on Aboriginal and Torres Strait Islander Issues*, Menzies Series Lecture, Sydney, 13 December 2000.

Hughes, R. 1996. *The Fatal Shore*. London: The Harvill Press.

Kapferer, B. 1988. *Legends of People, Myths of State: Violence, Intolerance and the Political Culture of Sri Lanka and Australia*. Washington, DC: Smithsonian.

——— 2000. 'Review of White Nation: Fantasies of White Supremacy in a Multicultural Society by Ghassan Hage', *Oceania* 70(3): 269–72.

Kapferer, J. 1996. *Being All Equal*. Oxford: Berg.

Lattas, A. 1985. 'The New Panopticon: Newspaper Discourse and the Rationalisation of Society and Culture in New South Wales, 1803–1830', unpublished Ph.D. thesis, University of Adelaide.

Lawrence, G. 1996. *Social Change in Rural Australia*. Rockhampton: Central Queensland University, Rural, Social and Economic Research Centre.

McKenna, M. 1997. 'Different Perspectives on Black Armband History', Research Paper 5, 1997–98. Canberra: Australian Parliamentary Library.

McQuilton, J. 1979. *The Kelly Outbreak*. Melbourne: Melbourne University Press.

Murray, L. 1996. *Subhuman Redneck Poems*. Potts Point: Duffy and Snellgrove.

Nicoll, F. 2001. *From Diggers to Drag Queens*. London: Pluto Press.

Sartre, J.-P. 1962. *Anti-Semite and Jew*, trans. G.J. Becker. New York: Grove Press.

Turner, I. 1982. *Room to Manoeuvre*. Richmond: Drummond.

Ward, R. 1958. *The Australian Legend*. Melbourne: Oxford University Press.

PART V
Afterthoughts

Afterthoughts

Ulf Hannerz

My country, Sweden, does not figure prominently in the preceding chapters, so let me begin these concluding comments by recalling that fairly brief period in the early 1990s when the party Ny Demokrati, 'New Democracy', made an appearance on the Swedish political stage.[1] Suddenly it was there – the product of a seemingly rather unlikely alliance between two individuals, both already fairly prominent on the national scene, although without very noticeable prior involvement in party politics. One was Ian Wachtmeister, from an aristocratic family, with connections to the royal court and no longer so successful in business, although he had once been the CEO of a major industrial concern. The other was Bert Karlsson, a conspicuous presence in the popular music industry, and a small-town boy grown into a man of the people. In the months leading up to the 1991 general election, the two embarked on a whirlwind tour of public appearances throughout Sweden, and succeeded in getting their histrionics widely reported in the media. Wachtmeister would wear an unusual hat, and they would illustrate their economic arguments by piling empty beer crates on top of each other. Partly through these acts, they became popularly known as 'The Count and the Valet', which was of course a way of referring to their contrasting class backgrounds. (One might have thought that a real valet would have shown a bit more social polish than Karlsson.) Officially, in the party structure, Wachtmeister was the party leader, while Karlsson was designated 'people leader'.

The election gave Ny Demokrati 6.7 percent of the national vote, and a considerable number of parliamentary seats, to the dismay of all other parties, not least the new centre-right, four-party coalition that was voted into power but which, to a degree, found itself dependent on the support of that new grouping, which was not regarded as politically respectable. While Karlsson engaged in his kind of protest politics by appearing in the halls of Parliament in inappropriate attire and reputedly making inappropriate bodily sounds, Wachtmeister was involved more in hardheaded politics. But then the two had a falling out, perhaps due to the inevitable internal contradictions between their perspectives, and Ny Demokrati rapidly crumbled. As Wachtmeister and Karlsson left their leadership positions (the latter returning to his music business, apparently no harm done), a series of new and rather improbable party leaders appeared, sometimes in competition with one another, selected through what could seem more or less like coups. By the time of the next national election in 1994, the party had largely become the subject of ridicule, and it disappeared from the parliamentary scene. In the election after that, Wachtmeister tried again, with an entity simply named 'The New Party', but that was largely a one-man show that garnered few votes.

It is tempting to claim that the Ny Demokrati interlude shows Sweden to be not just an exception, a country without a significant neo-nationalist political presence, but rather the first post-neo-nationalist nation: the first to pass, rather effortlessly, through a certain kind of political phase. But then, how should Ny Demokrati be most appropriately labelled? It was hardly particularly nationalist in the sense of appealing to a shared cultural heritage. It could certainly be viewed as populist. Through their personal alliance the two original leaders symbolically cut across the class structure in a striking way, even if it had more to do with cultural styles than with economic interests – after all, one was a new entrepreneur, the other a somewhat manqué representative of old capitalism. If one of the shadows cast was that of Margaret Thatcher and far-reaching neo-liberalism, the other could perhaps be seen, going further back in time, as that of Pierre Poujade and old-style protest against taxes and state regulations. The latter kind of protest movement shows up here and there in this volume. It also preceded the current forms of neo-nationalism in Denmark and Norway, and Gaillard-Starzmann notes that the young Jean-Marie Le Pen was a Poujadist.

It would seem true that 'nationalism' in 1990s European neo-nationalisms usually has less to do with any positive patriotic sentiments than with hostility towards outsiders. Yet it is not entirely easy to pinpoint what part immigration issues, which figure so prominently in the agendas of many of the groupings dealt with in this volume, had in the early success of Ny Demokrati. At least to begin with, anti-immigrant, more-or-less xenophobic agitation may not have been so conspicuous in the presentations of the two founding figures. Yet it was widely held among observers and the public generally that the party was a haven for such sentiments, and it appears that lower party echelons appealed openly to them in campaigning. In this notoriously protean, imploding approximation of a party, xenophobia soon became increasingly prominent in the pronouncements of the two original leaders as well, and one of their more improbable successors, a make-up artist, wondered out loud at a public meeting, her voice quivering, how long it would take before Swedish children were forced to turn their faces towards Mecca. Warm feelings for the motherland were hardly a major part of the message; this was more an attempt to mobilise resentment and fear.

In the longer term, however, what is perhaps most important is that the quick and very public self-destruction of Ny Demokrati is commonly understood to have for some time ruined the wider market for any other new right-wing/populist/nationalist/anti-immigrant party in Sweden.

The Contexts of Fear and Loathing

I wanted to begin with this sketch of the rise and fall of Ny Demokrati not just as a small additional ethnographic contribution, 'another country heard from' in this volume, but also because I will draw on the case here and there in what follows to try and identify even more clearly some of the themes in our anthropological approach to recent and present politics in Europe; and indeed, as the title of the book has it, 'beyond'. If the centre of gravity among the contributions is somewhere between Italy and Norway, it is surely useful and thought-provoking to also have the chapters on recent politics in India and Australia. In fact, as I read about Le Pen, Haider and Fortuyn, I make connections to yet further instances of personalised politics elsewhere, which perhaps also fit into the neo-nationalist framework. What about the flamboyant ex-novelist and governor of Tokyo, Shintaro Ishihara, co-author of *The Japan That Can Say No*, making threatening remarks about the trustworthiness of immigrant minorities? Or Patrick Buchanan, former Nixon speech writer, engaging (perhaps without much in the way of an organisational base, but nevertheless with some voter support) in a nativist quest, through Republican Party primaries, for the United States presidency? Again, these are people and episodes, often from the 1990s, at least partially contemporary with the phenomena under study in other chapters. Certainly the peculiarities of national context would make their stories in some ways different, but I sense significant similarities. Moving into the first decade of the new century, yet further leads appear, on the European scene and elsewhere. I will come back to that.

One recurrent concern in this volume is the complexity, the multi-facetedness of the cluster of politico-cultural ideas, interests and sentiments under scrutiny. Two points appear particularly important in getting away from an overly simplistic, even stereotypical view. Undoubtedly one major reason for a scholarly engagement with that wave of Western (including northern and southern) European national or regional movements that more or less suddenly and alarmingly increased their share of the political terrain at the end of the twentieth century was their tendency towards anti-immigration or even xenophobic stances of fear and loathing. For anthropologists, generally favourably disposed towards cultural diversity and whoever contributes to it, and critical of ethnocentric tendencies, this has surely mattered. Nonetheless, it becomes clear here that these movements are not entirely one-dimensional, and are best understood by taking rather wider contexts and sets of circumstances into account; these are not necessarily the same in each case.

This, for one thing, complicates labelling, and also makes it more difficult to place these phenomena on the political map. Can it be taken for granted that they are 'right-wing', as it has certainly been a strong tendency to assume? Are they always 'populist', in any meaningful sense? An earlier, pioneering scholar in this field, Douglas R. Holmes (2000), to whose work many references are made in this book, has used the term 'integralist', which he relates to the Counter-Enlightenment tendency in European history; but I note that he also describes it as protean, which happens to be a term I used above in trying to portray the character of Ny Demokrati in its heyday. Perhaps in the end, whichever label we prefer, we need to think of it, to use the term introduced to anthropology by Rodney Needham (1975), as a 'polythetic' category: it may involve a set of characteristics combining in different ways, so that at the extremes there may turn out to be no shared characteristics at all.

The other point, which to a degree likewise serves to shift some of the attention away from a narrow focus on anti-immigrant preoccupations, is to concentrate on those groupings that operate within more legitimate political arenas, such as in parliaments, and to leave the more extremist, sometimes criminal, violent fringe aside. Analytically, this seems to be a good idea in order to grasp a certain range of issues, although I would warn that it must not lead us to ignore the interrelations between the activities and imageries of some parties and some xenophobic violence. There is the critical question of what kind of social climate is created through agitation and in other ways. In Stockholm, for some months in 1991 and 1992, an unknown gunman soon referred to as 'the Laser Man' shot eleven people, all strangers to him but all of non-Swedish appearance, in ten separate incidents of urban terror; one of them died.[2] 'The Laser Man' was later caught and became the subject of a book; he noted in an interview that he had found support for his activities in the campaigns and pronouncements of Ny Demokrati – the party he had also voted for (Gellert 2002: 54). It would seem that when madmen listen, those who want to be identified as responsible participants in public life must choose their words carefully.

Nonetheless, we should also ask those broader questions about the loci of support for neo-nationalism in social structures. For one thing, it is interesting to note Gertraud Seiser's finding that, contrary to stereotypical expectations, Haider's FPÖ with its xenophobic tendencies is not met with much enthusiasm among Austrian farmers. I am reminded of stories I have heard, in Austria as well as Scandinavia, of local farmers who now go to Thailand or the Philippines to seek spouses who will give them a chance to keep their family enterprises going. It is probably not a large number, but apparently we cannot expect them or their neighbours to be among the pillars of neo-nationalism.

There are anxieties, however, that do seem to become entangled with neo-nationalist sentiments and antagonisms. Andre Gingrich identifies a couple of these. On the one hand, he points to the sense of vulnerability that comes with a threat of downward mobility. I suspect this is an area that deserves a great deal more scholarly attention. Perhaps it is still true that 'social mobility', as a concept established in the social sciences particularly during largely expansive phases in

Western Europe and North America, tends to mean upward mobility, and that we have not yet had a full view of the imagined worlds of those who experience, or fear, significant social and material decline. I recall here Sherry Ortner's (1991: 176) comment that in the United States, 'much of middle-class culture can be seen as a set of discourses and practices embodying the terror of downward mobility', and that these become especially noticeable, as both chronic friction and explosive potential, in parent–child relationships. In the American ethnography of downward mobility, there is also the work of Katherine Newman (e.g., 1999), but there would seem to be yet more to find out, for example, about how the fall of state socialism in Eastern Europe or structural adjustment policies in poorer countries, for a considerable number of people, have destabilised ways of life involving a modest level of comfort and some claim to respectability.

On the other hand, Gingrich notes that one source of support for neo-nationalism may originate in male uncertainties relating to changes in old gender roles, and the increasing assertiveness of women. That seems plausible, even though we find that a couple of the more prominent leaders of the kind of movement in question are women – Pia Kjaersgaard in Denmark and Pauline Hanson in Australia – and that the assertive gayness of Pim Fortuyn was hardly in line with old conventions of masculinity either.

A factor that I would still like to know more about in the context of neo-nationalist politics is that of age, or generation – a dimension of social life still surprisingly under-conceptualised and ethnographically neglected; although given current demographic changes, one may wonder how long it can remain so. In some of its more spectacular manifestations, xenophobia may seem like a youth phenomenon, as for example in skinhead culture in many parts of Europe. Young people (and especially young men), with fewer competing social obligations and less settled opinions, may frequently be available for more risky, dramatic engagements (which can also be part of identity experimentation). This may take them far right, or far left, or simply to soccer hooliganism; the intellectual component of these commitments may be variously large or small. Yet I wonder to what extent the combination of economic chauvinism and cultural pessimism that Andre Gingrich has found characteristic of neo-nationalisms, especially in smaller, relatively prosperous European countries, may also have a certain affinity with older age. Some years ago, when I and some of my Swedish colleagues became involved in a brief public debate over immigration, we noticed that a rather high proportion of the letters and phone calls we received (the total number was not very large) that were critical of immigrants and immigration policy were from older people. At their age, they were somewhat preoccupied with the quality of welfare institutions, and suspected that these would decline if newcomers were also making claims on common resources. And at the same time, having lived a large part of their lives in a period of considerable ethnic homogeneity and cultural uniformity in Sweden, and, in the way of many older people, being a bit inclined to nostalgia and out of touch and sympathy with ongoing cultural change, they perhaps experienced a number of things around them as alien and threatening – a kind of symbolic violence. (The value of *trygghet* Gullestad identifies in her chapter on Norway, 'a mixture of safety, security and control over one's life', is no doubt quite generally Scandinavian, and not least a concern of the elderly.) There is a certain irony in the fact that in much of Europe, some of the welfare institutions on which older citizens depend, such as hospitals, can now hardly function without immigrant personnel. With aging populations in many countries, a renewed sizeable import of migrant labour becomes a politically touchy prospect.

The resentment expressed in voter support for neo-nationalist parties, however, need not be seen as aimed entirely at alien new arrivals. It also seems to be a recurrent fact of European political life that in the post-Second World War period, in the absence of major upheavals, mainstream party organisations have often been seen as complacent and unresponsive. They habitually make deals with one another within the framework of some larger consensus, are inclined towards nomenklatura practices, reproduce through endogamy and familistic recruitment and proceed with policies that deny the facts of life familiar to 'ordinary citizens'. To what extent this offers an accurate portrayal of the working of party organisations, in everyday life or in crises, may not be entirely clear. (Perhaps we need some enterprising anthropologists doing intensive organisational ethnographies here?) But major, long-dominant parties often seem to be at least perceived to have such characteristics. Furthermore, media reporting on politics tends to favour the sort of 'investigative journalism' – or muckraking – that personalises political life along similar lines. The recurrent response to such political images seems to be populism in a fairly strict sense. In Sweden a term summarising the resentment against such tendencies has been *politikerförakt*, 'contempt for politicians'. The descriptions in this volume by Sunier and van Ginkel of Dutch party politics and by Fillitz of the Austrian situation appear to me to be examples of this kind of 'politics as usual' elsewhere.

Issues involving immigration, or understood to involve immigration, are obviously often among those instances in which the politicians representing established parties are taken to be unconcerned or ignorant about the situations facing ordinary people. As I have argued elsewhere (e.g., Hannerz 1999), there is a fairly widespread tendency, among politicians and other officials, to respond to criticisms of immigration or immigration policies, and to complaints about those everyday nuisances and irritations that flux and difference may bring about, with a habitual and no doubt largely well-intended celebration of the aesthetic and intellectual pleasures of cultural diversity. The latter almost appears to be seen here in terms of differing performances – to be enjoyed at a certain distance, from a good seat in the audience, as it were – rather than as a matter of ongoing, interactive, not always smooth mutual adaptation between established ways of life and thought. Undoubtedly the idea behind such celebrationism is to enlighten and to foster tolerance and respect. Yet at worst, if it appears to deny or belittle experiences people feel are very real, it may unwittingly provoke even more resentment.

Lessons for Anthropologists

Sometimes, neo-nationalist parties decline in popularity among voters, but it does not necessarily mean that their influence has entirely disappeared. At times it may seem that mainstream parties are not so impervious to outside influence after all, and shift to take on parts of the agenda of the unwelcome competitor. The occasional presence of the neo-nationalists could possibly even offer a useful alibi for a change of direction that was considered desirable anyway. Fillitz shows that Haider's Freedom Party was not alone in moving towards greater restrictions relating to immigration into Austria. Kapferer and Morris note that in Australia, when Prime Minister John Howard and his Liberal Party took part in the destruction of Pauline Hanson's One Nation Party, 'it was destruction by incorporation more than anything else' – and we have since witnessed Howard's government take some of the most dramatic actions against asylum seekers seen anywhere, as in the refusal, in 2001, to let the Norwegian ship *Tampa*, dangerously overloaded with refugees saved from another sinking vessel, enter Australian waters. In Denmark the harsh new stance towards immigrants was adopted by a centre-right coalition of which the neo-nationalist party was not actually a member.

What would have happened in Swedish politics if Ny Demokrati had not already imploded before its second national election campaign? Perhaps the party would have been able to stabilise with a sufficient voter base to keep it in parliament, with a more explicitly anti-immigration platform than it had in its first campaign. Then Sweden would have been more like a number of other European countries in this respect, instead of an exception. As things turned out, it became perhaps most like the Netherlands, with a loosely organised, personalistic party both rising and falling dramatically, even if the Dutch case involved the tragedy of a murder and the Swedish case more of a farce. Ny Demokrati as well as the List Pim Fortuyn demonstrate the weakness of organisations that come together extremely quickly, drawing together a following of people with very mixed backgrounds, and often with little in the way of organisational experience and skill, apparently having few opportunities or little willingness to check the credentials of supporters who may end up in visible positions before they turn out to have dubious opinions or biographies. Very soon then, too many things begin to go wrong, scandals attract adversaries and the media, which get into a feeding frenzy: what had first seemed like a force capable of remaking the political landscape may turn out to have had a more parenthetical presence there.

In contrast, there are those neo-nationalist parties that seem to achieve greater durability, and which usually appear to have achieved some greater strength only after a more extended period in which a nucleus of voter loyalty and an organisational base become rather more solid. Here and there neo-nationalist groupings have begun with the remnants of the totalitarian movements of the period between the World Wars. In Austria the FPÖ under Haider may have become a major national player only in the 1990s, but it had already been around, even if in somewhat different form, since 1956. In Denmark, again, the Danish People's Party was an updated, breakaway version of an old tax protest party that had never really quite faded away. In Norway the Progress Party had taken over from a small and rather idiosyncratic grouping, simply named after its leader, which had somehow managed to stay on the scene for a number of years.

Still, even when they turn out to be short-lived phenomena, parties (or proto-parties) such as Ny Demokrati and the List Pim Fortuyn can have an important part in the volatility of politics in contemporary national arenas, and we have reason to think about their characteristics in relation to what anthropologists can now contribute to the study of politics. Several of the chapter authors in this volume point to the drama, the theatricality, of neo-nationalist political activity. Haider certainly offers many examples, and Le Pen too. 'Charisma', perhaps now an overused word as it joins the popular media-supported vocabulary of celebrity and glamour, is a term at least occasionally applied to yet other neo-nationalist leaders. (While it is also true that some of those neo-nationalist groupings scattered over Europe that really do not seem to get anywhere have remarkably uncharismatic figures at the top.)

Consequently, what anthropologists can do with this kind of politics is to deal not least with its communicative forms, its spectacles – spontaneous but very often also staged – and with audience responses to them. Political anthropology here becomes an anthropology of the senses, an anthropology of emotion, an anthropology of the body, at the same time as it may retain many of the concerns and skills it has already cultivated. Not least does it have to be a media anthropology. Peter Hervik points to the striking cooperation between neo-nationalist politicians and a popular Copenhagen tabloid, and the movement of other Danish newspapers towards increasingly hostile storylines, especially towards Muslim immigrants. Mukulika Banerjee points to the part that the epic *Ramayana*, serialised on Indian television, came to play in furthering the Hindutva agenda. Finally, Silvio Berlusconi stands as an epitome of the entanglement of media and politics in Europe.

In sum, with so much of neo-nationalist politics requiring a multi-faceted tracing of the management of meaning and of meaningful forms, the critical response of anthropology has much to do with culture. It has to entail a subtle analysis of the symbolic modalities of present-day political action, but it also has to confront the current uses of the culture concept itself, the varieties of culturespeak (Hannerz 1999). Again and again, it becomes clear that notions of culture, cultural difference and cultural conflict have a part in neo-nationalist and related forms of political discourse. As Thomas Fillitz shows, in the case of the FPÖ, it may involve a cultural policy that, in its own way, can become quite elaborate and sophisticated. In a distressed reaction to such deployments of the culture concept, some anthropologists would now prefer to abolish it, to do anthropology without culture. My own stance is reformist rather than abolitionist: we can retain an emphasis on diversity and the human capacity for learning, unlearning and relearning, while developing our critique of old and new varieties of essentialism. To the extent that anthropologists are recognised as having any intellectual authority with regard to understandings of culture, such views and criticisms can be one of our contributions to public debate.

Such a scrutiny of culture and culture concepts in contemporary politics, however, may need to entail a critical stance not only towards some ingredients of political life itself, but also towards some of the assumptions and speechways of our academic neighbourhoods. The term 'political culture', as still often used in some disciplines, has implications of uniformity and stability, and we would not now want these to demarcate the uses of cultural study in politics. The quick successes of such political figures as Jörg Haider, Pim Fortuyn and the Ny Demokrati duo suggest that we should devote more attention to cultural turbulence, to the social organisation of rapid opinion shifts, to emergent expressive forms, to new uses of old symbols. For one thing, that may mean that we should try harder to close the gap between the study of 'culture', on the one hand, and the kinds of phenomena dealt with under such labels as 'collective behaviour' or 'moral panics', on the other. The work of Stanley Tambiah (1996) exploring riots in South Asia may not take on precisely this agenda, but it can still inspire further efforts in this direction. (In this book, it connects ethnographically most directly to Banerjee's comments on the Ayodhya affair.)

There are other lessons for anthropologists in this volume, to be noted in future work. Again, it is another building block in an endeavour to renew comparative anthropology (cf. Gingrich and Fox 2002), by gathering a group of scholars around a shared, but not too constrainingly directed, task of analysing parallel, convergent, yet certainly also sometimes divergent socio-cultural developments in a range of contexts. We could reflect, too, on the significance of this kind of effort to arguments about what may be the advantages and disadvantages but perhaps nonetheless the sheer necessity of multi-site ethnography in the contemporary world (see e.g., Hannerz 2003; Marcus 1995). Mostly, multi-site or translocal fieldwork – which tends to involve comparison, although also focusing on the interconnections between local sites – is assumed to be another variety of single-ethnographer research, in this case involving more mobility than usual. But surely an alternative is to have more fieldworkers, in a joint effort, distributed in space. The present book has not come about through research originally conceived as belonging to such a project, but we can sense that it could have. And in Europe at least, current preferred kinds of centralised research funding might encourage thinking about team projects along such lines.

We can also see that the book makes a contribution to anthropological method by serving, in large part, as an example of 'adversary ethnography'. The authors are not on the side of the neo-nationalists they write about. Of course, the situation is not unique; indeed a history of such anthropological engagements could now be written. Twenty years ago, to take one example, in the book *Waiting* (1985), Vincent Crapanzano portrayed the whites of a small South African town during the Apartheid Era. Yet further back, during the Second World War, those American (and other) anthropologists who studied cultures 'at a distance', and who were linked to the Office of Strategic Services as part of the war effort, were in large part engaged in trying to understand the enemy – the Japanese, the Germans (Mead and Métraux 1953). There are issues of field ethics involved here. Anthropologists have been accustomed to liking, or to being expected to like, the people in their fields. Gingrich and Banks, in their introduction to this volume, point to an essential distinction – 'empathy, not sympathy'. Those of the chapter authors who have been involved in something more like classic ethnographic fieldwork among the neo-nationalists and their followers have clearly kept this in mind. But the studies also bear witness to the fact that anthropological field and writing practices are now changing, towards styles that, somewhat like those of studying at a distance in earlier years, combine highly varied kinds of sources and data in an original synthesis. This is surely more than a way of approaching the unapproachable. It also points to ways in which anthropologists increasingly try to deal actively with issues of scale, and to build bridges between 'micro' and 'macro'.

What Now; What's Next?

The neo-nationalist phenomena described in the preceding pages belong mostly in the latter years of the twentieth century. While the streams of migrants and refugees that were made the target of hostile reactions came from varied areas of the world, in some parts of Europe these reactions were especially fuelled by the upheavals of the Balkans. This was likewise a period when there were serious divisions over changes in the European Union. If with time the Balkan situation became more stable, the processes of European economic and political integration continued to generate new contentions, involving the new shared currency and constitutional development. In Sweden, while memories of Ny Demokrati faded, the elections to the European Parliament in 2004 brought another surprise, as a new entity called 'the June List' drew considerable support. This was a rather anomalous creation, initiated by professional economists and people from the world of industry, who were critical of further European integration but not really inclined to start any new party, and who were far from populism and a more daringly expressive campaign style. To a degree its relative success merely showed again that because in much of Europe, comparatively few people still bother to go to the polls for European Parliament elections, the groupings most actively critical of past and future integration, and rather better able to mobilise their supporters, can sometimes do quite well. Yet the election results also showed that there was still some dissatisfaction with the ways the old established parties handled things.

Early in the twenty-first century, however, the political scene in Europe and elsewhere in the world has also changed in other ways not so visible in this book. If fear and resentment were behind much of the neo-nationalist activity, and were further stimulated by it, the date of 11 September 2001, with its attacks on the World Trade Center in New York and the Pentagon in Washington, DC, has come to mark another phase in the escalation of fear – a fear that may in part be rather amorphous, but which is otherwise quite sharply Islamophobic. If it is strongest in the United States, it is present elsewhere as well, and not least in Europe. (It seems worth noting, for one thing, that the Danish election that conspicuously changed the local political balance was held just a couple of months after that crucial date.) But then, on the other hand, the American reaction, and the growing inclination of the remaining superpower towards unilateralism, has in itself contributed to changing the landscape of political sentiments. In the United States, the 'war on terror' and the preoccupation with 'homeland security' carry overtones of neo-nationalism. The interpretation of the 2004 presidential election in terms of a 'red' and a 'blue' America (where the reversal of political colour codes, the blue standing to the left of the red right, seems like another example of American exceptionalism) again implied a deep domestic political divide. Meanwhile, there is also a new critical rhetoric of 'Empire', and there are scenarios of a West coming apart.

What political forces may find nourishment in this changing field, nationally or transnationally, we may not yet see too clearly. Perhaps an emergent macro-anthropology of politics and culture can offer if not forecasts then at least continued informed interpretation and commentary. Yet perhaps we can avoid ending these concluding notes only by voicing fears of our own? Andre Gingrich closes his chapter with a plea for visions that can serve as alternatives to the retrogressive answers of neo-nationalism. I would want to suggest that there may still be some grounds for hope.

A decade ago, the political psychologist Michael Billig (1995) identified a kind of contemporary nationalism of a rather different type than the neo-nationalisms we have been considering here. Not least in stable, prosperous societies a strong 'banal nationalism' can grow, largely benign and based on the recurrent practices and experiences of everyday life that come to define much of what it means to belong to a given nation state. I would suggest, as others recently have, that there is room for a parallel notion of a 'banal cosmopolitanism', which can gather strength as people feel reasonably at home in the world, as their ordinary, recurrent encounters and engagements with Otherness are not defined by suspicion and fear but by some confidence in their own ability to manage, and by mutual recognition and trust.[3] This would hardly have to be seen as some utopian, unworldly notion. In fact, I believe that some such banal cosmopolitanism is widely, although rather quietly, present out there, as an alternative to neo-nationalisms, not necessarily in the form of high-profile social or political activism, but growing as an increasing number and variety of people have work experiences, new links of friendship and kinship, memorable pleasures and challenges, in sites involving encounters with what is initially culturally alien. (Those Scandinavian farmers with Philippino wives should count among them.) Unspectacular as such developments may be, I would hope that anthropologists in Europe and beyond will also come together to map them.

Notes

1. My brief descriptive passages on Ny Demokrati here draw on personal memory and on Gellert (2002).
2. One of the survivors, an Iranian refugee student, Shahram Khosravi, shot next to the Stockholm University campus, later went on to become a professional social anthropologist, and I thank him for lending me his copy of *Lasermannen*.
3. On notions of banal cosmopolitanism or banal globalism, see Beck (2002) and Szerszynski and Urry (2002), as well as Hannerz (2004).

Bibliography

Beck, U. 2002. 'The Cosmopolitan Society and its Enemies', *Theory, Culture and Society* 19: 17–44.

Billig, M. 1995. *Banal Nationalism*. London: Sage.

Crapanzano, V. 1985. *Waiting*. New York: Random House.

Gellert, T. 2002. *Lasermannen*. Stockholm: Ordfront.

Gingrich, A. and Fox, R.G. eds. 2002. *Anthropology, by Comparison*. London: Routledge.

Hannerz, U. 1999. 'Reflections on Varieties of Culturespeak', *European Journal of Cultural Studies* 2: 393–407.

———— 2003. 'Being There ... and There ... and There! Reflections on Multi-site Ethnography', *Ethnography* 4: 229–44.

———— 2004. 'Cosmopolitanism', in D. Nugent and J. Vincent eds *Companion to the Anthropology of Politics*. Oxford: Blackwell.

Holmes, D.R. 2000. *Integral Europe: Fast-capitalism, Multiculturalism, Neo-fascism*. Princeton: Princeton University Press.

Marcus, G.E. 1995. 'Ethnography in/of the World System: The Emergence of Multi-Sited Ethnography', *Annual Review of Anthropology* 24: 95–117.

Mead, M. and Métraux, R. eds. 1953. *The Study of Culture at a Distance*. Chicago: University of Chicago Press.

Needham, R. 1975. 'Polythetic Classification: Convergence and Consequences', *Man* 10: 347–69.

Newman, K. 1999. *Falling from Grace*. Berkeley: University of California Press.

Ortner, S.B. 1991. 'Reading America: Preliminary Notes on Class and Culture', in R.G. Fox ed. *Recapturing Anthropology*. Santa Fe: School of American Research Press.

Szerszynski, B. and Urry, J. 2002. 'Cultures of Cosmopolitanism', *Sociological Review* 50: 461–81.

Tambiah, S.J. 1996. *Leveling Crowds*. Berkeley: University of California Press.

Notes on Contributors

Mukulika Banerjee is Lecturer in Anthropology at University College London. She is currently working on a monograph based on research into popular perceptions of democracy in India, in particular among illiterate but avid Muslim voters. Her first book, *The Pathan Unarmed: Opposition and Memory in the North West Frontier*, on a non-violent Pashtun movement, was published in 2000 by James Currey Publishers. Her second book, *The Sari*, is co-authored with Daniel Miller (2003). She is also editing a volume called *Muslim Portraits* to be published by Penguin.

Marcus Banks is Professor of Visual Anthropology at the University of Oxford, and has interests in race, ethnicity, ethnographic film and visual representation. He conducted his original fieldwork with a religious group of Indian origin in Britain and in India, resulting in an ethnographic monograph and an overview text on anthropological theories of ethnicity and nationalism. He is currently conducting archival research on British and Indian representations of India in colonial documentary film.

Thomas Fillitz is Professor in the Department of Social and Cultural Anthropology at the University of Vienna and Visiting Professor at Université des Sciences et Technologies of Lille. He has taken part in SOCRATES, teaching at various universities and is an expert at the European Commission. He has carried out fieldwork in Northern Nigeria, Ivory Coast and Benin. His research interests are in anthropology of art, post-colonialism, globalisation, knowledge transfer, and his regional interests are in West Africa and Europe. His publications include: 'Academia: Same Pressures, Same Conditions of Work?' In M. Strathern ed. *Audit Cultures* (2000); *Zeitgenösssische Kunst aus Afrika. Vierzehn Künstler aus Côte d'Ivoire und Bénin* ('Contemporary art from Africa. Fourteen artists from Ivory Coast and Benin' 2002); and 'The Notion of Art – Regional or General Comparison', in Gingrich and Fox eds *Anthropology, By Comparison* (2002).

Gerald Gaillard-Starzmann is Associate Professor at the University of Lille 1 and a member of the CNRS team: social dynamics and ethnic mobilisation. He grew up in Bouaké (Ivory Coast). He is the author of more than twenty articles and memoranda on psychoanalytical questions, the history of anthropology, development sociology and the ethnography and history of Biafada from Guinea Bissau. His books include *Répertoire de l'ethnologie française* (1990), available online at http://www.univ-lille1.fr/bustl-grisemine; *Dictionnaire des ethnologues et des anthropologues* (1997), published in English by Routledge; and *Migrations anciennes et peuplement actuel des Côtes Guinéennes* (2000). His most recent articles are: 'Then and Now: Teaching Anthropology in France', in Dracklé, Edgar and Schippers eds *Educational Histories of European Social Anthropology* (2003); and 'Islam et politique en Guinée-Bissau contemporaine', in Coulon ed. *Afrique Politique 2002.*

Andre Gingrich is Full Professor for Social Anthropology at the University of Vienna and a member of the Austrian Academy of Sciences. For his work on ideologies in Asia and Europe, he received the Wittgenstein Award 2000. His most recent publications include *Anthropology, by Comparison* (co-edited with Richard G. Fox, 2002), *Grammars of Identity: A Structural Approach* (co-edited with Gerd Baumann, 2004) and *One Discipline, Four Ways: British, German, French and American Anthropology. The Halle lectures* (co-authored with Frederik Barth, Robert Parkin and Sydel Silverman, 2005).

Marianne Gullestad is Senior Researcher at the Institute for Social Research, Oslo. Her many books and publications include: *The Art of Social Relations: Essays on Culture, Thought and Social Action in Modern Norway* (1992); *Everyday Life Philosophers: Modernity, Morality and Autobiography in Norway* (1996); 'Invisible Fences: Egalitarianism, Nationalism and Racism' (*JRAI* 8, March 2002); *Kitchen Table Society: A Case Study of the Family Life and Friendships of Young Working-Class Mothers in Urban Norway* (1984 and 2002).

Ulf Hannerz is Professor of Social Anthropology at Stockholm University. He is a member of the Royal Swedish Academy of Sciences and the American Academy of Arts and Sciences, and a former Chair of the European Association of Social Anthropologists. His research has been in urban anthropology, media anthropology and transnational cultural processes in the U.S., West Africa and the Caribbean. Most recently he has been engaged in a study of the work of news media foreign correspondents. Among his books are *Soulside* (1969); *Exploring the City* (1980); *Cultural Complexity* (1992); *Transnational Connections* (1996); and *Foreign News: Exploring the World of Foreign Correspondents* (2004). He was also anthropology editor for the *International Enyclopedia of the Social and Behavioral Sciences* (2001).

Peter Hervik received his Ph.D. in anthropology from the University of Copenhagen in 1992. A year later he was a postdoctoral fellow at the University of North Carolina at Chapel Hill. He is now lecturer in International Migration and Ethnic Relations at Malmø University, Sweden. He was also a lecturer at the Department of Social Anthropology, University of Oslo from 1999 to 2001. Hervik has conducted research among the Yucatec Maya of Mexico and in Denmark on issues of identity, categorisation, racism, nationalism, ethnicity, multiculturalism and the media. His books include *Social Experience and Anthropological Knowledge*, with Kirsten Hastrup (1994); *Mayan Lives Within and Beyond Boundaries: Social Categories and Lived Identity in Yucatan* (1999 and 2001); he edited *Den generende forskellighed. Danske svar på den stigende multikulturalisme* ('The Annoying Differences: Danish Responses to Emerging Multiculturalism' (1999), and *Mediernes Muslimer: En antropologisk undersøgelse af mediernes dækning af religioner i Danmark* ('Muslims of the Media: An Anthropological Investigation of the Media's Coverage of Religions in Denmark', 2002).

Bruce Kapferer is currently Professor of Social Anthropology, University of Bergen. He has held professorships and senior fellowships in Australia, England, Scandinavia and in North America. His anthropological fieldwork has concentrated in southern Africa, Sri Lanka and India, and Australia. His major research interests include the study of symbolic action in ritual and in politics, nationalism and urban processes. He is currently engaged in research into post-colonial state formation, religion, power and poverty in Asia and southern Africa. His books include *A Celebration of Demons* (1991), *The Feast of the Sorcerer* (1997) and *Legends of People, Myths of State* (1999).

Maryon McDonald studied social anthropology at Oxford University and then followed research interests that have ranged from nationalism to medical anthropology and questions of accountability. Her first book, '*We are not French!*' *Language and Identity in Brittany, France* (1989), was concerned with the persuasive constructions of certain post-1960s nationalisms, of the political left and right alike. She was formerly Reader in Social Anthropology at Brunel University and is now Fellow of Robinson College, Cambridge. Maryon McDonald has carried out ethnographic fieldwork in France and in EU institutions, notably the European Parliament and European Commission, and is the author of several papers and a forthcoming book on the anthropology of the EU.

Barry Morris is currently Senior Lecturer in Social Anthropology at the University of Newcastle, New South Wales. He has published on issues of indigenous polity and race relations. His current research is on the changing nature of contemporary racial politics in Australia. He is the author of *Domesticating Resistance: the Dhangadi Aborigines and the Australian State* (1989); and editor, with Gillian Cowlishaw, of *Race Matters: Indigenous Australians and 'Our' Society* (2000). His latest publication, as editor with Rohan Bastin, is *Expert Knowledge: First World Peoples, Consultancy and Anthropology*, in the Forum Series, *Social Analysis*.

Rik Pinxten is Professor of Cultural Anthropology and Comparative Study of Religion at the University of Ghent. He studied philosophy and was Visiting Scholar and Professor at Northwestern University and in the Summer Field School of New Mexico. He has done fieldwork with Navajo Indians, and is editor and co-editor of several journals in the social sciences. His publications include: *Anthropology of Space* (1983); *Evolutionary Epistemology* (with Werner Callebaut, 1987); *Culturen sterven langzaam* ('Cultures Die hard', 1994); *When the Day Breaks* (1997); *Goddelijke fantasie* ('The Creation of God', 2000); *De Aristieke samenleving* ('The Artistic Society', 2003); *Culture and Power* (with Ghislain Verstraete and Chia Longman, 2004).

Gertraud Seiser, after ten years of public service, is currently a member of the scientific staff at the Department of Social and Cultural Anthropology at the University of Vienna. She is conducting research on European peasants and on the impact of the European Community on economic concepts of marginalised rural areas. Her recent publications include *Explorationen ethnologischer Berufsfelder* ('Exploring the Professional Fields of Anthropologists'), co-edited with Julia Czarnowski, Petra Pinkl and Andre Gingrich (2003); 'On the Importance of Being the Last One: Inheritance and Marriage in an Austrian Peasant Community', in Schweitzer ed. *The Dividends of Kinship* (2000).

Jaro Stacul was awarded a Ph.D. in social anthropology from the University of Cambridge in 1998. He has been a Lecturer in Anthropology at the University of Wales, Swansea, a Research Fellow at the University of Surrey (Guildford and Roehampton), and is currently Assistant Professor in Anthropology at the University of Regina, Canada. His monograph *The Bounded Field: Localism and Local Identity in an Italian Alpine Valley* was published by Berghahn Books in 2003, and his latest book (co-edited with Christina Moutsou and Helen Kopnina) *Crossing European Boundaries: Beyond Conventional Geographical Categories* is in press with the same publisher.

Thijl Sunier studied Cultural Anthropology at the Universities of Utrecht and Amsterdam, and in 1996 published his dissertation, *Islam in Beweging: Turkse jongeren en islamitische organisaties* ('Islam in Motion: Turkish young people and Islamic organisations') on social and youth movements among Muslims in the Netherlands. He is currently attached to the Department of Cultural Anthropology at the University of Amsterdam and is engaged in comparative research on multiculturalism and citizenship in France, Turkey and the Netherlands. His most recent article is 'Post-migration Islam: Negotiating space in Dutch society' in

Sackmann, Peters and Faist eds *Identity and Integration: Migrants in Western Europe* (2003).

Rob van Ginkel studied sociology and cultural anthropology at the University of Amsterdam. In 1993 he published his dissertation on Texel fishing communities, *Tussen Scylla en Charybdis. Een etnohistorie van Texels vissersvolk (1813–1932)* ('Between the Devil and the Deep Blue Sea: An Ethnohistory of Texelian Fisher Folk'). He has since published several books on discourses on Dutch culture and identity, and on anthropological and ethnological debates on folk culture. His most recent research explored social cohesion in a Dutch 'New Town'. Recently, he published (with Barbara Henkes) 'On Peasants and "Primitive Peoples": Moments of Rapprochement and Distance between Folklore Studies and Anthropology in the Netherlands', *Ethnos* 2003, 68(1).

Subject Index

Name Index